THE OCCULT LIFE

OF

Jesus of Nazareth

EMBRACING

HIS PARENTAGE, HIS YOUTH, HIS ORIGINAL DOCTRINES AND WORKS,
HIS CAREER AS A PUBLIC TEACHER AND PHYSICIAN OF THE
PEOPLE - THE NATURE OF THE GREAT CONSPIRACY
AGAINST HIM - ALL THE INCIDENTS OF
HIS TRAGICAL DEATH,

GIVEN ON SPIRITUAL AUTHORITY,

FROM SPIRITS WHO WERE CONTEMPORARY MORTALS WITH JESUS
WHILE ON THE EARTH.

GIVEN THROUGH THE MEDIUMSHIP OF

ALEXANDER SMYTH

REVISED AND CORRECTED EDITION

CHICAGO, ILLINOIS.
THE PROGRESSIVE THINKER PUBLISHING HOUSE.
1899.

THE TRUE LIFE OF JESUS OF NAZARETH
THE CONFESSIONS OF ST. PAUL

Copyright © 1998 by Unarius

Printed in Hong Kong

Published in 1899—The Progressive Thinker Publishing House
The Occult life of Jesus of Nazareth and the Hull-Covert Debate

Revised Edition—1968 Hardcover, Softcover
Revised Edition—1998 Hardcover

Library of Congress Catalog-in Publication Data

Alexander Smyth
The True Life of Jesus of Nazareth, The Confessions of St. Paul

Includes:
The Crucifixion and the Resurrection of Jesus by an Eye-Witness
Library of Congress Catalogue Card Number: 98-60032
ISBN 0-935097-40-6

1. Original doctrines of Jesus
2. Conspiracy against Jesus
3. Parentage of Jesus
4. Saul of Tarsus
5. Judas Iscariot
6. The Sanhedrin

JESUS OF NAZARETH

NOTE

It was only after much pleading and persuasion—from myself and other Unarius students—with the Unarius Moderator, that he finally agreed to dictate this foreword, as he is a most humble and unpretentious person, and much prefers to withdraw or extract any personal inferences or innuendoes from the teachings; and wishes rather, that we place instead, all importance upon the principle he brings.

Nevertheless, we students are ever conscious of the great radiating power that is projected into all works coming through this Consciousness, and did not wish this book to be without this great inner benefit to the reader—although other students, along with myself, feel that great Minds "the Unariun Brotherhood on the Inner" worked with and aided those, (Saul and Judas), who gave the transcripts from the spiritual worlds.

Any sincere seeker can easily sense and see the constant similarity in presentation and in essence to the wondrous writings he has brought in the present dispensation.

Another unique quality ever present: his words convey and project into the mind of the reader, the very pictures of the word descriptions, a rare ability which was even existent with him as a small child!

To factually define or to completely describe all which the arrival of these two books has meant to me personally, and all that they have caused to happen to me would be like attempting to count all the stars in the entire celestial infinite!—so vast and tremendous have been its most profound and beneficial effects—physically, psychically, mentally and every other way; that to say the least, it has been an earth-shaking experience, lasting more than ten days duration! The major effects and benefits shall, we know, endure eternally—as is true with all persons who are thusly projected, seemingly from out a cannon into the future, thousands of years!

It has been thus fully realized the great repercussions which such information and discoveries shall have upon mankind in general, and especially with the religionists, when these factual truths, so long kept hidden, have come to light! Thus it is not in some personal glory that I have found such joy; but rather, with the inner knowing how it can, and shall, aid all mankind, from now on through all time!! Could we say more?

This book you will find to be the capstone in the arch of true understanding; it can well start you upon your personal "Second Coming" or "spiritual rebirth"—a more positive, regenerative, progressive, evolution!

And just here is an opportune time to relate a most profound prophetic line—a true "classic" which our beloved Moderator voiced just a few days hence the arrival of the "Life of Jesus" book; he said, quote:

"A TOUCH OF MIDAS IN THE SKY
THIS GOLD SHALL FALL BEFORE I DIE!"

Thus, here just within a matter of three days time, between the covers of this book, lies the "gold" to which was referred, and which did indeed fall right into our hands!

Of course, such a MIND would not be referring to the material wealth, but rather, unto the spiritual values which corrupteth not with time; but which shall, instead, endureth forever! This "gold" shall add great luster and brilliance to your life; and as the flame of life, now existing as but a tiny glimmer, is fanned by the light of true wisdom and understanding, does it ever grow the more brightly, to become a beacon shining in the darkened regions of the material worlds, beckoning those less illumined, onward—from out their wilderness unto the light of true understanding; uncontaminated by the lies, the derelictions of the negative forces of evil —to lead them instead, into the true "Promised Land," a land, not of milk and honey but, of the "Many Mansions," "The Kingdom Within," of which Jesus so often spoke and, referred to now by our Unariun Moderator as the "Inner" or "Interdimensions"—the Higher Worlds which are presided over by Super-Intellects, Master-Minds, great scientists of the ages and— which (Inner Dimensions) can be reached only through inner development, through personal attainment, through that rarely understood word —Consciousness.

May it be that this wondrous volume of Truth and Wisdom shall never again find its way unto the moldy archives of some ancient library, there to gather the moth and the dust of time; but instead, let it become that beacon of Light that shall lead mankind from out the wilderness of despair and ignorance in which he has been wandering, lo these many years—yea, even beyond the time of Noah!

And, if I may, take this opportunity to add my word of deep appreciation and gratitude to him, and to the Brotherhood who have aided in ever helping in my personal metamorphosis; and for the blessed privilege of walking by his side and serving in whatever way possible, not only in the present but in the distant past eons of time.

Ruth Norman.

UNARIUS

UNiversal ARticulate Interdimensional Understanding of Science

FOREWORD

It was during the closing months of the year 1967—just 13 years after the formal mission of Unarius had begun—a most noteworthy event took place; one of the greatest importance, not only to those more directly concerned with Unarius, but to the entire world as well. For indeed this event was a great valedictory which not only heralds the final closing chapters of the religions of the world, but even more strongly proclaims the Advent of the New World, the long-promised and soon-to-be Aquarian Age, and all other prophetic fulfillments; and in particular to those who have "come with their lamps filled," theirs is indeed the fulfillment through evolution of life in a higher world.

This event, while it would seem small and insignificant to many in the material world, was, however, to the immediate fraternity of the Unarius students, and in particular, to Ruth and the Moderator, the acquisition in the customary manner of materialization so often demonstrated, of two books; or more correctly, a book and a booklet which, as you will see by the titles, deal specifically with the life and death of Jesus of Nazareth. These two epistles have long remained hidden in obscure places from the eyes of religious fanatics who would have eagerly destroyed them, for these two works aptly and graphically portray the entire great hoax of the Christian religion. These books, however, do more than expose the machinations of frenetic religionists. They are in toto, a complete vindication of the entire concept of Unarius; and as it exists today, in the idiom of the scientific twentieth century, Unarius has already added great luster and meaning to the true purpose and mission of Jesus, which was to overthrow the old pagan Jehovan god and to reconstruct an entirely new concept in evolutionary creation.

In these books, and as you read them, you will be able to draw many exact parallels with the works of the Unariun Moderator. The similarities of language, the presentation of unalterable facts, the tremendous and over-reaching faculty of the Mind, as it was with Jesus and as it is with the Moderator, which in an instant's notice could reach into the most remote corners of the interdimensional universe and converse fluently on all known and unknown topics.

There are other parallels also which will give overwhelming and convincing proof, as many of the students who know the Moderator, know him as the Nazarene reincarnated at this most propitious time to polarize and to begin that long-awaited "Second Coming."

In this book you will read descriptions of the piercing, penetrating power which issued from the eyes of Jesus, the tremendous auric radiation also carried through the intonations of voice which transcended those of his time, just as in this, the Moderator's time; people also feel this transcending power, a sort of hypnotic trance or as an appropriate healing power which can cause some persons to break out in a violent breathless, perspirative condition or even cause almost complete im-mobility of the body. These power manifestations can be felt thousands of miles distant by those who are studying and in attunement. And, like the Nazarene, he too, has appeared to many people out of the physical body at bedsides in sickness, and at theaters; or even while driving a car by "remote control" without the physical body. He has, silently and un-seen led people in finding lost objects around the house, even though a thousand miles or more distance separated him from the seeker. He has described the exact location of lost or unknown cisterns, wells, springs, oil fields and mineral deposits. He has accurately described past, present and future to countless thousands of people, and on a number of occasions, actually described the circumstance of death even three or four years in advance.

On numerous occasions, for competent doctors, under test condi-tions, he has described and diagnosed physical and mental ailments of patients, in some cases unknown to the doctor. He has looked into the physical bodies of certain persons and described cancer and other diseases which had yet to make their appearance in the coming months or years; however, all of these incidents and many more will be described in the future biography, all of which most aptly and conclu-sively demonstrate a clairvoyant training and mind development which is far above and beyond any presently known or historical figures, save Jesus of Nazareth, who also equally demonstrated the same develop-ment.

One more massive piece of evidence is contained in the many thou-sands of handwritten testimonials by those who have had wonderful miracles happen to them, as they came in contact with and studied

Unarius.

Again, just as it was two thousand years ago, and just as the miracles truly happened in his time, and with the aid of the same Unarius Brotherhood, so did many wondrous things happen to those peoples who listened to his voice and had faith in what he said and came in contact with the great healing, radiating power which is the characteristic and the only one ever expressed in the world—as it was with the Nazarene, and the Unarius Moderator.

There is more, much more which could be written of this great historical epic, of the great and wonderful powers from the higher worlds who, unnoticed and unheralded, guide, aid and abet the denizens of these man-like creatures who swarm the earth; so do they proclaim their false gods, even while enjoying all of the munificent blessings projected by the Unariun Brotherhood from the Higher worlds. Yet, this has not been enough; for in the laws of universal creation, there must always be a polarizing agent, and so it has been through the epochs of history, one of the Unariun Brothers has walked the pathways of the earth; he has been called Amon Ra, Akhnaton, Anaxagoras, Zoroaster, Jesus of Nazareth, and finally the Moderator, or the Elder Brother, as he is known in the twentieth century.

In the final years of his earth-life mission an even greater contribution to this overwhelming testimonial will be contained in the biography wherein many more parallels can be drawn, many more facsimiles expressed, exact duplications in mannerisms, speech, expressions and ways—the power, the miracles, all of these parallels are the same, except that here in this twentieth century as a more fitting culmination as a rebuttal to the crucifixion and as an expressionary reagent to heavenly piety and compassion, have the Unariun Brotherhood multiplied seven times seventy-seven all of that which transpired near the sea of Galilee nearly two thousand years ago!

In contemplation, how great is the irony of this situation, while hundreds of millions of Christians await some sign, some fruitful beginning to the time of his return, He is already here; he has for many years walked among them, almost unnoticed and unknown and just as he did in that long ago, so he has walked upon all their footpaths and lived with them in all the ways of their lives, coming as a great blessing, a healing power, a polarizing agency. And as he walks away from all these sundry peoples, he leaves with them, burning upon the altar of their life, a tiny flame, one which will, if it is nourished and cherished, grow into the proportions of a new life, a new person, a new being living in one of those many mansions and forever looking into the face of the Infinite Creator.

And so, as it has been, as he has humbly and unknown, walked among them, it is his wish that he shall depart equally unknown, for how well does he know the foibles of human indispositions, the irascible malcontentions which arise in the minds of those who are confronted with the unknown, with the mandate of personal responsibility, unmitigated by professional religionists who promise salvation and immortality in the same breath they proclaim their false god! For, as he has often said, "If I ever become a mystic or that I am worshipped, so will our cause be lost,"—a cause which demands the utmost from every human who would aspire to one of the heavenly mansions.

How well then, in sagacity and wisdom is the challenge of this irony met, for just as it was in the long ago on the hill Golgotha and the minions of Caiaphas rent asunder his garments and perpetrated the greatest crime and iniquity in human history, where in turn, these traitorous villains succeeded in erecting the false superstructure of religion upon the death agonies of this man. How befitting then, in this, the twentieth century, in full knowledge of the creative law of incarnation did he resurrect his body to live among them, to speak of the same Creative Intelligence, the Father of all things, and to bring to all those who would listen, or that he, in some manner, touched them, bringing the same full measure of transcending power.

Yes, let the irony remain—the strongest and most graphic episode in earth's history, yet one with the fullest miter and measure of compassion for all those engaged in the metamorphoses of creative evolution.

The Moderator of Unarius
(The Elder Brother)

PREFACE

It has generally been conceded by all those who have read the New Testaments that the life of Jesus was indeed the greatest life ever lived, if this life is to be judged by its most unique character, and as it is so depicted in the Testaments. Also so depicted in these Testaments, this life presents the greatest enigma and an overwhelming contradiction, for it is impossible to compromise the concept of a man able to perform instantaneous miracles even bringing back the dead—that he did perform these acts without rhyme or reason other than, either as an exhibition of power or, as he was compassionately minded, etc., all against any wise and logical course of action which might be attributed to such power and intellect, i.e., that, psychologically speaking, such miraculous acts would also cause mass hallucinations, an addictive dependency on such miracles; or, again, that these miraculous acts were performed with the foreseeable, and the inevitable result that it would arouse the ire and wrath of the incumbent priesthood.

Furthermore, such miraculous acts are in direct opposition to the preachments of the same individual who always emphatically insisted that it was a personal responsibility of each individual to seek out the *Father within, so that all things could be added unto, or corrected. Also most apparent, in the great contradiction of this life is in the context of the mission itself, which was to overthrow the Jehovan god and to represent a true creative facsimile as posed by this Father image, which dealt specifically as the creative factor in all aspects of life; not the Jehovan god, an emotional, vindictive, even murderous god, who had led the Jews through a senseless forty-year trek through the desert, ending this pilgrimage in long years of war; to dispossess the Canaanites of their lands and homes.

These contradictions and enigmas have been the subject of heated debates, suspicions and malcontentions, both with Christians and non-Christians for many hundreds of years and until the present time, there was apparently no suitable historical recourse which could most adequately explain, and truthfully depict, the life of the Nazarene as it was truly lived.

In the many texts and liturgies of Unarius, much of this true information and background was presented; and to prove that Christianity, as posed in the Bible and Testaments, was a fabrication and presented the most obvious of all contradictions, that as this religion was actually founded upon the crucifixion and death of Jesus, it was so contrived and pre-

The Father as posed in the Creative power and substance which comprise all things—also spoken of by Jesus.

sented that in this death he died for all believers' sins! His blood washed them away, etc.!

Going still further into this contradictory fabrication, by representing Jesus in this tissue of lies and the resurrection, Jesus was represented as immortal, and the one and only son of this Jehovan-god despite the very obvious fact that he was crucified for trying to destroy this Jehovan religion!

In the presentation of the Unariun Concept and as it so constitutes a continuation of the doctrines of Jesus, there was also a lack of massive concrete historical evidence which could immediately dispossess and destroy these false illogical suppositions, the obvious fabrications of the Christian religion—as conditions were in the time when Jesus lived, most people were illiterate and could neither read nor write; moreover, conditions were extremely chaotic; the Holy Land and its people torn between two despotic governorships, the hierarchy of the Jewish temple and the Roman dictators, who had virtually conquered the country; as a consequence, very little, if any, literate histories were ever recovered from that time. One of these true historical accounts of the life before and after the crucifixion of Jesus is given in the "Eye Witness" account—a small book which survived the fire of the great libraries in Alexandria. This book was written by an Essene who knew Jesus and much of his life, which is recounted in this epistle.

Another book was, strangely enough, not written until 1800 A.D. This book was given in revelation to an especially-prepared individual, the account coming as a series of full color-visions in motion and action with a superimposed narrative given by the authors, Saul and Judas, as they recounted their parts in this most historical time.

By and large, these two accounts completely complement each other and any reader can, by reading, gain a comprehensive understanding which will dispel the contradictory miasma as it is depicted in the Testaments.

They will give a full and comprehensive meaning to the life of the Nazarene; and while there may be a few anachronisms, yet the entire context of these two books can be considered totally accurate. These two books will also most adequately reinforce and prove the entire Unariun Concept as it is so posed as a continuation and a vastly enlarged mission, as it was so started and presented by Jesus.

It should be noted here, any attempts to reconcile these two books and Unarius with any existing orthodoxies or with any historical researches as may be recorded in encyclopedias, etc., may lead to confusion, as none of these other accounts can be considered reliable. Only the true facts as they are recounted in the visions of Smyth and by "The Eye Witness" and the unimpeachable Unariun presentation which has, as one of its sources, the actual memory of a living man who was once the

Nazarene!

Briefly, in the revelations of Smyth, you will almost immediately perceive the makings of a dastardly plot contrived in the evil mind of Saul—a plot, like so many others so contrived, was aimed at attaining great power and prestige; and Saul, as he so plotted, foresaw the tremendous possibilities whereby he could—through the martyrdom of a man, through devious and skillful maneuverings—contrive to raise into the position of a Messiah, a miracle-man! Then, after the death of this superimposed Messiah, donned the fallen man's cloak, and as an apostle of this man, contrived to build a powerful religion and which he (Saul), as a virtual king and emperor over great masses of people, assumed a position quite similar to that occupied by the present-day pope!

How well he succeeded has been recounted over the centuries in Christianity; but for Saul, his position as the great religious emancipator, the dictator and Pope of the First Christian Church, ended abruptly when he was beheaded by Nero for the crime of assaulting his favorite concubine!

Read, then, the most adequate depiction of what is obviously the most villainous plot in the history of mankind—a plot which has at least equaled or surpassed any of those which has bloodied the pages of history!

A Historical Reference

According to the Encyclopedia Britannica, Herod, the First, was, preceding the birth of Jesus, both king and governor of Judea—so appointed by the Roman Caesar, Augustus, Herod I died in the year 4 A.D. and willed to his three sons, Archelaus, Antipas and Philip, three divisions—each one, a third of the land of Judea. It was Antipas who inherited the central portion of Bethlehem and other sites, historically linked with Jesus. Three years before his death, Herod I had ordered the execution of the first born in this central province, in an attempt to kill an illegitimate child, whose father was his son, Antipas (sometimes called Annanias), and thus remove the stain from the family name or to avoid certain other political or religious repercussions. This, however, is not recorded in the encyclopedia. Herod Antipas lived through the succeeding years and through the lieutenant-governorship of Pontius Pilate, 26-36A.D., which years include the crucifixion, 33A.D. His death is believed to have occurred in the year 39 A.D.

There is more, much more which could be gleaned from such documentaries and historical references, providing such research could be conducted with certain qualifications and with such comparative analyses which could separate the truth from much of the confusion which exists in such references. Such truth as so extracted would most strongly support the revelations of Alexander Smyth and "The Eye Witness Account of the Life of Jesus." Such historical extractions would also prove the arch-villainy of Saul—known later as Paul, the apostle—and the entire fabrication of Christianity!

The Moderator of Unarius.

CONTENTS

CONTENTS
(CONTINUED)

PUBLISHER'S INTRODUCTION.

We take great pleasure in being able to present to the world this unique work, "The Occult Life of Jesus of Nazareth," by the spirits, Saul and Judas, through the mediumship of Alexander Smyth. We believe it will be instrumental in removing much of the rubbish, superstition and perplexing problems that have from the start clustered around his eventful life. There has been a vast amount of discussion in regard to this remarkable personage, who has constituted the corner-stone of the Christian religion, and who has been the innocent cause of more terrific wars, persecutions, and bloodshed than all other agencies combined, and this book will in a great measure clear away the mists that have so long clustered around his eventful life and make clear many things heretofore badly obscured and but little understood.

J. R. FRANCIS.
Publisher.

DEDICATED

TO THE

CHRISTIAN CLERGY OF ALL DENOMINATIONS.

Reverend Sirs:—In compliance with the commands of my spirit friends, I am impelled to draw your attention to a subject of deep interest and vast importance to the Christian world. For eighteen centuries and more, gentlemen of your profession have undertaken to teach and expound the doctrines of the Christian faith. Sermons as numerous as the sands of the sea shore have been preached and books have been written, enough in bulk to build a large city, endeavoring to reconcile the Christian dogmas with truth and reason, without accomplishing the end in view; for the same mysteries and subjects of dispute and contention exist now, as in the commencement, shocking to every one of common sense who is desirous of knowing the truth. The reason of this is obvious. The New Testament, which is the text book of Christianity, when judged by the philosophy of the present day, is found to be a compilation of misstatements, misconceptions, perversions, and nearly every thing else opposite to that which it professes to be. The very character of Jesus as therein represented is a myth, a being of fabulous and impossible existence, of whom it is impossible to conceive in any natural and consistent light. But at length, it has pleased the Supreme Ruler of the universe that the truth shall be made known to mankind. The true character, history and doctrines of Jesus are now brought to light by spiritual communications through me, the truth of which cannot be successfully opposed, when all things pertaining to it shall have been made known. Therefore I respectfully request you, Reverend Sirs will suspend your judgments until you shall obtain a knowledge of the truth by investigating this book; then, if you do your duty to God and man, you will acknowledge the truth and preach the same to the world such being the desires and commands of the spirits.

In the hope and strong belief that your Reverend Order and the world at large, will greatly profit by the perusal of this book, I remain your respectful and humble servant,

ALEXANDER SMYTH.

PREFACE

Under a sense of duty which I owe to mankind, and especially to all those of the various Christian denominations, I feel myself impelled to issue this extraordinary book to the world. It purports to be The True History of Jesus of Nazareth, and is the first and only work in which is portrayed the true character of that much esteemed and beloved individual. In it he is divested of all the mythical and mystical surroundings and fabulous origin. He is presented to the mental view of the present age as a natural man whose traits of character were amiability, justice, truthfulness and benevolence, and who finally became a martyr to his love and good intentions towards mankind. The numerous incidents and startling facts pertaining to this history are given on spiritual authority, by a series of clairaudient communications and mental visions through the medium and author. The grouping of the characters, compiling of the incidents, description of the scenery and illustrations, are given in the words and style of the author, who has no other apology to make for any imperfections that may be found, than that he has done his best to make it comprehensive, important and interesting to all classes of readers. Some persons, not being favored with the new light of the age will probably discredit its spiritual authority. If so, that will not detract from the merits of the work, for all those who shall feel sufficient interest to peruse it, will find that everything therein stated is based upon physical and moral facts and probabilities. In accordance, then, with the duties and engagements by which I am bound, I respectfully submit it to the public. May it be productive of its great design, in dispersing from the minds of mankind the dark clouds of superstitious errors, such being the wish of the spirits, and of the humble individual who subscribes himself the

MEDIUM AND AUTHOR.

INTRODUCTION

In bringing this book before the public, I feel it to be my duty to give some explanation of certain things, which, forming a concatenation of cause and effect, gave origin to it. The matters I allude to are in relation to my own humble self, which, however disagreeable to me, I am constrained to do in some respects.

I am a man of humble circumstances, and have always been so—one who has always labored for his daily bread. My education has not been received from academy or college; nor have I had the assistance of a tutor except in my childhood, when I was taught to read the New Testament with a Sunday-school proficiency, so that as far as I have any learning, I am indebted for it to my own perseverance, though lately I find that the impulses of my nature have been modified and guarded by some spirit friends, of whose influence over me I knew nothing at the time.

I was of a nervous, sanguine temperament—ardent, hopeful and of blissful imagination. I left my native home when a youth with a firm resolution to see and enjoy the world. Thanks to the care of my kind mother, my morals were good. I had little to gain in that respect, but a great deal to lose. I wandered from place to place, seeking pleasures and information during many years. I partook of all things that the world presented, even to some of its vices, and in the course of my wanderings and adventures, I received a blight to my affections. I then became unhappy for a time, when, as a counteractor to sorrow, I contracted an evil habit. This state of things continued for a time as I continued to wander from place to place, feeling myself an unhappy creature whose affections and blissful hopes were nipped in the bud, whose noble aspirations were checked, whose desire of doing what seemed to me right, was blasted, and whose self respect was almost gone.

About the time that I was in my most distressed condition, I was aroused from my despair, torpor and lack of energy, by feeling within me some extraordinary experiences, so astonishing and astounding to me, that it absorbed the whole powers of my mind by day and night; my sorrows were forgotten and my evil habit was neglected. Then like Samson of old, I began to shake myself to see where my strength lay, and I said to myself, What is it? What is going to happen? I reasoned with myself, calling up my scanty amount of philosophy, but could not account for the phenomena. I went to several doctors, and revealed to them what I had experienced, from whom I received no satisfactory information; but they hinted that my experiences were nothing more than imaginings or hallucinations, and afterwards I heard it whispered about that I was crazy. After this I left the neighborhood, resolving to keep the subject hereafter locked up within myself, and endeavor, by studying the philosophy of nature, to find, if possible, the true cause of the phenomena within me. With this resolution I conformed passing my days in hard work, and at leisure times in study. In the meantime, the phenomena occurring to me frequently—how often I cannot say—I finally overcame my evil habit.

My life was now much more agreeable. I was industrious, studious and temperate; yet my old sorrow would now and then oppress me. After a time, the phenomena I have alluded to, entirely left me; but others not less wonderful and more agreeable, succeeded them, and continued with me for a great length of time. The latter were a source of great gratification to me; yet I was ever anxious to discover the cause; however, all my researches were in vain. I wished to impart to my neighbors these mysterious occurrences; but I was afraid to do so from fear of the results, so I kept them to myself until 1843, when I married. Then the phenomena ceased altogether, and did not occur until 1858, when I was again visited by them in the usual manner. Subsequently the subject of Spiritualism attracted my notice, when I proceeded to invest-igate its merits. After a few months' investigation of the subject, an idea occurred to me that I would inquire of Andrew J. Davis, the clairvoyant, concerning the mysterious occurrences pertaining to me. Accordingly I wrote him a letter, giving a description of my experiences, which was as follows:

Philadelphia, April 10, 1860

Mr. Davis — Dear Sir: —

Knowing you to be a man of learning, especially in spiritual and psychological subjects, I take the liberty to address you on a matter of great importance to me at least, and I hope when you shall have read this letter, that you will give me your serious opinion upon it.

For several years I have been the subject of a series of a most ex-traordinary and mysterious internal experiences or developments; I can-not say sensations, for I am well aware that what I have undergone did not come through the medium of my five senses. I am not an illiterate man, yet with all my philosophy I am unable to account for them. I have read many medical works, but do not find a case recorded similar to mine. I have conversed with many medical men, but could gain no other opinion from them otherwise than that it was "hallucination." I have also conversed with non-professional persons. The result was, they consider-ed me to be crazy! Since then, I have kept the subject locked up within myself, as I am not desirous of being considered either foolish or crazy. I will now relate the particulars to you, that you may judge:

About twenty years ago, when I was thirty years of age, I began to notice certain extraordinary occurrences within my person. Sometimes I saw or inwardly perceived the main branches of my nervous system burst forth suddenly into beautiful lights of blue and yellow; sometimes down my sides; sometimes along my arms; very often on one side of my face or across my brows. These appearances were as quick as a flash of lightning, during which I perceived the interior of the tubes through which the light passed.

Frequently when in my bed and about falling to sleep, a noise, sudden and powerful, would be heard in my head like the report of a pistol or the twanging of a large wire; then a flash of light would pass over the exterior part of the brain, when I could distinctly see the two hemispheres thereof. At times, an explosion would take place at the back part of my head; then I could perceive the medula oblongata and the ramifications of the cerebellum faintly illuminated. But the most beautiful and extraordinary of all the instances I experienced but once, as follows: One day I was lying on my back dozing, when my slumbers were interrupted by, as I thought, a large fly, which seemed to descend and buzz just between my eyes. Several times I was thus disturbed, when at last I arose, determined to destroy the intruder if I could catch it. I searched about, but could find nothing of the kind. Then, thinking that something else might be the cause, I returned to my previous position, resolving to keep on the watch.

As thus I lay for some minutes, without moving a muscle, my eyelids slightly opening, I perceived two yellow luminous specks; one at the inner, and the other at the outer angle of the eye, just beneath the edge of the eyelid. These specks were moving toward each other, the one at the outer angle moving the faster. At length they came into contact, when an explosion like the firing of a pistol took place, passing through my brain, and causing every particle of the substance to tremble. Then a beautiful yellow and blue light passed through my eyeball, along the optical tube up the brain, where I lost it. During its passage I saw distinctly the crystalline lens, the retina and the interior of the optical tube.

These extraordinary occurrences, with the exception of the last, happened frequently to me for several years. At length they ceased. For three or four years I felt like an ordinary man; but soon after this, a new development took place within me of a more pleasing nature, though not less extraordinary. I have never studied music, therefore I know not the names of the different parts, and shall find it difficult to explain to you what I wish, for my internal experience this time, consisted of vocal and instrumental music.

At this period of my life, I lived in the country, being the greater part of my time entirely alone. It seemed to me though I was sensible that it could not be so, that there was an instrument of music situated in the interior part of my brain. It performed entire pieces of music, with-

4

out pause or fault; and when it had finished an air, there was a pause for a few seconds, then it would re-commence with the same or another. It mattered not how I was engaged, nothing I could do would stop it; until it had finished its piece of music, it would continue without pausing. I resorted to various means to stop it. I worked hard, trying to think of nothing but my work. I visited my neighbors to pass the time in social chat. I took long walks and runs, but all in vain, for the music continued its sweet notes, performing whole pieces over and over in the most harmonious style, the tones resembling those of a small metallic organ or music box. This continued about a year, when it was succeeded by the music of voices; the latter, unlike the former, seemed to take place externally to me, and to be some distance above me in the air. I could distinguish three voices performing various pieces, sacred and otherwise, in succession, with great precision and harmony. Some of the airs were familiar to me and some were not; but all the tones were of the richest kind. I will observe in this place that some of the pieces performed, both vocal and instrumental, I had learned many years before, but had for-gotten them; while others, which I but partially remembered, my mys-terious powers performed without fault. At length the instrumental music died away, leaving me to be entertained by the vocal alone; the latter remaining with me for about three years, commencing as soon as I awoke in the morning, and continuing with but little intermission through the day, and to the last moment of my wakefulness at night.

Perhaps you may think there was some disturbance or disease either in my body or mind, but I assure you there was not. I had perfect health of body, was entirely sober and rational, and in a happy mood of mind, generally, though a poor man.

Frequently have I thought, when walking along the country road, listening to my musical powers, how pleasing it would be if I could be-lieve in the existence of good spirits! I could then have reason to think that I had found favor with some of them, who might be hovering above and around me, endeavoring to cheer me with their songs. At that time I did not believe in the spirit world, though since, I have felt inclined to admit the rationality of the doctrine. These mysterious visitings have left me for some time past. They were generally agreeable to me, and would have been more so could I have spoken of them to my neighbors, with-out fear of being considered crazy.

I have now to relate to you a new phase of their strange workings within me, which has completely astounded me, and for the first time produced an uneasy perplexity. I have been in the habit, since I have been married, of reading an hour or two after my family have retired for the night; so, it was generally near midnight when I sought my bed. One night last week, between ten and eleven o'clock, while reading as usual, my attention was withdrawn from my book by the shrill, lively notes of

5

an instrument which sounded to me like the shepherd's pipe of ancient days. It seemed to play a series of lively variations and quavers. Like the fluttering butterfly, it was here, there and everywhere; above and around me, when after about two minutes, they ceased, then all was still. I hurried into the yard of the house, looked around, but could discover nobody about at that time of night. Returning to my room, the next few moments were passed in awful suspense. This did not last long, however, for my attention was seized by hearing two persons discoursing, who seemed from their voices, to be of the male sex. I could not distinguish what they said, as their voices seemed to be too far above me, but I caught the names of several persons who, I knew according to history, had lived many centuries ago. Their discourse lasted a few minutes, then it ceased. There was a dead silence for a few seconds, during which I was rooted to the floor motionless, the powers of my mind and soul being absorbed in wondering suspense. Again I heard a few notes from the mysterious pipe, and then a voice, powerful and distinct, called me by name. As you may imagine, I was struck mute and motionless with astonishment. With suspended breath I anxiously listened in expectation of hearing more, but nothing followed that night, for I was too much afraid to respond to the call. Since then, I have abandoned my nocturnal readings.

Such is the substance of the letter I wrote to A. J. Davis, desiring him to give me his opinion and advice upon the strange matter. He published the same in his journal, the "Herald of Progress," May 12, 1860, and on May 19 he published an article in answer to it. The important points relating to my communication, are as follows:

"The case of Alexander S_____ is not new in the annals of mystery; the introverted action of the mind is possible, but rarely experienced. Swedenborg's condition was oftentimes not unlike that of Mr. S_____, showing the naturalness of such visitations whenever the mind's internal arrangements are propitious. In such experiences, it is absurd to reject the hypothesis of spiritual instigation. But it would be equally absurd to suppose the spirits were personally present, superintending each metamorphosis of internal action, as many persons are disposed to conclude from the mysterious novelty of the experience. In examining the mind's internal mechanism, we get at not only the actions of organs, but also discern the nature of the action. Each part of the mind diffuses a particular influence all over the constitution, and the influences that have emanated from all the parts, constitute "sensation," or the lightning of the nervous system, and inasmuch as human beings are organized upon the same principle, so it happens that an influence imparted to another, awakens in that other effects analogous to those felt by the one who imparted it. Thus a combative person, on his imparting his organal influence, will cause another to feel identical sensations. The same is true of every other organ.

"These facts are familiar to modern psychologists. They stand in the gateway between heaven and earth, preventing at once too much credulity and too much doubt; for such facts demonstrate the double nature of man, and at the same time, that he is not the cause of all spiritual phenomena. The automatic hemisphere of mind is quite as marvelous as the counter-hemisphere of voluntary powers, and when truly studied, man becomes as much a wonder before death, as when he returns in the estate of spirit.

"It would seem, judging from our correspondent's testimony, that his own spirit carried on the process originally instigated by the invisible intelligence. They had diffused an influence upon his nervous system, which entering into chemical combination with the sensitive elements, they (the spirits) could neither control nor extract from their subject. It is evident that many spirits have little knowledge of their own abilities to control the influence they cast upon mediums. The consequence was, that what should have been voluntary and under the control of the wishes or will, became instead, automatic and beyond management. The vibrations and concussive sounds, and the instantaneous representations of the nervous system etc., by means of beautiful lights, were inevitable effects, whenever his own and the foreign influences met, like two tiny thunder-clouds of opposite polarity. His vision was not with the eyes, but by means of the pervading optical influence; that is to say, the sensitive medium of physical sight was impressed with the internal facts and recurring phenomena. This explanation is intended to cover all cases of this kind; but one thing is remarkable, yet agreeing with our explanations; we refer to the repetitions or recurring character of his experiences. No other facts more clearly illustrate the occult operations of his own mental machinery. The spirit guardian, for example, would start a tune in his memory—perhaps impart an influence to the organal center where music is perceived by the mind, then the impressed and propulsed faculties would go forward with the operation. We have seen this phenomenon many times in persons who were impressed to address an audience, or to write a poem, etc. The spirit guardian of the medium would set the machinery in motion, and then retire; whereupon the medium's mind would take up the operation, and continue, as though it were an unthinking automaton. But there is evidence better, the hearing of one's name pronounced by tongues in the air. In this case, the spiritual ear is reached. The floors, roof and leagues of atmosphere vanish from the spaces between the speaker and the listener; they seem to stand in each other's presence. The whole ocean of human existence is stilled for the moment, and the person addressed by a voice from heaven, is either paralyzed with fright, or exuberant with gratification. Such a moment is sublime, because it seems to dissipate all doubt, and to reveal the external future. Heaven grant that all men may know the truth, and be free."

After reading Mr. Davis's reply to my communication, I considered myself much enlightened on the subject, much relieved of my timidity, and after some mature reflection, I resolved, that if there is a spirit wishing to communicate with me, I would avail myself of the opportunity, and with as much firmness as I could assume, invite the invisible intelligence to further proceedings. Accordingly, the following night, I was seated in my room alone, with writing materials and a book before me. The clock struck eleven. I endeavored to read, but it was a vain effort, for I understood not what I read; my mind being absorbed by subjects of greater moment. A thousand thoughts flitted through my brain; some of a hopeful, and some of a doubtful nature, and some fearfully speculative. "Is it possible such things can be?" I asked myself. "Shall I really hold communion with a spirit of the other world?" "Who can it be?" "What can be the purport of the visit?" Such questions occurred to me mentally. Oh! with what eager expectancy did I wish for the moment to solve their mysteries! Thus some minutes passed, all around me being silent as death, as I waited with an intense, uneasy suspense. At length, as though coming from a distant field, I heard the sweet, playful notes of the shepherd's pipe; faint and low at first, then increasing in strength as they seemed to approach me. This music, I allowed to be an announcement that my spiritual visitor was approaching me. As the first sounds of the pipe impressed me, all the powers of my mind and soul seemed instantly to concentrate themselves, and suspend their connection with my body. Still I heard the music, and I then became convinced that I did not hear it through the medium of my bodily ears. At length the music ceased, when a voice, the same I before had heard, called me by name.

"Who calls me?" I inquired mentally, with considerable trepidation.

"I am the spirit of one, who, like you in nature, once inhabited the earth as mortal man, far back in the history of nations," answered the voice, in a grave, manly tone.

"Make known your name, prove your identity, and then communicate your wishes," I replied, with a little more assurance; for I thought it prudent to know in the commencement with whom I was communicating.

"Here are two spirits present," answered the voice. "The one that addresses you is Saul of Tarsus, or better known to the inhabitants of earth as Paul the Apostle. My companion is Judas Iscariot, I presume you have read of us both, in that book called the New Testament. If so, I beg of you not to form any idea of us from that book, for it does not contain an item of truth relating to our true character or histories. That book, which received its origin through my influence, speaks of me as

8

being one of the best, purest, noblest and most pious mortals that ever lived; and of my companion, Judas, as one of the worst that possibly could be. The fact is, if you were to reverse the characters given of us in that book, you would come nearer the truth. It is true that Judas was a selfish man; and that he was guilty of ingratitude and cruelty in betraying the good man, Jesus of Nazareth, to the Sanhedrim; but however heinous his offense may appear to you, it will admit of extenuation when the truth is known. It was I, friend Alexander, who was the plotter and instigator of that horrid tragedy—the death of Jesus! Judas Iscariot was in my power. He acted at my suggestion, and did my bidding. He received the opprobrium of the evil deed, while I, the true actor, escaped with impunity. But that black deed was only one item of the many black crimes of which I was guilty during my career of pious hypocrisy while on earth, the facts of which I intend to bring to your notice; in so doing I shall prove my identity, for no man or spirit can unravel my wicked career excepting myself."

"How shall I know or believe what you say to be the truth?" I inquired of the spirit, "since you have given yourself so bad a character?"

"Friend Alexander," said another spiritual voice, which I judged to be that of Judas Iscariot, "you may believe what my friend Saul says to you, for he is quite a different personage to what he was when on earth. It is true, that then, he was one of the worst men, as a hypocrite, liar, defrauder and murderer. I also was not the most innocent and harmless of men; but since then, there has been a great lapse of time; thousands of worlds have been brought into existence, and thousands destroyed. In everything on earth, and in the spirit world, as well, great changes have been produced for the better; therefore you must not be surprised that Saul and Judas are no longer what they once were. Indeed friend Alexander, we are spirits of a much improved nature, since we acted our wicked parts upon the earth. We have had nearly eighteen centuries of isolation and separation from the harmonious society of the spirit world, which time we have passed in repinings, remorse and repentance, endeavoring to purge ourselves from the wickedness of our mortal lives, and to render ourselves capable of entering upon our spiritual career. I must inform you that we have not struggled in vain. There is but one other task we have to achieve, before we shall be entitled to take our positions among the exalted. My companion, Saul, will inform you what that is."

"What is the purport of your communication?" I inquired of the spirits.

"My friend, for so I must consider you, as I will explain presently," responded the spirit Saul, "Judas has informed you that we have passed many centuries in a state of isolation or separation from the happy spirits of this world, which became a necessary, self-inflicted punishment,

9

before we could become worthy of mingling in the social harmony of other spirits. You can have no idea of the nature and extent of the punishment we have undergone. No hell that ever was invented by earthly priest, can equal it in severity; yet there is no hell or torture inflicted in the spirit world. Every wicked spirit that comes here brings the means of his punishment with him in his own nature, which are the stings of his evil conscience. When a spirit passes from the earth to this world, every trait of his nature, habits, principles and passions are delineated on his spiritual features, so that lies and deceptions are totally useless here. The spirits are examined as they come, and then placed in society and positions corresponding to their natures which they possessed in their earthly life. When I made my appearance, after being killed by Nero's order, all the spirits who saw me were startled with horror when they discovered the many traits of my wicked nature. No society would receive me—all fled from me with loathing, and at length I was driven to a solitary desert spot on the outskirts of the lowest sphere, there to remain until my evil nature had consumed itself in sorrow, remorse, wailings, and a deprivation of that celestial pabulum which constitutes the food of the spirits in this world. I was cut off from all noble and intelligent society—cut off from the good and happy. All was gloom and barrenness around me. The light, heat and glory of God did not penetrate my wretched locality; the stings of my conscience and memory, with the hunger of my spiritual body, became so intense that I wished to be annihilated, but I could not die. Oh! the agony of ceaseless hunger is greater than all the other sufferings that can be endured! As Judas was my confidant and agent on the earth, he knew all my iniquities and wicked designs, and he served me with great zeal in the execution of my conspiracy against the good man, Jesus. I was therefore in the power of Judas in that respect. I was afraid that he might expose my crimes to the world, to prevent which, I rewarded his faithful, though sinful services, by taking his life. When I passed into the spirit world, I found that Judas, by the decree of our spiritual superiors, was to be my only companion during the long term of my spiritual exile and purification. Judge, then, if you can, the reception I met with from him when we met at the cheerless spot assigned us. With all the rancor, hate and vindictiveness that it is possible for a wicked spirit to possess, Judas assailed me. All my blackest deeds he continually brought to my remembrance; all my frauds, hypocrisies and meanness, he used as so many venomous stings, to wound my agonizing and remorseful conscience. I endeavored to retort in a similar manner, but he was invulnerable to my less powerful attacks, while I continually suffered under his lashes. Oh! my friend Alexander, mankind need not think that there is a hell in the spirit world to punish the wicked, for the wicked will carry with them hells sufficiently poignant to punish them for their misdeeds. So it was

10

with me and Judas. Our remorse, our mutual recrimination, our ceaseless hunger, and our hopeless state, rendered our immortal condition most horribly wretched. This miserable state continued from year to year, from age to age, and century to century, until the blackness of our hearts and the turpitude of our minds were gradually consumed by our anguish. After the lapse of more than seventeen centuries the powers above us who regulate our spiritual conditions relieved us from our dreary and painful exile. Finding us penitent, humble and completely changed for the better, they allowed us to go into the society of exalted spirits, and ameliorated our condition, by which we could receive comforts and continue to improve ourselves. We rapidly improved. Suavity, serenity and tranquil enjoyment succeeded our bitterness of nature. A love of truth and justice and a desire to do what is right succeeded to our past evil proclivities. A great thirst for knowledge possessed us, for we found that all who aspired to a higher condition must render themselves capable by a knowledge of all things. Thus nearly another century passed on, in course of which we have so improved in our natures that we are the very opposite of our former selves. We are now promised to be exalted to a higher sphere, after we shall have accomplished a certain task, which is the cause or motive we have in communicating with you."

"What may be the nature of that task, and how related to me?" I inquired of the spirits.

"We are requested," answered the spirit Saul, "as an act of atonement for our past wicked deeds, for the benefit of mankind, that we should descend to the earth, and seek out a man to act as our agent and confessor, and to him make known our misdeeds as connected with the conspiracy and death of Jesus of Nazareth; to make known to the world the true history of that good man who was the victim of our wickedness; to disabuse the world of the lies, errors and follies to which they render their faith and homage. Such is the task we have to perform before we are admitted to a higher sphere of exaltation; and the first step we have taken is to select you, Alexander, to be our medium and agent, through whom we will publish to the world the important truths which we have to make known."

"Why have you selected me to be your medium and agent on earth?" I inquired of Saul, being desirous to know his motive in so doing. "Could you not find a man more befitting the office than I? I have no influence or wealth to aid me in doing your bidding, even should I be enabled to furnish the talent and opportunity."

"It matters not," responded Saul, "you are the one selected, and you must comply. However, I have not any objections to acquaint you in part with the reasons why you are selected. If I were to tell you all the reasons they possibly might make you vain, which I do not wish to do. When our spiritual powers imposed upon us the task, they requested

11

that the man we should select for our medium should be one who had lived half a century at least, and that he should possess certain qualities, which I will not name. To these conditions we were obliged to give our assent, if we wished to achieve our own object in view, though we knew it would be very difficult to find such a man. However, we descended to the earth to look for our man, but after several years' wandering and searching, we found all our efforts to be in vain, for such a man was not to be found. We found many who were represented to be such as we wanted, but after minutely investigating their private characters, we found them lacking in the main qualities. We therefore gave up the search as a hopeless affair. Sometime afterward, Judas and I were holding a consultation as to what we should do, when casting our eyes below upon the mundane scene, we beheld a little boy reading the Bible to his mother, while she worked with her needle in her chair. Something in the physiognomy of the boy excited our curiosity, so that we drew near. As the boy read, the subject seemed to shock his sense of truth, for he left off reading and asked his mother if that which he read was true. The mother felt shocked that her child seemed to doubt what she considered to be the word of God. She accordingly told the child that it was true. The boy with great energy, replied, "Mother, I cannot believe it!" "That is a noble boy!" I observed to Judas; "his love and just sense of truth prevents him giving credence to the fables and lies of that old book, though his fond mother tells him it is truth itself."

"Saul," said Judas to me, with sudden vivacity, "an idea strikes me, by which we may accomplish our object. Suppose we were to take that little boy under our guardian care, screen him from all harm, and direct his mind in all matters necessary and good, protecting him until he shall arrive at fifty years of age, then we can make him our medium and agent. I thought the plan of Judas to be an excellent one; accordingly we took the boy under our tutelar care. That little boy, friend Alexander, was yourself."

"Ah!" I exclaimed, and said, "I do remember the incident. I was then about nine years of age. I was in the daily practice of reading the Bible to my mother at her request. I remember the chapter and verse, and from that day, I doubted the truth of the old book. But tell me, Saul, have you and Judas been my guardian spirits ever since?"

"We have," replied Saul; "and we have done you many services, unknown to you. We have saved your life several times. Once when you were a boy, you were in a tree, on one of the highest branches, trying to steal a bird's nest, when the limb gave way. You fell, and certainly would have lost your life had I not saved you. When you were a young man, you traveled in France, where we guided you through many dangers. When you were crossing the ocean, one of the ship's masts snapped asunder, when it, with the yards, sails and rattlings came down with a crash upon the deck where you were standing. There you certainly would have been killed, had we not saved you. You started from Charleston in the schooner "Sarah," for Mobile. When in Mobile Bay, you were tossed upon its boisterous waters, when the boom tackle broke; then the boom swooped round with a tremendous force. You were standing at the helm. Your head being on the same plane with the boom, your brains in another second would have been scattered to the winds, had I not thrown you flat upon the deck at the instant. We saved you from being robbed and assassinated in Mobile city one night. Once you were in a small canoe on the Mississippi waters, your intention being to get on board of a steamboat that was coming up the river. The officers of the boat did not perceive you, consequently they did not arrest the progress of the vessel. Your canoe was in a direct line with the boat, and would have been run under the water in another instant, had we not so guided it as to glide it off within an inch of the huge vessel. Then as the two vessels were moving in opposite directions, swift as the wind I infused into you a sudden impulse which caused you to spring like a grasshopper from the canoe into the boat. Thus you were saved a death by drowning. Do you not think we speak the truth, when we say that we have been your guardians for a long time past?"

"Saul," I made answer, "I now perceive that you have not only spoken the truth, but I find myself much indebted to you and your companion in gratitude for the services you have rendered me. All the instances of peril that you have related recur to my memory. They were considered by me as fortunate escapes, but I had no idea at the time that any spirit or power beyond this world was taking an interest in my preservation."

"I could mention many other instances wherein we have saved you from danger," resumed the spirit Saul; "but I will not take up more of your time than is necessary. However, there are some things I must relate to give you a correct understanding of our good intentions so as to establish your confidence in me and Judas. You remember the first time you loved one of earth's fair daughters; that love was unhappy in its issue. You were disappointed; your affections were blighted; you became a man of sorrow; you took to wandering, and fell into a bad habit, with the motive of mitigating the poignancy of your feelings. We could not eradicate from your breast the pains accruing from blighted affections, or we would have done so; however, we kept our guardian eyes upon you that you should not go to destruction. We left you alone for a time to pursue your wanderings, thinking that the new adventures you might encounter would be the greatest balm to a wounded heart. Time and change of scene did not produce the desired effect. We then thought it prudent to interpose and save you from destruction, for the course you were pursuing would have led you to that end. Accordingly we worked

13

upon your nervous system by means of magnetic and electric powers. You saw within you certain beautiful lights and many strange perceptions; you heard many strange sounds—to you very wonderful though to us in the spirit they were very simple. These impressions caused within you great astonishment. You became aroused. You saw your fallen condition. You became ashamed, and resolved to recover your self-esteem and social respect. We continued our process with you, and at length you began to search for the cause. You investigated matters of medicine and philosophy, and in time your mind became trained to study. In this process, your sorrow, your evil habit and despair were overcome. Having thus recovered you from your desponding condition, in order to prevent you from falling into the like state again, we thought we would produce within you something which would cause a happy state of feeling and joyous mind, and serve you under all cirumstances of life to cheer you onward. We accordingly acted upon that part of the brain where the faculty of music is situated. You were then internally entertained by a series of low, sweet tones, as though coming from a small instrument, performing all the good, lively airs that you had ever heard from your boyhood. By way of change we so worked upon your faculties that it seemed as if you heard singing of trio voices, externally to you, of the most harmonious strains. In fact, we produced within you that happy mood, that everything within and around you seemed filled with musical harmony. Thus we cared for you, and led you on until you entered upon the marriage state; then we withdrew our powers from over you, finding that you would have occupation enough for your mind of a domestic nature."

"Kind and worthy spirits," I exclaimed, as feelings of deep gratitude impelled me, "I now perceive that you have been my true guardian friends. You have now made clear to me all those mysterious occurrences that have been hanging over me so many years. As I am so deeply indebted to you, I consider that you have a just claim upon my gratitude, therefore command me in any respect. I will exert all my powers to do your bidding. Speak your wishes, and let me know how I can serve you."

"All explanations necessary having been made between us," responded the spirit Saul, "I will now proceed to inform you what Judas and I wish of you. You have now passed your fiftieth year, which is one of the conditions we are bound to in making our selection of a medium, and in all other respects, you are the man qualified to do us the service we require. We will now leave you for a while, to consult with our superiors; and when we shall communicate with you the next time, we will enter upon our intended task. Farewell for the present."

The preceding communication with the spirits was committed to paper from memory; but from fear of trusting too much to that faculty, I resolved for the future, to write down the most material points of the spirits' discourse, and afterwards to write them out in full, with such additions and illustrations as the subjects should require to make them understood. Accordingly, I made all necessary preparations when in the two following sittings Saul communicated to me the following;

INTRODUCTION

CONFESSIONS OF SAUL OF TARSUS.

SAUL OF TARSUS.

"Friend Alexander," said the Spirit Saul to me, at our next communion, who, at this time, seemed to be unattended by Judas, "since I was with you I have had an interview with our Superior Spiritual Powers, who regulate the affairs of this sphere in which I am placed. I made known to them my good fortune in having discovered you. I described your character: related some of the incidents of your life, and at length gained their assent to make you our medium and agent in the business I have alluded to. I will now give you a sketch of my true worldly career, which will be necessary in order to understand rightly the important narrative that is to follow it."

The spirit gave vent to a deep sigh, and paused for a few minutes, as though he were endeavoring to overcome some violent emotions. At length he said in a saddened tone of voice:

"It is a sad thing my friend, to confess that which I am about to do. To speak of one's self, concerning things and deeds, the remembrance of which fills me with horror; but such is the result of a sinful life, and therefore, however loathing and repugnant to me, it must be done. Bear with me, then, my friend, during my recital. Let not your just indignation break with me, but wait patiently to the end, and bear witness to the only atonement I can

16

make to outraged humanity for my past wickedness and follies.

I was born in Tarsus, a city of Cilicia, about two years preceding the birth of Jesus of Nazareth. This is important to observe, for after the death of Jesus, when my name is first introduced in the book of Acts, I am there represented as a very young man, supposed to be much younger than he was, when in fact I was his elder. The name given to me by my parents was Saul, after my progenitor through the line of Benjamin. My father was named Bathus; my mother Eunice. They were both pious people of the Jewish faith, and I was educated in the same principles.

My father was an active, persevering man, desirous of doing something in the world, but seeing nothing better or more available to him than common business, he limited his ambition to that, to which he applied himself with great energy, with the idea in view of becoming in course of time wealthy. He was a tent maker by trade, at which he prospered and gained riches.

After receiving the rudiments of an education at home, I was sent, at about twelve years of age, to Jerusalem to finish under the tutorship of Rabbi Rabban Gamaliel, a celebrated man, with whom I remained several years. I said that I was educated in the same religious principles as my parents, and during my youth I was an innocent believer in them; but when at the Holy City, surrounded by the priesthood, and having recourse to their books of law and traditions, a great flood of light gradually spread over my mind. I could not help perceiving the trickeries, knaveries, hypocrisies and selfishness of those holy men; and as well, the lies, fables and absurdities of the sacred books. I consequently became an infidel to the whole system and state of things, from the beginning to the end; but I had the prudence to hide my sentiments, and in course of time I became as great a hypocrite as the rest. I inherited from my father his persevering, active nature, and as I grew toward manhood, I felt a restless desire or ambition to do something in the world above common men, though I could not tell of what nature it should be. I could not reconcile myself to the idea of pursuing business and wealth as my father did before me; nor could I be contented with the limited and disgusting routine of the priesthood. I thought there was something greater destined for me to do than to be singing psalms, blowing trumpets, or gorging upon roasted meats, which were the general avocations of the holy priesthood. Yes! I felt an ambition within me to do something greater and more ennobling than this. I wished to be mounting up to a conspicuous elevation in the estimation of the world. I felt as though I could grasp in one hand all the minds of mankind, and with the other that I could lead them in fetters.

I continued my studies at Jerusalem until I had attained manhood, when I was suddenly called home, as my father had fallen sick. I returned to Tarsus. Soon after my father died, leaving me his business and a great portion of his wealth. At the solicitation of my mother and her friends I continued the business, though much against my inclination. However, as I had not any definite idea of any other course that I could pursue to my liking, I continued to follow in my father's steps for some years. In the meantime, my wealth was increasing. When I had attained my thirtieth year, my mother died; then I resolved to quit the business, leave my native city, and return to Jerusalem, for I longed to be one of the actors, if not the rulers of that distinguished city. I accordingly turned all my effects into money, took leave of my friends, and with one servant or bondman, I bid adieu to Tarsus.

About the time that I arrived at Jerusalem, Pontius Pilate was appointed Governor of Judea, and Caiaphas was shortly after made High Priest of the Temple. I had several friends in the city, among whom was my old tutor, Gamaliel, who proposed to me certain matters by way of occupation, but none of them met my views or inclinations at the time. Thus I continued inactive for the space of a year, wandering to and fro without knowing what it was I sought or wanted. At length in the course of my peregrinations, my curiosity and attentions were aroused by observing a wild looking man in an uncouth dress, preaching in various localities, a system of reformed theological doctrines. I listened to several of his discourses before the people, and found the main subject to be "The repentance of sins, and remission of the same through baptism of water." But that which excited my greatest curiosity was, that this preacher, who was called John the Baptist, during his preaching, several times intimated that somebody was coming after him, greater than he, who would have not only the power to forgive and remit sins, but would be enabled to cure diseases of the flesh, and open the heavens to all true believers. In fact, this John intimated that the time for the coming of the Messiah was at hand, and he would shortly appear.

As I said before, this part of the preacher's discourse aroused within me a great curiosity. I was desirous of discovering who this great personage could be that John was keeping in the background. I suspected that John was in colleague with somebody, who, under the assumption of the Messiah's advent, was going to make an attempt to change the theological views of society, and exalt himself into power. I was not credulous enough to believe in the appearance of any true Messiah. This set my mind in action. I endeavored to imagine their designs, doctrines and actions, until I became weary of reflection; and at length I resolved to sift the matter thoroughly and as quickly as possible. Accordingly I sought an interview with John the Baptist, in his retreat among the wilderness of mountains by the lake Asphaltez. I saw the man, and found him to be more of a fool and fanatic than a cunning impostor as I suspected. He was a wild ascetical fanatic, who had rendered himself crazy by studying the books of the prophets; yet he was sincere in what he said and believed. He said that he had found the Messiah in a certain man whom he was going to baptize on the morrow, when he would introduce him to the people. Having gained this information from John, I resolved to be present at this baptism.

On the day appointed I was at the place designated. I saw the baptism, and I saw the man whom John had brought forth to play a conspicuous part in life. I certainly never saw a more noble, amiable and handsome man in my life; and after hearing certain accounts of his skill or mysterious power in curing of diseases I considered him a fit person to assume the part that John in his religious fanaticism, considered he naturally inherited. All these things combined, suggested an idea to me, of what should be my future career. I hurried to my home and entered into deep reflection. Idea after idea, and plan after plan did I revolve and scan in my mind. At length my plan was decided upon. I sprang to my feet, and paced the room, exclaiming, "It shall be so! I will yet be a new star to dazzle the vision of mankind! They shall follow where I lead; they shall obey, reverence, and perhaps do me homage. Now, Saul, to action! Forward to the end in view, and crush down all things that obstruct thy path!"

In this sketch of my earthly career, I need not give you the particulars of my proceedings. I will merely state my design and its results, leaving all details until I give you the true narrative of Jesus, which is the great object I have in view.

My design was to make Jesus and his reform doctrines the means by which I would build a new religious sect, that should be acceptable and promising to the poorer and ignorant part of the community; and which should seem to be based upon the dim and ambiguous ravings of the Jewish prophets. In fact, by misconstruing and misrepresenting the discourses of Jesus with the aid of lies and deceptions, to represent him as the expected Messiah, and that he should represent himself as such, even in defiance of his own intentions and speech. This I found possible, with the assistance of others who worked at my bidding. After Jesus should have run his reform career for a time, it was my intention to bring him in collision with the authorities of the Temple and the Government. I said to myself: "He must then be removed and sacrificed to the principles and doctrines he endeavored to establish in society; for new principles take deep root in the minds of men, when they are well sprinkled with the blood of martyrdom." This I managed to accomplish by my evil schemings and workings. Jesus was sacrificed. The foundation was now laid upon which I built the superstructure of my ambitious desires. John the Baptist, while acting under his religious craziness, served my ends; but while in prison he returned to a sane state of mind, and began to see his errors and folly. From fear that he would recant what he had previously taught concerning Jesus, I caused him to be destroyed. Judas I slew with my own hands, as soon as I could dispense with his services, from fear that he would betray me to the world as he was the depositary of my secrets. There was now but one person of whom I was jealous, or considered an obstruction in my path; it was Stephen. I hated him for his virtues and talents, and I was afraid that while he lived I should not be the first to lead and govern the disciples of Jesus, and be considered worthy of their esteem. Accordingly I managed to have him denounced by the Sanhedrim, and sacrificed to their fury and my hatred.

Having accomplished all these preliminaries, I came forward in open day as an actor. With delegated authority from the Sanhedrim, I traveled towards Damascus, under the pretence of persecuting the new people; but in fact, it was to get into a more favorable locality where I could perform the first part of my open intended career. As I approached the city, a storm arose of thunder and lightning. "Here is an opportunity I must not lose," I said to myself. Then I threw myself from my horse— fell prostrate on the ground, and acted a pantomime of great terror. Indeed, with a little well performed imposture, I pretended that the spirit of Jesus had appeared to me, rebuking me for my wicked course, and commanding me henceforth to go through the world preaching his doctrines and principles. My imposture was generally believed by the disciples and followers of the late Jesus, and all those who knew other- wise, did not think it worth while to notice it. After a time, which I passed in reflecting upon my future plans, but which I represented as passed in repentance and prayer, I entered upon my travels, preaching certain doctrines of my own invention, which I gave to the world as being the doctrines of that Jesus whom I had caused to be murdered. My own fictions and lies I passed off as being the gospels of truth, as delivered from the mouth of the crucified Jesus, the Christ, the Son of God.

Oh! What a terrible monstrosity! What a mountain of vile imposition I have imposed upon the world! My deeds while on earth were black and heinous enough; but the wickedness of my doctrines, which I left to after ages of blind, credulous man, were ten thousand times more damning. What a contrast there is, my friend Alexander, between the doctrines taught by Jesus and those I represented as his! His discourses consisted of the purest and best of morality, calculated to establish among men a sense of love, justice, charity and humility. He endeavored to abolish all wicked and vicious habits, practices and notions; supplying their stead with a knowledge of physical truths and principles, all of which tended to harmonize mankind. His speculative ideas, if not real- ities, were beautiful assumptions, teaching that there was one universal, eternal God of love and mercy, who delighted in all that was good am- ong his children, rewarding all according to their merits. He taught that death was not to be annihilation, as some supposed, but only a transition state from our mortal to an immortal nature, where the emigrating spirit would he placed in a sphere of favorable conditions to carry out all its noble and virtuous aspirations.

The doctrines of Jesus were the principles of nature, simplified, easy to comprehend, and redounding to the benefit of man. In character, Jesus was a lover of truth and of his fellow men, full of charitable and benevolent feeling, mild and unassuming in his deportment, contented with little in this world, and depending upon God for all things, whom he, in his unknown orphan state, styled his Heavenly Father. Contrast with this character, friend Alexander, the ridiculous and absurd doctrines I preached concerning Jesus—all the nonsense of faith, grace and salvation by the redemption of sins through the blood of Jesus the Christ. Look at the books called the Gospels, the original one being written by Luke, at my suggestion and designing, from which all the others have been copied and imitated, with thousands of additions and omissions, to suit the notions of the various itinerant preachers calling themselves the teachers of the words of Jesus. Examine these books, and see the mass of confused and contradictory nonsense delivered as the teachings of Jesus. See the absurd and ridiculous light in which his character is represented, with qualities neither befitting a man nor a god, both of which he is represented to be. Coming into the world in a most ridiculous and unnatural manner; assuming to have a mission which he never performed; assuming to have power that he never exercised in defense of himself or his friends; assuming to be sent to a people, who would not receive him, and preaching his mission to those he was not sent to. He professes to be a man of peace, and that all mankind by him shall be blessed; yet he says that he was not sent to restore peace, but the sword. In one place he says he is equal with God, and in another, he says he is not equal. At one time he says his witness or record is truth itself; then in another he denies the same; and in general his character is represented to be deficient of all those qualities necessary to constitute a great and noble man, and much more, it is deficient of those necessary to constitute a God as he is represented to be. In fact, Alexander, if you examine the Gospels, my Epistles, and all the other writings of the New Testament, you will find them to be a compilation of lies, contradictory statements, ridiculous absurdities and mystical nonsense, too disgusting for any intelligent person to give credence or dependence to. I was the originator of the celebrated Gospels; but subsequent impostors like myself, added and altered my model to suit themselves, all of which have been palmed upon the ignorant world as the history and doctrines of Jesus.

There is one exception I must make, as regards my writings and preachings. I taught the doctrine of immortality after death. That is

actually true, as I have found it to be since my earthly career terminated, yet there is no credit due me for preaching that truth, as it had
been taught by many, before me or Jesus. I had no definite ideas concerning it, and cannot say that I believed it, as my wicked career will
testify, though I made it the grand theme of my teachings; but finding it
acceptable to the people, I laid great stress upon it, and by a little
sophistry I made it seem true to their minds. Oh! my friend! I wish all my
other impositions had been as happy in their results as this.

Thus, Alexander, instead of teaching the people the sublime and
happy morals, and the beautiful speculative ideas of Jesus, I wandered
over many countries teaching the detestable dogma to which I have
alluded, which I called the words of Jesus the Christ.

I pretended to work some cures in imitation of him, when with a little
jugglery and some lies, I gained the reputation of working miracles.
Whenever I wanted a new authority or wished to establish anything
new, I had a happy faculty of seeing visions, so that with a few mystical
figures or images, I construed things just as I wanted them to be.
Sometimes I pretended that miracles were wrought in my favor, in order
to establish my importance, and gain reverence from the deluded people.
Such, as when I was made prisoner at Philippi, through the assistance of
some friends, I bribed the jailor to let me escape; then the story was
told, in order to screen him, that I was set free by an angel. The silly
people forgot to think that in my subsequent career I was in more
difficult circumstances, yet no angel came to deliver me.

One great reason of my success in making proselytes and gaining
subscriptions, as I pretended for pious purposes, was the power of my
hypocritical simulation. I was all things to all men, as nigh as it was possible to be. With Jews, I boasted of being a Jew; with the Pharisees I
was a Pharisee. Before the Greeks, I was a Greek; and with the Romans
I claimed to be a Roman citizen. Before the Gentiles I preached against
the laws and ceremonies of Moses; and when I thought it to my interest
to enter the Temple, I shaved my head and conformed to all other ceremonies.

I preached meekness and humility in all cases, times and places; yet
there was no greater self-willed tyrant than myself, when I thought I had
the power. For instance, my dispute with Barnabas, Jesus, when before
his judges was mocked and otherwise ill-treated; but he bore all with the
mildness of the lamb. Although I taught the like conduct, yet I could not
conform to it, for when the High Priest ordered me to be smitten on the
cheek, I cursed him with all the rancor and ill-feeling of a demon. I
preached against all worldly interests, especially lucre, yet I was always
very zealous in making collections of money, to distribute to distressed
brethren at a distance, and in so doing I never forgot to take a share;
and sometimes, I was so covetous that I exited the suspicions of certain

rival apostles who made charges against my honesty, and sometimes their charges were true.

Toward the latter part of my career, many rival pretenders to piety and virtue, like myself, rose up against me; they had much envious feeling, suspicion and charges against me. They stripped me of a great many of my assumed virtues, powers and mighty works, representing me to be very much like what I really was—a selfish, ambitious, boasting impostor. This made me sick at heart, so that I almost repented of having entered upon my chosen course. But I found that I had advanced too far to recede. My course was chosen, and I was obliged to follow it, or suffer an ignominious fall.

Being naturally of a bold heart and full of assurance, I recovered courage, and continued my onward career repelling the charges of my rivals and enemies, and crushing all my opponents that came across my path. Thus I continued to wander for some years, making proselytes to my senseless doctrines, in the name of Jesus the Christ, and pretending to perform cures of a miraculous nature, establishing churches, of which I always made myself the head or principal.

In the course of my wanderings, having made a man of note and authority a convert, whose name was Paulius, I changed my name from Saul to Paul, as vanity suggested to me that it sounded of greater worth and importance. Thus I continued my career, it being generally successful and pleasing to my ambition, until I entered the Temple, and hypocritically conformed to the ceremonies which I had been preaching against. The people did not believe me to be sincere. They were aroused to anger against me. They seized me and brought me before the tribunal of the Sanhedrim, under the very same charges I had made against Jesus, at the same Sanhedrim a few years before. From that day the tide of fortune turned, and afterward evil was my destiny.

After much suffering and imprisonment, I was conveyed to Rome a prisoner, to plead my cause before the Imperial Senate. Nero was Emperor then. My cause was thought to be too trifling to be heeded, so that I was almost at liberty. I continued to preach and work miracles, making many converts, among whom was one of Nero's concubines. She professed herself a believer in the new doctrines and faith. I was always in daily communion with her, so that we were intimately acquainted. She was a woman of great beauty; in fact, it was not very extraordinary that my carnal passions should be aroused, and desires in conformity took possession of me toward her. Considering that I had full command over her mind, I was infatuated enough to make certain proposals to her. I found myself mistaken in the woman. She highly resented my proposals, and immediately acquainted her imperial master, and the result was, that in a short time, I found myself in prison. I did not remain there long, however, for in a few hours afterward I was led forth to execution. Thus

23

ended my ambitious and wicked earthly career.

Now, my friend Alexander, I have given a slight sketch of my evil deeds and misspent life while on earth. That it was one of great folly, error and wickedness, it will be useless to iterate; but that is not the worst of it. The results since my death have been ten thousand times more baneful to the cause of humanity than that which preceded it. For eighteen centuries the minds of men have been overspread with a gloomy, destructive superstition that I have entailed upon them. My dogma has enveloped them with the grossest and darkest of ignorance, and it has prevented them from making any advances in virtue, or intellectual improvement. Nearly all those who have endeavored to enlighten and liberate their fellow-men, have been crushed out of existence. Bloody wars have deluged the earth in every age and country for the space of eighteen hundred years. Men have destroyed each other individually with fire, sword, the rack and gibbet. The loathsome dungeon, torture and famine have swept millions of men from the earth, and all those who have been spared a cruel and untimely death, have been living in mental bondage.

Such were the awful results of the damnable doctrines that I preached to mankind, in the name of Jesus the Christ. Had I known the baneful consequences of my reckless ambition, wicked as was my nature, I could not have continued in the course which has proved the greatest curse that ever afflicted mankind. But I have suffered, greatly suffered, for my misdeeds! While the fools, hypocrites and knaves were burning incense, and shouting praises to Paul the Apostle for his good and pious deeds when on earth, I was shivering and writhing with the tortures of the hell within me. The poignant stings of guilt and remorse were piercing my soul through and through—curling me up with a ceaseless, excruciating agony. For nearly eighteen centuries did I hunger and thirst after the sustenance peculiar to spiritual life. While deluded mortals considered me to be enjoying the beauties and bliss of a happy exalted state in this world, I was suffering all the indescribable agonies of the self-damned. But time has passed. I have made all the atonement that is required of me here for my misdeeds while on earth, yet there is one duty I must perform to humanity. I must enlighten them concerning my history in connection with Jesus of Nazareth, and give a true narrative of that part of his life which terminated in a tragic death, of which I was the instigator. It is the only atonement I can make for the outrage I have given to mankind, and the injustice done to the injured Jesus. When I say this, I speak for Judas also, who sincerely joins me in the sentiments I declare; for he, as far as he was connected with this lamentable affair, wishes to make whatever atonement is possible to Jesus and mankind.

Before I proceed to impart to you the information which is to constitute the True Narrative of Jesus of Nazareth, I must give you a slight sketch of his early history, which being remote, and not necessarily connected with that part of his life in which I was an actor, I will not mingle it with the rest, but impart what I have to say, at present.

THE EARLY HISTORY OF JESUS.

Friend Alexander, I will not insult your intellect by supposing that you believe there is any truth in the vile and ridiculous account that Luke and I concocted when we wrote the history of Jesus concerning Mary, the virgin mother—the Holy Ghost in the form of a dove, acting as a proxy for the God of Heaven, in begetting a son who was to be equal to himself, and had existed through all time before he was begotten. I will not insult your reason, by supposing you to believe any part of these silly lies; but I will give you the true account of his youthful days as far as I received it from Jesus himself.

A short time after I had passed into the spirit world, being exiled from all society, in dreary exclusion, I received a visit from the spirit of the much injured Jesus, whom I had caused to be sacrificed to the hatred of the Jewish priests. I quailed before his benign and noble presence, feeling myself unworthy to meet his gaze. He gently rebuked me for the many evils I had done him, saying that he was informed of all by Judas, whom I had sent to the spirit world the same night that Jesus died. He told me that he forgave me for all my wickedness in regard to him, and then he spoke in sympathizing tones of my suffering condition. He said he could not mitigate my agonies, or he would, advising me to repent, aspire after righteousness, and strive to renew my nature for the better; that my wretched exclusion would be terminated in course of time, and I then would be allowed to mingle with the blessed. He then spoke of many parts of his history, enlightening me on many points I knew not before.

As regards his early days, he said that Joseph the carpenter and his wife, Mary, moved into Nazareth when he was not many days old. Nobody knew from whence they had come. They settled there, and gained the esteem of their neighbors as honest, prudent, working people. He never heard his parents speak of any mysterious or miraculous event in connection with his birth, yet as he grew up he perceived that there was some mystery or doubt concerning him, whispered among the neighbors. Some doubted his being the son of Joseph and Mary. Some went so far as to say that Mary never had a child; for little Jose, as Jesus was called in his youth, had been nourished on goat's milk, and the breast of Mary had never suckled a child, nor did she give any other indications of having become a mother. There were other instances the folks cited, as proof that Jose was not the son of Joseph and Mary. He

25

bore no resemblance in person, disposition or character to them. Whose son was he, then? Nobody knew, if Joseph and Mary were not his parents. However, the child grew in health, strength and great beauty of person. He did not take pleasure in the ordinary mischievous freaks and follies of children, the characteristics of his disposition being mildness, general amiability, and susceptibility to all grave and pious impressions. He was sent to school at the ordinary age to the synagogue of the village, where, as soon as he had mastered the rudiments of the language, he studied with great avidity the subjects of morals, metaphysics and religion, as then taught in the schools. He seemed to possess great intellectual capacity and comprehension, for at the age of fifteen he was pronounced the most intelligent youth and greatest disputer in the synagogue of the village and neighborhood.

As he approached manhood he became acquainted with a youth about his own age, whose name was John, who was the son of a priest, being educated for one of the priesthood. This youth was of a restless, erratic and visionary disposition, not content with the ordinary routine and views of things, for his mind was directed to a series of changes, innovations and reforms, which he was continually suggesting and advocating with the greatest of energy and confidence in his illusions.

The two youths—though very different in dispositions—became inseparable companions, for they found great pleasure in each other's company—not so much because their views in general assimilated, but they found an intense interest in contrasting their dissimilar ideas. They took long rambles together, sometimes being so interested in their discourses that they did not know whither they were going or where they were. Mount Tabor and its environments were frequently the scenes of their disputes and rambles.

One day they were taking a ramble as usual, and they discoursed upon certain moral subjects which were extremely exciting. They had been walking for hours without heeding their course. At length having made a pause they discovered that they were completely lost. They looked around them to discover indications of their whereabouts, but nothing could they see that they knew. The scene presented a grassy vale, along which meandered a small stream. At a short distance, at the foot of a hill, they perceived a small hut constructed of logs, the roof of which being covered with branches, rushes and soil. In front of this building they perceived a human being sitting on a rock. To him they directed their steps, with the view of inquiring their way back to their village. When they arrived at the spot they found the person to be a hoary-headed old man, enveloped in a long black robe, bare-headed, and feet without sandals. They soon came to the conclusion that they had fallen in the way of a recluse.

Having greeted the old man and stated their case, he, with a pleasing smile upon his countenance, gave the desired information, telling them that their case was not an uncommon one, for he had once been a youth himself, and had frequently lost his way, and the sight of realities around him in the pleasing contemplation of airy visions. He then invited them into his habitation, and set before them some food, telling them to rest and refresh themselves. He also invited them to tarry with him the night, as the day was far spent. The young men expressed their sense of his kindness, and gratefully accepted the hospitable invitation. The recluse then replenished his fire with sticks, which was burning in the center of the hut, and when the day was passed, they all three lounged around it, passing some hours in discourse. The old man seemed to be posessed of a great mind. Whether it came from experience, learning or supernal inspirations, they knew not; but most of his ideas were perfectly new to them, being of the most profound, philosophic nature, giving explanations and revelations of things, which to them had hitherto been as so many mysteries. He spoke of the great mysterious power pervading all nature under the name of God; of the multitude and magnitude of created things; of the different races of men; of their past and present errors; of the gradual progress and capacity of the human mind, and the probability that in course of time mankind will arrive at comparative perfection.

The two young men listened attentively to the old man's discourse, they never before having heard the like. Jose saw clearly that the recluse had got his ideas through experience and deep reflection, while John concluded that no man could speak as he had done unless he was supernaturally inspired. He said to himself, "Certainly this man is a prophet! I will question him, concerning myself."

"My worthy host," said John to the old man, "I must confess that I have never heard a man speak more startling truths than you have done. You certainly must possess the power of prevision and prophecy. I beg of you, if it be so, that you will try your powers upon me, and tell me what will be my career and end of life."

"Young man," answered the recluse, with a serious candor, "you are mistaken in your estimate of me. I candidly tell you that I do not possess the powers of which you speak; nor do I make any pretensions thereto, and all others who assume to be such I consider to be visionary enthusiasts or vile impostors. I consider it impossible with any person on earth, or spirit above, to see a thing that does not exist. Future events we all know do not exist, and as such, they consequently can not be seen or foreseen. But I will tell you what it is possible to do. A man is capable of speaking of probabilities according to the knowledge he may have of the thing in question. For instance, from the insight I have of you I can state some things that may probably occur to you during your lifetime."

27

"What may they be?" eagerly inquired John.

"They are to this effect," answered the recluse: "You will live a visionary life, meeting many disappointments and disgusts at what you will consider the perversity and wickedness of the world, because it does not prove to be such as you wish it or expect it to be. You will live an erratic and unsocial career, for your nature will find no pleasure in the general society of men. This disposition will lead you into many difficulties; your mind will become unhinged, and your end will be soon and unpleasant."

"Indeed!" exclaimed John, as he reclined himself back, with an air of one disappointed and mortified. "Your estimation of my career is not very promising or flattering. However, there is one comfort; you do not give them as facts, but only as probabilities. But what say you of my companion? he added, as he pointed to Jose. "Can you not say something better of him?"

"With regard to your companion," said the recluse, as he gazed into the eyes of Jose, "there may be something said of him of a very extraordinary nature."

"If you can foresee anything that will add to my happiness or of that of my fellow men, I pray you let me hear it," observed Jose.

"I perceive, my dear youth," responded the old man as he continued his gaze upon Jose, at the same time feeling of his hand, fingers and wrist with some mysterious motive, "that within you lies latent a great power, which, when brought into action, will influence the minds and act upon the bodies of your fellow men, producing the most extraordinary and astounding results."

Jose started, and a tremulous emotion passed through him at this declaration of the recluse.

"I mean," continued the latter, "that there is within you a mine of nervous power, which, when exercised upon your fellow men, will be capable of ameliorating many of their miseries, by producing the cure of their bodily diseases, and mitigating the severities of others; at the same time it will enable you to command their minds, to lead them from their errors and vices, to better conditions and understandings."

"Oh! blessed will be the day, if that shall prove true," exclaimed Jose as he sprang forward and seized the hand of the old man, which he pressed fervently from the impulse of his joyful excitement. "Make me acquainted with its nature, and convince me of its truth; then I shall be one of the happiest of men."

"There is a principle or power that pervades all animated nature, by some termed life, by others, spirit," observed the old man. "This power is not the same in all beings, especially in man. In some, it is weak; in others it is very strong. Some men who possess this power in an extraordinary degree, are capable of acting upon their weaker fellows, producing good or evil effects, as their dispositions direct them to act. The nature of the effects produced are very various; but when this power is exercised with benevolent designs, much good can be produced to our fellow men, in curing certain diseases, and influencing the mind in the right direction of virtue."

"Oh, most worthy sir," exclaimed Jose, his eyes beaming with enthusiasm and rapture, "make me sensible how I possess this power, for my delight of life is to do good to my fellow men."

"The power, as I said, lies latent within you," replied the recluse. "It requires some other external power to arouse it; and when once brought into action, it will continue in force during your life. I have the happiness to possess that power to a certain extent; and I think, if you give your consent, I shall be enabled to call forth that which lies latent within you."

Jose gave his consent, when he and the recluse rose from their seats, while John regarded them in speechless surprise as he remained in his place. The recluse desired Jose to stand erect against the wall of the hut. He then removed his garments, leaving his neck and breast bare; then placing his right hand upon the top of his head and taking his left hand in his other, they remained in this position for some minutes. Then he placed his right hand upon the back of his neck, and his left upon his breast, remaining thus for some minutes. Then he placed both hands upon the sides of his head, and moved them down to the soles of his feet; this he repeated several times. Then he placed both hands upon his shoulders, and slowly moved them down his arms to his fingers, which he repeated several times. At the commencement of this process, Jose felt a sudden icy chill pass through him, which was succeeded by a glow of heat and a tingling sensation all over him externally. All his vital organs seemed to expand and acquire force; his physical and moral energy seemed to become greater.

"Now," said the recluse, as he terminated the last mentioned actions, "let us see whether my anticipations are correct or not."

He then told Jose to stand in front of John, to fix upon his eyes his own steadfast gaze, and to will in his own mind that John should sleep, and then he gave directions to perform certain manipulations, all of which Jose performed accordingly. The result was as the recluse anticipated. John regarded his companion with an incredulous smile, as though he doubted the theory of the recluse; but soon his eyelids drooped, the smile vanished from his lips, his countenance became pale, and the relaxed state of his muscles gave evidence that he was no longer conscious of external things

"He sleeps," remarked the recluse.

"Wonderful!" exclaimed Jose, as he regarded the result with astonishment, and felt for the old man a degree of profound reverence.

"This sleep," added the recluse, "is very different from the ordinary one of mortals. The mind and all the powers of life are totally abstracted from the corporeal senses, and his individual existence is quiescent to all influences, save that of your own. In fact, his body is totally insensible, and his spirit is subject to your will in all respects, as I will convince you."

The recluse then took a small stick, with which he beat the sleeper over the shoulders and legs, without eliciting any signs of sensibility or motions. Then he gave Jose some directions how to exercise his will-power over him. Jose then stood in front of the sleeper, and with the concentrated energies of his will, commanded the latter to arise and follow him. Immediately the sleeping John arose and stood erect; then with a fearless step, he followed Jose around the hut, passed out of the doorway, and for a few minutes walked to and fro in front of it; then returning to the hut he was restored to his former position by the side of the fire.

Then Jose, having received instructions from the recluse, by certain counter manipulations restored John to his former state of wakefulness and sensibility. As soon as he had recovered his consciousness he looked around him with astonishment, and said: "Well this is strange! I really believe that I have slept."

"You have," responded the recluse.

"But did I sleep from my own nature, or from any power exercised over me by my companion?" inquired John.

"You slept," answered the recluse, "through the influence of a power possessed by your companion, which was existing in a latent state within him, and which I aroused to action. This power he has exercised over you, causing your body to become insensible to touch, and your mind and life-powers to concentrate themselves yet to become subservient to his will."

When the recluse had given this explanation, John raised his eyes to Jose, in which was an expression of reverence and awe; then raising his hands and clasping them together, he exclaimed exultingly, "Glory to the most High! His will is made manifest to me! My suspicions and anticipations are now become realities! The prophets have not spoken in vain assumptions; their words are true!" He then rushed from the hut.

When John had left, the recluse observed "the conduct of your companion is very strange."

"It is to those who know not his nature as well as I do," replied Jose. "He is naturally a great enthusiast, which has impelled him to gather up many chimerical and fanciful notions. From what he has just experienced, some new fanciful notion has just started in his mind concerning me; but I will reason with him tomorrow, and check its further growth."

The recluse and Jose passed some time discoursing upon the nature of the power newly developed in the latter. Full particulars were given by the recluse, according to his experience of its application to the benefit of men; the kind of diseases that would come under its influence; its mode of operation on the mind and body, and many other traits of its nature. To all of this Jose listened with intense interest and joy. Time became far advanced into the night, and as John did not return, they reclined themselves to repose.

About the break of day, John entered the hut, seeming to be much exhausted, as though he had passed the night in wrestling with intense emotions. The two companions then, after thanking their host, took leave of him, and departed for their homes.

As they went along, Jose imparted to John all that had taken place the previous evening concerning the induced sleep of the latter, and some important information he had acquired besides. He endeavored to impress his companion with the idea, that the power he possessed was a natural one, though not possessed by all men. John listened attentively without responding a word, but towards the conclusion of Jose's explanation, he shook his head, and looked up to his friend with an expression that seemed to doubt what he had heard.

"You seem to doubt what I have been saying," observed Jose as he caught the glance of his companion.

"I do, in one respect," replied John. "Your explanation of this mysterious power may be all true, excepting, as I think, your inference that it is natural to man. I doubt that."

"Then how do you view it?" inquired Jose with surprise.

"I have my ideas upon the subject," replied John, "but I do not wish to state them now. Let us cease to speak of it, and hasten home."

The two companions then continued their route in silence, each being absorbed in his own thoughts. As they came within a short distance of Nazareth, they entered a humble habitation by the roadside to see one of the neighboring families.

The people were poor, and the wife and mother was afflicted with severe neuralgic pains. As soon as Jose perceived the case of the poor woman, a thought struck him that this would be a good opportunity to test his mysterious power in the cure of diseases, and he therefore resolved to make the attempt. Calling the woman to him he addressed her in a soothing strain touching her malady; and when he perceived that he had wrought her mind to a befitting tone, he manipulated her from head to foot, exerting the full energy of his will to scatter the disease, and gently touched with his fingers the most afflicted parts. In a few seconds the woman declared herself relieved of her pains, and said she was cured. Unspeakable was the astonishment of the family, and great was their joy and gratitude. The eyes of Jose were lit up with great pleasure, while John stood with eyes fixed upon his companion.

"Come, John, let us depart," said Jose, as he took the latter by the wrist, and broke the spell that was upon him. They then passed into the road; but John, instead of walking by the side of Jose, followed a little in the rear.

"Why do you linger behind, John?" inquired Jose of his companion.

"It is not becoming in me to place myself on an equality with you any longer," replied John, in a troubled voice. "Hitherto we have been familiar companions, bound to each other by the bonds of friendship, but now a line of distinction must be drawn between us. Our companionship must give place to that of master and servant, and my friendship must be replaced by love, reverence and duty."

"By the Holy of Holies," exclaimed Jose, as he regarded his companion with the greatest astonishment. "Are you crazy, John? Whom do you take me to be?"

"The truth must no longer be withheld," replied John seriously. "The Lord has made his will and ways manifest to me this day, and the words of the prophet are come true, when he said, "Behold my servant whom I uphold; mine elect, in whom I am delighted. I have put my spirit upon him. Yes, Jose, you are the blessed one of whom the prophet has been speaking. That mysterious power you have of doing good, is supernatural, which is confirmatory of the truth. I can no longer doubt of your being the— "

John paused, as though he were afraid to utter the next word that would have completed his declaration. Then Jose seized him by the upper part of his tunic, and gazed intently into his eyes for a few moments, and then said, "The what?"

"The Messiah!" responded John, humbly and reverently.

There was a pause in their discourse as the two youths regarded each other for some time with great intentness, the expression of John's countenance being that of humility and reverence, while that of Jose, in the commencement, seemed to be astonishment and displeasure at what he considered John's infatuation. But as he continued his gaze the perception broke upon him that John was no longer of sane mind; then the sternness of his looks relaxed, assuming one of commiseration.

"John," exclaimed Jose at length, as he released hold of the former, "you certainly must be crazy to entertain so preposterous a thought. The foolish books you study have unhinged your mind. I beg of you, if you wish to be my friend and companion for the future, that you will never mention to me or anyone else the like again."

John made no response, but with a sullen air and dissatisfied feelings he followed his friend on their return to the village.

This event placed a restraint upon the friendly intercourse of the two young men, so that from that time their intercourse was much restricted. John confined himself to his studies, and Jose attended to his father's business. Nothing was known among the neighbors why the two young men were not so friendly as usual; but by some means it became known that Jose possessed a wonderful power of curing and mitigating certain diseases, which soon spread through the village and around the neighborhood. Jose was accordingly besought to exercise his power to the benefit of the afflicted. The result was, that many who were diseased were made sound, and many others were relieved, and by which he gained many friends bound to him in gratitude. Some persons there were who became jealous of his skill and popularity, and fearful of losing their own influence, thought proper to thwart and misrepresent him, so that while some were giving him all due praise, others were sarcastically hinting that he was a doubtful or bad character.

This state of circumstances surrounded Jose until he had arrived at the age of manhood, when an event happened which very much changed them. Joseph the carpenter, his reputed father, died. He had been prosperous at his business during his residence at Nazareth, one main cause of which was the industry and general good conduct of Jose, so that he had accumulated some wealth, which he had the good sense to divide between his wife and Jose.

Soon after the burial of his father, Jose converted all his means into money, and with the permission of his mother, he resolved to travel into distant countries to see the world and gain knowledge. His arrangements were soon made; but before taking his departure he had a friendly interview with his former companion John. They discoursed long together. John was sorely distressed upon this occasion. He ventured to express once more to Jose that he believed him to be the true Messiah as spoken of by the prophets. He begged Jose to acknowledge himself to be such, and to let him declare it to the world; but Jose remained inflexible to all his beseechings in that respect. At length they parted, with the compromised understanding that after a number of years, when Jose should return from his travels, if they should accord in their general views, they would go forth together, and preach to the world reform and repentance.

Jose then set out upon his travels. He visited Egypt, Greece and Italy, and some other countries. After some years, when he was about thirty years of age, he returned to Judea. When at Jerusalem he met John. They soon after made their appearance in public, under conditions as will be explained hereafter.

* * * * * * * * * * * * *

"I have now, friend Alexander," resumed the spirit Saul, "given you the early history of Jesus of Nazareth, which was imparted to me by himself at the time he visited me in my exile from the happy Spiritual societies. I shall now with the assistance of Judas give you his after history—that tragic narrative in which Judas and I were the principal actors. I shall not pretend to give you the incidents in detail and in such connection as to form a unity of the whole; but will deliver them as they

33

occur to my memory; nor shall I take up your time in description more than is actually necessary. My intent will be to furnish you with all the material facts and scenes, but leave the rest to your own taste, skill, learning and prudence, to make any addition, illustration or embellishment you may think necessary, to produce a united and comprehensive true history, such as will be easy of comprehension and agreeable to the people you live among. When you shall have accomplished this task, you will then issue it to the world, calling upon all Christendom to read it, that they may no longer live in error and misconception of the truths therein stated. The Christian clergy, after reading my historical revelations, will no longer have a just excuse in maintaining a system of baneful doctrines, which I, Saul, expose and denounce.

The task I have assigned to you is a laborious one for a man in your circumstances; but be not discouraged. It is a debt of justice due to humanity that I owe, and shall be enabled to pay through your labors. You will confer great benefits upon your fellow men, and though you may not meet with a just reward in your mortal life, be assured that you will obtain it in the world of spirits."

"Before I proceed to my task, I wish to ask a question," I said to my communicating spirit.

"What is it?" demanded Saul.

"I wish to know," I said, "what has become of the spirit Jesus."

"After his kind visit to me," replied Saul, "in which he made me acquainted with many secret points of his history that was not known to any other spirit or mortal, he took leave of me, and soon after was translated to the highest sphere of beauty and bliss; since then, I have not seen or heard of him."

* * * * * * * * * * *

According to the desire and commands of the spirits, Saul and Judas, I had about forty communications with them, in which they presented me a series of facts and incidents concerning the history of Jesus during the latter part of his career on earth, and the parts they performed therein.

These communications were given to me by the spirits taking possession of my mind about one hour each day, when, usurping all my mental powers and functions, they produced a series of visions similar to beautiful and well connected dreams. Scenery, characters or personages, dialogues and actions transpired in regular succession and order, like a performance upon a theatrical stage. I was the only spectator, though I had no other conception of myself than that of a conscious perceptive essence, with the power of perceiving the hidden feelings and unspoken thoughts of the visionary personages before me, the medium.

The True History of Jesus of Nazareth

JESUS OF NAZARETH

VISION FIRST

The mystical powers of the spirits descended upon the medium. His inward self gradually withdrew from his corporeal senses, when he seemed to become a conscious existing essence. His being appeared to consist of a passive consciousness, exquisitely sensible to all that transpired before the soul's perceptive eye. At first a greyish mist passed before his vision, which soon gave place to a bright light that presented to view a scene of the earth where certain persons acted a part of life's true history, which opened the series of revelations about to be disclosed. The voice of Saul was heard at intervals in explanation of what the medium saw, the nature of which is detailed as follows:

About the sixteenth year of the reign of Tiberius Caesar, emperor of Rome, when Judea was suffering under the tyrannical sway of Pontius Pilate, her fifth Roman Governor, two men on horseback were traveling along the road that skirts the valley and plains along the western bank of the river Jordan. They were proceeding due south. On their right were the fertile plains, with the barren, gloomy Judean mountains in the distant back ground,—the latter seeming to converge towards the river, as the travelers progressed on their way. On the left was the river, fringed with the graceful oleander, the drooping willow and fern-like tamarisk, interlaced with many vines that embellished the scene with their many flowers of crimson, yellow and blue. Beyond the river, in the east, was the tall rugged line of gloomy, barren, dark brown mountains of Ammon. As the travelers proceeded on their course, the river gradually enlarged in width, and became divided into several channels, with several small islands intervening, which were covered with canes, rushes, briars and thistles.

At length the course of the river was obscured by a wide extent of marsh, which was covered by a dense growth of reeds, canes and rushes. The travelers now found themselves at the mouth of the Jordan, which opened through various channels upon that scene of physical and fabulous terrors, the lake Asphaltis, or the Dead Sea. In the course of a short time a scene of solemn grandeur burst upon their view. The great expanse of bitter waters lay stretched out before them motionless, like a basin of molten lead. The mountains curved outward in the form of an amphitheatre; those on the west gradually sloping to the bed of the lake, while those on the east rose almost perpendicular, without a vestige of vegetation or sign of life. At a slight elevation from the waters, there was a thin, purple haze; but the sky was completely cloudless, through which the burning rays of a midday sun poured down unobstructed. Not a breath of air was stirring; not a living thing was to be seen; not a sound was heard but the tread of the travelers' horses; all was as silent and inactive as the imagination could picture the valley leading to the realms of death.

When the travelers came to the open view of the lake they halted for a few moments, and cast their eyes around the scene, but no visible emotions of admiration or terror were depicted upon their countenances, as would have been the case with many others, under the same circumstances. To it, they seemed indifferent, as though the scene was not new to them; they looked rather for the route they were to pursue on their journey. With a few observations to each other they turned their course to the right, leaving the lake and approaching the base of the mountains on the west. After traveling some time over a loose bed of pebbles and boulders, they entered a ravine which was walled in by perpendicular masses of limestone rock between which ran a small stream of fresh water bordered by several stunted trees and jungles of reeds, canes and vines.

As the bottom of this ravine was strewn with fragments of rock that had fallen from the sides of the mountains, and the debris of rushes, canes and branches of trees, the progress of the travelers was of necessity slow and difficult; but in the course of time they arrived at a spot which was more open and less encumbered. A willow tree of more than ordinary stature, with its delicate branches, was gracefully drooping over the margin of the stream. The water under its protecting shade seemed to run its course with crystal clearness and refreshing coolness. For several feet around this tree was a mossy verdure, so pleasant and inviting from its rarity in the barren wilderness, that the travelers' attentions were arrested, and they halted.

The travelers presented many points of great difference in appearance, though not of absolute contrast. One of them rode a beautiful light grey steed of great mettle. He was the younger of the two, who seemed to have just arrived at the full development of young, vigorous manhood; perhaps his age was thirty, or a little over. He was smaller than common in stature, but was well formed; his limbs indicating great strength and activity. His complexion was much fairer than was common in that country, being a mixture of white and red, denoting a preponderance of the sanguine temperament. His features denoted that he was of that type, from which nearly all bold, daring, brave and ambitious men have sprung. His forehead was high and expansive; his nose long, and almost perpendicular with the former; his mouth small; lips thin and sensitive of emotion. His eyes were dark brown, expressive of great intellectual energy, and a restless disposition, as though the spirit within was dissatisfied with its surroundings, and desirous of finding a sphere more genial to its nature. His beard and moustache were dark brown; small, but neatly trimmed, his hair being of the same color, hung in massive curls around his neck and shoulders, confined around the head by a band of dark cloth, worked with threads of gold, from which a purple cloth passed over his head, and falling over his left side. His under-garments were of fine white wool, reaching from the neck to the knees, over which he wore a white silk tunic reaching to the middle of the leg, and fastened around the waist with a girdle of several bright colors. His legs were covered with buskins of red cloth, richly embroidered with threads of gold, and his feet covered with sandals. Over his left shoulder was thrown a mantle of green cloth, which he drew around him as temperature or occasions required. Altogether, his dress denoted gaiety and richness, befitting one whose worldly means were far above those of the common lot of mankind. His air and demeanor denoted him to be not only superior to his companion in appearance, but also superior in his self-estimation and standing.

The other traveler seemed to be about the middle age of life. He was of darker complexion than his companion, with reddish-brown hair, in short, thick, curling locks, with short, thick beard and moustache of a lighter tinge. Deep, arching eye-brows of the same hue overshadowed deeply sunken dark eyes that twinkled with shrewd intelligence of the world. His forehead was broad and oval, projecting over his aquiline nose; his mouth large, and lips thick, indicating a disposition prone to sensuous and vicious indulgences.

The shape of his garments were similar to those of his companion, but more humble in their pretensions. His head was covered with a red cloth fastened with plaited cords of silk; his tunic was of dark brown cloth fastened around the waist with a leathern belt. A grey mantle hung over his left shoulder. His legs were covered with leathern buskins, and his feet with coarse sandals. He rode a black horse of very strong build, that not only carried the rider, but likewise a large leathern bag containing provisions and other conveniences of travel, which was strapped over his back, so that the contents balanced on either side behind the rider. The general appearance of this person indicated that he was subordinate to his fellow traveler, as a servant or bondman. Though his deportment was humble and submissive, there were at times certain glances of the eye and motions of his upper lip, which indicated that he considered his position a degraded one, and that he would rebel against his master if he had the power to do so. Such were the two travelers in personal appearance.

Having arrived at the verdant spot, and viewing the inviting shade around the willow tree by the running stream, as before mentioned, they halted, and the younger of the two, with an expression of pleasure on his countenance, turned to his companion and observed: "Let us alight at this spot, Judas, to rest and refresh ourselves."

"The words of my worthy master shall be obeyed," responded the other, who was addressed as Judas, as he placed his right hand upon his breast, and reverently bowed his head. Then instantly springing from his horse, he led it in company with the grey his master rode, who by this time had dismounted also, to the patch of grassy verdure around the tree, to graze at their pleasure.

The younger traveler then spread his mantle upon the verdant spot, on which he reclined himself with his head resting on his hand. In this position he soon seemed to be absorbed in deep thought. In the meantime the servant Judas having taken his leathern bag from his horse, soon emptied it of its contents which he proceeded to place in order for his master's repast. He spread a white napkin upon the ground, upon which he placed several barley cakes; then unfolding another cloth he exposed to view a joint of roast sheep which he placed by the bread. Then came preserved figs and other fruit which found a proper position on the cloth; then he poured from a leathern bottle some delicious wine made from the palm tree from the celebrated wine country of Jericho, some of which in a silver goblet, he placed ready for his master. This done, he took another goblet, ran to the stream and filled it with water, and quickly returning he placed it alongside of the wine; then perceiving that everything was ready he bowed in reverence before his master, and said in a tone of humility:

"Will my master be pleased to partake of the repast? All things, are prepared for his will and pleasure." He then retreated a few steps, where he stood in attendance with his arms crossed on his breast while his master should satisfy himself with the food before him, according to the usual custom of inferiors before their superiors. Little did he think at the moment, of the extraordinary turn relations between him and his master were about to take, that would break through all humiliating customs, changing his position and reversing his feelings.

When Judas invited his master to the repast, the latter started suddenly from the spell of deep reflection, into a consciousness of his true position. Arousing himself from his recumbent posture, he seated himself in front of the refections, and taking the goblet of water he drank it off at a draught; then presenting the goblet to Judas, he told him to refill it. The latter immediately obeyed, but when he was about to replace it the master said: "Take it to thy own side, Judas. Drink, and let us partake of this food."

Judas looked up to his master, with doubt and surprise depicted on his countenance. He doubted whether he had heard his master's words aright, or whether the latter was serious in his commands, which Saul observing, remarked:

"Be not surprised at what I request of thee, Judas. I am serious in what I say, and have good intent. Join me in this repast, and think not of the breach of customs, or the relation between us."

"Does my worthy master think that I, his humble inferior and bondman, shall thus presume?" Judas timidly responded.

"I know, Judas, that thou art my bondman," rejoined the master; "and thy objections are considered just and prudent in one of thy position, by the people of the world; but in considering thyself my inferior, I know thou beliest thyself, for thou dost not think so. Thou hast too much intellect not to know that God made us all equal, and that it is society which has made us unequal. Thou hast a sense and feeling which can quickly perceive an insult given to thee, as well as the humiliation of being a bondman; and I know, Judas, that thou hast a bold heart that would resent all indignities heaped upon thee if thou wert free to do battle."

"Oh! master, master Saul," exclaimed Judas in a piteous tone of voice, with painful emotions depicted on his countenance, as thus he added: "Why has my master chosen this course to try his servant? My master has spoken the truth; but why drag from my mind my most secret thoughts, and rip from my heart my most sacred feelings? Is it to cover me with new indignities and sufferings?"

"No, Judas," responded Saul—such being the name of Judas's master—in a tone of sympathy and kindness. "I wish not to add to thy sufferings in any way, but to relieve thee, and give thee an opportunity to assert thy sense of right and manhood, which I know to exist within thee. I have been long aware that thy relation to me as bondman is galling to thy feelings, and I am sensible that thy merits deserve a better lot. Finding myself influenced through these views and feelings, I have resolved to ameliorate thy condition, and perhaps in the course of a short time, I shall accord the full extent of thy wishes. When I cast my eyes around this rude scene of nature, and view the stupendous walls of rock on either side of us, I cannot help being impressed with the idea how small a thing I am when compared with these majestic masses. Then I cannot help seeing the vanity and inconsistency of my lording it over my fellow atom."

These sentiments were delivered by Saul with apparent seriousness of manner, and humble tone of voice, while Judas regarded him with increased astonishment, his mind being perplexed between hopes and doubts of his master's sincerity.

"Come, Judas," Saul added, "we are alone in this wild solitude, with none but Jehovah to look down upon us. We are equal in his sight. Let us then put aside customs and social relations, and be equal to each other for the present. Come and join me in this repast, for I have much to tell thee, and much counsel to ask of thee."

"I have always been true to the master since I have been his bondman," Judas mildly replied in his usual mode of addressing his superior in the third person, such being the custom among servants and bondmen in his time and country. "The master has only to command, and I to obey."

Judas then with some degree of diffidence seated himself on the ground with his legs crossed, opposite his master, with the provisions spread between them, when Saul, taking a cake of bread, broke it in two, one-half of which he presented to Judas, and at the same time a small vessel containing salt. This ancient ceremony finished, they both began to eat.

The mind of Saul fell into a train of reflection, while Judas was occupied—independent of his eating—with the thoughts and new feelings consequent upon his new position, and nothing was said for the first few minutes by either of them.

It was difficult for Judas to guess what was passing in the mind and breast of Saul, so various were the expressions of his countenance.

Sometimes it would seem very grave; sometimes lively, sometimes there would be a smile upon his lips accompanied by a general expression of good nature; sometimes a smile of scorn accompanied by an air of hauteur. At length shaking off his mood he declared that he had eaten enough, and then desired Judas to pass him the wine cup. The latter complied, and at the same time declared that his hunger was satisfied. The other goblet was then filled, which Saul presented to Judas with seeming courtesy. Then their manners to each other began to assume the appearance of true fraternal friendship.

Saul was a native of Cilicia. He was born in the opulent city of Tarsus, where his father, Bathurst, an industrious tradesman, had accumulated much wealth by the humble occupation of tent-making. Saul being the only child of his parents was sent to Jerusalem to obtain the best education that could be obtained in those days, where he remained under the tuition of Gamaliel, a celebrated man, until he was about twenty years of age, when he was recalled home by his father, who constrained his son to learn and superintend the business by which he had made his wealth.

This course of proceeding was very much disliked by young Saul, who, during his studies in the great city, had imbibed too many exalted ideas from his proud, wealthy and high-minded associates, to fit him for the humble calling of his father. However, there was no alternative. Saul was obliged to submit to his father's will, or risk his displeasure and evil consequences; the latter he resolved he would not do. Thus he reluctantly pursued his humble calling for several years, while his mind would be soaring and fluttering in the realms of fanciful ambition, achieving in imagination deeds of daring and priceless worth. Wealth and social respect Saul was enabled to obtain; but that was not sufficient to quench the thirst of his ambitious soul. Power and Fame were the greatest attractions in life to him, and the greatest compensation for toil and death.

Thus Saul continued to pine after a more congenial sphere wherein his ambitious nature would be enabled to develop itself, and his soul to imbibe the flattering comments of men. At the age of thirty both his parents were dead, and he found himself at length free to act according to his own will.

Saul soon converted the wealth he inherited from his father into shekels of gold and silver, and having made all necessary preparations he bid adieu to his native city, and turned in the direction of Jerusalem accompanied by one servant. He was determined to seek new scenes and adventures wherein his restless spirit and ambitious desires would enable him to find congenial employ.

His servant, Judas Iscariot, was once a man of good estate, but owing to vicious and reckless conduct in his youth his dependence became squandered, and he by some means became indebted to the father of Saul. The debt remained unpaid for some years, and at length the creditor becoming impatient he laid claim to the person of Judas until the debt should be paid; and when Saul's father died Saul inherited the claim in conformity with the laws and customs of the country, and Judas became the bondman of Saul.

Judas when a youth, though careless and vicious in general, possessed some virtuous qualities. He was generous, liberal and benevolent; but after he had squandered his substance and began to feel the adversities of his changed position his nature became changed, for he gradually became the reverse of that which he formerly was. He considered his former virtues to have been the causes of his calamities; he therefore closed his heart and mind to all principles and considerations of honesty, liberality and benevolence. The acquisition of wealth by any means in his power was the object of his schemes and toils. With gold in his possession he thought he could once more become a freeman! With gold he could once more be happy! Such was Judas.

Saul having drank his goblet of wine, replaced the vessel, and then, with a countenance expressive of sincerity and candor, proceeded to address Judas.

"Judas, it will be unnecessary to explain the causes and conditions by which the relation between us as master and bondman has been established. These things are too well impressed upon thy mind to be forgotten."

"True, master," replied Judas as a sudden shudder seemed to overcome him, while his countenance paled, and a glance bespeaking fury and malignity was suddenly awakened within him, which he endeavored to suppress. Then turning his regard to the ground and striking his breast, he added: "'Tis true, too true, to my sorrow and shame! Had I possessed less generous impulse in my nature, and more of the worldly fox my master would not have reminded me of my present degradation."

Saul perceiving that his allusion to Judas' bondage had produced within the latter bitter feelings, assumed an expression of sympathy on his countenance, and observed in a soothing tone of voice: "Believe me, Judas, I do not speak of this as a vain man who blazes forth his claims over another whom human laws and unfortunate circumstances have placed within his power. No! Nor is it with any intent of arousing within thee any painful feeling that I have spoken, but it is of necessity that I mention it as it is the basis of that which I am about to say concerning thy welfare."

The irritability of Judas subsided. He raised his eyes to his master with an expression that seemed to say: "I wish I could believe in thy sincerity, but I still doubt thee." After a few moments had elapsed, in which the master and bondman regarded each other, endeavoring to

42

discover the inward man, Judas replied: "Proceed, master, Judas will listen in humble attention."

"To bring this matter as fairly to thy comprehension as possible," said Saul in resuming, "I will give the results of my thoughts without stating any preliminaries as I intended to do. It is my wish and intentions, provided it shall meet with thy wishes and approbation, to so change our relation to each other and society as to make thee an agent to do my bidding on a free and equal standing with myself, instead of rendering me servile obedience as a bondman, and to the rest of the world thou shalt be a freeman."

As soon as Saul had spoken these words Judas sprang to his feet, his whole frame quivering with an intense excitement. Clasping his hands together above him for a moment or two, he seemed to be uttering thanks to the Great Jehovah; then suddenly throwing himself upon one knee he took up the border of his master's tunic, which he pressed to his lips and ejaculated: "Master, kind and worthy master, let Judas be not deceived in thy words! Let him be convinced that such is his master's will and resolution! Let the claims of bondage be removed from his person, and then his heart will be forever the true slave of gratitude to his master!"

"Calm thy emotions, my faithful Judas," returned Saul mildly, "and listen to me. That I am sincere in what I have said the reasons I shall adduce will convince thee."

After a little while Judas managed to tranquilize his transport, and resumed his seat, and Saul continued his discourse.

"Thou art acquainted, Judas, with the history and conditions of my late parents. Thou hast seen also something of my nature to know how incompatible was the course of life I was constrained to lead in conformity with their desires and commands. In fact, my daily routine was burdensome and painful to me, though in obedience to my father, and in prospect of inheriting his wealth I forced myself to pursue it. My life was worse to me than a bondage, for I felt an impulse within me for other occupation than that of tent-making. My ambition and ideas pointed to something of greater significance. I longed to launch out upon the world to see what part I could play among the great, honored and powerful men who, like giants, stalk to and fro looking down upon their inferior fellow mortals, feeling an exulting pride in their own greatness. As such was the nature of my desires an intuitive idea told me that such would be my destiny."

"No doubt the Spirit of Jehovah has stirred up the soul of my master to some great deed or career, that will fill the four corners of the earth with his greatness. If so, I know he is capable of fulfilling the same from the depth of his mind and the nobleness of his principles," observed Judas in a low tone of voice, and with gravity of countenance.

Saul smiled his thanks for Judas's approval and good opinion, and then resumed: "Now my parents rest in peace in their tombs, having left me their wealth as a reward for my filial obedience. I have no longer a restriction to the bend of my wishes. I am now free, Judas, as thou wert once, and shalt be again, if thou wilt accept of my proposals." Saul then suddenly reached forward, when seizing Judas by the wrist, he stared at him with great intensity of gaze, as he resumed: "Judas, we will both be freemen! We will both act together, and share equally in the results of our actions." Judas started, and looked upon his master in astonishment, for the manner and words of Saul had somewhat confused him. "Yes, Judas, thou shalt no longer be a bondman. I feel the want of a trusty agent and faithful companion to whom I can entrust my secret thoughts and feelings, who can aid me in my projects, adventures and interests; who will plan and execute for me in my absence as well as in my presence. Say, Judas, wilt thou change thy present relation to me for the one I propose? Thou shalt be declared free in society, and shalt be equal with me in my presence. Thou shalt have the use of my wealth according to thy wants and desires, and after a while the document of bondage I hold against thee shall be put into thy hands. Now, speak, Judas; wilt thou accept of my proposal?"

"Master, I accept," answered Judas, who with difficulty could utter the words so great was his astonishment and emotion. Then raising his hand above him, he added: "And before the Great Jehovah I declare to devote all my energies to my master's welfare, to be trustworthy and faithful."

"Then this is to be a compact understood and agreed between us," said Saul, as he also raised his hand and placed the other upon his breast. "Now, Judas, thou must not any longer address me as master, nor speak in the strain of an inferior. In all respects thou must deport thyself as my equal. We will now consider the object I had in view, that has brought me to this rocky wilderness."

After a few minutes had elapsed, which was passed in reflection by Saul, and by Judas, who endeavored to calm the excitement within him, which had been produced by his change of condition, the former observed: "Thou must remember, Judas, that in the course of our wanderings a few days since we stayed at a small village named Enon, on the Jordan. We saw there a collection of people listening to a wild-looking, middle-aged man dressed in a very uncouth style, who was preaching to them some new religious doctrines; whether of his own conception or any other authority I know not; and afterwards he descended to the river, followed by the people, when he immersed some of them in the waters. Didst thou pay attention to that man? They called him John the Baptist. He seemed to be a wild, religious enthusiast, a crazy man or knave—I know not which he most resembled."

"Perhaps all these qualities were combined in his character," replied Judas with a scornful curl of his lip. "I noticed the man, and listened to his discourse."

"After he had declared the points of his doctrine and exhorted the people to observe them, didst thou observe anything peculiar that he said?" inquired Saul.

"Yes, sir," answered Judas. "I noticed towards the end of the discourse he said: 'There was another coming after him greater than he!'"

"That is the part to which I wish to bring thy attention," said Saul with manifest interest in the subject. "What dost thou think or understand by that assertion of his?'"

"I think it a very probable one," replied Judas, as his lip gave another slight curl; "for as I think there is nothing very great in John the Baptist, it cannot be a very difficult matter for one greater than he to come forward."

"Truly," said Saul, smiling at Judas' opinion of John the Baptist, "the man does not seem to have much capacity for exciting another man's envy; but that is not the point I wish to arrive at. To whom dost thou suppose he alluded, when he said that?"

"I know not, sir," answered Judas; "but I heard him allude to the same person when he discoursed at Jerusalem. He said at that time there was one coming after him whose sandal he was not fit to untie. I thought to myself that he was not fit to preach God's word, if he were not fit to untie a man's sandal."

"I think so, too," observed Saul; "but I must confess to thee that he has excited my curiosity very much in respect to this unknown person he speaks of. I wish to find out who he is, and what is the connection between him and John. I have a suspicion that there is a deep scheme or plan laid between them, in which they both intend to play a part presently, either of interest or self-aggrandizement. If it be so, as I suspect, I wish to become acquainted with this person, and the subject they are going to venture on. I wish to see if I cannot take a part or perform a character to my own satisfaction. With this desire I have inquired where this John the Baptist can be found when he is not wandering over the country. I am informed that he secludes himself in a cave somewhere up this ravine; therefore I have come here to seek him and make what discoveries I can concerning his unknown friend. Judas, we will now depart in search of him, and for the present, thou must continue to be my servant."

VISION SECOND

JUDAS

Saul and Judas, now companions under a new mutual tie of sworn friendship, interest and sympathy, having mounted their horses, started up the rocky ravine in search of the recluse, John the Baptist. Their progress was slow and fatiguing, as stated before, for every now and then they had to scramble over masses of rock, or turn aside and choose their way in another direction; besides, the branch, though generally running along the middle of the bottom, was frequently turned from that course by rocks and collected debris, forming other courses in various directions, so that they were often obliged to plunge through water and mud. The ravine was about one hundred feet in width at this spot, with walls of gray limestone, nearly perpendicular, and of an immense height. The sun's rays penetrated this rocky cavity but for a short time during the middle of the day, while on the mountain-tops they were seen to glitter from morn to eve, when all space below bore the aspect of cheerless gloom. Nothing was to be seen bearing the signs of life, excepting the scanty, stinted vegetation along the margin of the stream or in the clefts and ledges in the massive walls some dwarfish trees stood out, which were nourished from the decomposition of the walls' rocky substance.

At length the travelers came to a ledge on the south-western side of the ravine, about twenty feet from the base, and a few feet in width. Above they saw the openings to several caves. There seemed to be no other means of mounting the ledge, than by climbing over a confused mass of rocks at its nearest end.

"This must be the spot, or somewhere near by, where our recluse has thought fit to make his home," said Saul to Judas. "I think he need not fear the temptations of the world, or wiles of the Evil One in this locality; for any one who should venture here would be in danger of breaking his legs or neck."

"I cannot conceive," remarked Judas, "how any man can forsake society, bad as it is, to live in such a dreary, miserable wilderness as this."

"There are several causes to account for it, Judas," replied Saul. "Religious fanaticism, ignorance, error and madness combined, are the general causes by which these poor self-deluded mortals forsake society. But there are many others, every one of which lack common sense, right reason, and the love of their fellows."

The party now came up to the ledge, which they found impossible to mount with their horses, so they alighted and tethered them to a small tree by the branch. Then they approached the huge pile of rocks, and climbed from one to the other until they reached the top of the ledge, where they soon discovered a narrow foot-path winding its way among rocks and scanty herbage, lengthwise along it. Along this path the travelers took their course with a cautious, quiet step. Saul in the meantime produced a short sword which he had under his garments, and Judas imitating his example, took out a long knife.

"It is well to be prepared in case of danger," said Saul. "We possibly may come upon a mountain robber and his family, instead of a recluse."

Their cautious preparations were unnecessary, for the path soon led them to the mouth of a cave in the rock, when they heard a voice in a loud exhorting strain, which they recognized to be the voice of the recluse John. Softly they approached, and attentively listened, when they distinguished the following words:

"And there shall come forth a rod out of the stem of Jesse, and a branch shall grow out of his roots; and the Spirit of the Lord shall rest upon him; the spirit of wisdom and understanding; the spirit of counsel and might; the spirit of knowledge, and the fear of the Lord. Again, what says the prophet? Behold my servant whom I uphold—mine elect, in whom my soul delighteth! I have put my spirit upon him. He shall bring forth judgment to the Gentiles. He shall not cry nor lift up; nor cause his voice to be heard in the streets. A bruised reed he shall not

47

break, and the smoking flax he shall not quench. He shall bring forth judgment unto truth!"

There was a pause for a while, but at length the voice resumed: "Again, my brethren, what sayeth he further? For unto us a son is given, and the government shall be upon his shoulders; and his name shall be called Wonderful, Councilor, The Mighty God, The Everlasting Father, The Prince of Peace!"

The voice ceased, when Saul whispered to Judas: "John the Baptist is haranguing an imaginary audience or congregation. Put up thy weapon, Judas, and let us enter. Remember, thy speech and actions must be in conformity with whatsoever character I assume."

Judas bowed in assent, when they both entered the cave. The entrance to the cavern, which was at the base of the wall of the ravine, was about six feet high by three wide, with a slight descent into a kind of a passage; at the farther end of it was another opening on the right leading into a spacious, irregularly formed chamber about fifteen feet high and as many broad in the most narrow part, with twice the number in length. The walls and ceiling were of rock, of nature's molding, excepting the wall at the farther end, which seemed to be artificially constructed from rude fragments of rock of various sizes and shapes.

The floor of this chamber was tolerably smooth and clean, but no furniture was to be seen excepting a coarse cloth suspended over the entrance, which was used to screen the indweller from the night air. There were a few vessels, such as a water vase and some cups and dishes of earthenware, and in one corner a quantity of rushes covered with a coarse cloth, which served the recluse for a couch. At the base of the artificial wall there was a small fire burning, which seemed to be made of rushes and broken pieces of brushwood that had been gathered from the debris swept down by the stream. Over this fire, by means of two cross-sticks, a cooking vessel was suspended, containing something intended for food, and a few feet from it, seated upon a stone, was the occupant of this wild solitary abode, who seemed to be intensely absorbed in reading a roll-manuscript or book.

As the two visitors were about entering this chamber the recluse resumed his harangue:

"Thus, men and brethren, speaks the Holy Prophet. What shall we understand by his words? What shall we think and say of them? What—"

"Peace to all within here," exclaimed Saul as he entered, by way of salutation.

"Blessed be this abode in the name of the Lord," said Judas in unison.

The recluse was so absorbed in the subject of his contemplation that he did not see the visitors enter, but as soon as he heard their voices he started and instantly sprang to his feet throwing himself in an attitude of proud defiance. Whether he thought that the great arch fiend had come, or enemies of a more earthly nature, to attack him, it is not clearly known; but it is evident he expected something of a hostile nature. His body was slightly bent backward; his right arm extended, holding in his hand the manuscript book, as though it was a sword he flourished, and his left hand was placed upon his breast, while from his dark, sunken eyes beamed forth glances of mingled astonishment and terror, and his long black hair was scattering in wild disorder. His features were of the true Arabian type. A high forehead, long thin nose, small compressed lips, projecting cheek-bone, a dark olive complexion and very meager, a thick moustache and long un-trimmed beard, added to his wild and savage aspect. There were several wrinkles around his eyes, some around his mouth, and two long ones running down the cheeks to the lower part of his chin, which were not produced from old age, but rather the effect of an ascetic life and a disturbed mind.

He wore a dark brown dress made of camel's-hair cloth of very coarse texture, reaching from the neck to the ankles, with a kind of cape over the shoulders reaching to the elbows, and fastened around the waist with a leathern belt. His hairy, sinuous legs, arms and feet were entirely naked. Such was the recluse, John the Baptist, a young man of about two and thirty, though in appearance many years older.

The parties viewed each other for some moments in great aston-ishment, without saying a word, when at length Saul bowed low, and addressed the recluse in a mild, complacent tone of voice,—

"Be not alarmed at our presence, holy sir. We are travelers and friends."

The amazement and terror of the recluse subsided, and the hostile attitude gave place to one more humble and placent, and he inquired in a tone of voice more courteous than was to be expected from his previous hostile demonstrations; for as he glanced at the elegant dress of Saul and the more humble one of Judas, he soon perceived that the former was a person of consequence, and the latter his servant:

"What purport, my friends," he said, "may you have in this visit to my humble abode?"

"We have no particular object in view, holy sir, in this our visit" replied Saul. "I am traveling for pleasure, curiosity and information. I have today been exploring the scenery of this wilderness, and having passed up this ravine from the direction of the lake, I perceived some caves above this ledge, and knowing that the day was drawing to a close I thought it would be well to select one of them wherein to pass the night. Thus, holy sir, thou must attribute it to accident and not design, that has caused us to intrude upon thy pious meditations. However, as we are here, we will tarry for the night, with thy good leave, and avail ourselves of the benefit of thy holy company."

The recluse, nothing doubting, received the explanation of Saul with good grace. All suspicion and alarm seemed banished from his dark, sunken eyes, hither to so repellant, for they assumed a placent and kindly expression, as in a tone of meekness he replied to Saul and his companion:

"Strangers, it is not in the power of poor John of the wilderness to accord you such hospitality as is customary in the world, and such as your habits and station require. But, if you deem fit to share with me the shelter of this rocky cavern and my humble food, I shall most gladly make you welcome."

"Most thankfully we accept thy proffer of a shelter for the night; with it and thy sage discourse we shall be enabled to pass the time to great advantage. As to food, we are not unprovided."

The host then went to one corner of the cavern, from which he brought forth a long board which he placed upon the ground near to the fire. Then placing a large stone under one end and covering it with the mantle of Saul, he formed a rude couch. Then he told his visitor to repose himself. Saul did as he was requested, and Judas seated himself on a large stone near to him.

The first thing of consideration that occupied their thoughts was the care of their horses, and as soon as the host understood this he told Judas to take them a little higher up the ravine, and he would find a cave to the right where they could be secured for the night.

Saul then entered into conversation with the recluse upon various unimportant matters, with the view of ascertaining as well as he could the nature of the latter before he entered on the subject of his designs. They were like sailors, who, when they are entering a strange harbor, drop the lead and line and ascertain the depth of water and the most favorable points, in order to enter in safety.

In the meantime Judas left his company with the intention of attending to the horses. With hasty steps he traversed the ledge and descended to the bottom of the ravine; then, looking cautiously around him, and taking a deep inspiration, he exclaimed: "Ah! by the God of my Fathers, I am once more alone!" Seeming to feel a degree of relief from this ejaculation, he said to himself:

"I can now think and speak, if I choose, without fear of that master of mine. Freedom of thought and speech must be a luxury to any one like me who has so long been deprived of it. To think freely when in his presence, I am afraid, for somehow his keen eye can penetrate to my thoughts. How then, can I speak freely when I have not freedom of thought? But why need I be afraid any longer? Has he not told me that

I shall be his equal in his presence? Did he not say that I shall no longer serve him as a menial, but shall be his trusted agent in all matters, wherein I am to serve him with liberty of speech, and shall share his wealth according to my wants and wishes; also that in a short time I shall be made a freeman in fact? O! glorious change that will be. It seems too great to be true! I wish I could penetrate the depth of his mind and heart, as he can mine. Perhaps he has some design to accomplish at present, requiring my trusty services, and when that is accomplished he will not be true to his word. Ah! that thought is perplexing. How shall I be sure that he means well to me? How shall I secure him?"

Thus Judas communed with himself as he proceeded to the spot where the horses were tethered-up to which point of time his thoughts seemed incapable of making any farther progress.

"Ah! how shall I secure him?" he repeated; but not being able to find an answer to his query he seized the horses and led them up the ravine, with a slow, steady step, as he conned over that important sentence. At length having traversed about a hundred yards he arrived at a cave on the opposite side of the ravine, the opening of which being low down and of sufficient size to admit the horses. It consisted of one chamber, quite convenient to shelter the animals and keep them secure.

He led them into the cave, and then taking the bag containing the provisions, he took therefrom two barley-cakes which he broke into pieces and placed them before the beasts. While they were eating he gathered many fragments of rock with which the floor was strewn, and with them he built up in the entrance-way a barrier, so that they should not be able to make their escape. This done, he stood before it a few moments to see if his work was efficient, when the difficult question of his previous train of thoughts recurred to him, "How shall I secure him?" Slapping his hands in an ecstasy of joy, his eyes glistening with triumph, he exclaimed. "I have it! I will serve my master the same way I have served the horses. I will feed him with everything that his vanity and ambition shall desire. I will secure all his secrets and designs, and while he is enjoying his anticipated ambitious achievements, I will gradually raise around him certain barriers through which he shall not be enabled to advance or retreat without my assistance. Thus he will be dependent upon my will, secrecy and circumspection. The fulfillment of his word with me will then be secure. This is a happy thought. Now, Judas, proceed to action!"

Judas seemed much elated at the solution of his difficult question. He then took up his bag, and was about returning to his company when another train of thoughts entered his mind that caused him to arrest his steps.

51

"I feel convinced," he said to himself, "that master of mine has more deep designs upon that recluse than he chose to make known to me. I am determined to find all out; therefore I must keep my eyes, ears and thoughts alive, while at the same time I will feign an utter indifference. They may talk late into the night; therefore a fire-light will be necessary. Perhaps the recluse is not well supplied, therefore I will gather some fuel."

Thus saying, or thinking, Judas once more deposited his bag and commenced gathering a quantity of dry rushes and sticks, which were to be found along the margins of the stream, of which in a few minutes he made a good-sized bundle; then placing it upon his shoulder, and his bag under his arm, he bent his way towards his master and the recluse.

When Judas returned to his companions the last ray of the sun had departed from the crest of the mountains. All was gloomy and misty in the ravine, and darkness filled the caves, excepting the one where the recluse's small fire cast a light for a small space around. Judas entered and deposited his bundle of fuel at the feet of the recluse.

"Thou hast done well," observed the recluse to Judas. "Thy forethought and care are commendable, as we may need it before the night is through." Then turning to Saul who was still reclining on his couch, he remarked: "Thy servant seems trustworthy and vigilant. Is he free or a bondman?"

"He is a bondman," replied Saul; "but his merits cannot be esteemed too highly. Practically there are no bonds between us but those of affection and mutual interest."

"It is well," returned the recluse. "It would be a great good if all men held the same relation to each other."

While this short dialogue was going on Judas was endeavoring to recruit the fire by putting on fuel and blowing it; but the commendation he received from his master so excited him to laughter that he had great difficulty in restraining himself. "They little think," he said to himself, "that I thought only of my own convenience when I procured the fuel. Henceforth when I serve another I will think of myself first; such shall be my maxim."

Judas having recruited the fire, an agreeable warmth compensated for the chills of the evening, and a good light was shed around a great portion of the cavern, while the cooking vessel above it sent forth volumes of steam, and emitted a bubbling sound.

"I wonder what is in that pot," said Judas to himself as he eyed the vessel over the fire. "I have heard that John the Baptist fed on locusts and wild honey. It certainly cannot be that, for I never heard of locusts being stewed. Perhaps the old wizard has had a presentiment of our visit, and is preparing something extra for our repast."

Judas's doubts and curiosity were soon satisfied, for the recluse perceiving that the day was spent, observed that it was now time to repair the waste of the body by partaking of food. He then brought forward a large board which he placed about a foot from the ground by supporting it with several large fragments of rock, forming a rude table. Taking the vessel from the fire he poured its contents into a large wooden bowl which, upon investigation proved to be a kind of bean or seed taken from the long pods of a species of locust tree, which he had made into a stew by adding some barley-meal, water, and a gum taken from the leaves of several wild shrubs known to most people in the country as wild honey—altogether making a savory mess, palatable and nourishing.

This preparation the host placed upon the table, and afterwards he disinterred from the fire-ashes two barley-cakes; from another locality he produced some dried figs and a vessel containing water. Having made these preparations he turned towards his guests and said: "Come, my friends, share with me this humble repast. God has made us of the dust of the earth, and so far as our bodily wants require he has made us dependent thereon. He commands us to eat of its fruits in order that we may live to glorify him."

"With good will, holy sir, we will partake of thy food," replied Saul as he rose from his couch and stood before the host, assuming a courteous and graceful demeanor. "But there is one request I would ask of thee before hand. As we are provided with what is necessary during our stay in the wilderness, thou must allow us to make with our provisions a common stock, so that if we partake of thy food, thou must partake of ours in social friendship."

The recluse seemed to hesitate for a few moments before he replied, and he cast a rather suspicious glance upon Saul, then upon Judas, and lastly upon the big traveling bag, as though he would fain know what they had to eat. At length he replied, "Be it as thou wilt, my friend."

By order of Saul, Judas soon brought from the bag the remains of the roast sheep, some preserved fruit, cakes and sweet-meats, all of which he placed upon the table. The leathern bottle he disengaged, and also the goblets, and placed them aside in readiness when they should be called for. Saul and the recluse now seated themselves upon stones by the table, while Judas stood in attendance. The host crossed his arms, bowed his head, and muttered a few words of thanks to the great Jehovah. Judas took two goblets, filling them with water, one of which he placed before the host, and the other before Saul; then with his knife he cut in pieces the roast meat, returning it to the board, when the repast commenced with mutual courteous attention to each other's well-being. The recluse presenting to Saul one half of a bivalve shell, told him to partake of the locust stew, assuring him that it was very good, and of which the latter availed himself, pronouncing it excellent—far beyond his anticipations. The host then helped himself to some of the same; but during the process of mastication he cast several glances towards the roast meat, and Saul perceiving this, he pushed the platter containing it towards him, and in a persuasive tone invited him to partake thereof.

"It is contrary to the customs and precepts of the Order of Priesthood to which I belong to partake of meats," remarked the recluse, as he cast another glance at the roast sheep.

"Why so?" inquired Saul, with feigned astonishment. "Do we not eat roast lamb at the Paschal Feast?"

"True, my friend, we do in that case," returned the recluse; "but that is a holy ordinance by the express command of God through Moses, to show the purity of our hearts and souls, in keeping in religious remembrance God's mercies to our forefathers."

"That may be as thou sayest," rejoined Saul; "but if the eating of roast lamb can have such a good effect upon the soul at the feast of Passover, it certainly cannot have an evil effect at another time. We know from experience that it is not so, and there is not any holy ordinance to forbid it as a sin."

"My scruples do not proceed from the idea of committing a sin," rejoined the recluse, "but from prudence, as it is thought by our order, that by abstinence from flesh our minds and souls will be better prepared for profound and holy meditation, but in the present case I will make an exception to my rules. I will set apart this evening for friendly converse with thee, and I will partake of the good cheer thou hast put before me."

Thus saying the recluse helped himself to the roast meat, which he ate with a great relish and a keen appetite. No sooner had he eaten the first piece than it seemed to have aroused within him the hunger of a wolf or vulture for flesh; piece after piece he demolished without the accompaniment of barley-bread or his favorite dish, the locust stew, until the whole of the meat disappeared; then drinking off his goblet of water he removed a little from the table, panting and swelling with the fullness thereof.

"I thought the old wizard could not resist that nice bit of lamb," said Judas to himself, as he looked on at the carnivorous voracity of the recluse, "but I did not think that he would have deprived me of my share."

Saul having satisfied his appetite with bread and fruits, gave Judas a signal, when the latter brought forward the leathern bottle and filled the two goblets with wine. In the meantime the host and his visitor retired from the table, the former seating himself upon a stone by the

fire, and the latter on his couch. Judas having completed all his necessary offices, betook himself to the table where, though he was somewhat chagrined at the absence of his roast lamb, he managed to make
a supper from the remaining eatables.

"That roast flesh of thine was of most excellent quality," remarked
the recluse to Saul as he continued to suck his teeth and lick his lips,
as though he wished to prolong as much as possible the savory taste.

"I am glad thou wert pleased with it," answered Saul.

"I am sure there never was a finer lamb ever entered the temple of
the Lord as a burnt offering," added the recluse. "But I am afraid, my
friend, that I have been too inordinate in my eating. When the pent up
appetites are let loose they get beyond our control. So it has been with
me, I have fasted a long time from flesh, and now that I have eaten I
have taken too much."

"Make thyself not uneasy, dear sir," replied Saul, "but follow my
example. I am accustomed after my meals to take a cup of wine. It
promotes digestion, gives a pleasing exhilaration, and in many other
respects is a good medicine."

Saul then went to the table and brought forward the two goblets of
wine, one of which he presented to the recluse, as he continued to
observe: "Now, sir if thou drinkest this wine it will do thee good in pro-
moting digestion, warming thy blood, and— "

"But dost thou know, my friend, that wine is forbidden by the order
of which I am a member?"

"Call it not wine, then." replied Saul. "Let it be medicine. I will be
thy physician to prescribe for thee, to aid thy digestion."

"Thou art inclined to be humorous, my friend," observed the recluse
as the austerity of his countenance relaxed a little, and a slight smile lit
up his stern features. "However I think thou hast good reason in this
particular. I really think something is necessary to aid me in the digestion of my supper."

There was a pause in which the speaker seemed irresolute, as was
shown by certain nervous actions. At length he suddenly seized the
proffered goblet, and said: "I will do thy bidding and follow thy example. Let it be understood that this night I devote in friendship to
thee; besides, our compact was that each one should share the other's
food."

Saul then drank his wine, and the recluse did the same with a deep
gasp, indicating that his draught was a long and powerful one. He
handed Saul the goblet, and then he arose, paced the chamber to and
fro with one hand on his breast, as though he felt a force within him
that impelled him to more than common action.

"By the God of our Fathers!" exclaimed Judas mentally, as he saw
the recluse quaff the goblet of wine. "I wonder what the old wizard will

be prevailed upon to do next. Twice he has broken the rules of his Order through that sweet-tongued master of mine. I should not be surprised if Saul should persuade him to dance!"

Judas having at length finished his supper, glanced towards his master, from whom he received a signal to re-fill the goblets with wine, which order he immediately executed, placing them upon a smooth flat stone near to his master. The recluse in the meantime had discontinued his pacing to and fro, and had seated himself by the fire into which he gazed with great intentness. There seemed to have been a marked change come over him, for his eyes were glassy and wild in their expression: the veins of his forehead were fuller, and the general aspect of his features sterner than before, while his fingers, as his hands were clasped together, seemed to be endowed with a spasmodic twitching. For a few minutes he seemed unconscious of the presence of his guests, as he was totally absorbed in the train of thought and feelings within him.

"May I be bold enough to inquire, worthy host." said Saul, with great suavity of tone in his voice, "what are the reasons that influence thee to lead this solitary life in this wilderness? Is it that thou viewest the ordinary attractions of life—the pleasures, conveniences and interests of society is unbecoming and repulsive to thee; or art thou afraid that their temptations would withdraw or interfere with thy pious meditation?"

"I am not afraid of such temptations," replied the recluse, as he withdrew his gaze from the fire, and fixed it with an expression of severity upon the questioner, and then added: "I am not insensible to the attractions, pleasures and interests of society; but I know there are some circumstances more favorable to that course, by which a man ought to prepare himself for his destiny. With this view, from my own free choice, I have become a denizen of the wilderness."

"But how can a man know his destiny, my dear host?" Saul asked in surprise. "What man is there can know today what tomorrow will bring forth concerning himself or others?"

"That may be the case with most men," gravely responded the host; "but as regards myself, my course, my duty and destiny are known to me, for they were foreordained and marked out before I was born."

"Indeed!" exclaimed Saul in apparent astonishment who nevertheless was not at all surprised at what he heard, for he was now confirmed in his previous ideas, that John the Baptist was a religious monomaniac. "Whom, then, have I the honor to address, for I am ignorant to whom I am indebted for this night's hospitality?"

"Hast thou not read the books of the Holy Prophets? They speak of me," answered the recluse.

56

"I have," replied Saul, "but I know of nothing therein stated that alludes to thee, that I know of, for I know not thy name. Tell me who thou art."

"I am the voice of him that crieth in the wilderness: 'Prepare ye the Way of the lord; make straight in the desert a highway for our God'" the recluse uttered in a loud piercing voice. Then suddenly springing to his feet he went to the niche in the wall, from which he brought forth his book. Unrolling it before Saul he pointed with his finger to a passage, and remarked with an air of zealous triumph: "Thus sayeth Esaias when foreshadowing the precursor of the Messiah. I, John the Baptist, am that voice in the wilderness!"

"John the Baptist!" exclaimed Saul in dissembled surprise. Then looking at the passage pointed out by John, he nodded with the intent of expressing his belief of the wild statement made by the speaker. The recluse then unrolled the book to a greater extent, and pointing to another passage he remarked:

"And what says Malachi, The Prophet of the Lord: 'Behold! I will send my messenger, and he shall prepare the way before me; and the Lord whom ye seek shall suddenly come to this temple—even the messenger of his covenant whom ye delight in. Behold! he shall come with the Lord of hosts.'"

"Then thou art John the Baptist the precursor of that Mighty One who is to appear among us," inquired Saul with a degree of reverence in his voice.

"I am the man to whom the Prophets allude," replied John the Baptist emphatically as he quietly crossed his naked arms upon his breast, and looked down upon Saul with an air of pious dignity. "To whom would the prophets allude unless to me? Do I not realize them in person, nature and circumstances? Do I not realize them in spirit? Are they not realized in time? For it is now, according to the visions of Daniel, that the time is come when the Messiah shall make his appearance to Israel; and I, John, am his precursor to prepare the minds of men."

"Most holy man," said Saul rising from his couch and bending before the recluse in a reverential manner, "I have heard of thy holy fame, but knew thee not. I am now indebted to accident for the benefit of thy valuable discourse and enlightenment on this mysterious subject. Nothing doubting of the holy mission to which the prophets allude, I wish to know, holy sir, who is this mysterious one, and what is his nature, of whom thou sayest thou art the precursor? Deign to give me, sir, the enlightenment I ask in confidence, and I will be an attentive listener to thy words. But—"

Here Saul stooped down and took up the two goblets of wine, one of which he presented to John, and resumed:

57

"As the request I make of thee may be too exhausting, I pray thee to drink with me another cup of this palmy juice, in holy communion and friendly confidence, as it will give thee strength to perform the task."

John looked suspiciously at the proffered goblet and then at the countenance of his guest, but seeing nothing repugnant in either he withdrew his gaze and remained a few moments in hesitation. The previous goblet of wine which he had drank had warmed his blood, aroused his nerves, and caused his ideas to flit with rapidity, producing within him a seeming energy of body and mind, as well as a glorious thrill of feeling. However, as some time had elapsed since he had taken it, there was an abatement of the stimulus, leaving a thirst in the throat and a hankering desire to repeat the potation. Under all these influences it is not surprising that the holy man should once more succumb to the pleasing temptation. He did so. Stretching forth his hand he seized the goblet with eagerness, and said: "Be it as thou sayest." The wine disappeared; a quickening fire glowed through his blood and nerves; the muscles of his face twitched; his eyes glared, seeming to emit beams of holy fire, and he felt a power within him capable of encountering Satan and all his hosts.

At this instant a powerful snore was heard to issue from Judas, who, being seated on the floor, reclining against the wall by the fire, wrapped in his mantle, with his head bowing upon his breast, seemed to be in a very deep sleep.

"My servant sleeps soundly," observed Saul. "Thou mayest now impart to me in confidence all thou knowest concerning the Great Mysterious One, who is to come among us, and of whom the prophets have spoken."

"My friend," replied John in a serious tone of voice, "the intelligence that I have to impart is not to be given in confidence to one more than another, for it concerns all the tribes of Israel and even the Gentiles to have their ears open, as it is to the salvation of all mankind to hear of the coming of the Great Prince and Mighty King who is to be; who is to gather the scattered children of Zion and re-build the throne of David; who shall seize the scepter of Judah, to restore the reign of harmony and peace, which was the design of God for his chosen people; who is to enter the Holy Temple, the House of God, to purge it from its corruptions, to drive hence its polluters, impostors and great sinners; to reinstate God's holy ordinances; to purify his holy altar, and offer up sacrifices more acceptable of Israel. God has spoken of this holy mission and of the Divine Prince who is to come through his inspired prophets. From them we must gain our information, and on them we must depend for our authority, until our eyes may be blessed with the sight of the Messiah's presence. The prophet Isaiah says:

"And it shall come to pass in the last days that the mountain of the Lord's house shall be established in the mountains, and shall be exalted above the hills, and all nations shall flow unto it, for out of Zion shall go forth the law, and the word of the Lord from Jerusalem. In that day the branch of the Lord shall be beautiful and glorious, and the fruit of the earth shall be excellent and comely for them that are escaped of Israel. And it shall come to pass that he that is left in Zion and he that remaineth in Jerusalem shall be called Holy, even every one that is written among the living in Jerusalem. For unto us a child is born; unto us a son is given; and the government shall be upon his shoulders. And the Spirit of the Lord shall rest upon him; the spirit of wisdom and understanding; the spirit of counsel and might; the spirit of knowledge and the fear of the Lord. And he shall set up an ensign for the nations, and shall assemble the outcasts of Israel, and gather together the dispersed of Judah from the four corners of the earth. In that day when the Lord cometh the eyes of the blind shall be opened and the ears of the deaf shall be unstopped. The lame man shall leap as an hart, and the tongue of the dumb shall sing. And the people of the Lord shall return and come to Zion with songs and everlasting joy upon their heads; they shall obtain joy and gladness, and sorrow and sighing shall flee away."

By this time, John the Baptist, from the pious ardor with which he had delivered his discourse, had wrought himself to a high pitch of excitement, which was greatly increased by the stimulus of the wine he had drank. His voice was high and piercing; his words uttered with great rapidity, accompanied with a restless motion of his legs and frantic gestures of his arms and hands, while the expressions of his features were wild and terrific.

"Again the holy prophet sayeth," John continued, "Behold my servant whom I uphold,—mine elect in whom my soul delighteth. I have put my spirit upon him; he shall bring forth judgment to the Gentiles. He shall not fail or be discouraged until he has set judgment on the earth, and the isles shall wait for his law. He shall go forth as a mighty man; he shall stir up jealousy as a man of war; he shall prevail against his enemies. He shall say to the prisoners, go forth; to them that are in darkness, show yourselves. They shall feed in the ways, and their pastures shall be in high places. They shall not hunger or thirst, neither shall the sun smite them. In their affliction he will be afflicted, and the angel of his presence will save them. By his love and his pity he will redeem them. Comfort ye then—comfort ye my people, sayeth your God. Speak ye comfortably to Jerusalem and cry unto her that her warfare is accomplished, and that her iniquity is pardoned; for the Messiah cometh who is to save her. Hear ye then, the voice of him that crieth in the wilderness: Prepare ye the way of the Lord; make straight in the desert a highway for your God!"

John the Baptist paused for a few moments, during which he looked intently upon Saul as he pointed with his forefinger to himself and then added in a much lower tone of voice:

"I am the voice in the wilderness. I am the messenger of whom the prophet spoke, who is to go forth and proclaim the coming of the Messiah. This I have been doing through all the countries from north to south bordering on Jordan, preparing the people to receive their Lord by preaching to them repentance of sins, and remission of sins by baptism. My task is now nearly done, for the time draweth nigh."

John the Baptist ceased. With his eyes intently fixed upon Saul he seemed to be trying to make out what effect his last declaration had upon his hearer. During the whole time that he was delivering his discourse, Saul listened with grave attention, as though he gave full credence to all he heard. Now and then he would utter an exclamation, or give a motion of his head in approval of the statements made by him. But Saul was a man of great self-control. When he had an end in view which he wished to keep secret, he did not allow his features, his words, or his actions to betray it; consequently the part he played before John was not natural and sincere. He did not believe any of the prophecies cited by John to be true, though he pretended so. He viewed them rather as the wild ravings of ignorant, gloomy, fanatical men, whose minds were crooked through disappointed ambition and religious phrensy. He made no exception even with John the Baptist, for from the acquaintance he had of him he was confirmed in the opinion that he was a gloomy fanatic, and actually crazy on some points, with not sufficient learning or common sense to see the errors and inconsistencies of his doctrines. However, as Saul's design was to make discoveries, he pretended to be a believer in all that John advanced, giving no opposition, but gradually leading him to the point at which he wished to arrive by putting a question now and then.

When John the Baptist said that "The time draweth nigh," and paused, Saul sprang to his feet, seized John by the hand, and pressed it fervently in both of his; then with great earnestness of expression and tone of voice, he said:

"Tell me, holy man, when that time is to be, for my eyes wish to see the glory of that day."

John the Baptist placed his hands upon the shoulders of Saul, and regarded him for a few moments with an air of triumphant zeal, and at length said:

"Thou shalt be happy in thy wish, my friend. According to the vision of Daniel, the seventy weeks have just expired, when the Messiah is to make his appearance; therefore the time is come, and he, the long expected Lord who is to rule over the House of Israel, is come! Yes, he is come! for mine eyes have seen him."

Judas gave a terrible snore, and changed his position. Saul started; this time his action was not feigned. He had at length, and unexpectedly, brought the recluse to the very point he had been aiming at, with greater success than he anticipated, and could now afford to listen to him with a truly intense interest. He remained silent for a few moments, seeming to revel in pleasing emotions. A presentiment seemed to impress him that something was about to transpire which was to open to him a sphere of glorious future action.

"How wonderful are the ways of the Great Jehovah," piously ejaculated Saul. "Tell me, holy man, what thou hast seen of this mysterious and holy personage. What he is like, how he deports himself, whence he came, and all else concerning him."

John the Baptist seemed to hesitate for a few minutes in his reply to Saul's questions, but after pacing to and fro across the chamber two or three times with his arms crossed on his breast in deep reflection, he replied:

"The time appointed for his public declaration and entering on his mission is not quite yet; till then I thought it wise to keep him unknown; but as I have thus far spoken in confidence to thee, I will still further speak, depending upon thy discretion in the matter of what I shall further say."

Saul promised the recluse to be discreet and confidential upon all secret matters entrusted to him, when the recluse resumed:

"This mighty personage we have been expecting under the name of the Messiah, is two-fold in his nature. He is both man and God; man in his external nature and form, and all divine within. His person is human, though far superior in beauty and grace to ordinary men. His deportment is most amiable; meekness and benevolence glance from his eyes; words of wisdom, kindness and sympathy flow from his lips, and when he puts forth his hand, everything he touches receives a virtue impressed."

"How!" exclaimed Saul in surprise, "is there more virtue in his touch than in that of other men?"

"There is," replied the Baptist. "It is by this means we know him to be the promised Messiah."

"This is strange," said Saul to himself. "I began to suspect a collusion and a grand scheme of imposture between this pretended messenger and this Messiah; but now I know not what to think."

"Listen to what I have seen with mine own eyes," continued the recluse. "In times past I saw poor afflicted mortals with loathsome diseases, all corrupt within and disgusting without. This divine person of whom we speak placed his hands upon them, gently gliding over their deformed members, sometimes once, twice, or several times. The sores of the afflicted have drawn up; they soon dried, scaled, and shortly became as new flesh, and all without and within became healthy."

"This is truly wonderful," said Saul audibly, whose interest began to be greatly excited regarding the person spoken of. "But what meanest thou by saying "In times past?" Hast thou known this strange personage in former times?"

"Even so," replied John the Baptist. "We were companions and fellow students in our youth."

"I see!—I see!" said Saul to himself as his eyes brightened with the sudden development of some new ideas. "This John and this pretended Messiah are old acquaintances. They have had time enough to understand each other. They have had time enough to invent and bring forward some great scheme of imposition, which they are now about to bring before the public. Yet it is possible that there may be something singular and uncommon in the nature of this new comer, upon which the scheme of their Messiahship is founded. However, I must see farther before I make any rash conclusions."

"When was it," said Saul to the recluse, as soon as the preceding reflections had passed through his mind, "thou didst discover this miraculous power that thy divine companion possesses? Was it in his childhood, youth, or manhood?"

"It was at the time when childhood ceases and manhood begins to develop itself, that I made the discovery. From my studies and profession as one of the priesthood, I became convinced that it was a divine power developing itself within him; and after a farther investigation I became confirmed that in him we were to behold the Messiah as promised by the prophets. It was not so with him; he acknowledged the divine power within him to a certain extent; but his modesty was so great that he would not acknowledge himself to be the divine person spoken of by the prophets. With this declaration he left me to travel in distant countries, promising me that after he should have improved in knowledge, he would return to his native country; and if he still possessed that miraculous power he would use it to the greatest extent for the benefit of his fellow men. He has now returned, and is prepared to declare himself to the world as a teacher of morals and true religion, aiding his discourses with his other powers as a physician. But mark me, my friend, though this divine man cannot consent to be considered the Messiah, yet I, John, am convinced that he is the promised one; for it is now the time expires according to Daniel's vision of seventy weeks, when he said the Messiah should come. This I know, and I consider it to be my duty to make it known; as the prophets expressly state that I shall declare it to the world."

From the latter part of John the Baptist's statement, Saul was enabled to take a comprehensive view of the whole affair. He saw that he himself was wrong in considering either John or his companion as impostors, and was better enabled to see the motives of their actions. John he considered to be under the influence of a superstitious and fanatical zeal, while his companion, whoever he was, seemed to be impelled through noble principles of honesty, truth and benevolence. Saul therefore felt gratified with his present discoveries.

"I doubt not all thou hast said to be the truth concerning this divine man," observed Saul to the recluse, as he wished to make him believe that he was of that opinion. "His modesty, as thou hast said, prevents him from acknowledging his divine nature; but if the prophets speak truth, and thou art not mistaken, he certainly must be the Messiah."

"Thou hast spoken well," replied John, his eyes sparkling with great pleasure.

"But when, holy sir, shall I have the unspeakable pleasure of beholding this remarkable personage?" inquired Saul.

"Three days from the present, he will appear at Bethabara, on the Jordan," answered John, "where he condescends to receive the holy rite of baptism at my hands. Though he is entirely pure from all sin and vice, and needeth no cleansing, yet he is willing to conform to this holy institution as an example to others."

"At Bethabara, three days from this," said Saul, repeating the words of John as though he would firmly fix them upon his memory.

"Yes," replied John, "be thou there before mid-day, when thou shalt behold him of whom the prophets have spoken, and who is to take up the sceptre of Judah, and gather her scattered children unto the House of the Lord."

"Believe me, I will be there," answered Saul.

Nothing further of any consequence was said between the recluse and his guest that night. They soon afterwards betook themselves to their night's repose. Saul wrapped in his mantle slept on his rude couch, and the host betook himself to his bed of rushes in one corner of the cavern.

"Ah! what a wonderful dream I have had," said Judas to himself, as he roused up from his sleepy position to put some fresh fuel on the fire. "What wonderful disclosures of wonderful times! Wonderful men, wonderful secrets and wonderful doings, predicting a wonderful future! Ah! we shall see. I must go to sleep in earnest now, or I shall not be fit to play my part tomorrow."

Judas then placed himself as comfortably as he could, and slept soundly till the morning, when he and his master made an early departure, after taking a cordial leave of the recluse, John the Baptist.

VISION THIRD

LAZARUS

The meridian sun in dazzling splendor rode high above the Mount of Olives, the last fertile mountainous ridge that separates the Holy City of Jerusalem from the great wilderness of the East. The top of this mountain was formed of three mounds, the centre one being the highest, which were covered with thick forests of oak, pine, fir, cedar and other trees. The western side descended gradually in gentle slopes down to the valley of the Kidron, which was the eastern boundary of the city. These slopes were covered with the olive, fig, palm and myrtle, and many open spaces presented vineyards and orchards, bearing delicious fruits. Along the base were summer residences pertaining to the wealthy inhabitants of the great city, surrounded by gardens, redolent with the odors of fig, balsam, pomegranate and mulberry. On the eastern side of the mountain, separated from three mounds by a slight depression, was a rocky ridge, nearly barren, gradually rising at the centre mound, and terminating at the northeastern end by a deep ravine; and at the foot of this ridge on the eastern side was a village called Bethany, consisting of a few flat-roofed houses built of stone. This village formed two lines of habitations separated by the road or street, in the center of which was a small aqueduct conveying water into every house and garden from the mountainous rills; and on each side was a row of trees of olive, fig and others. The inhabitants of this humble place were generally of the working class, consisting of a few mechanics and artisans;

but the greater part were cultivators of gardens and vineyards whose sites of occupation were on the other side of the mountains. There were three roads leading from the village; one passing round the south-western shoulder of the mountain, then descending over uneven, stony ground down to the Kidron; another making a steep ascent over the ridge, and thence over the top of the mountain, and descending to the north-eastern end of the same valley. The other, after leaving the village and turning a bluff, makes a rapid descent eastward down to the valley of the Jordan, and being the main road to Jericho from Jerusalem.

The view from this spot eastward is of vast extent, over barren mountain ridges and deep gloomy ravines, line after line, down to the plains of Jordan; the course of this river could be traced by a line of verdure, but the waters could not be seen. A little farther southward could be seen the open space containing the sullen waters of the Lake Asphaltis or Dead Sea, resembling a gigantic basin of molten lead. Beyond in the background are the lofty mountains of Moab, rising peak above peak in great majesty. The air was so clear that the sea and mountains seemed quite close, though many miles distant. The country below presented a scene of complete desolation, the hills being bare and red, cut into deep ravines as far as the eye could discern; the mountains back of these form a stupendous wall, whose outlines seemed as smooth as a work of art.

The habitation at the south-eastern corner of this village of Bethany was a larger house than the rest, it being a public inn for travelers passing between Jericho and Jerusalem. It was a rectangular building of stone with a flat roof, having several rooms below and some above, the entrance to the latter being by means of a staircase on the outside. The house and grounds were surrounded by a stone wall, one portion of the latter forming a garden which was arranged into fanciful sections for flowers and herbs. Here and there were fruit trees giving forth delicious odors and bearing luscious fruit. In front of the house was an open casement or window surrounded on the outside with a trellis-work covered with creeping plants bearing beautiful and sweet scented flowers. The entrance to the house was by a door immediately under the stairs, with a covered porchway or piazza some feet in extent. There were stables, out-houses, and a yard intervening between the house and the garden, all of which bore the impress of neatness and good arrangement.

The proprietor of this establishment was a man by the name of Lazarus, a widower with two daughters, who was a tanner by trade. He worked at his business in the upper part of the village while his daughters kept his home and gave entertainment to travelers passing between the city and Jericho. He had formerly been a resident of a village in Galilee named Nazareth, but being discontented with his circumstances he removed to Bethany in Judea, where he was near to the Holy City, and where it was more convenient to make purchases of skins from the slaughter houses of the Temple, owing to the vast quantity of cattle that were made a sacrifice to appease the carnivorous appetite of the Great Jehovah; so that between the two callings of tanning and innkeeping he and his family were doing well in life, though not rich.

Lazarus' two daughters were the greatest treasures he possessed, whose filial love and amiable devotedness to his wishes compensated him for the loss of his much-beloved deceased wife. They were both maidens of agreeable person, good natural sense, and possessing as much intelligence as their circumstances would permit. Martha, the elder, whose age was about twenty-eight, was a tall, noble-looking female of full womanly development, with jet-black hair, eyes and eye-brows, and oriental cast of features, with russet complexion. Her whole person gave evidence of great power and endurance, yet graceful and symmetrical in form.

Mary, the younger daughter, was about twenty-five; who was less in stature, and more delicate in appearance than her sister. Her hair, eyes and eyebrows were of chestnut brown; her visage more oval, and her features more rounded. Her complexion much fairer, being a mixture of pink and olive; her skin more transparent, exhibiting a vermillion tinge on her cheeks and lips. Her bust was smaller, the outlines of the most graceful curves; and all her limbs, though light in structure, possessed the greatest symmetry. Her eyes beamed glances of tenderness and amiability, while her words were of sweetness, encouragement and sym-pathy. Martha's noble person could command respect and admiration, while Mary, with less pretensions to beauty, with her sweet voice and gentle beaming eyes, could gain the love of all around her.

In the principal chamber of the house on the lower floor the two maidens were together, their father being absent on business at the Holy City. The apartment was spacious, the rude walls being covered with ornamented leather, and the floor with a thick matting made of rushes. At the open casement were rich hangings of silk, striped with various showy colors. Along one side of the chamber at the base of the wall was a kind of mattress elevated about a foot from the floor, with several thick cushions covered with black leather, which was used as a place of general sitting or lounging; and on the opposite side was an alcove a few feet deep, and elevated from the floor about two feet, around which was a mattress and cushions covered with red silk, and hanging curtains in front of the same material, looped up at the sides. A small window admitted the light that looked out upon the rear part of the building. Within this alcove, the two sisters, Martha and Mary, were seated.

Mary was habited in a vestment with wide open sleeves, open at the neck and breast, reaching a little below the waist of rich silk, in various colored stripes, from underneath which fell a short skirt of white linen reaching a little below the knees. Around her waist was a red silken girdle, and her lower limbs were inducted in full trousers of fine red wool, fastened around the ankles. Her beautiful small feet were bare, though slippers of exquisite workmanship stood by her side ready for use when occasion required them. Around her wrists were golden bracelets; in her ears were golden rings of exquisite workmanship, and on one of her fingers she wore a ring of plain gold. She was reclining upon the cushion with her eyes shut, in natural, unconscious ease, either asleep, or in a half-dreamy, dozing state.

Martha was habited in a dress of similar style to that of her younger sister, though of coarser and more humble materials, for she being the elder and of greater strength, was in the habit of attending to the more laborious part of domestic duties. She was seated opposite to her sister in the alcove, with her lower limbs crossed beneath her, in the oriental style, as she was sewing upon a garment that lay in her lap. As she progressed with her work she cast an eye of solicitude upon her younger sister now and then, as though she was uneasy about her, and then continued her work and her reflections. Presently a change seemed to come over Mary; her slumbers no longer seemed easy; her respirations were difficult; a slight quivering of the lips was seen, and a slight moan issued from her now and then as though her dreams or thoughts produced within her distressing emotions.

"I wonder what can ail my dear sister today?" Martha said to herself, as she glanced towards her sister, and perceived that her sleep was uneasy. "There is something, I am sure, more than common. She spoke this morning of spirits depressed, and evil presentiment. What can she mean? Hie! what nonsense! What reason has one so pure and innocent as she is to anticipate evil?"

Martha's reflections were interrupted by hearing a piercing shriek burst forth from her sister. Immediately casting her eyes in that direction she saw Mary spring from her recumbent position and rush to the verge of the alcove; then turning with her hand placed upon her breast, her eyes fixed on vacancy, she uttered another shriek, and exclaimed in a most piteous tone of voice:

"0! save, save my pretty bird!"

"Mary, my dear sister," exclaimed Martha, as she rushed towards her, feeling much terror at the singular occurrence. Then seizing her hands, she shook her as she added, "Awake, awake, my sister! Thou hast been dreaming a bad dream. Look around thee and see where thou art!"

The terrified, vacant stare of Mary subsided as she became conscious where she was, and that her distress proceeded from a dream. At length being convinced of her situation, she heaved a deep sigh, and burst into tears, while a tremor seized her.

Martha, as soon as she perceived her sister restored to consciousness, rushed from the chamber into some other part of the house; but she quickly returned with a goblet containing a cordial which she presented to her sister, and made her drink.

After a while Mary became composed, when raising her eyes to her sister with a serious expression, she observed:

"Is it possible that all I have seen and felt is no more than a dream!"

"Nothing more I assure thee, my dear sister," responded Martha, "but what can possess thee to conjure up so terrible a dream? Now Mary, my love, I know that something must be on thy mind. Thou must make me thy confident in the place of our dear mother, and I will advise thee with all the wisdom and loving consolation that I possess. Come, my dear, be not scrupulous in letting me know what it is that disturbs thy mind and feelings. But first let me know what was thy dream."

Mary remained silent for some minutes to all the solicitations of her sister, with her eyes cast down and her bosom heaving with great emotion. But at length, looking up to Martha with reawakened interest, as a faint smile played around her sweet lips, she said with sisterly affection and candor:

"I am sorry to trouble thee, Martha, with my silly thoughts and feelings; but as it is thy wish I will tell thee all."

The two sisters then seated themselves side by side, the head of the younger resting on the bosom of the elder; nestling and embracing each other with true sisterly affection. Mary not only felt for her sister a true sisterly love, but a degree of deference as she viewed her in the light of a mother, owing to her age and superiority of experience. And Martha found that not only the impulses of sisterly love bound her to her younger sister, but the responsibilities and solicitude of her deceased mother, to render her sister happy, devolved upon her.

"Come, Mary, relate to me that horrible dream," said Martha as she smoothed the nut-brown hair of her sister on either side.

"Thou must remember, sister," said Mary in a timid voice, "that I told thee this morning I felt very much depressed in spirits, which I considered a foreboding of coming evil, or something strange that is about to happen. Thou dost not believe in presentiments, sister, but I do."

"I know nothing of presentiments," responded Martha tartly, "and I cannot believe what I cannot comprehend. Now proceed with thy dream."

"Well," resumed Mary, "I continued under these sad impressions all the morning until wearied, I reclined upon the couch. For some time I lay dozing, but at length fell asleep. Then I dreamed that I was a little girl as I used to be when we resided at Nazareth. I thought I possessed a little bird of most beautiful plumage, that warbled most harmonious music. It was my pet. I prized it above all other things on earth. To gaze

upon the brilliant colors of its plumage, and listen to its heavenly harmonious notes, filled me with unspeakable pleasure."

"A change took place in my dream. I thought that by some means
my bird flew away to the woods on the mountains. I followed in pursuit,
weeping, sobbing and tearing my clothes. As I wandered on over hill and
dale, penetrating through the wild dark woods. I thought that I grew
taller, larger and older, until I became the person I now am. At last I
perceived my bird. It was fluttering in agony over a limb of a tree. I
rushed towards it, and endeavored to coax it down, but it seemed
spellbound to the spot. All my efforts were in vain. At length, casting my
glance towards the trunk of the tree I saw an enormous serpent with
distended jaws and its eyes intently glaring upon my bird. My poor little
pet was fascinated and could not escape. At length the head of the
serpent moved slowly along the limb of the tree. The bird still fluttered,
and gradually came closer and closer within the influence of its fascinating eyes, and at length, to end its miseries, it flew into the serpent's
open mouth. I saw it disappear. O! great was my agony! I shrieked and
awoke. Such is my dream, dear sister."

When Mary had finished relating her dream her trembling and tears
were renewed. Martha bent down, drew her closer to her breast, and
kissed her repeatedly, endeavoring to console her with fond embraces.
Both remained silent for some minutes.

"What dost thou think of my dream, dear sister," said Mary, at length
breaking the silence which, like a baneful spell, seemed to exercise its
influence over both of them. "Dost thou think there is any confirmation
of my impressions of this morning?"

"Thy dream is a strange one, and rather saddening," replied Martha.
"But rest assured, my dear sister, it has no connection with future
events. According to my experience I find dreams to be the result of our
previous state of mind and affections. They are the pictures of our
private thoughts and feelings, according to our past impressions; and
consequently are not, as is commonly believed, to be the good or bad
omens of future events."

"Thou art an unbeliever of the prognosticating power of dreams
also," said Mary reprovingly.

"The fact is, my dear sister," returned Martha, as she imprinted another kiss upon the cheek of Mary, "we must look into ourselves for the
causes and nature of our dreams. Now if it were possible for me to know
all the little secrets of thy mind, all the affections of thy little heart, and
all the mysterious impulses of thy soul, then I should be enabled to
explain thy dream in all its parts."

Mary heaved a deep sigh, and her eyelids drooped.

"Now, my dear sister," added Martha in a lively tone, "as I have been
so far a good physician, in pointing out thy ailment, let me continue the

good office, by advising thee to get married."

"Married!" exclaimed Mary pettishly, as she raised her head and regarded her sister in surprise.

"Yes, my dear sister," returned Martha, "marriage is the only remedy in such cases."

"I think my sister Martha had better avail herself of the counsel she gives me," observed Mary curtly.

"True, my sister!" responded Martha, "I have no objections to marriage as regards myself; but thou knowest that I have made a vow to remain single as long as our dear father exists. I am bound to tend and care for him all his days in the place of our lost mother."

"And I have made a vow to remain single," replied Mary, with emphasis on the two last words, as a blush suffused her countenance and her eyes shone with greater brilliancy. Then raising her hand to her lips she kissed the ring upon her finger, which was noticed by Martha.

"Is it possible, my dear sister," said Martha, inquiringly, "that thy mind and heart still dwell so seriously upon the remembrance of that youth who was thy companion and playmate so many years back? I should have thought that his absence for so long a time would have effaced him from thy memory and affections."

"Impossible!—never, never!" exclaimed Mary, as she burst into tears. Then throwing her arms around the neck of her sister she continued to weep and sob for some time. At length finding herself somewhat relieved she released her embrace, and observed:

"Thou didst not know that youth, Martha, nor did I as I do now. There was something so different in Jose from all other young men that I ever saw, or have since seen. Far superior was he in personal traits to all others of his sex. Most amiable and kind was he in disposition; most graceful, grave and natural was he in all his actions. When he spoke, his voice was a stream of harmonious music that moved my soul in sympathy with all his feelings and sentiments of joy or sadness. And there was a power in his clear dark brown eye, that I cannot describe, though I felt it often. Whatever his harmonious voice spoke upon, seemed to be depicted within his brilliant orbs of vision; and as I gazed upon them, I would soon be drawn within the sphere of their mysterious influence. All opposition, resistance and self-control would succumb. Motionless and powerless the conscious soul became absorbed within his heavenly fascination. 0! sister, sister! shall I ever behold him again?"

Mary once more threw herself upon the neck of her sister, when tears like crystal drops flowed afresh from her hazel eyes.

"Console thyself, dear sister," soothingly responded Martha, as she drew her sister closer to her breast, and endeavored to chase her tears away with kisses; for she was deeply moved with sympathy in her sister's despondent love. "Remember, my dear Mary, that it is many years since that cherished companion of thy childhood left thee to travel abroad. It is highly probable that he no longer lives upon the earth. Thou must cease to hope for his return, and endeavor to banish that fond remembrance of him from thy memory."

"Never, sister, never!" replied Mary with great energy.

Further conversation between the sisters was prevented by the entrance of an old man into the chamber, who approaching the maidens with a hurried step, shouted in a loud voice:

"Good news, daughters! Good news!"

This old man was Lazarus, the father of the two maidens. He was small of stature, though of robust form, who seemed to have seen three score summers at least, for his long beard, thick moustache and arching eye-brows were perfectly white; beneath the latter his small dark eyes shone with considerable vivacity, indicating that the zest and powers of life were not much impaired. His nose was slightly aquiline, with prominent cheek bones; his complexion a dark olive, with a ruddy tint on the cheeks and lips, giving assurance that he was in perfect health. With the exception of a few wrinkles across the forehead and around the eyes, his age seemed to have borne lightly with his person. The general expression of his countenance was a lively shrewdness and a capacity for worldly business matters; yet when occasions called into force the traits of his nature there were unmistakable evidences that he possessed true affection and kindness for his family, and a fair sense of justice, propriety and charity for all mankind.

He was habited in a long loose robe of dark brown cloth, with large sleeves and a large silk girdle around his waist, in which he carried his purse of money. Over his left shoulder and across his breast was wrapped his brown mantle. His legs were naked, but the feet were covered with coarse sandals, and his head covered with a close-fitting skull cap, around which was twined a figured shawl. In his hand he held a stout stick which he used partly to facilitate his traveling over the rough, mountainous roads, and partly for self-protection. Such was Lazarus, the father of the two maidens, Mary and Martha.

"Good news, my daughters," exclaimed the old man, as he rushed into the presence of his children flushed with excitement and animated with joy; but as soon as he perceived his younger daughter in tears, all the expressions of his joy immediately vanished, and those of alarm succeeded.

"What! my daughter Mary in tears? What has happened, Martha?" he anxiously inquired.

"Nothing, dear father, of any consequence," answered Martha smiling. "Mary has only been telling me some of her little secrets. Father, thou knowest what a little spoilt child she is; so full of affection; so full of sensibility, that her little overflowing heart has to find vent in tears now and then, whether of joy or sadness."

"Come, my darling daughter," said the old man, as soon as he had divested himself of his mantle and head dress; when raising Mary he pressed her to his bosom and fondly kissed her. "Come! chase these unworthy tears away, and listen to the good news I have to tell thee."

"Good news for me, father, sayest thou?" inquired Mary, as she wiped away her tears, and looked at her father doubtingly.

"Yes, my dear, good news for thee, for Martha and me, and I know not how many more," replied the father.

"0! what can it be? Do tell us quick, dear father!" said Martha, anxiously.

"Now, daughters, do not be in a hurry. I intend to make you guess a while," said the father, with the intention of arousing their curiosity and wit.

"Perhaps thou hast made a good sale and purchase of skins. Is it that, father?" inquired Martha.

"I have done very well in that respect," replied the father smiling; "but that is not my news. That is nothing!"

"Hast thou been honored with an interview with the High Priest?" inquired Mary.

"Yes, I have, but that is not my news. That is nothing" answered the father; when suddenly checking himself, he said: "God of my Fathers, what am I saying? I must not speak disrespectfully of the High Priest!"

"Hast thou found any gold, treasures, or jewels?" inquired Martha.

"No, I have not, but gold, silver or jewels are nothing in comparison to what I have found."

"Then pray, father, tell us what it is thou hast found," said Martha coaxingly.

"I have found a man who will bring joy to your hearts and peace to this house," returned the old man in a tremulous voice.

"Who—who is he? Speak, father, quickly!" demanded Mary as she placed her hand upon his shoulder, and gazed intently into his eyes with great excitement visible in her countenance.

"Daughters," said the old man seriously, "I have found your old acquaintance and companion of your youth, Jose of Nazareth!"

"Our long lost Jose?" exclaimed Martha in astonishment.

"The same," replied the father.

"0! father, father! Mary has fainted!" exclaimed Martha in affright.

The previous sad emotions and gloomy anticipations, followed by the unexpected joyful tidings, were too overpowering for the great sensibility of the fair maiden of Bethany. For a few minutes the nervous centres of her system were paralyzed, refusing their accustomed offices to the heart, then all consciousness and power ceased for a time. The insensible maiden was laid upon the cushions in the alcove, and the distressed father stood over her with tears of anguish in his eyes. Martha turned away with the intention of fetching restoratives, and the servant maid to give assistance; when, as she crossed the room and was about passing out at the door-way, she staggered backward uttering a shriek of surprise and joy. At that instant a tall, majestic figure crossed the threshold of the door, and stood before her. She was struck mute with astonishment and admiration.

"Peace to all in this house!" exclaimed a rich, manly voice.

Lazarus turned, and beheld his former youthful friend and neighbor.

"Welcome to the home of Lazarus and his family," said Lazarus to the visitor, as he advanced and bent lowly before him.

"Welcome to this house and all that is in it." Then pointing to his elder daughter, he added, "My daughter Martha."

"Martha, dearest maiden, friend and associate of my youthful days, dost thou know me?" said the visitor in soft persuasive tones of friendship as he advanced with open arms towards her.

Martha had been for some moments gazing in silent admiration of the noble person before her; but as soon as she heard him address her she recognized the voice. She instantly rushed forward and embraced one of his extended arms, while he drew her to his breast and imprinted a kiss upon her forehead.

"Jose! Jose! my long lost friend and acquaintance!" ejaculated Martha, her eyes sparkling with exuberant joy. "Praise be to the God of our Fathers for the pleasure of once more beholding thee!"

The person addressed as Jose was a tall handsome man, several inches above the full stature, who seemed to have just attained the full development of perfect physical manhood. His age was about thirty, or perhaps thirty-two, though some persons would judge him to be younger when viewing the perfect freshness and perfection of his manly beauty. The brilliancy of his eyes; the transparency of his skin, without a wrinkle or spot; the rich carnation of his beautifully formed lips, and the tinge of health upon his cheeks; his expansive, smooth forehead, through the skin of which could be easily discerned the frontal vein, the minute ramifications of veins and arteries, and the mature development of the reflective faculties; his nose and mouth of the most exquisite symmetry, expressive of the most refined and chaste sentiments and emotions of natural purity; his hair of raven blackness, soft and fine, presenting a variety of shades as parted on the forehead, falling in long natural tresses around his gracefully curved neck, and couching agreeably over his broad shoulders,—all these made his appearance very impressive.

His moustache and beard were of the same darkness as his hair, the former small, curling forward; the latter parted in two like a fork, of prominent and uniform thickness, reaching two or three inches below his chin. Beneath his beautifully arched dark brown eye-brows vividly shone his eloquent eyes expressive of wisdom and high aspirations of thought, with mildness, serenity and sweetness of disposition.

The crown of his head was covered with a blue cloth, and a shawl of many colors entwined his brows. His symmetrically formed limbs and body were covered with a long close fitting coat with large open sleeves reaching from the neck to the middle of the leg; and around his waist was a girdle of several colors, from which it hung in graceful folds. Over his left shoulder and across his breast, drooping in folds by his side, he wore a green mantle. His hands and legs were bare and his feet were covered with sandals.

Such was the personal appearance of Jose, the early part of whose history has been made known in Paul's confessions.

"The blessing of God be upon thee Martha" replied Jose to Martha's greeting. "In friendship and brotherly love I salute thee."

As soon as the greeting between Martha and Jose had terminated, Lazarus directing the attention of the latter to the insensible Mary, said to him in a dolorous tone of voice:

"Behold my younger daughter Mary. She lies in a swoon. The emotions called up by a knowledge of thy unexpected return were too powerful for her sensitive nature to control. O! help her, Jose, if thou canst."

Jose cast his eyes upon the unconscious maiden who, with the pallor of death in her countenance and her symmetrical limbs extended, lay stretched upon the cushions in the alcove; and her inspiration being imperceptible she seemed to have departed from this life. He placed his hand upon his breast as though he would check an emotion that suddenly arose within him, as he half audibly exclaimed:

"Ah! my Mary!"

Then turning to Lazarus he said in a soothing tone of voice:

"Be not distressed, friend Lazarus. Thy daughter shall soon recover to embrace thee."

Then Jose divested himself of his head dress and mantle, and kneeling by the side of the unconscious Mary took hold of one of her hands, which he felt for a few moments. Then he placed his hand upon the back of her neck where he let it remain for a few seconds; then drawing it gently over her shoulder and across her breast, let it remain for a short time over the region of the heart. This process he repeated, when certain favorable effects were produced. The prostrate form of the maiden lost all rigidity, inspiration began to be perceptible; the eyelids and lips quivered; her fingers began to move, and at length her eyes opened. Again they closed, and again they opened. Then suddenly rising from her recumbent position she looked around her with an expression of astonishment, and said in a dubious tone of voice:

"Do I dream, or is it real what I see?"

"It is all reality, my child" answered Lazarus with joy in his eyes.

"Yes, Mary, my dear sister" said Martha, "it is a happy reality. Look up, Mary, and see if thou canst recognize this friend."

Mary raised her eyes toward Jose on whom she fixed her gaze for some time; then, suddenly rising from her couch, she rushed towards him and fell into his arms, as she exclaimed:

"Yes, yes, my long lost Jose! My long lost friend and companion of my childhood."

She could say no more, for joy overpowered her. Her head drooped upon his breast, and she burst into tears.

With gentle soothing words, Jose reduced to a sober measure the high wrought feelings of Mary's ecstatic joy. Then general greetings and congratulations took place among all present. Refreshments of wine and cake were brought in and partaken of. They seated themselves in social harmony within the alcove, supported by cushions of silk, Mary being near to Jose. Then they discussed in a happy mood the reminiscences of the past, when they were happy companions and neighbors in Nazareth of Galilee.

Thus passed the first hour of this happy, social group. At length Jose was requested to relate his travels and adventures from the day of his departure from Nazareth, which he consented to do. It would be impossible to describe the spell of interest Jose exercised over this innocent and honest family, as he proceeded in the relation of his adventures and travels—especially Mary who was reclining upon a cushion by his side, and occasionally leaning her delicate arm upon his knee. How the music of his voice commanded and absorbed her attention while gazing upon his manly countenance, changing its expression according to the nature of his discourse, and filling her with emotions of sympathy in his behalf. How carefully she watched every minute motion of his handsome lips as they uttered words of glowing eloquence when describing scenes of intense interest. How her bosom would heave with painful emotion when he described some of the hardships and disappointments of life he had encountered, and the misfortunes, vices and miseries he had seen others experience during his travels over the world. How her heart would rapidly beat with joy and her eyes glisten with pleasure when he related instances of pure love, charity, benevolence and justice among some men that he had seen, and of his own noble endeavors to ameliorate the condition of mankind.

Thus held in rapturous thraldom in listening to the intensely interesting adventures of Jose, Lazarus and his daughters were unconscious that the sun had sunk below the mountain, until they found themselves in darkness, and then they all arose, and passed into another chamber to partake of the evening repast.

VISION FOURTH

JESUS AND MARY

The dazzling orb of day had for hours disappeared below the horizon, and the less lustrous lamp of night was suspended high in the heavens above Mount Olivet, diffusing her silvery beams of tranquil light and soothing influence over and around the humble village of Bethany, which, like an eagle's eyry, was perched in the cleft of the mountain.

Within the vast expanse of the celestial vault myriads of stars with ceaseless light, unobstructed by cloud or mist, contributed their powers to illuminate and adorn the scene of night. The air was soft and agreeably tempered, redolent with numerous agreeable odors exhaled from trees, from blossoms, from healing shrubs and beauteous flowers. All lights were extinguished in the humble dwellings; all was peace and quietness, for all the worthy people, excepting two, had retired to rest from the toils of the day.

With noiseless steps and hand in hand that two emerged from the dwelling of Lazarus, crossed the enclosed yard, and entered the garden near by. One was a man of tall, commanding figure and majestic mien; the other a female much less in stature, of delicate, sylphlike form, whose sparkling eyes told a tale of love and present happiness. Both persons were enveloped in their mantles which covered their heads, shoulders and busts as a means of guarding against the night dew.

As soon as they had entered the garden the female leaned upon her companion's arm, and her eyes beaming with pure affection looked up to him, seeking an exchange of glances. The man with looks of tenderness and solicitude gently supported her delicate form, as in a voice sweet and musical he poured into her ears words of sacred intelligence, tales of interest, and declaration of secret thoughts and feelings congenial to her soul. As thus they discoursed they paced to and fro the smooth walks belonging to this beautiful parterre, or under the fruit trees on the borders thereof.

"Mary," said the female's companion, as he raised his hand and eyes towards the firmament with a serene expression of countenance, "does this scene not impress thee as being one of great beauty and magnificence?"

"Yes, Jose," replied the maiden in great sweetness of tone. "This scene of night is truly beautiful. This night seems to impress me with its beauty and magnificence more than any night I have noticed for many years. I know not how it is, for I am of simple mind, not knowing how to appreciate such scenes of grandeur; but I know that I have frequently paced this garden in the tranquil hours of night, and never have I felt as I do now. When I gazed upon the starry firmament with all its glittering lights, and endeavored to imagine what they were, I found my mind a blank. I seemed to be an insignificant speck not included in any of the great systems of greatness and grandeur. All things impressed me with a chill; the forest-covered hills and green sloping valleys seemed cheerless. I felt a sadness of heart. I found myself, as it were, alone in the world and unhappy. Ah! how great the change this day and night since thou hast returned to me, Jose! Now all things seem bright and smiling. My mountain home looks picturesque and beautiful. Mount Olivet never looked so gay, with her olive and fig trees, her orchards and vineyards with their luscious fruits. Even the red barren hills eastward down to Jordan, the dread Lake Asphaltis, and the mountains of Moab seem more cheerful to my view, while the humble dwelling of my father I would not exchange for a palace. Ah! Jose, my heart is now overflowing with happiness so exquisite and ineffably sweet! Tell me, Jose, how all this change is produced within me."

As Mary uttered the latter part of her speech her companion seemed to undergo great emotion, as though some feeling or sentiment that his good nature prompted him to acknowledge he was about to reveal, yet prudence compelled him to suppress. His eyes became averted from the loving gaze of the fair maiden, and a slight tremor passed through him. After a few moments' silence in which he struggled to gain his composure, he replied with calmness:

"Mary, I am happy to perceive that the reminiscences of our youthful days are not obliterated from thy memory, and that the brotherly love and pure friendship we formerly entertained for each other burns as brightly and as holy as ever in thy pure heart. That it is so I am convinced from the pleasure and happiness thou dost manifest at my presence, giving to thee that happy tone of feeling which makes all things around thee appear so bright and beautiful; it is the reawakening of thy sisterly love and pure friendship."

"Sisterly love and pure friendship!" exclaimed Mary, repeating the words of Jose in a tone of aversion. "I have a sincere love for my sister, a deep filial love for my father, and a great friendship for all mankind; yet none of these are like unto the affection which I entertain for thee, Jose."

"Mary, thou art all innocence and pure affection," replied Jose, as he placed his arm around the maiden and pressed her to his breast. "Thy love is beyond all price, and happy will be the lot of that man who shall possess and enjoy it. I am aware of the tender relations that exist between us, the claim and command I have over thy pure affections; yet, Mary, there is a Being greater than I who ought to command thy attention and share thy love before me; a Being who is the source or fountain of all love under whatever form it is manifested on earth. Every passional emotion of love that vibrates in the heart or thrills through the nerves, emanated from and once formed a part of that great mysterious power which we all feel, yet whose perfect nature we know not. Let us then for the present, Mary, cease to talk of our egotistical love, and talk of Him from whom all love cometh."

"Dost thou mean the God of our Fathers, Jose?" inquired Mary.

"I mean the God of the Universe, Mary," replied Jose sternly.

"I have been taught," said Mary, "to believe in one great God, Jehovah by name, who made this world and all mankind; who selected the Children of Israel as a choice and favored people; who sent his servant Moses to lead them from the bondage of Egypt, and then gave to him a table of laws, by which they should be governed. To this God I have been taught to render due homage, praise and glory. Such are the limits of my understanding thereon."

"Mary," replied Jose in a tone of gravity and with an expression of solemn earnestness, "I wish not to shock the self-reliance of thy young inexperienced mind; but the love of eternal justice and immutable truth as well as my duty to thee compel me to declare that all thy conceptions of the Deity, which thou callest the God of our Fathers are but so many gross errors, that have no existence in the nature of the true God of the universe, who is the Master and Father of all things around us."

"Errors!" exclaimed Mary in surprise and trembling. "Errors sayest thou, Jose! Are not the words of our priesthood, and of our holy books all true? They declare that there is but one God, Jehovah, who descended upon Mount Sinai, and amidst lightnings and earthquakes made compacts for his favored people."

"No, Mary," answered Jose emphatically; and his eyes became expressive of an aroused energy and zeal. "It is all imposture, fiction and lies so gross and absurd in their nature that to connect them with the idea of the true God, is to utter blasphemy and wickedness.

"The God in whom thou hast been taught to believe under the name of Jehovah, is nothing more than a figment of the human imagination, bearing a correspondence in its nature and attributes to the traits of character and peculiarities of man. The Gods as worshiped by mankind in every country and in all ages, have been represented in their natures according to the gross conceptions of the people of the time and place. They are the ideal images designed by certain cunning men to represent and account for the various mysterious phenomena of nature of which man has hitherto been ignorant. Mankind in their primitive savage state worship the phenomena of nature under various hideous and fanciful forms; and as they progress in their social relations and expand in mind, so do their Gods make a corresponding change of form and attributes.

"When a nation of people are savage, cruel, fickle and unjust, the Gods of that people are the same, and as the nation advances in intelligence, virtue and reason, their conceptions of their Gods make a similar advance. This relation between mankind and their Gods has proven true in all times and countries, and is the case with the race of people of which we are. What were the Gods of our forefathers before the time of Moses? Were not our forefathers ignorant savages in bondage to the Egyptians, so void of intelligence that they knew not their origin? Did they not render homage to beasts, birds and reptiles as their Gods? Yes, such was their gross, groveling state, and such their gross conceptions of the superhuman powers!

"This state lasted for ages, and until one among them who had been reared under more favorable circumstances, possessing some intelligence, vast cunning and a bold spirit, called his brethren together, broke their bondage and led them forth in triumph from their masters, to seek a new country where he could establish them as a nation. This was Moses who, seeing the necessity of uniting his people by some powerful tie, seized the occasion to establish a new God. And what was this God, this Great Jehovah, but an ideal figment that originated in his mind, whose attributes correspond in nature to the character of Moses' self; a being of absolute rule—bold, terrible, cruel, vindictive and unrelenting; possessed of firmness and weakness; of power, and yet impotent; of justice, and yet unjust; of love and hatred; of steadfastness and fickleness; of intelligence, and yet ignorant; of truth and falsehood; and of all other qualities, some good and some evil. Such was the God established by Moses, and such was Moses in character. This God as established by Moses was good for the people under the time and circumstances in which they were placed, as it was somewhat superior to their previous state of gross ignorance. But now the times have changed; there is more knowledge existing in the minds of men than before; and the evils arising from this barbarous superstition are more apparent and more grievous to bear. Therefore it becomes our duty to discard the relics of previous barbarism, and to lift up our thoughts in search of the True God of Nature."

While Jose was delivering the preceding discourse, Mary continued to gaze upon him with the greatest astonishment, and with some degree of terror in her countenance, it being the first time she had ever heard sentiments expressed so opposed to the education she had received. In the simplicity of her mind she had never doubted or questioned the truth or origin of the Jewish theogony; and had they been uttered by any other lips she would have considered them as the greatest blasphemy; but coming from him whose word she had hitherto considered as truth and wisdom she felt confounded for a time, not knowing what to think or how to decide—whether to renounce the belief to which she had been educated, or admit the truths as delivered in Jose's words.

For a few moments there was silence in which Jose gazed penetratingly into the face of the maiden to discover what effect his words had produced, while she was struggling to collect her thoughts and regain sufficient composure to form them into words. At length, drawing closer to her companion and placing her right hand upon his shoulder, as she looked up to him with great seriousness of expression, she said in a grave tone of voice:

"0, Jose, what strange and fearful words are these thou hast uttered? Is it possible that thou art serious and true in all thou hast said, and that all my education on these matters is nothing but a system of error and imposture? Is it possible that the great system of Priesthood and all pertaining to it, as established by Moses and continued to the present day, is no more than a grand scheme of imposture and knavery? Is it possible that I, a true believer and humble devotee of the Great Jehovah, know nothing of the true God of the Universe?"

"It is even so," replied Jose in a tone of great sweetness. "Let not the truths I utter affright thy young mind. Look at them boldly, and thou wilt find that truth is more inviting and amiable when once seen, than error and falsehood, though the latter may be better known to thee. In that which I have said, I have spoken in seriousness, with a sense of its responsibility. Thou knowest I never speak otherwise. It is also true that the priesthood of Jerusalem's Temple and all pertaining to it are nothing but a grand scheme of imposture and knavery, and that its devotees know no more of the true God than the babe just born."

"0! Jose, Jose," cried Mary piteously. Reclining her head upon his breast, she clung to him as though for protection. "Have mercy upon my ignorance and weak nature. I have no reason to doubt thy words, for they have always had the power to sink deep into my mind, leaving there the impress of truth and wisdom. But now, dear Jose, this discourse of thine has wrought me great uneasiness. I feel a void in my mind since thou hast destroyed the main structure of my education. I feel as nothing compared to my former self. Do not, therefore, deprive me of those errors and false notions that I have been taught to believe sacred, unless thou canst fill up the void with something of greater substance and beauty. Give me at least one idea of that true God of whom thou hast hinted, but not yet fully spoken."

"I will, Mary," answered Jose quickly. "Let now all thy senses awaken to receive impressions from the beauteous and magnificent universe. Let thy soul open and expand its recipient powers so as to embrace the brilliant truths which the phenomena of nature shall present to thee. Let thy spirit awaken and expand its wings, soaring with me to various realms, where the beauty, power, wisdom and magnificence of the Universal God are displayed."

Jose then extended his right hand towards the starry heavens, and added in a tone of voice, calm and grave, as his countenance seemed to be illumined with a sacred fervor, while the glance of Mary following in the direction indicated, was of an absorbing, solemn interest.

"Behold, Mary, the vast expanse of firmament above and around us! Regard this beauteous moon whose silvery tranquil beams serve as a lamp of night to illumine this earth in the absence of the lustrous orb of day; and notice the twinkling stars whose numbers are innumerable, which not only contribute their share of nocturnal light, but give to the celestial scene a solemn beauty and grandeur. What thinkest thou, Mary, constitute the substance and nature of these celestial lights? In other words, what are they?"

"What are they!" exclaimed Mary in surprise at the question. "Are they not what our reverend Rabbi have taught us that they are? Is not the moon a great light to rule the night as the sun does the day? Are not the stars so many smaller lights, like so many torches attached to the vault of the firmament, to light up and adorn the scene of night?"

"Such is the answer I expected from thy innocent but misinformed mind, Mary," replied Jose in a tone of gentleness, though a smile slightly curled his lip. "But mark me, such a view of things is erroneous. They are fabulous notions taken from the mystical lore of the Rabbi. I who have traveled and conversed with sages of many countries, have reason to know better. I, therefore, declare to thee, Mary, what thou considerest as so many lights to rule and adorn the scene of night, are so many suns and worlds, similar to the one we live in."

"Worlds!" ejaculated Mary in astonishment as she regarded Jose doubtingly for a moment, and then with steady gaze she peered into the starry firmament.

"Yes, Mary, worlds," resumed Jose. "Worlds and suns innumerable! Families of suns, worlds and moons similar to our own, so numerous that it would be as easy for a man to count the particles of sand in the desert as to number the worlds that exist through the vast extent of universal space. To thy naked eye these starry luminaries seem no larger than a common torch, and according to the deep and profound learning of the Rabbis they are represented as such, yet the smallest of them is nearly as large as the earth we inhabit, while the greater portion are hundreds and even thousands of times greater in bulk. Of such vast extent is the distance of the nearest star that a bird of the swiftest wing could not fly the same extent of space in many thousands of years. All these suns and worlds possess peculiar motions, giving the changes of night and day as well as seasons, which are continued incessantly to all eternity. Moons, around worlds, worlds around suns, and suns with their families of worlds, making a gradual revolution around some central spot in the universe. Within this central spot we may suppose exists that Great Power, that Great Soul and Mind which is the source of all life that exists throughout the boundless expanse of matter and space; He, the great God of life, of light, of love and motion, whom all mankind feel and acknowledge, but whose nature and person no one has been enabled to define!"

"What wonderful and fearful ideas thou bringest to my view, dear Jose," said Mary in a tremulous tone of voice. "How different are thy conceptions of these mysteries to that of our Rabbi!"

"Thou sayest truly, sweet maiden," replied Jose. "The God of our Fathers as represented by our Father Moses and his successors, was the creation of their ignorant minds, possessing all the weaknesses, limited powers and turbulent passions of the people of those days. But the great God of Nature, as I will represent him to thee according to my intuitive ideas, is a much different being to the Jehovah of Moses.

82

"Thus, Mary, thou must endeavor to imagine the mighty power, greatness and wisdom of this Great God who could and has done all these mighty works, for words will fail to describe them. Compare the mightiness of this great God with the absurd and ridiculous representation of the great Jehovah as given by our forefathers who waged a petty warfare with an Egyptian King to obtain the release of our forefathers from bondage. Consider how the great Jehovah entered into a contest with the Egyptian jugglers to see who could work the greatest feat; the palm of success being at length conceded to him by his producing some vermin of the meanest and most loathsome kind. After all the display of his mighty powers he could not bend the Egyptian King to his wishes, so he caused the Children of Israel to flee by night. Then he induced them to wander in the deserts for many years searching for a home where they suffered all kinds of deprivations and miseries. On the top of Mount Sinai he declares himself to his people, giving to them the Decalogue which he had inscribed on two tablets of stone; and though it is said he made the earth and whole universe in six days yet it took him forty to make the inscribed tablets. Under the guidance of this God and his servant Moses our poor ignorant forefathers wandered and suffered for forty years, when at last they were enabled to seize some land where to establish a home by murdering and robbing the Canaanites. This God of our forefathers is not only cruel and unjust to other nations, but he is full of wrath and vengeance to his favorite people, for at times he slaughtered them by thousands with sword, disease and famine.

"How great is the contrast, Mary, between the God of our forefathers and the great true God, whom I am endeavoring to bring to thy comprehension."

Jose paused for a few moments and regarded the countenance of Mary, to discover the effect of his words, while she, raising her beautiful hazel eyes, met his glance half-way. No terror or superstitious awe was expressed in her glance as before, when the name of Jehovah was mentioned, but the expression was indicative of rational thought and firmness, as she observed with a sober energy of voice:

"Jose, I now perceive that my education has been one of error and imposture. I now begin to comprehend some of the startling truths which thou hast endeavored to impress upon my young, misguided mind. Things which were taught me as sacred, I now begin to view in their true shapes and colors, as things of distorted imagination, ignorance and imposture. I henceforth discard all such absurdities, as lies and impositions, and I shall hold myself impressive to all the lights of truth, pertaining to the true and only God of the universe.

"0! Jose," added Mary after a slight pause, in which she drew herself closer to him, regarding him with a look of mingled love and reverence, "when I look upon thy noble person, hear the music of thy voice and consider the wisdom of thy words, it seems to me that I am in the presence of one far greater than human. I feel a spell come over me filling me with mingled love, admiration and reverence. I pray thee, then, to continue thy teaching, scattering a few more seeds of intelligence upon my simple mind, that they may take root and spring up like beauteous flowers, exhaling delicious odors, in honor of the great God of whom thou hast been speaking."

"0! Mary," replied Jose in a tone of great tenderness, "pure and innocent as thou art, thou art worthy of the love of thy Maker, and as such art capable of understanding his nature. Thou art now enabled to perceive that the God as worshiped by our forefathers and our present people, is a figment of barbarous imagination, worshiped only by such as are lost in ignorance and insensible to noble manhood; but the Great God of the universe is a Divine Father, by whose divine love all passive matter has been endowed with life. His wisdom and goodness conceived the plan which extends from the time of acting through all eternity. It was his divine essence of love that united atom to atom in bonds of sympathy and holy wedlock; from which sprang minerals, crystals, vegetables and animals of every kind, hue and figure. This ascending and progressive work of organization was prosecuted by a series of successive spheres of developments bound together by the bonds of mutual interest and dependence. The higher being developed from the combined energy of all the lower, until the powers of each sphere were developed to the ultimate design. When the organization of man became sufficiently developed and matured, it became qualified to receive the impress of the positive spirit of God upon the tablet of its interior life, and by which he became developed into a spiritual intelligence which constituted him an offspring of the divine essence of love and mind. It is thus by the development of this interior spiritual intelligence mankind became the children of God. When God's children can be no longer sustained upon earth, he receives them within his own mansion under his own especial care, where the elements of their spiritual being become developed into a still higher state of perfection, and they become more worthy of their Maker.

"Yes, Mary, the great God I am endeavoring to bring to thy notice is the father of us all as well as the life spring of the universe. His inherent and unchangeable attributes are power, wisdom and love. By his divine love, he felt the impulse to awaken and form all passive matter into the beauteous universe, as we behold it. By his infinite wisdom he was enabled to plan and design it to go into operation; and by his almighty power, he was enabled to put it into execution. By his fatherly solicitude for all that he had produced, he has controlled, and still continues to govern every thing in order, with the hope that his magnificent works will ultimately redound to his glory and satisfaction."

84

"Is the love that is felt in the human breast anything akin to the love of this divine Father?" inquired Mary timidly.

"It is, though not in the same degree," replied Jose. "It springs from the same source, modified to suit every sentient being of the earth. It comes from the divine essence of our heavenly Father's self. It penetrates through all material things, thrilling throughout the being, and swelling the bosom of our mother Nature. The most minute atoms are brought into holy alliance by its divine sympathy, and every germ of the vegetable world that bursts into life, expanding in beauty, kissed by the beams of light, and nursed by the honey dews of heaven, is conceived in love by this divine essence. Every creeping or aerial being, fly or insect, reproduces its kind from the same power. Every innocent bird with beautiful plumage that coos, bills and mates, is under the same divine influence; and all other animals are bound to transmit their kind to succeeding times by this process of love and parental solicitude. In mankind there is a modification of this passion of love which adds to his bliss and exaltation.

"The passion of love with all other animals is confined to the earth, dying out with the animal when it has run its course; but in man it is not so. The conjugal love of man and woman, coupled with pure and holy desires, develops all the divine affections which are necessary to man's happiness on earth; and when it is commingled with noble aspirations and exalted ideas, aspiring to all that is beautiful, lovely, good and magnanimous, then it will open to him an inheritance in the realms of bliss, after he shall have passed his terrestrial career. Then he enters the presence of his divine Father, to receive a welcome to his new home and state of everlasting bliss."

"Oh, Jose! dearest Jose!" exclaimed Mary in a tone expressive of great excitement, as she disengaged herself from his arms, and stood at a small distance before him, with one of her hands upon her breast and the other extended, her whole person seeming to be wrought up to an ungovernable pitch of intense feeling, her cheeks glowing with the vermillion blood; her nostrils expanding and quivering, inhaling deep draughts from the external air; and her eyes gazing upon him with an intensity of love and suspense. After a few moments' pause, in which she endeavored to lessen the throbs of her heart, she added:

"Jose, pardon me if I do or say anything unseemly in thy sight, for the subtle powers of my nature are now beyond control. Eagerly have I listened to the wisdom of thy words, in bringing to my untutored mind a knowledge of the true God. Clearly and justly do I appreciate thy explanation of his divine nature; how his divine love is the active principle which has brought all things into existence, continuing them from age to age by the same power. With rapture have I understood that it is this same love that exists within the breasts of all mortal beings, the ties that

85

bind us to each other, the parent to the child and the child to the parent; man to woman, and woman to man. All this I can appreciate, therefore I know that thy words are true.

"Yes, Jose, for years has this subtle mysterious passion been nestling and growing within this breast of mine. From day to day and year to year has it been increasing in strength and purity, praying for the happy moment when it should burst from its concealment, and declare itself to the object of its adoration. That moment is now, Jose. I will not and cannot suppose that thou art ignorant as to whom my love is devoted; for thou with all thy wisdom can easily penetrate the innermost secrets of my heart, yet from some secret prudence thou hast delayed to call forth the confessions of my soul, therefore I am compelled to declare that it is thou, Jose, who art the object of my love. Think not amiss of me if I make this confession. If this love, as thou hast taught me, comes from the divine nature of the great God of the universe, is it not holy, just and pure? And if it be natural to all beings of our kind why should I conceal it? If thou seekest for a love of the highest type which shall open an inheritance for thee to that immortal blessed state of existence hereafter of which thou hast spoken, have I not a just plea in defence of my love? All my pure desires, noble aspirations and exalted ideas are concentrated in thee. Wilt thou accept my love, Jose?"

While Mary was making her passionate declaration Jose remained immovable, devouring with greedy ear the outpourings of her innocent and ardent love; but at the termination of her discourse he averted his eyes for a few moments, which he passed in reflection, and recovering the equilibrium of his emotions, he at length raised his eyes, which beamed with great tenderness, and replied in a tone of voice tremulous with emotion:

"Beloved maiden, the time, as thou sayest, has come when the ties that bind our hearts together should be defined and understood. When we were children strolling over the hills of Nazareth, we loved as children allied by the ties of brotherly affection; but as we grew older our attachment grew closer, more sacred and interesting; then we termed it friendship. Since our separation at our native village our attachment has become greater, deeper, more fervid and dependent upon each other for worldly bliss. Our hearts, though separated by distance, have communed with each other, and our two souls have mingled into one, like commingling dew drops on a flower. Our desires, our hopes and aspirations have reflected each other's image. Our hearts have beaten in unison, and our spirits spoken with the same tongue. In all this there has been a rapture too deep, heartfelt and abiding in this mysterious mutual feeling, to be expressed by the cold word of friendship. What then is it but love?"

"Then thou dost love me, Jose?" interposed Mary in a state of thrilling suspense.

"With a pure and holy love I love thee, Mary," answered Jose. Then a wild shrill shriek of joy was uttered by Mary as she sprang forward and threw herself upon the neck of Jose, who with loving fervor clasped her in his arms.

Some minutes elapsed in silence, during which the two lovers in close embrace intermingled that mysterious magnetic aura which under various external demonstrations produced the thrilling sensation of love.

At length when their ecstatic feelings of joy had somewhat subsided and consciousness returned to inferior objects of sense, Jose gently raised his head, after imprinting his lips for the last time upon those of the now happy maiden, and addressed her in tones of the greatest tenderness.

"Mary, beloved maiden, whose love is as pure and ardent as the rays of light emanating from the dazzling sun, long have I anticipated this happy moment, and long have I feasted in imaginary bliss that I should enjoy when our mutual love should be made known to each other. But perhaps thou hast thought me remiss or somewhat mysterious in my conduct if I loved thee, that I should be so long absent from thy side. Let me therefore explain."

"Jose," responded Mary in joyous emotion as she threw her arms around the neck of her lover, and gazed upon his manly countenance with a look of fond devotion; "Jose, I have no complaint to urge against thee. Since thou hast accepted my love and acknowledged a return, I feel myself extremely happy; all my past grievances, anxieties and suspense are banished forever, and I may say that I never felt a pang during thy absence that my present bliss does not more than repay."

"Sweet maiden," replied Jose, "thou art worthy of all the joy of which the human heart is susceptible. This I can declare in truth, that ever since we parted at Nazareth thy image has ever been present to me. Three objects have influenced and impelled me during my wanderings in foreign countries, which I have ever considered as so many sacred duties. One was to investigate and inquire as far as man possibly could into the nature of the Deity. Another was to render myself worthy of his love; and the other was to render myself worthy of my Mary's love. With a knowledge of God, possessing his love in heaven, with my Mary's love on earth, I thought I should be extremely blessed. This has been my aim and achievement. But now, Mary, I have something to say that will not be so pleasant for thee to hear."

Jose then proceeded to inform the maiden more in detail of the objects of his pursuits during his travels, which were to discover men's notions or positive knowledge of the Deity. That after ten years' travel and study he had been enabled to gain considerable knowledge thereon—at least enough to infer that the Jewish system of theology and theogony were base, vicious and absurd. He had, therefore, determined to return to his country, and would endeavor to enlighten his people as to the nature of the true God, and the vile system of things taught by the Priesthood and their books.

He told her also that since his return he had seen John the Baptist, who had invited and pressed him to receive baptism at his hand. He stated, that though he did not admire the character of John or his doctrines generally, yet as to baptism he saw nothing very objectionable. He thought it might possibly have a good effect on and among the people, therefore he consented that John should baptize him. After that he intended to commence his task of teaching the people.

Mary expressed her uneasiness at the prospect of being again separated from the object of her love; but Jose soothed her fears and reasoned away her objections by telling her that he would not be far away, nor long at a time; and after a while when he should have made some progress in establishing his views among the people, he would return to unite their loves in holy wedlock.

Mary at length gave her assent to all Jose proposed, agreeing to wait with cheerful resignation the deferred time of their happy union. Jose then stated that he must take his departure on the morrow for the neighborhood of the Jordan, to prepare for the forthcoming ceremony of John's baptism.

With a firm reliance on each other's love and faithfulness, with joyous hearts at the present, and blissful anticipations of the future, the two lovers returned to the house, and separated to their respective chambers.

VISION FIFTH

JOHN THE BAPTIST

Bethabara was the name of a shallow part of the river Jordan, which from time immemorial had been used as a ford between the eastern and western banks; with the exception of this particular part, the margin of this river as far as the eye could discern was adorned with the graceful oleander, the low and weeping willow, the fern-like tamarisk, canes and shrubs of many species decked with blossoms of gorgeous hues, emitting the sweet odors of an early spring. From this ford on the eastern side of the river a track or rough road led up through ravine and gorge, over the vast ranges of barren mountains into the country of the Ammonites. On the western side a road after ascending the river's bank stretched out in a southwestern direction, crossing the broad fertile plain of Jordan, passing along many cultivated fields and vineyards decked here and there with clumps of trees, which generally surrounded the homesteads of the proprietors; thence the road, extending over hill and dale and gradual ascending slopes, led on to the city of Jericho.

This ancient city was celebrated for its strong fortifications, its beautiful gardens and groves which surrounded it, and for its excellent palm wine. On the eastern side of the city a forest of pine extended nearly to the river, and on the western side stretched the Judean mountains, over which the road passed to Jerusalem.

Here and there on the western side of the ford was a rude habitation, generally used as a caravansary for the accommodation of travellers or other purposes connected with the location.

The sun rode high in the heavens, seeming from its position to be near mid-day. Many watery clouds crossing its luminous disk mitigated the intensity of its burning rays. The air was temperate and moist, so that a multitude of people who had collected on the western bank did not feel any oppression from the elements. Groups of people—generally of the poorer sort—between the river and the rising bank, stood here and there discoursing, while others were reclining under trees, reposing on verdant spots. Others were partaking of refreshments at a house on the roadside close to the edge of the bank, but the larger portion of the multitude surrounded a tall gaunt man with flowing beard and bare head, who was elevated upon a small mound of earth and stones, and preaching to them with a wild vehement eloquence, accompanied by energetic and frantic gestures. This person was John the Baptist, who presented the same rude wild appearance as before described. As he proceeded in his harangue, his dark tangled locks floated in the wind; his long sinuous arm moved to and fro in rapid action; his dark eyes flashed or rolled with fanatical phrenzy and piety, and his loud shrill voice struck terror to his hearers, producing upon them a powerful effect, making them feel a compunction for their sins and a desire for repentance. As he continued his preaching the scattered people gradually gathered around him; among whom were Saul and Judas, who were seen to approach closely enveloped in their mantles, and mingle in the crowd around the preacher.

Shortly afterwards two other persons made their appearance, some-what distinguished from the rest by their dress, having on long black robes with white cloths twirled around their heads over black skull caps, with long white beards, presenting grave and venerable aspects.

These persons proved to be two officers deputed by the Sanhedrim at Jerusalem to ascertain what were the doctrines and designs of John the Baptist, which they were to report to that body. The Sanhedrim, though deprived of all political power by the Roman Government, still retained all authority over religious matters, and could inflict all their usual punishments, excepting death, on any person or sect whom they deemed to have departed from the orthodox theology of the Holy Priesthood. As John, about this time, began to make many converts to his system of repentance and baptism, the vigilance of the Sanhedrim began to be aroused, so that they sent their officers to discover and make report concerning John's doctrines. These men having descended the bank, mingled among the multitude of John's hearers without exciting any particular notice.

In the meantime John continued in his bold energetic style to harangue the people, denouncing the iniquities of the times and the awful state of corruption that had crept among God's people. He pointed out the vast number of sins and derelictions of duty that were common among them; their heedlessness; their want of compunction and sorrow for their evil doings; their foolish reliance that their sins would be forgiven, provided they made the customary offerings at the altar of the Temple. "Thus they continued." John said, "from year to year, committing sins to be atoned for by their offerings and making offerings that they might be at liberty to commit more sins without improving in their hearts or minds or making any nearer approach to God."

John launched out in strong invectives against the priesthood of the Temple, who received from the people the offerings of lambs, sheep, kids, beeves, poultry, oil and wine, and all the other good things of the land which the priests love so well, yet pretend that they sacrifice them to the Lord in order to turn him away from his wrath, and cause him to forgive the people their sins. He told them that the priests were jugglers, cheats, knaves and impostors, who robbed the people of their offerings, and devoured them while the Lord got nothing but the greasy smoke and stench thereof as a sacrifice. He said the Lord was very wrathy at the continuation of such iniquities; that he had punished his people by giving them over to a strange nation to be ruled, and that he would still further punish them unless they reformed. He told them that the Lord desired a reform among his people, and that the Lord had revealed to him what that reform should be: a perfect repentance of their sins; then a remission of the same should be given through the means of baptism, which should be in place of burnt offerings. John then wound up his discourse by telling the multitude that all those who truly repented of their sins and wished to have them forgiven, must follow him into the river where he would administer the holy institution of baptism to them.

John then descended from his elevated position, and with solemn gait betook himself to the river (followed by the multitude), into which he waded a few paces until the water reached his breast. Then some of his disciples, taking the hands of the first sinner who wished to receive baptism, entered the water, leading him close up to John. The latter, in a solemn, impressive voice then invoked the presence and mercy of the Lord, declaring that the sinner present was sorely repentant of his sins, that he was willing to renounce the world and all its abominations, to enter into a new life of purity and righteousness. He, therefore, called upon the Lord to cleanse him of all his past iniquities through the medium of holy baptism. John then raised some water in the palm of his hand, which he poured upon the head of the sinner, at the same time giving him a new name, telling him that as he was about to enter a new life he must also bear a new name, so that he should be as much as possible withdrawn from his former self.

This part of the ceremony being concluded the disciples suddenly plunged the new convert under the waters of the Jordan, when he was withdrawn to the shore and handed over to his friends. The ceremony was performed upon another, and another, until a great many had undergone John's process of regeneration. There was a pause in the proceedings for a time, for nobody else seemed inclined to accept of the new institution. Then John came out of the water and mingled with the people, among whom he seemed to be searching for somebody, with an expression of uneasiness in his countenance. At length he came close to the two deputies from the Sanhedrim, one of whom with an air of hauteur and in a tone of authority thus addressed him:

"By what authority doest thou these things?"

John, regarding the officer with a bold and defiant air, replied: "I would also ask a question. By what authority did Moses strike the rock in the desert, and give water to the Children of Israel to quench their thirst?"

"That was by the authority and power of the God of our Fathers, the God of Abraham, Isaac and Jacob," answered the officer.

"Even so it is with me," returned John with a glance of triumph. "By the power and authority of the same God do I preach the repentance of sins, and give remission of them through baptism of water."

The two officers seemed confused and confounded by this answer of John. They knew not why he should not have the authority of the Lord for doing what he did, as well as Moses. They did not believe John had any authority from that source; but if they denied it in his case it would be as easy to deny it in the case of Moses. They looked at each other with an expression of dismay, not knowing what to say farther. At length the other officer being less disconcerted and knowing that something must be said to support the dignity of the Sanhedrim, said to John, with seeming indignation:

"Dost thou, rash man, presume to say that the law as given by the Lord to Moses and the Holy Priesthood his successors, is not complete and efficient for the government of his chosen people, but that he has made other laws and established other institutions?"

"Why should I not speak thus?" demanded John.

"Because," returned the officer, "that would be to charge the Lord God Jehovah with inefficiency of power and changeableness of mind, which would be blasphemy."

"Then if thou sayest it is not so, thou art ignorant of God and his works," returned John with great energy of voice and gesture. "Did not the Lord make heaven and earth, and all upon the earth, even to man, which work he pronounced good, and blessed it?"

"Truly so," responded the officer.

"Did not the Lord say," resumed John, "that he repented having made man and the earth, for everything was evil therein and an abomination in his sight, excepting Noah and his family? Did he not bring a flood of water over the earth, and destroy everything he had made, excepting what was in Noah's ark? Tell me, then, you proud ignorant man, if this be not changeableness in the Lord."

The two officers were thrown into the greatest consternation. They shrank back aghast from John, and knew not what reply to make.

"Even so," resumed John, "as the Lord brought a flood of water over the earth to destroy the works of his own hands, which he once pronounced to be good, so shall he bring a new dispensation upon the earth, which shall destroy the Law, the Priesthood and the Temple that he ordained to exist forever among his people."

"What manner of man art thou, who speakest in this wise?" demanded the first officer in a perturbed tone of voice, for he seemed somewhat afraid of John. "Art thou a prophet'?"

John made no reply, though he seemed inclined to do so.

"Art thou Elias?" inquired the officer; but still John made no answer.

"Perhaps," observed the other officer in a sneering tone, and with a contemptuous air, "it is Moses, or Micah, or Daniel, or Esaias, who speaks through his mouth."

"Yes, scoffer, thou hast spoken truly in naming the last," replied John in a boisterous voice, his countenance expressive of great indignation as the peculiar points of his religious belief or monomaniacy burst upon his mind, arousing him to an uncontrollable phrensy. "Truly hast thou spoken, though thou didst not mean it. I am he, of whom the prophet Esaias has spoken, when he said: "The voice of him that crieth in the wilderness. Prepare ye the way of the Lord." Then John, stretching out his hand, pointed to the road that led down from the bank above, added in a loud exultant voice: "Behold the chosen of the Lord cometh! The Savior cometh, of whom the prophet hath commissioned me to speak! He cometh to the baptism, yet needeth no repentance, for in him there is no sin."

At this announcement by John, the officers and the multitude cast their eyes in the direction indicated, when they perceived the person called Jose, in company of a very young man, descending the bank and approaching the multitude below. The officers were very much puzzled and astonished, not knowing what to understand or think of what they saw or heard. But the multitude generally having had intimations from John of the coming of some great personage, were not so much taken by surprise; yet they all gave evidence of feeling an interest and curiosity on seeing the new comers.

93

At length Jose and his companion made their approach, the latter being a very fair complexioned youth of about eighteen years of age, without beard or moustache, with golden colored hair hanging in long tresses over his shoulders, and confined around the head by a black silken fillet. As they approached the multitude no one obstructed their way; but all excepting the two officers gave respectful salutations. Some gave the common salute of friendship, by slightly bending the body; while others bent their bodies so low that their fingers touched the ground, thereby expressing reverence as well as friendship. John the Baptist left the officers, approached Jose, and bent in great reverence before him; then rising, he kissed him on either cheek. When this last incident took place, Jose observed to John in an undertone of voice:

"Brother John, it seems to me from the deportment of the people towards me, that there is something more than an ordinary salutation or courtesy shown. I hope thou hast not failed in the promise thou hast made me."

"Master," replied John the Baptist submissively, "the restriction thou hast placed upon me has sorely tried me, but I have endeavored to fulfill thy wishes."

The restrictions alluded to by John, was the circumstance spoken of in the confessions of Saul, concerning the youthful career of Jose and John the Baptist. It was stated how that mysterious healing power was discovered in Jose, and how John, being possessed of great superstition and religious zeal, had considered Jose to be something more than common humanity; and how he had come to the conclusion that he must be the Messiah spoken of by the prophets. When Jose discovered the sentiments of John, he endeavored to convince him of his error, but failing to do so, he forbade him to mention anything of the kind in public. John promised to comply, but still remained firm in his opinions. Thus the two companions separated, and Jose started upon his travels.

When Jose had returned to his country, he had an interview with his old companion, when he renewed his former restriction; and by way of giving him encouragement in his religious pursuits, he promised to sanction the doctrine of baptism by receiving it at his hands. He also gave him to understand that if he should break his promise, by speaking of him in public as the Messiah, he (Jose) would forsake him, and denounce him to the world as one bereft of his reason. Such was the understanding between Jose and John, at the time the former was about receiving baptism.

"If thou hast been prudent, it is well," returned Jose. "But now, dear brother, let us proceed to the performance of this holy ceremony; for, as I judge from the appearance of the heavens, it will not be long before we shall have a storm."

As Jose made this observation, he cast his eyes upward, when he perceived that vast masses of clouds had gathered around and completely obscured the sun, which seemed to be well charged with electric matter, as they twisted and convolved with great commotion. Jose then took the hand of his young companion who had accompanied him, and observed to John the Baptist:

"Let me acquaint thee with our younger brother. His name is the same as thine: John—the son of Zebedee of Galilee, an old acquaintance of mine."

John the Baptist regarded the young man for a few moments with a pleasing expression of countenance, though there was a slight roguish twinkle in his eye; then placing his hands upon his shoulders he kissed and blessed him; and immediately afterwards said to him in a whisper: "Do not let him know that we were formerly acquainted."

Preparations were now made for the baptism of Jose. John the Baptist entered the river while the former divested himself of his mantle, head dress and outer clothes, which were given in charge of his young friend. Then two elderly men taking Jose by the hands led him into the water, when the multitude impelled by a lively interest rushed forward to the river's brink. John the Baptist then called attention to the necessity of true repentance previous to baptism, even should the conformant not be of a sinful nature. He said: "All mankind are liable to temptations and frailty; therefore a decided renunciation of the world and all its contaminations is necessary to insure salvation by baptism; for without a consciousness of our weakness and a desire of purity of heart, baptism would be of no effect; therefore, baptism is to be considered as a glorious symbol, that we have defeated the machinations of Satan, and accepted the mercy and will of God." He then uttered a few pious ejaculations, calling upon God for his approbation of the proceedings, praying him to admit the conformant to his divine love and confidence. Then he spoke in eulogistic terms of the conformant, of his many virtues, his noble aspirations, his desire to enlighten his fellow men as to their errors, vices and sins; how he designed to devote his life and energies to bring all his brethren of the flesh to a knowledge of the true God, that they might inherit salvation. Therefore, as the conformant had renounced the world and sacrificed all its interests with the intent of working man's salvation, he should give him a name in accordance with his benevolent and meritorious design."

Then John took up some water in the palm of his hand, which he poured upon the head of Jose, and said: "I therefore name thee Jesus. Be thou the light of a new dispensation which shall bring man to a knowledge of his God." Then the two attendants immersed the conformant in the waters of the Jordan. In an instant after a vivid flash of lightning burst from the deep masses of clouds, followed by a crash and a terrific peal of thunder which rolled through the heavens and was echoed for many seconds along the ranges of the mountains. This occurrence affected the multitude in various ways. The generality being deeply interested in the proceedings enacted before them, paid little heed to the turbulence of the elements, and were consequently greatly startled when the lightning burst so suddenly upon their view. Some immediately left the spot and hastened to their habitations on the bank to seek shelter, while others being struck with a superstitious terror remained trembling and undecided what course to pursue. In the meantime, Jose, who henceforth must be called Jesus, was led from the river by the attendants, and as soon as he had advanced a few paces on shore, he knelt upon the ground and entered into communion with his God. While he was in this position a dark cloud which obscured the sun was suddenly rent asunder, and the solar rays, like so many golden threads, streamed down over and around the head of Jesus.

John the Baptist, who had remained standing in the river as one struck mute and powerless from the moment he heard the terrible clap of thunder, now rushed to the shore and hastened to the spot where Jesus was kneeling in prayer, exhibiting in his countenance great excitement. With his arms elevated, his lips quivering and eyes rolling, expressive of wildness and phrensy, he gave evidence that his mental powers were at that moment unbalanced and his monomania predominant. From the moment the thunder burst over his head, all reason, prudence and self-control left him. His wild superstitious visions, his stern bigotry, and his false, though indomitable sense of duty, were powerfully strong within the deluded man, so that he found it impossible to do otherwise than speak and act according to the impulses of his craziness. In the peals of thunder he thought he heard the voice of Jehovah confirming him in the idea that Jesus was the Messiah, and in the sun's rays that poured down upon his head he thought he saw the spirit of the Lord descending upon him. As soon as he arrived at the spot where Jesus knelt, he cried in a loud exulting voice:

"Glory! glory! glory to the great Jehovah! Great is God! He is great and true, for this day hath he fulfilled his promises as given through the mouths of his prophets. Glory to God! He promised us a Redeemer, a Messiah, and this day has he made true his words. Behold, 0 Israel— behold, my children, your Messiah! Why should we be afraid to speak? Why should we keep it hidden? Has not the Lord declared to us in a voice of thunder that this is the chosen one to redeem Israel? In the words of thunder I heard him declare, saying: "This is my Son;" and now behold the spirit of the Lord descending to confirm his words!" John pointed to the beautiful rays of the sun that were streaming down upon the head of Jesus.

Any further harangue of John was prevented by Jesus rising from his knees, and covering his eyes with his hands and slightly bending his head, he seemed to be undergoing some grievous emotion. But he soon recovered his composure, and regarding John with a look of mingled pity and reproach, he said to him:

"John, thou hast broken faith with me, and by so doing thou hast sorely grieved me. I pity thee and blame thee not, but henceforth thou must not seek me. Peace be with thee."

"Master," replied John, as he threw himself upon his knees before Jesus, "be not angry with me, for the Lord hath willed it so. I do his bidding, which has been foretold by the prophets."

Rain now began to fall in large drops, and the clouds gave indications that a heavy shower would fall forthwith. The remainder of the people hastily left the scene, and Jesus having hurriedly re-adjusted his dress with the aid of his young companion, left also. But there were two persons who did not seem inclined to follow the example immediately, and wrapping their mantles closely around them, they took shelter under a willow tree close by the river, and entered into conversation.

"Now, Judas," observed one of the persons to his companion, "we are out of hearing of these fanatics. We can now converse; but I must be brief in what I have to say to thee, for our time is precious. What dost thou think of the scene thou hast just witnessed?"

Judas cast his eyes over the countenance of Saul, endeavoring to glean what effect the scene alluded to had made upon him, before he would venture to reply; and having satisfied himself, he said: "Indeed, sir, the scene has been an extraordinary one, and to me deeply interesting."

"Judas," said Saul, with pleasure glistening in his eyes, "I tell thee, man, that I am more rejoiced with what I have seen and heard today than if I had found a treasure. I feel richer today than when I received my father's wealth. I feel like a fortunate miner when he has struck a rich vein of gold, who sees a prospect of gaining the object of his wishes, and anticipates the pleasure and happiness he will be enabled to obtain therewith."

"There were some curious incidents transpired, which a man of deep mind could turn to his advantage, no doubt," remarked Judas, as he eyed his master with a searching glance.

"Yes, Judas," returned Saul smiling. "I think I have this day found materials with which to lay a foundation upon which I can build up a structure suitable to my taste, talents and ambition. Yes, yes, it shall be so! I will convince the world of this and future ages, that Saul, the son of the tent maker, was not an idiot, a lout, or a dullard. I shall now begin to feel an interest in life, for I have found a stimulus to the powers of my body and mind."

"I cannot imagine, sir, the objects to which thy words allude. Thou must be more explicit," observed Judas indifferently.

97

"Not at present, my friend Judas," replied Saul in an exceeding courteous tone, at the same time his left eye gave a slight twitch. "I have not
time to do so, my friend. I want to call thy attention to that man who
was the last to receive baptism at the hands of that crazy John the
Baptist—Jesus, as he is newly named. What thinkest thou of him?"

"I think," replied Judas seriously, "that he is the most beautiful spe-
cimen of perfect manhood I ever saw; and if his interior is as noble as
his exterior indicates he must be too good for this world."

"Thy estimation, I think, is a very correct one," returned Saul. "I never
saw a man that has aroused within me so great an admiration. I think he
must be destined for an important career in this life, and under such a
belief I wish to join my career with his, whether it shall prove to my
praise or shame. Now, Judas, the private services I wish thee to render
me are now to commence according to the agreement we have made
between us."

"In what way can I serve thee?" inquired Judas. "Speak and I will
obey."

"Thou must follow that man," replied Saul in an earnest and impressive manner, "and endeavor to find out his abode. Then thou must
beg to be admitted into his service, or allowed to be one of his followers,
for he intends to be a religious instructor of the people,—giving them
some new doctrines concerning matters which they and everybody else
know nothing about." Saul then placed a bag of money in the hand of
Judas, and resumed: "Present this bag of money to him and tell him it is
all the wealth thou possessest, that thou desirest to make it common
stock, if he will allow thee to follow him to listen to the wisdom of his
words. Should he consent to receive thee, then thou must find out all his
ways, doctrines and intentions as far as possible. In all other respects
thou must exercise thy wit to invent tales to suit thyself and circumstances as occasion shall require. As soon as thou hast gained all the
information thou canst obtain, before he can put any plan in operation,
thou must come to me and learn my further wishes."

Judas told Saul that he understood his wishes, and that he would
fulfill them to the best of his capabilities. He then took leave of his
employer, and hurried from the scene in quest of Jesus, while Saul made
his way to his residence in Jerusalem.

VISION SIXTH

ROMAN SENTINEL

The dazzling orb of day had passed over the Holy City, and sank from view behind the western hills. The busy crowds of people had left the streets and retired to their homes to feast and rest, recuperating for the toils and strifes of another day. The Holy Temple was deserted; the courts were void of priest and people; the fire of the holy altar had burned down to embers, and the offerings of fatty smoke and blood no longer regaled the nostrils of the great Jehovah. He, the great God of the Jews, was under the necessity of abstaining from food till the morrow, while the holy priesthood, his immaculate servants, were at their homes feasting on roast meats of beef, lamb and kid, and imbibing copious potations of wine and oil which had been brought to the Temple as offerings to their angry God, to appease his wrath.

It was night, about the sixth hour, when no one was seen or heard, not under shelter, excepting the Roman sentinels who grimly stalked before the gates along the battlements, and around the towers of Jerusalem. Saul was in his chamber which was a spacious and handsomely decorated apartment in one of the public inns of the city. It was lofty and wide, the floor being covered with a thick matting. The walls were hung with rich tapestry of red silk. The entrance-way and a window casement were covered with blue hangings. On one side of the room was an elevated couch covered with purple stuff, with cushions of the same. Around the apartment at equal distances were marble pedestals on which lamps were burning. In one corner of the apartment was a square piece of furniture made of precious wood, with several small drawers and doors, which contained articles of precious value, as money, books, papers, etc.; and on one of the pedestals near to the couch was a small simple constructed vessel designed for the division of time by means of water oozing through a small hole out of one part of the vessel into another, which may be termed a water clock.

Saul was reclining upon his couch, but not asleep, in his night dress, consisting of a long linen robe of the purest white. Several times did he turn himself, seeking a more easy position, and each time endeavored to compose himself to sleep, but all in vain. Being so much impressed with the adventures of the preceding day, he found it impossible to arrest his mind's continued flow of thought. A new life and augmented vigor seemed to have taken possession of him; a new field was open to his view for the display of his ambitious daring; so that thought succeeded thought in rapid whirl before the conscious eye of his mind. Time! time!—that which he a little while before found so difficult to pass over, now he considered to be one of the most valuable things in existence. He wanted time to review all his plans, schemes and suggestions. He wanted time to give them a trial; time to put them into execution; and a long course of time would be necessary to achieve all he contemplated and desired.

"Oh!" he mentally exclaimed, "had I possessed these ideas ten years ago, and persevered in the execution of them, I should have by this time been enabled to realize my grand design. Fool that I have been thus to lose ten precious years when I might have gained unlimited power among men and obtained an imperishable fame! Ah! that mysterious handsome person I saw yesterday baptized by John; what a glorious career he is about to enter! With his noble mien, his well stored mind, and the persuasive eloquence of his voice and words, and that mysterious power he has of curing diseases, with his many other virtues, will gain him the hearts and minds of the people. He will be enabled to do much good, and thus immortalize his name, even should he not strive for self-aggrandizement. He is still young, seeming to be about my own age. Ah! I seem to have a presentiment that his and my mortal career and posthumous fame are somehow dependent upon and connected with, each other. Let me reflect further. I will search into the most obscure recesses of thought until I find some way to accomplish my wishes. Farewell to sleep for this night!"

Thus saying Saul sprang from his couch, drew his robe closer around him, and then paced up and down his room with a quick unconscious step, for his mind being so deeply absorbed in his reflections, his senses, though receiving external impressions, did not transmit them to his brain.

Having paced his chamber for some minutes he stopped before the piece of furniture before mentioned. He opened one of the drawers and drew forth a vessel containing wine, of which he took a small measure full, and then returned it to its place and resumed his pacing. Again he sank into the meshes of thought and as he continued his restless course the workings of the outward man sometimes indicated what was passing within the interior one. At first his glance was stern and fixed, with features rigid, as though he was penetrating the depths of thought to discover the means to accomplish his design. Then a compression of his thin lips and restless motion of his eyes seemed to indicate that difficulties embarrassed and puzzled him, and the knitting of the brows and quivering of the lip portrayed some fearful image had risen up that shook his soul with terror. Sometimes he would suddenly halt when all his features betokened his surprise as a new thought sprang up unexpectedly; and then a smile or frown would glide over his countenance, according as it seemed favorable or otherwise. According to the index of the water clock, an hour had passed as thus he continued to search, select and adjust his thoughts in some degree of order; his reflections were then in a more regular train, and according to clairvoyant perceptions were of the following cast:

"At length," he mentally said, "I have worked through this chaos of thought which at first seemed impossible to reduce to order. Yes, yes, I see the course that is necessary for me to pursue to gain the cherished objects of my ambition, power over the minds of my fellow men, and fame that shall last during my life, and extend to future ages; a fame that shall be built upon assumed virtues and the sacrifice of every noble principle. But, ah! there are questions I ought to ask myself in all sincerity before I proceed to action. Should I achieve all the desired objects of my ambition, will the gratification resulting therefrom repay me for the labor and sacrifices I shall have made? Will the good or benefits that I shall give to society compensate for the crimes I shall commit in producing them? Such questions are difficult to answer, for no man can foresee the result of his own actions. What use, then, will there be in hesitating? Why not content myself with the idea that the object I have in view is a glorious one, and leave the results to unforeseen chance? Why should I be afraid to enter upon this course which seems to be the only one that will give me a zest for life? What is there to stay my progress? Is it the moralities of justice, honesty and truth that shall check me? Ah! ah! they are but fictions that bold and cunning men use with which to cheat their neighbors to their own advantage. Is it priest-craft and religion that shall arrest and defeat me in my design? The first is an imposition by which the priests cheat the people, and the latter is an imposition of their invention, with which the people cheat themselves. All the powers by which a people are governed are impositions and tyran-

101

nical force. There never was a nation governed by any other means, therefore I may conclude there never will be. What good would it effect to preach to an ignorant people of honesty, truth and justice? It possibly may do some good in a family or small circle of intelligent men, but no farther. No legislator ever governed a people by such powers, and no history can be adduced as an instance. By what power did Moses bring our forefathers out of the land of Egypt? By the power of lies and imposition. By what power did he establish his system of theogony and laws? By the power of imposition and the sword. By what power did our forefathers gain this land we live in? By fraud, treachery and the sword. By what powers have all our previous monarchs, judges, high priests and magistrates reigned over us? By fraud, treachery, imposition and the sword. By what power are we now held tributary to Rome? By the power of the sword only. Consequently we have now the most conscientious tyrants to rule us that we ever had. Why, then, should I be different from the rest of mankind? Why should I not follow the examples of all the illustrious great men who have preceded me in our own and all other nations? Moses established a belief in a wrathful and vindictive God, and a code of sanguinary laws by lies and the sword. Why should I not destroy his system, and establish another of a milder nature by similar means? Moses resorted to any means in his power to accomplish his ends, and why should I not do the same?"

Saul halted before a mirror which was suspended to the wall, when perceiving his image he seemed to address it as he resumed: "Yes, Saul, such is the nature of mankind, and of those in particular who wish to distinguish themselves by a bold, laudable ambition. But suppose my contemplated designs be achieved; suppose the time shall come when I shall stand in the zenith of exultant, successful ambition, will the changes in society that I shall have produced be of a worse condition than they are now? Will there be no amelioration? It is impossible! I am not so witless; I am not so callous of heart, with all my faults, that I shall not strive to improve the condition of my fellow men. Let the result be what it may, society cannot be worse than it is now."

Then Saul, making an encouraging gesture to his image in the mirror, his eyes beaming with pride and triumph, added in a voice of exultation: "Onward! onward! brave son of Bathus! Pursue the course for which thy nature has befitted thee and thy talents have enabled thee to achieve. Be thou worthy of all power and greatness, according to thy noble aspirations. Let not dastard fear nor silly sentiment of refined moralities check thee in thy pursuit; nor let mistaken sympathy prevent thee from striking low whomsoever shall cross thy path as an opponent. Let— "

Saul's self-exhortation was interrupted by hearing a knocking on the outside of his chamber door. Hastily taking a lamp from one of the pedestals, he proceeded to open it, when Judas made his appearance.

"Most welcome, dear Judas," cried Saul in a lively voice, as he inclined his person as though he were paying due respect to an equal.

"How times and conditions do change in this world!" said Judas to himself as he noticed his master's courteous deportment. "Two or three days ago I was Saul's bondman, subject to all his insults and caprices; now he treats me as a free gentleman equal to himself. I scarcely know how to speak or act before him, this change so confuses me. However, I must do my best and endeavor to support my dignity."

"I have long been wishing for thee, Judas," added Saul.

"Hast thou?" replied Judas, curtly, with an air of indifference. "Then why didst thou not attend to my summons sooner? I have been rapping for several minutes. Hast thou anybody with thee, for I heard loud talking?"

"I was merely addressing a few words to my own image in the mirror, for want of better company," replied Saul, somewhat ashamed at confessing so trifling a matter.

"If that were the case," returned Judas, smiling, "thou and thy audience were very much of the same mind, and thou didst not fear much opposition."

"Let us talk no more on such trifling matters. But tell me, Judas, if thou hast succeeded in the request I made of thee," said Saul, in a tone that seemed partly authoritative and partly persuasive, for he was in a state of nervous anxiety, without the full command of himself. But Judas did not seem in a great hurry for communication, and taking a cushion from the couch he stretched himself upon the floor, when placing it under his head and arm, he reclined himself at his ease; then raising his eyes to Saul, he replied:

"I have traveled from the white mountains near Jericho, sir, since the sun has dipped into its watery bed: the road was dusty and hard, and I feel much fatigued, therefore thou must not think of receiving much information from me until a goblet of thy wine shall loosen this parched tongue of mine."

"Wine!" exclaimed Saul with a start, as though he had suddenly discovered that he had been forgetful of the respect due to his visitor. Then he hastened across the chamber, thrust open the private recess, and immediately brought forward the vessel containing the wine and two goblets which he placed upon a small stand close to Judas. The latter immediately filled a goblet and drank off its contents at one long draught, which, from the working of his features, seemed to have given great satisfaction; then re-filling, he drank another more at his leisure, which seemed to restore him to his usual state of vigor, caution and speech. Having replaced the goblet, he raised himself up to a sitting posture and observed:

"Art thou sure there is no one within hearing?"

103

"Fear nothing; all is right. Proceed," answered Saul.

"Well, sir," said Judas, "according to thy orders I followed the young man that John the Baptist had just baptized and given the name of Jesus; he was much in advance of me, but making inquiries of several who were returning from the baptism, I traced him into the white mountains, and came up with him just as he and his young companion were about entering their grotto. He has a small dwelling built of stone in the midst of a patch of verdure on the plateau of the mountain, about one hour's travel from the Jericho road—being a fit retreat for a student or a recluse, and a little more civilized in appearance than the cave of John the Baptist. I accosted him in the most humble and respectful manner, which he returned and invited me into his dwelling. I then proceeded to inform him that his person and character, so far as I had seen and heard, had aroused within me the greatest admiration and reverence, so that I had determined to attach myself to his person and fortune, if he were willing to receive me as a servant, a follower, or a disciple, as I understood he was going to travel about the country, and teach the people the nature of true piety and the true God. I then threw my bag of money at his feet and begged him to receive it in support of the common welfare. For a few minutes he hesitated what answer to give me, as though he doubted my sincerity; then again regarding the bag, he seemed to think that if I had any selfish or sinister end in view, I would not have risked my money; he, therefore, after a slight deliberation with his young companion, whose name is John, agreed to receive me as one of his followers, and appointed me on the spot, custodian and steward over all affairs of buying and selling. The bag he returned to my charge. I stayed with him that night, gleaning all the intelligence I could concerning him, and helping him in counsel concerning his intended travels. I have grace of absence for a day or two, which I devote to thy service.

"Judas, my friend, thou hast acted discreetly in this matter," remarked Saul, as he advanced to the former and kissed him on the forehead, with great semblance of true friendship. "Henceforth thou shalt be to me as a brother; thou shalt share with me all my good fortune and my secrets, and whenever we encounter trouble we will give each other assistance."

"Mutual interests and mutual dependence make mutual friends," observed Judas with a sly glance at Saul, and a slight curl of his lip.

"Thou sayest truly," replied Saul, with a slight laugh. "Now let us take a little wine, and then thou canst tell me any discoveries thou hast made concerning thy new master, Jesus, as he is now named."

They then filled their goblets with wine and drank, when Judas remarked:

"As regards the character of the man, from what little I have seen of him I will vouch that he is everything that his noble person indicates him

104

to be. He is simple, plain and unaffected in his discourse. He has a well stored mind, and is a great admirer of everything that is beautiful and true in nature, and there is no doubt that all his principles are founded in honesty, truth, justice and charity in all their phases. He seems imbued with a true religion, and his piety does not seem to be like that of other persons, consisting of creeds and formalities; his seems to be the reverence of the Great Author of our existence, and the practice of virtue for the benefit of his fellow men. He does not speak of God as a person, or in connection with our people's history, but simply as the Great Power of universal nature. This makes me think that his God is not the same our priesthood call the Great Jehovah. Whatever his ideas may be of God, there is no doubt in my mind that they are of the most exalted and rational kind."

"There is no doubt that he is a high-minded, noble man." remarked Saul in a serious mood. "It is a great pity that he is such."

"How?" exclaimed Judas, regarding Saul with surprise. "Dost thou think that there are too many high-minded, noble men in this world for its good?"

"No, that is not my meaning," answered Saul. "It is that I admire the principles of such men; but I know that their noble-mindedness generally comes athwart certain men of opposite principles, and then they are sacrificed to the interests and ambition of the latter. Now, this Jesus, according to thy views, is one of those noble natures, and thus it is I pity him because I admire him. Now, although I admire this Jesus, yet if he should come athwart any object I have in view, I should consider it my duty to myself to sacrifice him. Dost thou understand me, Judas?"

"I think I do," answered Judas with a shudder; "but it seems to me some what paradoxical."

"Did he give any explanation of what took place between him and John the Baptist at the conclusion of the baptism?" inquired Saul.

"I think he made me sensible of the true state of the case," replied Judas. "Although it is a matter of some intricacy, yet I think we can understand it, knowing what we do of the nature of John the Baptist. When we visited John in his cave we found him to be a wild, superstitious fanatic, who was under the delusion that he was commissioned by the Lord to prepare the way for the coming Messiah. This Messiah he said had come, and was to be baptized at his hands. We found afterwards that the person he baptized and named Jesus was the person he alluded to. Now it seems that this Jesus was aware that John entertained such ideas concerning him many years past, but he being a sensible man, and one of the strictest probity, knew that there was no truth in any of those wild notions of John's. He, therefore, endeavored to convince John of his error, but failing to do so, as John is really crazy on that point, Jesus forbade him to mention anything of the kind to the people.

105

"During the absence of Jesus on his travels the subject remained in silence; but as soon as he returned John again importuned him on the subject, and also he desired Jesus to receive baptism at his hands, as he thought it would recommend the institution to the people. Jesus consented to comply with John's last request, provided the latter would promise to keep to himself his notions about the Messiahship. John finally gave his word that he would, and the baptism took place as we have witnessed. All went on well until the thunder, lightning and sunshine came, when John's crazy notions were again excited. So convinced was he that he heard the voice of Jehovah in the thunder, he could contain himself no longer. He burst forth exultantly, declaring that this Jesus was the Messiah the prophets had spoken of. When Jesus rose from his knees, he told John that he had broken faith with him, and henceforth he must not seek him to renew his acquaintance.

"Such is the nature of the case as well as I can understand it. Jesus feels himself much grieved at the crazy declarations of John, but he persists in denying or assuming any such pretensions, for he is too honest and noble in his nature to palm himself upon the people for that which he is not. He said he was not surprised at John's conduct, for he knew him to be crazy upon that point, therefore he can but pity his state."

When Judas had concluded his narrative there was a pause for a few minutes, during which he helped himself to some more wine, and Saul remained in deep thought. At length the latter raised his eyes to Judas with an expression of great sternness, at the same time placing his hand upon his shoulder, he observed in a serious tone:

"Judas, we have made a compact between us of mutual assistance and interest, the particulars of which we need not recapitulate; but I wish to know if thou art still of the same determination to fill thy part of the agreement."

"I am," answered Judas, emphatically.

Well, then, I will open my mind clearly and distinctly to thee, that there may be no misunderstanding between us," said Saul as he erected himself, seeming to be relieved from a momentary suspense. Then placing the cushions one upon the other, he reclined upon them at his ease, and resumed: "When thou wast describing to me the character of this Jesus just now, I observed to thee that I admired and pitied him; in the first place, for his noble nature, and in the other case, that his nobleness of nature would render him adverse to others of different principles. I also told thee the duty a man owes to himself when he is thwarted in his designs or interests. There is also another duty a man owes to himself, which I must bring to thy notice. When a man has a certain object in view and wishes to obtain it, it becomes his duty to avail himself of all opportunities, means and persons to obtain that end,

106

whether it be detrimental to others or not; for self-interest is the first and greatest of laws that govern a man of the world. Now it so happens that this Jesus, though I admire his character and sympathize with his designs, is one whose person, character and talents I can avail myself to accomplish the designs I have in view; in fact, he is the very foundation upon which I can build up a structure that shall ensure my notoriety and future fame. The consequence of these measures to him, I have nothing to do with; it is sufficient for me to know that in him I find the means to accomplish my designs. I feel myself justified by natural rights to seize upon them and use them to my purpose."

Judas started and averted his eyes from Saul, which being immediately perceived by the latter, he observed:

"Thou must not allow any refined sense of sympathy to interfere with thy action in any matter like this, where thy self-interest and safety are at stake. Such would be imprudent, for it is a great obstacle in the way to the accomplishment of great deeds. Our worthy ancestors in the time of Joshua when they took this land from the Canaanites, pulled down their walled cities, slew their warriors, plunged the sword into the hearts of the old men and matrons who could not fight. They ripped up the women with child, and trod the unborn babes under their feet. They dashed out the brains of children against the walls, and took the young maidens to themselves for their own pleasure—they were not deterred by feelings of sympathy in such acts as these."

"No, nor by justice," interposed Judas.

"Truly so," responded Saul. "Many persons would think such doings of desperate wickedness; but we ought to remember that our ancestors were in desperate circumstances. They were fighting for a home under captains and generals of savage, brutish natures; besides, they were taught to believe that their great God Jehovah ordered and guided them to do so. Had they been an enlightened and refined people, moved by moral sympathies, they never would have been enabled to do so; they would have remained and perished in the desert. Thus we may see that their savage natures, their ignorance and lack of refinement, and all their immoralities were so many virtues for them, by which they were enabled to accomplish their ends in view."

"Saul, thou art a great reasoner," remarked Judas as his upper lip slightly curled. "I really believe thou couldst persuade the King of Ethiopia that he was Emperor of Rome."

"Possibly," answered Saul in a gay tone, and he gave a short laugh. "Thou must attribute my powers that way to my schooling, for I received my instructions from the priesthood—Rabbin Gamaliel was my tutor. But let us return to the subject we have in view. I said that in this Jesus I find the means to achieve my designs. But how is this to be done? thou wilt naturally ask. I will answer in this wise: This Jesus is about to mingle among the people to teach them better morals, better views of religion, and a more rational conception of God. Now as far as I understand this man, I think he is quite capable of doing all he proposes. His handsome person and amiable manners will gain the good will of the people; his great intelligence and moral justice will arouse their attention, and his mysterious power of healing diseases will command their admiration, conviction and influence, consequently he will make many proselytes and gain power over them. Now comes the important point to which I wish thee to pay attention, Judas. John the Baptist has taken it into his crazy head that this Jesus is the true Messiah as spoken of by the prophets, and that he is commissioned to prepare the way before him. Now, although we know that this idea of John's is no more than nonsense, yet it is the very point on which hinges all my wishes and designs. The idea that Jesus is the true Messiah and the real son of God, I wish to be disseminated among the people, for I wish them to believe it. I would also like that Jesus himself would believe it, or would assume as much. I know the last two points are not impossible to achieve, if he were surrounded by some cunning interested agents. There is no man, let him be ever so intelligent, if he possess a mysterious power of curing diseases as this Jesus does, who may not be persuaded that he is something more than human; or if he cannot be convinced to believe such, it is yet possible, by appealing to his self-interest and aggrandizement to prevail upon him to assume that he does so. Jesus we think to be a noble-minded man, yet he may have weak points, and possibly may be overcome through them to our wishes. He also may change in his views of interest and prudence, and in the course of time through our influence he may consider it best to assume another character before the people than the one he now bears. His future conduct, therefore, will materially depend upon the influence exercised by those around him."

"I begin to perceive the part thou wishest me to perform," remarked Judas, as he glanced at Saul with a sly significant expression.

"I am glad, my dear Judas," resumed Saul with great sweetness of tone, "that thou canst perceive my meaning. I therefore shall have less difficulty in suggesting all the points that will be necessary for the task I wish thee to perform."

"If I understand thee rightly," remarked Judas, "thou wishest me in the first place to follow this Jesus whithersoever he may go; then to construe and misconstrue his doctrines so as to make them seem evident to the people that he is something more than a mortal man; in fact, that he is nothing less than the Messiah."

"Yes, Judas, that is it precisely," replied Saul joyously, as his actions gave evidence of his great pleasure.

"I think I can perform this task in course of time, with patience and perseverance," remarked Judas. "I will mark all the available points in his doctrines as will admit of construction that will suit the end thou hast in view. And when he shall produce a cure through the means of his mysterious power of healing, I will magnify it before the people, and invent tales of others so great and wonderful that he shall appear before them as a very God. Such, I will disseminate far and wide unknown to him. Besides, I will study out many other inventions to put into execution according to circumstances. I will engage that before long the crazy notions of John the Baptist shall be more extended and believed in than the doctrines of Jesus himself."

"The very thing," exclaimed Saul, the sparkling of his eyes betokening his great satisfaction. "My dear Judas, thy wisdom and cunning is greater than that of Solomon, and thy services to me are inestimable. Whence did thou get thy schooling, my dear Judas?"

"My schooling has been that of adversity," replied Judas gravely, "and my tutor was Saul, the son of— "

"Enough! enough!" hastily interposed Saul. "I am glad thou hast availed thyself of thy opportunities, and proved thyself an apt scholar. Depend upon it, Judas, thou wilt yet be a man of great notoriety. But to return to our subject. I must say that I think thy plan of proceedings to be excellent, and there is no doubt in my mind but that it will accomplish our end in view. With regard to our mutual interests and secrets, I think we understand each other."

"I think we do," answered Judas as he raised his eyes to his companion. Then the glances of the two conspirators encountered, with a forced expression of confidence and candor; at the same time there was a suspicion of insincerity lurking in the heart of each against the other. There was a pause of a few seconds in the discourse of the companions, which at length was broken by Saul, who said:

"Before thou takest thy departure, Judas, there is another subject on which I wish to consult thee."

"Speak on, worthy Saul," said Judas.

"I have been thinking," resumed Saul, "that when a man is about entering upon a great enterprise, in which he stakes his worldly reputation, wealth and happiness, it would give him more courage and daring if he could be assured or foreshown that he would ultimately succeed. Although I have good hopes and prospects of my designs being successful, yet I would like to be made more confident by taking a glimpse of the future. Now, I understand that somewhere in the neighborhood of the city there is a wise woman or sybil, who is capable of foretelling future events. Art thou acquainted with such a woman, and wouldst thou advise me to task her skill?"

Judas remained silent for two or three minutes with his eyes cast to the ground, seeming to be in deep thought; but at length turning his regard upon Saul, he replied:

109

"I have heard that there is a sooth-saying woman somewhere in the environs of the city, but I know not where. Thou askest me my opinion on this matter. It is this: I would advise thee to question this woman. When she answers, I think it will be easy to ascertain whether her words are probable or not. If she should answer thee favorably, it would be giving thee confidence and great satisfaction for the present. I also shall be glad to know the result of things, for I am an interested party."

"Then it shall be as thou sayest," said Saul emphatically. "Wilt thou find out this woman's abode tomorrow? Then we will visit her together."

"I will do so," answered Judas.

The two conspirators then took another goblet of wine, when Judas took leave of his companion, and sought out another chamber to pass the remainder of the night.

VISION SEVENTH

JUDAS DRINKING WINE

In a small, private room, at an inn of low repute somewhere situated in the eastern extremity of the Holy City, Judas was reclining upon the mattress and cushions that extended along one side of it. Before him, elevated about a foot from the floor, was a long board or table covered with a dark coarse cloth, upon which were several vessels containing wine and cakes. At one end of the room was a door opening upon a corridor leading to various apartments and to other parts of the house, and at the other end was a window casement looking into a yard in the rear of the building where stabling for horses and cattle was kept.

The furniture and general appearance of this room was of the plainest and most common kind, making no pretensions to anything but common public service.

Judas was reclining on his right side supported by cushions, with his legs extended at ease, his eyes being cast downward and his brows contracted, seeming to be in profound reflection.

"God of my Fathers—if God there be—to what awful fate am I doomed?" mentally exclaimed Judas, as he grit his teeth in agony. "Is this the result and punishment of my youthful frailty? Frequently have I thought while pining as a bondman that could I once more obtain my freedom I would live a reformed man demeaning myself with that propriety which would gain my own esteem and stand right before God and man. But now, how is it with me? On one hand perpetual bondage, insult and misery; or, on the other, all my hopes and good wishes blasted, my soul sold to iniquity for the prospect of freedom and wealth! 0, Saul! Saul! thou art a demon in human shape, callous at heart to all virtue and sympathy with what is good, thus to take advantage of my unfortunate condition to make me the tool of thy cursed ambition. Is there no possibility of escape? Are there no means to shake off the trammels which are about to entangle me with the most damnable of wickedness? No! there is none. If I fail in the compact I have made with him my life will be the forfeit, for I am the repository of his heinous secrets. 0! wretched, wretched, is my lot! But remorse and sad reflection will avail me nothing. I must submit to my destiny and endeavor to harden my heart that I may commit acts which my sense of justice cannot approve."

Judas then sprang from his cushion, seized the vessel containing wine, poured out a goblet full and drank it off. At that instant somebody on horseback rode into the yard, when Judas, hearing the arrival, hastened to the casement and looked out, when he exclaimed, "Ah! it is Cosbi. I must now shake off my gloomy mood and prepare for his company, for he is a merry, reckless fellow, who could not be made sad if all the people in Judea were so many Sauls."

Scarcely had Judas finished his observation when the door burst open, and a gaily dressed young man, with great exuberance of spirits, and a wild merry eye, rushed into the room and sprang forward to Judas, when the two friends embraced by kissing each other on the cheeks.

"My dear friend Judas," exclaimed the new comer.

"Dear Cosbi," returned Judas.

The person under the name of Cosbi was a young man of about two and twenty, of a fair olive complexion, with black hair, eyes and eyebrows; his eyes shining with great brilliancy, restless and wild in expression. A small, black moustache curled at the extremities, surmounted two pouting coral lips, rather libidinous in their expression; a carnation tinge on his cheeks denoted good health and vigor; his forehead was smooth, but not expressive of any great mental powers, from which gradually inclined outward a delicately formed nose. Altogether, his features were more pretty than handsome, and his dress seemed to correspond. On his head he wore a cylinder-shaped black covering about four inches deep, with a large jewel in front; from beneath which his dark hair flowed in massive locks around his neck and shoulders. His coat was of light blue cloth reaching to the knees, fastened around the waist with a silk girdle of gaudy colors, open in front; beneath which a pink silk underdress was seen, fastened around the throat. His legs were covered with buskins of red leather, and his feet with sandals ornamented with studs of silver. His arms, beneath the wide sleeves of his coat, were covered with the silk underdress. On his fingers were several gold rings, and a large pair in form of hoops were suspended from his ears; and across his shoulder he carried a dark mantle. Altogether, he resembled a butterfly—light, airy, gay and thoughtless; full of wild activity, sipping here and there the sweets of life without suspecting there were any bitters.

"Didst thou receive my message, Cosbi?" were the first words of Judas after embracing his friend.

"Indeed I did," replied Cosbi with a laugh, "or how should I be here? When I did so I was so anxious to see thee that I immediately asked permission of the Seeress, and having obtained which I took a horse and galloped over hill and dale at the risk of killing the poor beast. When I came to the old wall of the city I felt inclined to leap over it, but remembering that it is over seven hundred feet high from the bottom of the valley to the top, I thought I could not do it at one leap, so I was obliged to take time and enter by the gate, and here I am."

"Well, and how dost thou and the world agree," said Judas, affecting gaiety of mood. "I see from thy gay and merry appearance thou hast not much cause for weeping."

"My dear Judas, didst thou ever see me weep?"

"I think not," replied Judas.

"No," said Cosbi with assumed gravity. "Before such a doleful event could happen all the aqueous vapors of this world must dissolve to waters of agony, and then by some mysterious power I must be compelled to imbibe them all and then I must be squeezed tight in the hand of horrid fate before a tear could be forced from my eyes."

"Thy expression speaks more of poetic extravagance than sound worldly philosophy," returned Judas. "But come, let us take some wine and be seated, then we can talk at our ease."

The two friends accordingly took wine and seated themselves.

"Ah! that wine is good" said Cosbi. "I would rather have a draught of that wine than all the philosophy in the world. I despise all those abstract, refined and grave speculations called philosophies, and the various schemes of ambition by which men are withdrawn from true enjoyment to seek after ideal ones that end in disappointment and misery. I do not speak thus from my own experience of them, but from what I see in others. All these pursuits of men under the names of philosophy, religion and metaphysics, are only so many spurs to their ambition for knowledge, power, fame, titles, glory and aggrandizement above their fellow men, which carry with them cares, anxieties, disappointment, sorrow, remorse and misery as the results. I will not follow any of those pursuits, and consequently I shall be free from the results. I was born to live. I live to enjoy, and I enjoy today with the hope of

113

enjoying more tomorrow."

"Are there no things or circumstances in which care and solicitude are necessary before action, and regret, sorrow and remorse after action?" inquired Judas.

"Nothing of the kind with me" replied Cosbi. "I live for the day, and that is for enjoyment. I care not for the morrow or its results. I act to-day with the best intent; that is, to enjoy, and care not how it may affect others. I think and act for myself, and others must do the same. I take all things for the best, and see nothing the reverse. Like a moth or butterfly I flit to and fro from one flower I sip. I say it is good. I go to another, and say it is excellent. I sip of another, and say it is better than all. Thus I am continually changing my enjoyments, and with every change I am better pleased. What is the world for but for enjoyment when a man is in the right mood, and not to be making one's self miserable in pursuing schemes of philosophy and ambition, which end in nothing but disappointment, remorse and misery. Look at me, I am contented to have what can be enjoyed in this world, such as gay clothes, fair maidens, good food and wine, an agreeable companion or two, and a contemplation of all the beauties and poetry of nature. Such as these I seek, and such I enjoy, in fact, Judas, the generality of men know not how to live; they forsake the good things they can obtain, and run after that which is ideal and delusive. Come, let us once more taste this delicious vintage, and then tell me how the world fares with thee, for I forgot to ask thee before. I see that some change has occurred with thee, for thou makest another appearance to that which I saw thee when last present."

"Yes, Cosbi," responded Judas, "there has been a change in my circumstances since I saw thee last. I was then a bondman, and now I am a freeman, or taught to believe so."

"That is good," observed Cosbi, evidently pleased; and then he said: "Art thou still with thy former master?"

"I am acting for him in a certain business as his agent, for which he remunerates me well," replied Judas.

"That is good also," remarked Cosbi.

"But," resumed Judas, "I am about serving a new master, from whom I get no pay."

"That is strange," remarked Cosbi; "but perhaps thou hast something good in prospect."

"I will explain all that presently," answered Judas. "But now tell me how thou likest thy office as page to the Seeress."

"Ah, my dear Judas," said Cosbi as a slight change came over his merry countenance. "The time I have passed with my kind mistress has been an interesting time to me. Her confidence in me is great, and her kindness knows no bounds. I have learned more of human nature and the secrets of persons than I ever knew before, since I have been in her service. I have pried into the philosophies, religion, morals and ambitions of all classes of men, and found them all to be hollow and false, from which I have constructed a philosophy of my own to suit myself."

"I thought," replied Judas, "thou didst denounce all philosophy just now."

"And so I do," answered Cosbi, "all except my own, which is simply this: I believe nothing as it is represented to be, but take every thing as it is. If thou wert in my office thou wouldst be initiated into this species of wisdom, and discover its beauties, truth and value. To speak in confidence to thee, my dear Judas, the system of soothsaying as foretelling future events, which is followed by my amiable mistress, is no more than a system of cunning imposition."

"Such I always judged to be the case," remarked Judas.

"Yes, it is true that it is imposition on the credulity of fools," resumed Cosbi. "Though such is the case, my mistress does not follow it like others, for the sake of the shekels of gold and silver. She has some secret design in it that I cannot understand, and a secret grief that I cannot fathom. On all other subjects she is open and communicative to me. But that is not what I wish to bring to thy notice. Speaking of the secrets we acquire of persons I will tell thee how we get hold of them. I mingle among families and persons of note under different disguises, learning their histories, relations, offices and pretensions, which are recorded in a book. If a stranger should come to ask questions, an answer is evaded until we can obtain some intelligence of him. Then the questioner by the nature of his question points out the object of his ambition or desires, which when added to the knowledge we have of him in the book, will enable us to give an answer with some degree of probability, if not altogether truth. This is the art of soothsaying. The fools who come to question us gain their answers, and are more or less satisfied. We gain their gold and silver; besides, we gain a knowledge of their true nature, which is generally in great contrast to their pretensions. It is thus that I have constructed my own philosophy: Not to take men as they are represented to be, but to take them as they are."

"And what is thy estimate of men, according to thy philosophy?" inquired Judas.

"The greater part of mankind may be divided into two classes," replied Cosbi; "The first as fools and idiots; the others as liars, knaves and monsters. There are a few exceptions which we may consider as good men, though they incline to one or the other of the classes."

"Then in what class are we to include ourselves?" inquired Judas.

"0, my dear Judas," replied Cosbi somewhat puzzled by the question, which caused him to give Judas a peculiar wink, when he replied: "We, of course, are among the exceptions a little inclined to the latter class."

"0, indeed," responded Judas laughing, "I believe there is some truth in thy philosophical classification. Thou art a merry and candid fellow, Cosbi. I was going to say knave, but I will not be so rude of speech."

"If thou hadst done so," responded Cosbi laughing, "I should not have been offended, for I always like to hear things called by their right names."

"But dost thou think," observed Judas, "that it is a great pity for a man of thy talents to be passing his time as a page to a Seeress, when if he would go upon the world he could find offices of greater advantage, and adventures of greater interest?"

"I have passed a happy and profitable time with my mistress," replied Cosbi; "but the truth is I do begin to feel weary for the want of a change. In one respect I feel my confidence and trust infringed upon, as it were; that she will not discover to me the cause of her secret grief and the design she has in continuing the imposition of soothsaying, which I know she despises, and does not follow it for the sake of lucre. If she would make all known to me I should take pleasure in soothing her sorrow with all my sympathy and good offices; but as she will not I believe I must forsake her. I cannot live where there is sorrow that I cannot assuage."

"Let us take some more wine, Cosbi," observed Judas, "and then I will explain what I meant when I said that I was going to serve a new master without pay."

The two friends then proceeded to partake afresh of the wine, and after a few minutes being passed in this indulgence, they continued their conversation.

"The man to whom I was lately a bondman," observed Judas in a serious tone and manner, "has made me his agent to carry out in part his designs. Part of my service will be to travel with another person, a very extraordinary man of great beauty, talents and virtue, who designs to teach the people of Judea and other countries, with the view of producing a general moral reformation. The intent is that I am to watch his proceedings and exercise my influence over him in certain matters which I cannot now explain. In filling this office I shall want somebody to follow me at a small distance, whose services I can call in as occasions shall require to fill the part assigned to me; and I know of no one more capable, as I think, of doing what I need than thyself. If thou thinkest proper to accept the office, I now make thee the offer in preference to others."

"What is the nature of the duties or the part I should have to play?" inquired Cosbi.

"I have heard thee say," replied Judas, "that thou hast been in the habit of disguising thyself and assuming various characters. I presume thou art good at mimickry."

"There is no character or person that I cannot imitate, from the beggar to the High Priest," answered Cosbi, as he looked up to his friend with great curiosity.

"It is well," replied Judas; "but the persons and characters required by us will be more easy to imitate: such as blind, deaf and dumb men, cripples and madmen."

"What a noble cast of characters thou givest me to perform," ejaculated Cosbi, bursting into a hearty laugh, "and their costumes so expensive!"

"The more simple the character and less expensive the costume, the better," observed Judas. "But now thou understandest the task assigned to the office, wilt thou accept? Thou shalt be well paid for thy labor and trouble."

"Before I answer thee," said Cosbi, "I will ask thee a few questions."

"Certainly," said Judas.

"In the first place," said Cosbi, "this new master of thine, whom thou art going to serve as a spy upon his actions and sayings, and be to him a counselor of confusion, is going to preach to the people with the view of reforming them."

"Yes, that is the idea he entertains," replied Judas.

"Well, that is good, for the world needs reforming," said Cosbi laughing. "The Great Jehovah thought so himself when he concluded to drown all mankind excepting Noah and his family. But his experiment did not succeed, for the first thing Noah did after the flood was to get drunk and show his nakedness, and his descendants through all the world need as much reforming as ever. But, as regards our subject, I presume thy new master intends to reform all classes, from the beggar to the High Priest and the Governor, making them all exceedingly wise, honest, just and benevolent? Well, that will be glorious! I hope I shall live to see it."

Then Cosbi gave another laugh.

"Such is the intent of this good man so far as his power will go," responded Judas.

"I do not doubt it," rejoined Cosbi. "Then he intends to reform all lawyers, and make them honest, all doctors, and make them learned and candid in speech, and all amorous women and demireps, making them pure in heart and mind, if he cannot in body? O what a glorious state of society we shall have! How I do like the idea!" and Cosbi laughed again.

"He certainly will try to do all these things," said Judas.

"Then he will endeavor to give the people some better ideas of a God?" resumed Cosbi. "He will endeavor to establish one who will not tempt his people to commit sin; one who will not get angry with his people, and will not afflict them with diseases, or smite them with the sword, or destroy them in any other manner; one who will not require to be fed by earthly mortals with roast beef, mutton, kid and poultry; and one that is not fond of oil, wine, frankincense and barley bread? O, Judas, when thy new master shall make this reform, we also ought to become pious and render homage to his God!"

"I think such a reform is needed, which my new master will endeavor to establish," answered Judas.

"Does thy new master intend to try his powers upon the Priesthood?" inquired Cosbi. "Does he think he will be enabled to make them speak the truth? To be honest, charitable and just? To have a sense of noble, manly dignity? To spurn all meanness, imposition, illiberality and fornication? To do all this, will be to achieve a great work indeed! I shall not be surprised to hear next that he has made a convert of the sun, putting out his light and making him travel home in the dark." Then Cosbi gave another laugh.

"The Priesthood," observed Judas, "though the most infamous of humanity, may yet be affected by the preaching of reform. At least my new master will endeavor to reach their corrupt hearts."

"But my dear Judas," continued Cosbi in his questioning, "what does this reformer intend to do with the blind, deaf and dumb, the cripples and madmen? I do not understand this part of his reform."

"This is an arrangement between my late master and me," replied Judas in a low tone as he bent towards Cosbi; "the design of which is to give this new master of mine a greater confidence in his powers, and to spread his fame among the people as one who possesses superhuman power."

"I cannot see how that is to be done," remarked Cosbi.

"In this wise," replied Judas: "This extraordinary man possesses a mysterious power by which he can cure a great many diseases, but that goes only to a certain extent. Now I and my late master wish to make the people believe that this power is unlimited; that, in fact, he can cure the blind, lame, deaf and dumb, besides crazy folks who are thought to be possessed with evil spirits. Now if thou shouldst personate a lame man, and my master should say to thee "Walk," it will be easy for thee to do so; and if thou shalt personate a blind man, and he shall say to thee "Receive thy sight," it will be easy for thee to do so."

"Oh!" exclaimed Cosbi, as though something had suddenly hurt him. Then puckering up his mouth, drawing in his cheeks, raising up his eyebrows and projecting his eyes, he presented a ludicrous figure of stupid astonishment, which having indulged in for a few seconds, he relaxed his features, and added in a low tone of voice: "I see! I see! Why, Judas, thou hast cast the scales from my eyes. I was blind, but now I see. O what a brilliant idea! It is worthy of its originator, and the originator worthy of praise. What an excitement will be among the people! What glorious fun for me when I drop my crutches and run at the word of command; or when I open my eyes and stare around me after being cured of my blindness!" Then Cosbi burst into another laugh and continued the same demonstrations of hilarity for several minutes, when at length he said: "I need scarcely say, my dear Judas, that I accept thy offer, and will do the best to the extent of my powers to render thee service. Thou must let me know when I am wanted. I must now return to take leave of my mistress, and study the parts I have to perform."

Cosbi rose preparatory to departure, when Judas arrested his attention by observing:

"Stay yet a few minutes, Cosbi. I have been so interested in our discourse that I had almost forgotten the principal business, concerning which I wished to see thee. Let us once more partake of the wine, and then I will inform thee what it is."

The two friends once more indulged in the vinous fluid, and then Judas observed:

"My late master having undertaken this great enterprise, of which I am to be his agent, is naturally anxious about its results. He is desirous of knowing whether he will succeed in his designs, and although he is a learned and astute man, yet he is fool enough to believe in soothsaying. He accordingly desired me to inquire about a Seeress who can answer his questions; therefore, Cosbi, I sent for thee to make arrangements for my master's reception by thy mistress, as he intends visiting her this night. As I feel interested in the answers thy mistress shall give to his questions, I thought it best to give thee a clue that she may be enabled to answer him to his and my satisfaction."

"My dear Judas," responded Cosbi, "I understand thy wishes. In the name of my mistress I say we will be ready to receive thy master at the fifth hour tonight, and accord to him that mystic intelligence of future days, which as yet is not conceived in the womb of time."

The two friends conversed a little while longer concerning the items of intelligence that Cosbi was to convey to the Seeress, to enable her to answer Saul's questions. Mutual secrecy being enjoined, they embraced and parted.

VISION EIGHTH

THE SEERESS OF SCOPUS

The dark shades of night hung over the valley of Jehosaphat, and the adjacent hills and ravines to the northeast. The progression of the stars indicated that it was nigh to midnight, and their twinkling light revealed the outlines of a large, lonely mansion that stood at the foot of a hill. All was dreary and lifeless without. Soon the facade of the building vanished before the mental eye, when a scene of singular beauty and splendor presented itself.

There was a lofty chamber, octagonal in shape, with a pillar in every angle supporting a concave roof. These pillars resembled palm trees, the spreading branches at the tops forming the capitals. Around the body of every tree an enormous serpent twined the entire length from bottom to top, its head with glaring eyes and forked tongue being surrounded by the foliage.

The roof was decorated with glittering stars on a dark blue ground, and the walls were hung with rich drapery of light blue silk, which nearly reached to the floor, and which was bordered with a golden fringe. The floor was covered with thick matting, soft to the foot and noiseless to the tread; and at four divisions of the chamber, between the pillars, were four couches covered with purple cloth elevated about two

120

feet from the floor. In the other four divisions of the walls were two doors and two windows, but all covered with the drapery. At four equal distant spots were four pedestals, on the top of which were four lamps burning sweet scented oil. Over one of the couches there were rich hangings of scarlet cloth, in form of canopy; the folds being looped aside, presented to view a female reclining in luxurious ease and pensive reflection.

Presently she arose, and with solemn stately steps paced the chamber in a silent, pensive mood. Now and then she placed her hand upon her brows, or over the region of her heart, denoting the subject of her thoughts to be pregnant with anguish and sorrow.

She was tall in stature, of lithe and symmetrical form. She was pale and haggard, seeming to be advanced in age more from the ravages of cankering sorrow than by number of years. Her hair, which once had been as dark as the raven, was now streaked with silvery whiteness, being formed in bands around her head, over which was thrown a short white veil. Though her countenance bore the effects of time and sorrow, yet there were relics in her features which gave evidence that she once had been a commanding beauty. Her forehead denoted lofty and noble sentiments; her nose of the oriental type, with her small mouth and gracefully curled lips, bespoke a spirit of firmness and one used to command; and her eyes still retained a lustre, though subdued to a melancholy expression.

Her dress consisted of a black skirt hanging in graceful folds to the ground, slightly trailing behind, and over which a short purple robe was fastened around the waist by a girdle richly embroidered in gold. Pendants of gold in her ears and a gold bracelet on her right arm adorned her person. Her feet were covered with white slippers, curiously ornamented with threads of gold. Such was the person called the Seeress of Scopus.

For some minutes she paced the apartment in solemn silence. At length, being moved with great poignant emotion, wringing her hands and upraising her eyes, she ejaculated:

"Great God of the Universe, under whatever name we poor mortals adore thee, hear thou the humble petition of thy erring, though repentant child of earth! Restore to me my long lost and neglected child before death shall close my eyes to this world of woe and misery! Let me see him, if it be but once, that I may declare to him his parentage! Forgive me the sins of my youth, under consideration of the repentance and sufferings of my after days! Grant, great God, the desire of my heart, and ever afterwards with gratitude and humility I will bend to thy will!"

Having thus addressed the Father of the Universe, the poignancy of her feelings became subdued to comparative calmness; then, with her arms crossed on her breast and head bowed low, she continued to pace

121

to and fro as she communed with herself in a low tone:

"It is all in vain; either there is no God of mercy or he heeds me not. What will it avail me, then, that I continue to besiege heaven with my prayers for God's mercy and favor, declaring my repentance and humility, if the boon I ask is forever to be denied? Is it not better to believe in a blind inexorable Fate, whose decrees if not swayed by the prayers of mortals, are at least impartial and sometimes favorable to their wishes? For twenty years have I daily put up prayers to my God, asking for mercy and forgiveness for my past follies and sins, and petitioning that he would direct me to the discovery of my child, but no mercy, no boon, no hope have I received after a penance of so long a time. I will pray no more. I will strive to steep my mind in oblivion of the past, and become indifferent to the present and future. I will render my heart callous and insensible to the poignancy of my woes, the sense of my shame, and all the finer emotions of my nature. The raging fires which once made me the victim of libidinous desires, have smouldered and died out, and passions which once raged within my breast for the miscreant who seduced and deserted me, no longer excite or burn within me—all have sunk into apathy. But there is another passion that has risen within me more powerful than all the others—a mother's love for her child! Can I conquer or extinguish it? No! As long as I live its holy impulse will quicken and command me to search the world over, praying and crying aloud in hope of yet beholding my beloved child. Ah!— "

The soliloquy of the Seeress was interrupted by the drapery moving aside, when Cosbi entered the chamber, who making his approach, bent before her with great formality and etiquette, and said:

"Sweet mistress, the worthy citizen of whom I spoke to thee has come. He desires an audience, if it will meet thy pleasure."

"Let him be admitted, Cosbi, and be thou in attendance," said the Seeress. Then Cosbi retired, when she observed to herself: "Again am I mortified, self-humiliated and self-despised in practicing this system of imposture; but as the love of a mother is holy, almost any means are justifiable when they are devoted to the cause of her child. Thus I exonerate myself for imposing upon the ignorant and superstitious people, who reveal to me their innermost secrets, when they think they are prying into the secrets of fate or futurity. From this mode, I hope to find a clue to the discovery of my child. But now comes this Saul of Tarsus, to question me. Cosbi has given me the clue to his desires, and tells me that he is a cunning and learned man. Well, I must meet him with a bold front and great pretensions."

The Seeress then returned to her couch where she reclined herself with the abandonment of imperial indifference.

Cosbi, followed by Saul, now entered the chamber, when the former pointing to the Seeress, with a graceful bow to the latter, retired from

122

their presence.

Saul was closely enveloped in his mantle so that his features could not be seen. He gazed around the singular and magnificent chamber with evident surprise and admiration mingled with a great curiosity to discover, if he could, any traits of character of the Seeress in the novel scene around him. Having at length taken a general view of all around, he said to himself: "Here is wealth, refinement and a singular taste displayed in this apartment. She cannot be a common impostor, who by juggling tricks, palms upon common minds her cunning answers as oracles from the Gods. No! She must be a true prophetess, who by an inward sight or intuition, can trace out the events of future days—for such I believe there are. However, I will test her."

Saul at length approached within a few feet of the Seeress and bowed low before her, when the latter, rising from her couch, returned the salutation, and said in a courteous tone of voice:

"Stranger, what wouldst thou with the Seeress of Scopus?"

"Art thou a prophetess," answered Saul in a sneering tone, "and knowest not who I am, and what my business?"

"Do the supernal powers take notice of mortals before they declare themselves and their wishes?" replied the Seeress in a tone of severity, and her eyes flashing with indignation. "Presumptuous man, this much I know of thee without questioning the supernal powers: Thou art rude and uncourteous to those from whom thou wouldst ask favors. Thou judgest others according to the measure of sincerity and virtue thou seest in thine own mind and heart. Thy ancestor and namesake of the tribe of Benjamin, of which thou art, was more humble and courteous to the witch of Endor when he sought the information preceding the battle that sealed his fate."

Saul started, and an indefinable dread seized upon him as he said to himself, "By the God of my fathers! she knows me." Then throwing the mantle aside he humbly bent before her and said:

"0 Woman favored by the Gods, pardon my temerity. Not from ill will did I thus speak or desire to be uncourteous, but from the prudent motive of testing thy genuineness, the veracity of thy wisdom, and medium powers between the Gods and men."

"Enough!" interjected the Seeress, feeling satisfied with Saul's apology. "Now state thy wishes, and if my powers can aid or satisfy thee, I will."

"0 woman, whose knowledge and power transcends the sphere of common mortals, deem me not presumptuous or base if I unfold my mind and heart before thee. Man is a restless and discontented animal, full of fancies and follies at the best; and when he is favored by circumstances to be placed above the common wants and pursuits of men, it is then he becomes the most discontented with life. The general occu-

123

pations and scenes of life become stale and flat, he looks around for something new to give him interest and occupation, such as shall bring him honor, fame, wealth and aggrandizement. I pretend not to be superior to our mortal nature, by being passive to such ambitious impulses, for, alas! I feel myself too sensitive and desirous of worldly greatness. Such is my nature, and such my circumstances. To meet the requirements of the one and the deficiencies of the other, I have designed and entered upon a grand enterprise which will procure me all the excitement and occupation so necessary to my nature. Besides, I anticipate that in course of time it will procure me honor, fame and glory. But mortals such as I am cannot foresee future events. I feel anxious to know the result of my endeavors, therefore, O Seeress, I wish to acquire of thee a little information to the few questions I shall propound. In the first place, shall I succeed in the enterprise I undertake? Will my works and character gain the approbation of posterity? Will my renown extend far into posterity? Such are the points to which I crave solutions through thy mystic powers. Accord them to me, I pray, without diminution of the truth."

"It is not in my power to answer thee unaided," observed the Seeress. Then placing her hand in the bosom of her dress she produced a gem of a light blue color and transparent, about the size and shape of a hen's egg, which she presented to Saul, and added: "I must bring thee in connection with the supernal powers. Gaze upon that gem with all the intensity of thy vision: and at the same time, call up in thy mind in successive order the various parts of thy grand enterprise which thou designest to enact and establish, accompanied with the questions thou wouldst have solved. Do this, then the supernals will take note of thy desires, and make known their answers through me; then return to me the gem."

Saul having received the gem from the Seeress, looked upon it with a fixed intensity of gaze as he revolved in his mind the various schemes, projects and achievements of his intended enterprise. At the same time the Seeress gazed upon him with a glance as fixed and powerful as a serpent upon its prey. Every slight motion of his eyelids or quiver of his lips was taken in by her absorbing gaze. She seemed to have found an entrance to his soul through which she peered, and stood spellbound in awful contemplation of what she saw.

After a few minutes had thus transpired, Saul took his eyes from the gem, returned it to the Seeress, and observed: "The task is done."

Then the latter crossing her arms upon her breast and gently closing her eyes, seemed to be undergoing a state of supernal inspiration. At length returning to her ordinary position and regarding her visitor complacently, she addressed him:

"Saul of Tarsus," she said in a low but distinct voice. Saul started when her voice fell upon his ear; then he bent forward to listen, his countenance expressive of the most intense interest as she added: "It has pleased the supernal powers to deign answers to thy questions through me their humble servant, and thus I answer thy first query:

"Thou wilt succeed in thy enterprise to a certain extent. The seed of thy enterprise will be sown, and thou wilt live to gather a part of its fruits."

"Live to gather a part of its fruits," said Saul, following the words of the Seeress. "Well, that is favorable. It shows that I shall not be cut off in the commencement of my undertaking."

"As regards thy second question," resumed the Seeress, "the answer is thus: Posterity will receive the institutions founded by thy labors, with greater reverence and esteem than of worth. Posterity will also highly esteem thy character as given to them, on which they will pay great eulogiums and praise. But thy true character will not be known by them."

"Will receive with great reverence my labors." said Saul to himself. "Well, that is favorable. But my true character will not be known by them. Well, that is favorable also; for if they knew my real character, I do not think they would have much reverence for me."

"As to thy third question," resumed the Seeress, "the answer is thus: Great will be thy renown through many ages of posterity. Millions now unborn will eulogize thee in singing thy praise. Institutions founded on thy doctrines and labors will extend through many countries, even to nations not now in existence. Some centuries will elapse, and still thou and thy works will impress the world. But as all institutions established by men, however great, are doomed to eternal change, so the time will come when thine will pass away and be forgotten."

"Some centuries will elapse, and still thou and thy works will impress the world!" repeated Saul to himself. "Well, that is quite favorable and glory enough! But the time shall come when thine shall pass away and be forgotten. Had she spoken otherwise, I could not believe her."

"Such are the answers as I have received them from the powers above. Art thou satisfied?" said the Seeress.

"Great and noble woman!" replied Saul in a tone of great suavity, "thou hast given me new strength and confidence in my undertaking. The answers I have received are cherishing to my heart and enlivening to my mind, and they bind me forever in grateful remembrance to thee and the superhuman powers." Then Saul taking a purse of money from his girdle and approaching nearer to the Seeress, he added: "Let me as a testimony of my thanks and satisfaction, lay this at thy feet."

Then the Seeress striking upon a small metal basin that stood upon one of the pedestals near her, a shrill sound vibrated through the chamber, when Cosbi immediately made his appearance. Saul then making a graceful obeisance took his departure and was conducted out of the mansion where Judas was ready to receive him in attendance with horses.

"That man is an ambitious knave," said the Seeress to herself when Saul was gone. "It requires not much assistance from the supernals to divine his ambitious desires and probable career, especially as I received a clue thereto from Cosbi. I can read his heart and mind in his eyes."

Cosbi again made his appearance, when his mistress beckoned for him to approach her. He did so, when she said:

"Knowest thou aught of this man personally, and of his ambitious designs?"

Cosbi seemed to hesitate for a few moments, but at length replied: "I know a little by report, but nothing definitely."

"What is that little thou dost know? Let me have it, Cosbi," said his mistress.

"My dear mistress," answered Cosbi in seeming perturbation, "it will be with great regret that I shall comply with thy wishes in this instance."

"With regret?" exclaimed the mistress in surprise. "What dost thou mean, Cosbi? Art thou not my confidential servitor, bound to me by interest and gratitude to impart to me all thy secrets?"

"My dear mistress," exclaimed Cosbi with great emotion as he took her hand and pressed it to his breast, "I must declare all to thee, though it distresses me to do so."

The Seeress looked upon him with speechless surprise, but offered no opposition to his enigmatical conduct.

"That man who has departed just now has an agent in his employ, with whom I have engaged to travel and to serve."

"Then thou wouldst forsake me, Cosbi," exclaimed the mistress in surprise and indignation.

"I am sensible, my dear mistress, of thy kindness towards me, for which I have endeavored to show a just appreciation; but notwithstanding I must beg to renounce thy service."

"For what reason dost thou desert me?" inquired the mistress in a tremulous tone, as though she felt a painful emotion at parting with her faithful servant, for whom she felt almost as great an affection as for a child. "Tell me what there is in my service that displeases thee."

"I will endeavor to do so at thy bidding," answered Cosbi, "though to do so of my own accord I should consider as trenching on sacred ground. Thou knowest, my dear mistress, that I am of a joyous nature, endeavoring to make myself happy and all others around me. I have imparted to thee all my secrets, and thou in return hast given me general confidence; yet there is one secret thou wilt not impart to me, the cause of thy continued grief. I daily perceive that thou hast at thy heart a secret sorrow, and I cannot mitigate it or give thee comfort because thou

126

wilt not impart to me its source. I have lived with thee in hope that I should in course of time prevail over thy delicacy to become thy confidant, and be enabled to restore thee to cheerfulness; but as all my endeavors have failed therein, I cannot remain here any longer to see thee suffer a pang that I cannot assuage."

When Cosbi had delivered his last sentiment the Seeress remained silent for some time with her eyes averted, seeming to be in a pensive mood and absorbed in reflection. At length arousing herself to a sense of her position she remarked to Cosbi in a mild but sorrowful tone:

"Cosbi, I believe thou art justified in wishing to leave me, though I must confess I much regret that it must be so. But as thou art determined, a thought has struck me that thou possibly may do me a service, and at the same time pursue thy own happy course."

"Any service that I can render my beloved mistress will only enhance my pleasure," replied Cosbi.

"I believe so, my dear friend, for such I must now consider thee," returned the Seeress sighing; then extending the arm on which was the golden bracelet, she said to him in an expressive manner: "Look upon this bracelet, Cosbi—mark well the jewels with which it is set, and the workmanship."

Cosbi examined the bracelet minutely, wondering at the time what could be her intention in drawing his notice to it.

"I am now," resumed the Seeress, "going to comply with thy wish, on the eve of our separation, and do that which I have hitherto refused to do, by imparting to thee the cause, in part at least, of my settled sorrow; therefore listen well to my words."

Cosbi was all attention.

"Some years ago there was a person on whom all my affections were concentrated. I will not state what was the tie or relation between us. Let it suffice to say that I loved that individual with as pure and ardent a love as a mother could love a child.

"Circumstances became such that my beloved object was parted from me, and in his possession was the fellow bracelet of this—the precise counterpart to the one I now wear—and never have I seen the person or the bracelet since. Much have I travelled and many inquiries have I made, but all in vain; no clue have I been enabled to trace of the lost loved one. As a last resource I adopted the art of soothsaying, and assumed the character of a Seeress, thinking that by acquiring the secrets of the wealthy I should be enabled to discover a clue to my lost beloved one. As yet I have been unsuccessful, and thus continues my sorrow without mitigation. This, so far as I have related it, is the cause of my poignant grief. Dost thou think, Cosbi, thou couldst recognize the counterpart of this bracelet if thou wert to see it?"

Cosbi expressed his belief that he could.

127

"Well, then," resumed the Seeress, "as thou art going to leave me to travel with thy new master, it is possible that thou mayest discover the counterpart of this bracelet worn by some female; or thou mayest see it among the collections of those who traffic in such articles of merchandise. At any rate if thou shouldst discover it I wish thee to make inquiry and trace it, if possible to the original owner. Shouldst thou make any such discovery then thou must communicate the same to me, and possibly I may discover the person for whom I grieve, or ascertain his fate."

Cosbi gave the Seeress repeated assurances that he would make every endeavor to fulfill her wishes in every respect, and after sympathizing and condoling with her for some time they separated.

VISION NINTH

THE GENIUS

High up among the Judean mountains, on one of the most eastern ranges, not far from the city of Jericho, situated midway between the mountain top and the ravine's deep abyss, there was a plateau containing a small fertile spot, being an oasis in the desert of the mountains. Several springs gushed from the mountains' sides, and spreading over the small plain and mingling with the debris, a scanty supply of mould was produced, from which grass, shrubs, trees and moss sprang up spontaneously. This fertile spot was a miniature forest of pine, cedar, tamarisk, oak and palm trees, interspersed with grassy plats and running water. Near the centre of this small verdant locality was a habitation or grotto, the cylindrical wall being constructed of rocky fragments, and the roof of rushes in the form of a cone; in the front of which, near to the entrance and under the shade of a tamarisk tree, was a long rude bench which seemed to be used as a seat or lounge.

This lonely smiling spot in the desert was suitable to the resident, who seemed to avoid the busy turmoil of society, and courted this lovely scene for uninterrupted meditation. This was one of the retreats of Jesus of Nazareth when in the neighborhood of the Holy City.

The sun had passed the meridian, diffusing with undiminished splendor its life-inspiring rays upon the scene around, causing the air to be dry and sultry. At such a time all animals withdraw to shade and repose to avoid exposure to the sun when in the zenith of its power.

With his head pillowed upon his mantle, under the shade of the tamarisk tree, Jesus reclined upon the bench in front of his grotto. From early watching and fatigue of deep reflection, his bodily senses became exhausted and slumber gradually stole upon him, until his senses were lost in oblivion, and he was unconscious to the scene around him. But from certain passing motions and alternate expressions of his features, it could be seen that the inward man or spirit was awake and active. Jesus was asleep and dreaming; and as the mysterious vision flitted before the mental eye, so strong were the sympathies of the soul with the senses of the body that it would, unbidden, impress them upon the features of the corporeal man. Alternately his features expressed surprise, admiration, love, reverence, fear or horror, which according to the medium's perception, shall here be portrayed:

In the panorama of his mental sphere, Jesus saw himself wandering alone in the wilderness of the barren mountains, seeming to be in a reflective mood upon the approaching time, when he designed declaring his intentions and doctrines to the people. Some time he had wandered over plain, hill and gorge, without heeding whither he went. At length looking around him he perceived the scene to be unknown to him, and knew not the way to return. Some time he stood perplexed and undecided whether to proceed or endeavor to retrace his steps. All was barren, desolate and dreary around him; no signs of life or indications to any route. Long ranges of barren hills and mountains stood before and behind him; deep ravines and unfathomable abysses impeded his progress, without a prospect of succor from any living being. He gave himself up for lost. For a few minutes he remained still with great uneasiness of mind, when at length he thought he saw something approaching him. Nearer and nearer it came; at length a venerable old man of a stern aspect and clothed in a loose dress, burst upon his view and stood before him.

"My friend, I am lost." said Jesus, addressing the old man in a courteous tone of voice, and with a salutation of the body.

"So I perceive," replied the old man complacently. "As thou hast not wandered very far from thy abode, it is possible to regain it before the day expires; but if thou shouldst go much farther thou wilt be irretrievably lost. This scene is a type of thy mind. At present thou art in doubt how to proceed; but if thou pursuest thy inclinations thou wilt be lost."

"How!" exclaimed Jesus. "Dost thou pretend to know my mind?"

"I do not pretend," replied the old man with a smile "but I actually do know thy mind, and as a friend who admires thy virtuous inclinations, I come forward to give thee warning so as to arrest thee from destruction. In the same manner I am capable of directing thy safe return to thy abode."

"Thou fillest me with amazement," cried Jesus, looking upon the old man with intense interest. "Give me some proof that what thou sayest is true before I talk with thee any farther."

I can easily do that," replied the old man, as he gave a peculiar disagreeable leer at Jesus, who felt an indefinable shudder pass through him at the time. "It is thy resolve before many hours shall have passed to start upon the world with the laudable intent of reforming mankind. Is it not so?"

Jesus gave an involuntary start and retreated a pace from the old man, regarding him with fearful amazement.

"Tell me," he cried in a hurried and excited manner, "tell me who thou art, for I believe thou art something more than mortal."

"I am," replied the old man seriously; "yet all my sayings and doings are connected with mortals. I have lived from the first. I live with the present, and I shall live forever as long as man liveth, for I am the Recording Genius of Humanity. I trace the progress and aberrations of nations, and record them in a book which I call Experience. I note the gradual progress of mankind from barbarism to refinement, and sometimes from refinement to barbarism; and I can assure thee that when I reflect upon the various acts of man that I have recorded, many exceedingly wise axioms are brought to my view. Now, as I admire thy noble intentions of doing good to thy fellow men, I wish to give thee the benefit of my experience and reflections, which I will do in a few words. Forbear to put into execution thy designs, but return to thy simple and virtuous private life, and study to make thyself happy."

"I cannot conceive," replied Jesus rather indignantly, "that it is a man's duty to live for himself alone. A man is but a small part of mankind, yet there is a mutual dependence and connection upon each other, either for good or evil. As one drop of water in the ocean is connected and dependent upon the whole mass, so is the mass affected by the single drop, either for good or evil. How, then, if a man be honest, virtuous, intelligent and full of love, can he do no good for his fellow men by teaching his principles and giving them his good examples?"

"All thy ideas are very good, according to their intrinsic worth." replied the old man. "They may do good between one individual and another, but when thou talkest of applying it to a nation of people, that is quite another thing. The great difficulty will be to execute them, which thou wilt never be able to do. There never was a nation of people governed by preaching to them honesty, virtue, intelligence and love. There is not one now that acknowledges these principles as the rule of their government; and I may venture to say that it will be many, many centuries before there ever will be."

"If such be the failings of our rulers," remarked Jesus, "is it not possible to establish a virtuous power among the people by instructing them and setting examples?"

"That would be still more difficult and impossible," returned the genius. "An individual it is possible to reform and bring to a certain degree of refinement, but not so a people. In the first place, when thou goest to preach thy doctrines to the people thou must be assured that their minds are prepared to receive them. They ought to have a sufficient mental capacity to comprehend any abstract or obscure point thou mayest bring before them, for unless they have such, thou mayest as well preach to a flock of goats or sheep. In the second place, some portion of the people may be able to conceive thy doctrines in part, and misunderstand a part; then there will be misunderstandings and misconstructions, giving a general confusion of errors. Another portion of the people may understand thee well, but their habits, vices and petty interests will prevent them from following thy instructions; and lastly another portion of the people may understand thee thoroughly, but their opposing interests will generate hate against thee. They accordingly will misrepresent and villify thy doctrines and instructions, and then proceed to persecute thee, resting not until they procure thy destruction. Such has been the fate of nearly all those who have endeavored to enlighten the people; and such will ultimately be thine, if thou wilt persist in following their footsteps in neglecting the warning I give thee."

"Great God!" exclaimed Jesus in a commiserative tone of voice. "if such be the fate of those who endeavor to improve mankind, how will the world ever be made virtuous and happy?"

"The Great God of Nature made man," replied the genius impressively. "If he should think that mankind needs improving, he, no doubt, will do it himself, or cause his work gradually to improve itself. It certainly looks presumptuous for a man to think himself capable of improving what God has made before he understands his own nature or the nature and design of mankind whom he wishes to improve. Leave God's work to God, and let every man who thinks himself superior to his fellow mortals, endeavor to improve himself. The Great God of Nature works by efficient means to accomplish his own ends, and no doubt mankind after passing through a succession of self-exalted grades, will ultimately arrive at that state to which he is destined."

"Then thou thinkest that an appeal to man's sense of reason and virtue will be of no effect in producing an amelioration in his condition?" observed Jesus inquiringly.

"Certainly not," replied the genius. "I know it would be quite futile. There is no such thing as a general perception of reason and virtue among a people; every one has his own perception of things that he thinks will suit himself, which he calls his reason and virtue, and which will be quite different to those of his next door neighbor. All others will be quite different, one to the other; so that there will be as many perceptions of reason and virtue as there are people. Now, as this is true, would it not be vain and futile for a man to preach virtue, religion, morals and metaphysics to a nation of people, thinking to arrive at a general result, when left to their free minds to decide? It would be worse than futile—it would be absurd. The only possible way for a man to enlighten and benefit a nation, is for him, first, to seize and concentrate all the power of that nation within himself, and then if he should be a wise and virtuous man, he can coerce his people to do what is good for themselves, but not otherwise.

"Did Moses liberate his brethren from Egyptian bondage by preaching virtue and reason to the Egyptians? No; it was by force of numbers and arms. Did he establish his ideal God—the Great Jehovah—among his people, by preaching refined and abstruse doctrines among them? No; it was by the terror he created among them with his artificial thunder and lightning, the blowing of a brass trumpet, and the slaughter of a few thousand of his brethren. As long as Moses and his successors possessed this power over the Children of Israel, so long were they a people corresponding in character to the stern, cruel, fanatical and indomitable spirits that ruled over them. Thus it has been with all nations; thus it is with the present, and possibly will be the same of the future. The mass of mankind cannot be governed by appealing to their moral sentiments; they have no capacity to perceive the fitness of things for the general good; they have no gratitude for benefits conferred upon them, nor a just sense of manly dignity to lift them above petty interests, vices, frauds, or vindictive passions. There is but one thing they all acknowledge and bow to—that is Force."

"Thy views, as thou hast stated them," observed Jesus," may be the legitimate deductions of man's past history, and the present may seem to confirm them; but tell me, is man to continue always in this state of vice, ignorance and misery? Is there to be no starting point from which a new era is to commence, in which he shall make efforts to advance and improve his condition? I am of the opinion that era has now dawned. Opportunities are now great when a leader endowed with fortitude and good principles will not labor in vain in revolutionizing and reforming his fellow men. I cannot conceive that it will be displeasing to the Ruler of the Universe that one man shall endeavor to improve his fellow men by giving them enlightenment concerning the true principles of a happy and just life. With this view, I consider it my duty to run all ventures in undertaking the task, and with God's permission I will do it."

"Mark my words," said the genius in a stern tone of voice, though the glance he threw upon Jesus was one of commiseration, "from the admiration I conceived for thee and thy virtuous intentions, I wished to save thee from the fatal consequences of an error. I gave thee warning

133

to desist; I gave thee my reasons, and cited instances from the past history of man to confirm them; but thou dost still persist in thy infatuation to rush to thy own destruction. One other trial will I make, and then I will leave thee to do thy will. Suppose thou enterest upon the course thou designest, and meet with success at first, which is probable, I will now portray a picture of the future, which shall be as true to probability as the calculation that tomorrow's sun shall rise.

"Thou shalt teach the people thy principles, consisting of the purest morality, relating to their nature and duties in life. Thou shalt give them the most exalted conceptions of a Deity, and enlighten them concerning the laws of the Universe; teach them their duty one to another; obedience to their rulers, and inculcate within them a love for all mankind. By this course thou wilt make many converts; some will understand thee, and some will follow from example. Thou wilt become popular among the people, having power over their minds. Thus far thou wilt be successful, but mark well what will follow:

"The truth of thy doctrines and thy popularity among the people will make thee enemies; some, from envy of thy power over the minds of the people; some will consider their interests injured by thy doctrines and works; others, who are dependent upon the institutions of the day, will be afraid that thy enlightenment of the people will ruin them. Then they will all combine to persecute and destroy thee. Misrepresentations and vile accusations they will disseminate concerning thee; charges will be preferred against thee, and then thy doom will be condemnation, ruin, and perhaps destruction by thy enemies."

Jesus shuddered.

"That," continued the Genius, "will be the evil result to thyself only. Now see what will follow to mankind at large:

"Thy death will give a new impulse to the dissemination of thy doctrines, or those which will be passed under thy name. Thou wilt be considered a martyr; which will make new converts daily. Ambitious and interested men will rise among them as leaders and expounders of thy doctrines and intentions; some additions and some omissions will be made. Then some misconceptions and misconstructions will take place; then a few fables and a great many lies will be added, so that, at length, there will be scarcely a precept, a principle, or a fact of thy original doctrines that will be taught by thy successors; yet every teacher will utter his fables, his lies, his vulgarisms and misconceptions in thy name, and call it gospel. Every teacher will gather what few facts he can concerning thy history, and add to them what fiction and lies he thinks proper, so that in course of time there will be a thousand histories of thee consisting of the most absurd and monstrous fictions,—each one differing from the others, and scarcely an item of truth in the whole. As time passes on new converts will be made who will disperse themselves far and wide into many countries. New forms and additional doctrines will be added to thine until thy original principles will assume a dark, gloomy and absurd system of superstition, which will be called a religion. There will be a wild fascination in it, which will create a fanatical zeal in its followers. In the commencement the converts of this new religion as they spread themselves over the world, will encounter great persecution from the old established authorities of previous systems of superstition. Tens and hundreds of thousands will undergo martyrdom in thy name, thinking themselves happy to die possessing thy doctrines, when at the same time they will be entirely ignorant of thy principles.

"The time at length will come when thy followers will predominate in the land; then a grand system of priesthood will be established with a supreme head, who, possessed of political power, will arrogate to himself a spiritual one. He will assume to hold the keys of heaven, pointing out the way for others to go, forgiving sins, and damning all who do not follow his suggestions and commands. The rage or persecution will now be turned; thy followers will be the persecutors. In thy name will they condemn the innocent, the just, the philosopher, and exterminate them with the sword, the rack, the gibbet and fire, calling upon them to repent and confess that thou art the Holy One, for whom all these murderous acts are consummated. The time will come when schisms will arise on doctrinal points, when one part of a people will believe this, and another that; the people of one nation will prefer this doctrine, and the people of another nation will believe that doctrine; then hatred will arise among nations. They will go forth to battle, mutilate and destroy each other in thy name. Each party will put up prayers to thee in the supernal world, calling upon thee for thy assistance to help them slaughter each other, and when one party shall gain an advantage in battle they will sing praises in honor of thee for the help thou hast given them in destroying their fellow men. Thus the world will be deluged with blood. Mankind instead of progressing will retrograde in their nature and become demons. The earth will become a slaughter-house, all to the glory of thy name. The minds of men will be filled with gloom, fanatical zeal, and a base, absurd superstition. They will live in dread and die in terror. Arts, sciences, literature, and all refinements will be banished from society temporarily; for nothing good will be enabled to exist where man is so cursed by the horrid superstition which will be built upon thy original virtuous principles. Like a huge demon it will ride upon the neck of society, making all mankind wretched and the whole earth a hell. Thus, however noble and benevolent may be thy intent, thy doctrines and name will prove for many centuries the curse of mankind!"

* * * * * * *

135

With a piercing shriek Jesus awoke from his unquiet sleep. Terror was depicted upon his countenance, and he trembled in every nerve. The external scene of his abode and locality impressed his senses, when he found that all he thought he had just experienced was no more than a dream. Still the vision was fixed in his mind, and the voice of the Genius still rung in his ear: "The Curse of Mankind!" He shuddered at the awful thought.

Just at this point of time, John of Galilee, the young companion of Jesus, and Judas in company, were approaching the grotto, when perceiving Jesus they saw that he was in a troubled state. They immediately rushed towards him and seized him by the hands.

"Dearest brother," cried John with much alarm expressed in his fair youthful countenance, "what aileth thee?"

"Dear master," said Judas, as he endeavored to assume an expression of fearful solicitude, "tell thy devoted servant and follower what it is that disturbs thee."

Jesus leaned upon John's shoulder, and with his right hand covering his eyes, he remained silent for a time, endeavoring to recover his thoughts and composure, but at length he replied:

"My friends, pardon me for having given you any alarm. I have been sleeping, and have had a dream so replete with terrible images that it shook me to the soul; and since I have awakened I find my nerves sympathetically affected by the same; but all will be well in a little time."

"Impart to us, dear brother, the nature of this dream," said John in a soft child-like voice. "Perhaps we can give some interpretation of it, or at least give comfort by our counsel."

"Let us be seated, then, and I will do so," returned Jesus as he bent his steps to the grotto, followed by his attendants.

The interior of the grotto was a plain circular chamber, without any furniture excepting a part being elevated around the wall, which was covered with rushes and coarse cloth, serving as seats and couches.

The parties entering, seated themselves and reclined at their ease. Jesus, after receiving a refreshment of wine and water at the hands of Judas, commenced to relate his dream; and as he proceeded in the narrative, the large blue eyes of John were expressive of wonderment, while Judas gave many demonstrations of being equally affected.

John of Galilee was a great believer in spirits visiting mankind to guard or interrupt them in their doings and intentions. Some of these spirits he believed to be of a friendly, and some of a malignant nature so whenever anything of an extraordinary nature occurred to men, John endeavored to account for it by his philosophy of spirits. Thus when Jesus had related his dream, John observed:

"My dear brother, there is no doubt that this dreadful dream has been produced by one of the evil spirits—perhaps the great Arch Fiend himself—for he is capable of assuming any character and speaking in any strain. He can pretend to be as pious as the High Priest, or he can speak with the wisdom of a philosopher. There is no doubt it was he who appeared to thee. He has been enabled to see the good thou art about to do for mankind, and as he wishes men to continue in their old ways of wickedness, he wishes to prevent thee in thy design of reforming them by impressing thee with the idea that evil will come of thy labors instead of good."

John then appealed to Judas to know if he did not think that to be the true solution of the matter, when the latter, after a few moments reflection, in which he found it would suit his purposes, gave John to understand that he was of the same opinion.

"It may be as thou sayest, John," replied Jesus, "for I am not much acquainted with the nature of evil spirits; but I rather think that my dream proceeded from some doubts and conflicting ideas I had previous to my going to sleep."

Some time afterwards this dream was given to the people by Judas in a modified state. He represented the Arch Fiend tempting Jesus in the wilderness, offering him all the world to forego his intentions.

There was some further conversation upon this subject, which at length was lost sight of by Jesus observing:

"My friends, it is my wish that we depart from this locality tomorrow. We will commence our travels, and wend our way to my native village in Galilee—to Nazareth where I will commence the great task I have imposed upon myself. May God give me strength to proceed, and success in my undertakings. John, thou must attend to my person and be the first officer between me and others. Judas shall carry the bag, and be our provider in all things necessary to us on our journey and when we sojourn. After a while, I will take to me more followers who shall aid me in my endeavors; for we know that the greater the number of workmen in the vineyard the greater will be the produce. Then let every thing be prepared, and by sunrise tomorrow we will bid adieu to this, our abode."

137

VISION TENTH

HOUSE OF THE VIRGIN IN JERUSALEM RESTORED

Fifteen hills with verdant slopes surround a fertile spot wherein a village stands, which is bordered with stately palm trees and rich gardens, hedged around with prickly pear, that radiate from the village to the base of the hills. Mount Tabor with its rounded dome is seen in the north-east; Mount Hermon's white top in the distant north; in the west is Mount Carmel, and on the south stretches the broad plains of Esdraelon.

The village inhabitants are not numerous, consisting principally of agriculturists, with a few tradesfolk. The habitations are rectangular, built of stone and timber, with flat roofs, and mostly painted white. There is one building larger than the rest enclosed by a wooden fence, between which and the building is a smooth green sward bordered with flowers. This edifice is the village school and synagogue. At the north-west of the village is a large spring, which is arched over with stone, and not far from the south-west end of the village there is a sudden descent into a deep ravine. The ground at this spot consists of massive rocks, the brow of which overhangs the deep abyss below; about a hundred feet to the eastward of this, there is a gradual descent, where a road leads on to the plains of Jordan and the lake of Genesareth. This village was Nazareth, recorded as the place where Jesus had been bred from his infancy, and where he had received the rudiments of his education.

The glorious orb of day had nearly run its daily course; its golden disk and dazzling sheen were fast sinking from view behind Mount Carmel, when three weary travellers arrived at the spring of Nazareth, with the intent of quenching their excessive thirst. There were several females around the well with their vessels to obtain the cool water for their families' evening consumption. Some of them were young maidens, and some matrons of elder years; all of whom as soon us they saw the travellers and understood their wants presented their vessels to them to drink from. One of the young damsels, a finely formed brunette, with dark hair hanging in wild profusion around her naked neck and shoulders, wearing a single garment of blue stuff, passing over her left shoulder, girded about the waist and hanging in folds to her ankles, approached the tallest of the travellers and presented her vessel for him to drink. The traveller, with graceful bow to the lovely maiden, availed himself of her offer; when, having satisfied his thirst, he returned the vessel to her hands and addressed her in tones of great sweetness:

"Sweet maiden," he said, "I thank thee for thy welcome favor. Tell me of what family thou art in the village."

"Sir," replied the maiden timidly, "there is no family in the village I can claim as mine, for I am a poor orphan."

"With whom dost thou live, then?" inquired the traveller.

"I am living, sir, with the matron Mary, the widow of Joseph the Carpenter," replied the maiden.

"Ah! she lives, then?" exclaimed the traveller; and then he added: "She is well, I hope?"

"Alas! sir," responded the maiden, in a solemn tone, "my kind mistress is far from being well; she has been sick for several days, and now it is thought she is on the couch of death."

The traveller gave a sudden start, and his expression bespoke great distress of feeling. After a few moments, in which he endeavored to recover from his painful emotions, he said hurriedly:

"Hasten thee to thy home, and I will follow thee there."

The maiden instantly placed the water-vessel upon her head, and with a quick yet graceful step, took her way to the village.

Then Jesus, for it was he, turning to his two companions, John and Judas, said to them:

"My friends, I must leave you for a while. Go to the village inn and abide there till I come."

Then wrapping his mantle carefully around him that his person could not be distinguished, he, with hasty steps, followed the damsel into the village, and into the house whither she went.

139

Within a chamber of one of the dwellings in Nazareth several of the neighbors were assembled around the couch of a dying woman. They were mostly females, though several of the other sex attended occasionally. One of the males present was the Rabbi of the village, who was distinguished from the others by the long, black robe he wore, and the white tire or twisted cloth around his head. His long, white beard and moustache, and the solemn expression of his mien, were in character with his office, whether in conformity with his own or not. These good people had assembled to attend to the invalid's last wishes, and to administer all the comfort and consolation it was in their power to do, to smooth the path by which her spirit was to depart from this world to the dark shades of death.

The sick woman seemed to be a person in the first step of declining age. She lay upon her couch with the pallor of death on her countenance, breathing with short, quick inspiration, as though the machinery of life was making strenuous efforts to retain the vital spark. Her bust was elevated by means of several pillows, with her head thrown back and her eyes closed, though awake and sensible to all around her.

The worthy Rabbi had just terminated a pious exhortation, in which he endeavored to impress the idea that she would soon find relief and recompense from all earthly troubles, in the bosom of Father Abraham. Then there was a silence of some minutes, occasionally broken by the sobs and wailings of the visitors. At length the eyes of the sick woman opened, when turning her feeble gaze upon one of the women present, she told her to get something from under the pillow of the couch and give it to the Rabbi. The woman did as she was requested, when she produced to view a small casket of ornamented leather, which she put into the hands of the Rabbi. Then the sick woman, turning her eyes towards the latter, with great effort, managed to address him in a feeble voice:

"Rabbi, one reason I have for thy presence here, is to commit to thy charge and safe-keeping some documents and a relic which are to be placed in the hands of my long lost boy, Jose, should he ever return to his native village. Tell him, if thou seest him, to pardon me for not making the communication before. Tell him that I have done all for his happiness, as I thought, and that I could not die in peace unless I should declare all the truth to him at last. Rabbi, wilt thou promise to fulfill my request?"

"Dear sister," responded the Rabbi, "be thou comforted on that point. I solemnly promise to do all thou wishest me, if he ever returns to this village during my life."

"I am grateful, Rabbi," answered the dying woman. "Now I am more at ease; but I could wish, had it pleased God, to see my dear Jose once more before I die."

During the delivery of the last few words the door opened, when Jesus entered the chamber and approached the couch of the dying woman. He then fell upon his knees at her side and cried affectionately:

"Mother! dearest mother! it is I."

Then seizing her hand he pressed it to his lips as the tears trickled fast down his cheeks. The dying woman, on hearing his voice, suddenly sprang up to a sitting posture, and gazed upon his countenance with wonder and great joy. Then raising her eyes to heaven, she uttered one loud, shrill shriek of exultation and fell back upon the pillows. Her last effort expended the remaining sum of her strength; her vital spark then fled, and the lease of her earthly tenement was terminated. Her features relaxed, for she was a corpse; and Jesus accompanied the departed spirit to the Throne of God with his prayers.

An hour at least had passed, when Jesus arose from his prostrate position. He looked around him and found that all the visitors had left excepting the Rabbi, who, in a tone of solemn sympathy, observed, as he held forth the casket:

"It would be presumptuous in me to check or disapprove of the natural outpourings of sympathy and pure love which thy tears demonstrate —tears of regret at the departure of a near and dear relative, suggesting in their course a multitude of fond remembrances that existed between you in by-gone days. Tears of affection are a just tribute to the worthy dead—a divine soother of our inward sorrow, rendering us humble and calm, enabling us to view justly the decrees of God, and appreciate the precarious tenure of our mortal state. My friend, just before thy appearance thy mother confided to me a trust, which I solemnly promised to guard and fulfill. She gave me this casket to keep in safety, with strict injunctions that if ever thou shouldst return to thy native village, I should place it in thy hands. It contains something of importance, of which she has kept thee in ignorance. She begs of thee to forgive her for what she has done, as she said she did what she thought best for thy happiness. I now acquit myself of my trust."

Then the Rabbi placed the casket in the hands of Jesus, who received it, wondering what could be the nature of its contents; but suppressing his curiosity for the time he expressed his thanks to the Rabbi for his services, and appointed him superintendent over his mother's funeral, and took leave of him for that time. Jesus then quietly wended his way through the dark village to the public inn where he found his companions, with whom he passed an hour, relating what had occurred since he left them. After a while, he sought an opportunity to be alone, when he eagerly opened the casket and saw what it contained.

*   *   *   *   *   *   *

Several days had passed, in which Jesus buried his mother and mourned her loss in sincere sorrow, according to the usual rites and customs. It was now the Sabbath day; the synagogue was open, and the villagers congregated there to pray and hear the morning services read. Thither Jesus and his companions went.

Again the scene before the medium's mental eye undergoes a change. The scene presented the interior of the synagogue,—a rectangular building of very simple structure, and void of ornament. Light was admitted from the upper part of the walls through window casements. From the walls a few feet inward a passage was formed along the four sides, and in the middle of the building a square space was divided off with a balustrade on the four sides, in the centre of which was a rostrum or speaking desk elevated two or three feet from the floor. Between the balustrade and the exterior passages the space was filled up with plain wooden benches, on which the people could sit, recline, or kneel at their choice.

Nearly all the villagers were present, and many persons from the country around, for a curiosity had been aroused in consideration of the strangers presence among them, especially of Jesus who claimed Nazareth as his native place, and was known to the greater part of the people under the name of Jose. It was also whispered among the people that this Jose was going to address them at the conclusion of the morning service.

At the usual time the services commenced by a young student entering the enclosure habited in a long white robe, who held in his hand a scroll or book called the Esdreth, from which he read a number of prayers in a shrill recitative tone, accompanied by the people in certain parts repeating the same. This lasted a few minutes, then an aged Rabbi entered the enclosure and mounted the rostrum attended by the young reciter of prayers. The latter presented the Rabbi a book called the Shema, from which he read in a distinct, impressive voice several chapters or parts. He then read from another book called the Book of Law several parts, and concluded from another of the Prophets. He then announced to the people that the services being over, any one was at liberty to speak or ask a question. Then Jesus arose from among the people, and with a steady unassuming gait entered the enclosure and mounted the rostrum which the Rabbi had just left. The Rabbi inquired of Jesus if he wanted a book, when the latter replied that the Book of the Prophets would do.

There was now a general stir and excitement among the people, all eyes being placed upon the handsome and dignified person before them. For the first few moments a general buzzing, whispering noise was heard; but as soon as Jesus spread open the book and intimated that he was ready to address them, all present became as silent as death. Jesus uplifted his eyes for a few moments as though invoking the Divine Power, then glancing around at the people he pointed to a passage in the book, and read it in a mild, distinct and impressive voice:

" 'The Spirit of the Lord is upon me, because he has enabled me to preach the true light to the poor; to bring good tidings unto the meek; to build up the broken hearted; to proclaim liberty to captives, and break their prison bonds.' Thus spoke the Prophet Isaiah.

"Brethren, I do not presume to say or hazard a conjecture as to what were the designs or impressions of the Prophet when he made this declaration. Some may think that he alluded to himself, and others may think that he alluded to another that is to come. Whichever way it may be I shall not heed it in that respect; but I will endeavor to show you what is the meaning of it, and whether it be applicable to the present time and circumstances. In contemplating this declaration by my own inward light, I am enabled to see the design of the Prophet, the meaning of the declaration and its applicability to the present time, all of which I will explain and make clear to your comprehension.

"In the first place, this declaration must not be understood in the present sense and literal meaning, word for word. I shall therefore divide it into several subjects, and explain them separately; by so doing I shall be fulfilling in a measure the design of the Prophet. 'The Spirit of the Lord is upon me.' What is meant by the Spirit of the Lord? When I say Lord, I mean the great God of the Universe, the great Father of us all, and not the absurd, irrational, vindictive being our forefathers gave us to worship under the name of Jehovah. The Spirit of the great God of the Universe, what is it? As the great God exists within the vast universe contemplating his mighty works, he issues a divine essence which he diffuses through all the boundless space to all material and spiritual nature, whether it be a single atom or congregated masses of worlds, imparting to all his divine will and power. To the primitive masses he imparts his power of motion and design, which ultimate in the formation of worlds, of minerals and vegetables. Then to these he imparts physical sympathies and appetent carnal powers, which ultimate in animals of low degree. Then to them, by gradual degrees, his divine essence imparts the powers of conception, the formation of mind, of reason in various degrees, until man is at length established. Thus, man is so constituted, that he balances between his corporeal cravings and the impulses of divine intelligence. If his corporeal nature predominates, he is a brute; and if the divine impulses of intelligence predominates, he is a man allied to God who made him, in his divine spiritual nature. If, then, a man shall live a pure and rational life in this world, giving so much attention to his corporeal nature as his wants require, and devoting the remainder of his energies to the improvement of his spiritual part, then the latter will become expanded, ennobled and refined,—always struggling for, and aspiring to, the grand, sublime and holy.

"A man thus living becomes in body pure, chaste and healthy, under due submission to his spiritual part. His intelligence becomes greater than that of other men; and that spark of divinity of which his soul consists, becomes sublimated, having the power of diffusing itself like a ray of light far into the universe, when at times it comes in contact with the divine essence as coming from the Divine Father. The spiritual part of man thus situated is then in communion with the Spirit of God, and thus is explained that part of the Prophet's declaration: 'The Spirit of the Lord is upon me.' Such a state of man's spiritual exaltation is true inspiration.

"The Spirit of the Lord is upon me because he has enabled me to preach the true light to the poor.' Now, brethren, let us examine what is the true light, and who are the poor. By the true light, we may understand a knowledge of God's works as pertaining to man. This knowledge will embrace many subjects, the least of which is of great importance. We will say for instance, that it is necessary man shall know the design of God in creating him; then he should know how to live a pure and righteous life; how to improve and perpetuate that life bodily and spiritually; what is dissolution or death, and if there be a future existence after death for man, what are the necessary preparations to insure this after life. These items of knowledge constitute the true light as pertaining to man, and the source by which they are revealed is true inspiration. But where, brethren, is this true light to be found? Where is the true source that gives it—the truly inspired man? Shall we find it in those books called sacred? Shall we find the truly inspired man among those men the books call the Prophets? No, my brethren, those books contain not the true light. They do not contain the least true idea of the nature of God, his designs in creating man, or man's true nature; neither do they contain a code of wise laws teaching how to live purely, justly and righteously, or give a rational glimpse of the life hereafter.

"Shall we look to those Prophets for a source of true inspiration? for lives of purity, for words of wisdom and knowledge beyond the common sphere of life? No, my brethren. The Prophets were very common, ignorant men,—ignorant of those things of which they pretended to prophesy. Examine the books, then, and you will find that the God by whom these Prophets were inspired, as represented by them, is no more than the portraiture of a tyrannical king, absurd, fickle, cruel and ignorant. If such be the God Jehovah as they have portrayed him, what are they themselves? The greater part of them were cunning impostors; some, fanatical zealots; some, perfect madmen, and all gloomy minded and desperately ignorant, who were continually denouncing woes to man. I do not wish you to understand, my brethren, that there never were any truly inspired men, but I wish to convey the idea that they are not to be

144

found among those mentioned in the Sacred Books.

"Whatever claims other men may have to true inspiration, I know not. I will not dispute the assumption that there are such, for when I examine my own nature I am enabled to say that it is possible. Yes, my brethren, it is possible. You behold in me one who under the supernal favors of the Divine Father, has undergone more than a common mortal's experience on these matters. Many years have I devoted to the arduous study of our common nature, of God and the Universe; many times have I been exalted above my common nature; many things have I seen that other men see not; many things have I learned that other men can not learn, and many things I do that other men can not do. Yet I am not so conceited or crazy as to consider myself more than mortal. But, notwithstanding, I can place my hand upon my heart and solemnly affirm, in the words of Isaiah:

"The Spirit of the Lord is upon me, because he hath enabled me to preach the true light to the poor."

"But now my brethren what are we to understand by the poor? Are we to understand those who have not worldly wealth, consisting of rich garments, fine houses, lands and shekels of gold and silver? No! Such is not the meaning. It has reference to the spirit. A man may have all the riches of a Solomon, and still be poor in spirit. A poor man in this sense is one who does not know that he possesses a spark of the Divine nature within him; he is entirely ignorant of his nature, of God and the universe; he knows not the design of his existence, or how to live purely and justly; nor can he perceive or appreciate the great changes that take place through death, leading to a more exalted life. All his ideas and aspirations are limited to the earth. Like one of the lower order of brutes, he gropes his way through life with his head down, seeking for something to satisfy his animal nature; he seeks for nothing to change the dull monotony of his life, but such things as engender petty strifes, envy, and low ambition. Such a man, my brethren is poor indeed, for that divine jewel that God gave him is buried and lost to him in the depth of his ignorance, being covered with the rubbish of this world. Such is the poor man, whether he be a beggar or a king. 0! my brethren, if there are any among you who feel thus poor, and wish to forsake so wretched a condition, let me, humble as I am, enlighten your understanding as to what are the true riches of life. Let me aid you to disinter that divine spark of immortal life, the divine soul that God gave to you, that lives, though buried and lost within you. That precious immortal thing, disenthralled and brought to your view, will make the sparkling diamond seem dull in comparison by its surpassing lustre. Its divine light will guide you through all the dark paths of this world of evil deeds and tribulation, revealing all the true riches of this life, worthy of pursuit and possession. Then, my dear brethren, with the assistance I shall give you by my future discourses, you will know what is true life; you will become rich in health and purity of body and innocent enjoyments. Your minds will become rich in intelligence, of great ennobling ideas, comprehensive of your own nature, and of the true God. Your nerves will vibrate in unison with the harmonious symphony of all the magnificent phenomena of the Universe. You will be rich in hope, which will triumph over the dark shades of death, and rich in anticipation of that happy state which all, who are just in heart and exalted in mind, will enjoy in future.

"Such, my brethren, is the meaning of the true light that I shall preach to the poor, and the good tidings I shall bring to the meek. Now let us examine the other part of the prophet's declaration:

"To bind up the broken-hearted and proclaim liberty to the captives."

"Who are the broken-hearted and the captives, but those who suffer daily and hourly in this wretched state of society, through the instrumentality of the tyrants and impostors who abuse and shackle their understandings? There are many men who can see their mental and spiritual degradation, who would willingly strive to shake off the shackles that bind them, but they dare not. Their minds are so enthralled by gloomy superstition and stern, cruel customs, that they know not how to proceed to regain their freedom; yet they sigh for a change of condition; their wishes and hopes flee before them, and dark despair fills up the void. These are the captives and broken-hearted, to whom I proclaim that freedom is nigh, and an ointment prepared for their wounds.

"Our ancestors, were slaves to the Egyptians until Moses arose among them, when he changed that species of bondage for one of another kind. Ever since then our people have been held in mental slavery under the dominion of a vile selfish priesthood. Yes, brethren, your minds are locked up within the bounds of a base destructive superstition. You are debarred by this priesthood from receiving the true light; your minds are darkened by the grossest ignorance, which prevents you from perceiving your true nature, as designed by the true God of the Universe. But the time shall come, brethren, when all these mental bonds shall be rent asunder; then you will be enabled to come forth to the true light of day. You will cast your eyes around and see the disseminated rays of God-like intelligence, which will enable you to see yourselves and all other things; then you will be enabled to lift up your heads with the true dignity of manhood. You will then learn the fact that the creator of man is not Jehovah, the God of the Jews, but the true God of the Universe. Yes, my brethren, you will see and feel the true God-head in all the magnificent phenomena of nature; you will learn that he is the Father of us all; that Universal Nature is our Mother, and that we are their children, and as we progress in life, by living in purity and spiritual exaltation, we may ultimately lay claim to be the true sons of God."

Any further discourse by Jesus was now prevented by a great clamor arising among the congregation.

In the commencement of his address the people seemed excited with a lively curiosity, and as he proceeded to bring to their views the many new ideas and important truths, which he delivered with impressive enunciation, they became greatly interested, many expressing their convictions of the truth by sudden involuntary exclamations. But towards the latter part when he bore severely upon the vileness of the priesthood, the grossness of their superstition and mistaken views of the true God, then their old prejudices were awakened and a reaction took place. A visible emotion of displeasure was manifested by blowing, hissing and spitting, while many cried aloud, "blasphemy! blasphemy!" At length, when Jesus had delivered the last sentence, the Rabbi of the Synagogue, with distorted features and eyes flashing with indignation, sprang upon a bench, shouting "blasphemy! blasphemy!" Then he seized his long, black robe with the desperation of a madman, and rent it from top to bottom, and afterwards seizing his long white beard with both his hands, he tore a portion of it out, which he scattered among the people, calling aloud upon them to avenge the God of Moses.

The whole congregation were now in the greatest commotion and confusion, being separated in many groups, in angry altercation and violent gesticulation. Jesus perceiving that he could no longer be heard, made no further attempt to continue his discourse. He raised himself erect as he stood in the rostrum, and waving his hand around, he said in a loud commanding voice:

"Peace, brethren, peace!"

Whether the people were struck with awe by the commanding tone and aspect of Jesus, or whether their commotion settled down by a newly awakened curiosity, they, however, became immediately quiet and calm; their eyes were intently fixed upon Jesus as he descended from the rostrum and quietly approached the Rabbi who was still standing upon the bench, violently vociferating and gesticulating, hurling charges and imprecations against Jesus. As the latter approached and confronted him, in a loud, imperative voice and commanding mien, he said to him:

"What wouldst thou?"

"'I would expose and denounce thee as an impostor, a liar and blasphemer," replied the Rabbi with increased rage.

"Wherein have I merited these angry expressions of thine?" demanded Jesus coolly.

"Thou hast blasphemed," answered the Rabbi, "in denying our Great God Jehovah, denouncing all our Prophets as impostors, and spoken vilely of our holy priesthood. And forsooth, although thou art known to all our people as the son of Joseph, the carpenter, yet thou hast the audacity to represent thyself as the son of God."

"Not as the son of Jehovah whom in thy ignorance thou callest God," rejoined Jesus; "but the living, true God of the Universe I claim as my father. Dost thou dispute my word?"

"I do," answered the Rabbi with terror in his eyes, "and denounce it as a blasphemous lie."

"Then I will make thee from thine own mouth confirm the words that I have spoken," returned Jesus sternly. "I call all the brethren present to bear witness."

Then Jesus caught the glance of the Rabbi's eyes, and from a glance of his own he beamed forth an unseen subtle power; like a serpent charming a bird, his figure was erect and bold, and eyes immovable. At the same time he stretched forth his hands, holding them for a few moments on a plane with the Rabbi's head, and then drew them gently downward. The invisible power was all-subduing. The Rabbi started as though he had received a sudden shock; his countenance expressed great terror, but it soon subsided; his arms fell powerless by his sides; his eyes closed; his features became composed, and he seemed like one standing in a sleep. Jesus relaxed the severity of his countenance as he moved towards the rostrum, and at the same time the Rabbi descended from the bench and followed him. With quiet and simultaneous steps they both entered within the enclosure, when Jesus pointing to the rostrum, the Rabbi mounted the steps and stood before the people, unconscious of all around him.

While these proceedings were going on between Jesus and the Rabbi, the people seemed to be equally spellbound. Not a sound was heard or a movement seen, for they were all gazing in breathless astonishment at what took place before their eyes. So mystified and awe struck were they, that Jesus was regarded by them as something more than mortal man. Perhaps he was a God, they thought; perhaps a demon, or an enchanter at least. About a minute after the Rabbi had stood in immovable submission, Jesus spoke to him in a loud voice, and said: "Rabbi, declare to all present my claim to parentage." Then the Rabbi, in a solemn and distinct voice, said:

"Jesus of Nazareth is not the son of Joseph and Mary. He knows not who is his earthly father, but he claims the true God of the Universe as the father of his spirit. He is truly a son of God in a spiritual sense."

"Now, my brethren," said Jesus, addressing the people, "bear testimony of this man's words to himself."

Then Jesus waved his hand towards the Rabbi, who immediately became restored to his natural self, when Jesus left the enclosure and passed through the people to depart from the synagogue.

As soon as the Rabbi was restored to his natural state some of the people rushed up to him, and questioned him concerning what he had said in the rostrum. He denied any knowledge thereof, and said it must have been a trick of the Evil One, by whose agency this Jesus had worked. He then became more enraged than ever against the latter, and advised them to seize him and throw him over the brow of the precipice, as a worker of sorceries and mischief. He soon collected a small party, and rushed forward in pursuit of Jesus, whom they overtook at the door of the synagogue. They accordingly took hold of him, and with wild cries and shouts, they hurried him through the village to the south-west end, at the brink of which was the ravine, where they would have thrown him down. But as they approached within a few paces of the spot four men armed with clubs rushed from behind a hedge, and immediately fell upon them with great force, so that within a second or two, six or eight were laid prostrate with broken heads. The remainder of the party finding such an unexpected onslaught, became seized with terror, and accordingly fled from the scene as fast as they could, leaving Jesus alone and unhurt. Two of the rescuers immediately took Jesus by the hands, and hurried him to the eastern road that led to the plains below. One of these was John of Galilee, and the other was John's brother, James; a tall, robust young man, with a long beard and hair of a sandy color, who happened to be at Nazareth at this time on a matter of business. The other two rescuers were Judas, who acted as captain of the band, and Cosbi his private aid. These brought up in the rear, taking care that Jesus should not be under the necessity of receiving any more such inhospitable receptions as that given to him by his loving townsfolks.

VISION ELEVENTH

SIMON

The noon-day sun dispensed its rays of light and fructifying power down upon the sparkling waters of the lake of Genesareth, whose fair bosom was dotted with many fishing and trading vessels returning with the profits of the morning's toils, or exchanging wares between shore and shore.

On the eastern shore the view is bounded by the tall, even line of mountains, which of yore bounded the land of the Ammonites; on the west by the long, uneven range of Judean mountains, the long, arched line of Tabor is seen, and the square-shaped hill with two tops, called the Hill of Beatitudes. Commencing from the shore at the north, the western mountains recede inwards in the form of a half-moon for about seven miles along the lake leaving a plain about five miles wide, well watered by springs. This was a beautiful, fertile spot, well cultivated and well inhabited, there being several neat villages around; the remainder of the plain being divided into fields, orchards and gardens. This spot was called the land of Genesareth.

At the northern extremity of this spot the town of Capernaum was seen, and below it, south, bordering on the lake, the small village of Bethsaida; on the opposite shore there was another of the same name. Between the lake and the cultivated plain was a broad, open, sandy beach, with a border of thorn jungle between it and the former. The most north-eastern point of view presented the dome-shaped hill from which issued several warm springs that sent their steaming waters over the beach into the lake. The most southern point of view is where the Judean mountains curve in towards the lake at the extremity of the cultivated plain before spoken of.

Along the edge of this lake a level beach runs the whole way round, from north to south; the southern end is roughly strewn with black and white stones of volcanic origin. But the central or northern part is formed of smooth sand and a texture of shells and pebbles. Shrubs, too, of the tropical thorn, fringe the greater part of the line of shore, mingled here and there with the bright pink color of the Oleander. On this beach which runs like a white line all around the lake, the hills plant their dark bases, descending nowhere precipitately, but almost everywhere presenting an alternation of soft grassy slopes and rocky cliffs. Such was the scenery of the lake of Genesareth at the epoch here alluded to.

The Bethsaida situated on the north-western side of the lake was a small hamlet consisting of a few houses occupied by the fishermen and their families, they being of the most humble description. The walls were of stone; the roofs flat, and covered with rushes. There was an open piazza, with a few trees for shade, in front of each dwelling.

The largest house in the place fronted the lake, from which an extensive view could be taken over this inland sea, to the dark line of the Ammonite mountains in the background of the opposite shore. In the front of this house a covered piazza ran the whole length of it, along which was a rude bench used as a place of sitting and lounge. This part of the dwelling was shaded by a row of locust trees which were planted at a few feet distant, in a large yard, the latter being bounded by a low stone wall. Within this yard were several appurtenances connected with the fishing business, and for the use of the family.

The proprietor of this dwelling was one Simon, a tall portly man, with ruddy complexion and blue eyes; forehead broad, and rather low; nose nearly perpendicular, and gently rounded at the extremity; his mouth and lips small; chin rounded; dark brown hair flowing around his neck and shoulders, and his moustache and beard small, but full; he, in all respects, indicated a sanguine temperament and an expression of countenance generally agreeable.

His physiognomy would indicate that his moral qualities were boldness, self-confidence and a desire to progress in worldly affairs. He seemed to be one who could do a charitable act; to have a keen sense of justice, yet would have no objection to sacrifice the latter, if necessary, to any end that he thought would conduce to his advantage.

His dress consisted of a loose shirt and nether garment, of blue stuff, the latter reaching to his knees, with a leathern belt around his waist, in which was stuck a large knife, on the left side; his legs, arms and feet

151

were bare, being very much browned by exposure to the sun. Simon, upon particular occasions, wore a kind of loose vest and a mantle, for his body, a white tire for his head, and leathern buskins and sandals for his legs and feet. He was considered by his humble neighbors to be rich—for he owned two or three boats, the house he lived in, and a large stock of dried fish. Besides he was the master fisherman who had most of the others of Bethsaida in his employ. He was consequently considered in that small society as a person of consequence and importance.

Simon was sitting under his piazza surrounded by his men—a rough, hardy, sun-burnt, loosely clad set of fellows, with naked feet and legs, with ragged beards and tangled hair of various colors, uncombed and uncovered. Some of them were reclining on the bench, and others under the shade of the trees, reposing from their labors. They had just returned from their morning's fishing. Having met with fair success, their boats were hauled upon the shore, and the produce of their toil carried in baskets to the dwelling of the proprietor, where they were disposed of in the out-houses in the large yard.

Simon seemed to be in excellent humor, for the success of that day's fishing was greater than usual, and more than he expected.

"How many fishes didst thou say there were, brother Andrew?" inquired Simon of a tall robust man with short curly hair, who bore a resemblance in features to the speaker, though somewhat younger in years, for he was a brother.

"I counted forty, brother," answered Andrew, "and a very good number it is, considering the weight of them."

"But art thou sure there were forty?" inquired Simon with a lively interest expressed in his tone of voice.

"Yes, brother, I am sure," returned Andrew, "for I counted my fingers and thumbs four times over, and so I cannot be mistaken."

"Well, now, this is very singular," observed Simon, giving great emphasis to his words so that his hearers should not mistake what he was saying. "This day is my birth-day, and I am exactly forty years of age this very day. This I call a curious and lucky event."

All his hearers gave an exclamation of surprise and looked up to him wondering.

"Thou mayest well say a lucky event," remarked Andrew in a sulky tone, as though he were displeased with the turn of events in his brother's favor. "Thy life seems to be full of these lucky events. I know not how it is that God should favor thee more than me, yet so it is. Thou hast become rich while I with all my struggling to do well am no more than thy servant. I shall not be surprised if thou some day shouldst become the governor of a province."

Simon was a little displeased with the remarks of his brother, as they evidently showed that Andrew was envious of his prosperity; but as in his last remark he suggested the idea that he possibly might arrive at some distinction, that restored him to good humor, for he began to entertain the hope that such a thing was possible. Then turning to his brother with a smile upon his countenance, he said as he patted him upon the shoulder:

"Come, Andrew, let us not quarrel with our fortunes, but thank God for all things. If I have prospered hitherto, perhaps it will be thy good fortune by and by. Come! as this is my birth-day, and I have been lucky enough to take an extra draft of fishes, suppose we take an extra draught of wine, and make ourselves merry and contented."

To this proposition by Simon, Andrew and all the others quite willingly agreed; then jokes and good humor prevailed, and while the former ran into the house to get the wine, the latter banished his envious thoughts for the time.

In a few minutes Simon returned bearing upon his shoulder a large black goat skin containing about five gallons of wine, and in one hand he held a panier containing drinking cups or goblets made of beeves' horns. Placing the articles upon the floor, he called all his men around him, telling them to partake of the exhilarating juice to their heart's content. He then distributed the cups, and untying the neck of the goat skin bottle, poured out the crimson beverage and filled every man's cup to the brim. As easy as fishes could quaff water, so easy could these fishermen quaff wine; and in the ratio of quantity they poured down, so did the thermometer of their blood go up, until they attained such an easy state of good humor that jokes, stories and adventures were exchanged among them, which, to their simple minds, possessed a deep and marvellous interest.

Thus the party of fishermen continued in their hilarious enjoyment for the greater part of an hour, when another personage made his appearance on the scene. An old man entered the yard leaning upon his stick as he walked. He was bare headed, with long flowing white hair, bald on the top, very much tanned with the sun and wrinkled with old age.

As soon as he came within view, Simon caught sight of him first, when he exclaimed:

"By the God of Moses! here comes old Zebedee!"

Then he instantly prepared another cup of wine. In a little while the old man approached the party, when he made a general salutation, which was acknowledged by the others with vociferous demonstrations of welcome.

"Come, father Zebedee, take this cup of wine before thou speakest one word," said Simon as he proffered the cup. "I am sure this sultry day must have parched thy tongue. Come! thou art welcome."

The old man did not seem willing to reject the offer of friendship, for taking the cup of wine he made one long draught of it, which nearly deprived him of breath so great and powerful was it. Then said Simon as he patted him on the shoulder:

"Now, old father, tell us the news; but first of all, hast thou heard of thy son John?"

"Well, worthy Simon," replied old Zebedee, "I have news from Nazareth of a most wonderful nature."

"Oh! what is it?" exclaimed Simon and the others.

"And I have heard something of my son John," continued the old man, "but I know not which to begin with, so I must think a bit."

"Give us the news from Nazareth," said some of the party, while others wished him to state what he had heard from his son John.

"Patience, my good folks," cried the old man, as he seated himself upon the bench. Then all the party collected around to hear him. "I must tell it my own way, so do not interrupt me."

All parties being reduced to order, there was a general silence, when the old man spoke as follows:

"You all remember that some time ago John the Baptist was in this neighborhood preaching. I never liked that preacher, for he looks and speaks as though he were crazy-like, and I believe a great many folks who listen to him become so, too. Well, this old John preached many strange doctrines. One thing I remember in particular. He said there was somebody coming after him greater than he was. Well, I did not understand what he meant by that, whether he meant the one that was coming after him would be a giant, or whether he would be more crazy than John. However, so it was. My son John up to that time was a very steady boy, though he used to stay out all night sometimes, talking poetry to the moon; but he had a long talk with John the Baptist before he left, and two or three days after, my son John ran away from me. Well, it was ever so long before I heard of my son. At last I heard he had been seen in the company of a man that John the Baptist baptized and named Jesus. Then a few days ago I heard that there was a man arrived at Nazareth calling himself Jesus, who intended to deliver a discourse to the people of that village. Then I said to my son James: "Go to Nazareth and see this man; perhaps thou wilt find thy brother there; if so, bring him home." So James went according to my word; since then I have not heard from him. But I have heard something very strange from Nazareth. Well, it seems this man came to Nazareth, and proved to be a person who had been reared in that village from his infancy, by the name of Jose, son of Joseph the carpenter, and Mary his wife. No sooner did he come, then his mother died; he buried her and mourned for her some days, then he entered the synagogue and preached.

"Now comes the astonishing part of my news. It seems that this Jesus preached many strange things, so that the people were shocked. They cried out 'blasphemy!' and the Rabbi did the same. He accused Jesus of

154

saying that he was the Son of God. Jesus told the Rabbi that he would make him confess and declare the same before all the people. The Rabbi bid Jesus defiance, when Jesus cast a spell over him—made him mount the rostrum and declare to the people that Jesus was the Son of God. Jesus, after doing what he wished with the Rabbi, released him from the spell, and then was about leaving the synagogue, when the Rabbi caused the people to rise against him as a sorcerer. They took him, and would have thrown him down the ravine, but he escaped somehow. I understand my son John is with him. This is all I know about the affair, my friends. Perhaps we shall know more in a few days. I hope my two sons are safe, and will return to me."

All the parties were deeply interested in the narrative of old Zebedee, and completely astonished when the last act of Jesus was related. They knew not what to believe or how to comprehend it, but continued to express their wonder by various comical ejaculations.

"Well! did I ever hear anything like this before," cried Andrew, whose protruding blue eyes denoted the effect of the marvelous tale. "Well! this beats brother Simon's story of the big fish. This man Jesus, or whoever he is, to do the like of that, must be an enchanter, a sorcerer, or a— "

"Hold, Andrew, hold!" cried Simon, interrupting his brother in what he was about to say. "Do not say anything disrespectful of a man thou knowest not. I think I know a little about this Jesus, or Jose, that I will tell thee. Several years ago when I used to visit Nazareth, I was somewhat acquainted with a lad by the name of Jose. If this Jesus be the same person I knew under the name of Jose, we ought not to say anything wrong or disrespectful of him, for I am sure he can not deserve it. The lad Jose I speak of was very handsome, amiable, kind and gentle; besides, he was very learned, or thought to be so, and I am sure he was incapable of becoming an impostor, or anything bad."

Simon paused for a moment as he cast his glance in the direction of the yard gate, when he added:

"But look! Here comes one who can give us information. He is well acquainted with the people of Nazareth."

By Simon's last remark, all eyes were turned towards the entrance of the yard, when they perceived an old man advancing, with a very peculiar shaped head that bore some resemblance in form to an inverted bell, and which was covered with short, white curly hair, very much like sheep's wool. His head was broad and bulging at the top; his forehead and temples tapering down until joined by a long, narrow, meagre face, which seemed to have the expressions of doubt, suspicion and acerbity of temper.

This new comer, when he approached the party in the piazza, gave a short, surly nod of his head by way of salutation, then glanced around him with seeming distrust and disapprobation of the company.

155

"Well, Nathaniel, how are the times?" inquired Simon, by way of a leader in conversation. "I have just been speaking of thee."

"Oh!" exclaimed the old man with great indifference, "nothing good I judge, for one person seldom speaks good of another behind his back."

"I was merely stating that I thought thou couldst give us some information upon a certain matter," added Simon.

"Oh!" again ejaculated Nathaniel. "People do not want information, they want confirmation of their own notions and ways."

"Do not be so snappish and surly, Nathaniel," remarked Simon, "We merely wish to ask thy opinion of a certain man, of whom we think thou knowest something. We want to know something of his history, nature and qualities, for he is now about making some excitement in the world."

"Where does he come from?" demanded Nathaniel with great assurance and a dogmatical air, as though the question when answered, was a perfect criterion to decide upon any man's character.

"He has been bred a Nazarene, and comes from that locality," answered Simon.

Old Nathaniel gave a diagonal twist of his mouth and a horrid leer with his large leaden eyes, and then replied:

"Can anything good come out of Nazareth?

"Why not?" demanded Simon indignantly.

"The fact is, brother," remarked Andrew in a jocular tone, "our friend Nathaniel is prejudiced against Nazareth. He thinks nothing good can come from thence ever since he took that young wife of his from that locality, who curls his hair so nicely."

A general burst of laughter followed this remark by Andrew, while the thin visage of Nathaniel was dreadfully distorted with anger. Before the company could recover from their merriment another fisherman whose name was Philip, a tall, awkward, simple looking man, hastily approaching the party, and announced that he had seen the two sons of Zebedee in company of two stranger's, approaching the house, one of whom was a very handsome, dignified man, as much so as King Solomon.

"Thanks be to God!" exclaimed old Zebedee, as he arose from his seat in the excitement of his joy. "I shall once more behold my darling boy John; and possibly one of these strangers will prove to be the much talked of Jesus."

The company was now thrown into considerable commotion. All boisterous hilarity was dispensed with, every one drawing himself up and assuming the best attitude and countenance he could, for they had an indistinct idea that somebody superior to themselves was coming in their midst, which caused them to wait with a slight trepidation the approach of the great man.

In a few minutes the two sons of Zebedee, John and James, entered the yard, followed by Jesus and Judas. When old Zebedee saw the party advancing, he jumped down from the piazza, and with tottering steps hastened to meet them. Then John perceiving his father coming towards him, left the side of Jesus and ran to meet him, when the father and son, falling upon each other's neck, embraced one another with great affection.

"0! my son!" exclaimed the old man, "how couldst thou leave thy old father?"

"Dear father," responded John, after kissing his sire on both cheeks, "be thou silent for a while and I will explain all to thee. I must now introduce my new master, Jesus, to Simon."

John, leaving his father in the company of James his brother, and rejoining Jesus and Judas, then advanced towards Simon, who was standing outside of the piazza, when he, with the most respectful formalities of the time and country, introduced them separately to the master fisherman. Simon made the most profound bow to Jesus; so low did he bend himself that his fingers touched the ground; then rising, with an air expressive of great reverence, he said:

"Most worthy and learned sir, the fame of thy wisdom and most wonderful powers have outstripped thy speed of traveling this way. I have heard of thee, praise be to God! I consider myself happy in living that I can testify my respect to thee. Be pleased, then, to accept the use of my house, for all therein is at thy command, and I will be thy servant."

"I thank thee, my friend, for thy hospitable reception," replied Jesus, who seemed to be much pleased with the manner of Simon. "There is something in thy face that tells me thou hast a good heart. What is thy name?"

"My name is Simon," answered the host.

"Simon," repeated Jesus musingly. "I like it not—it is not expressive enough of thy character—it is too passive. I see something in thy nature upon which I would like to lay the foundation of my hopes, firm and steadfast as a rock. Ah! if thou wert one of my followers, I would like to call thee Cephas."

"Worthy sir," returned Simon, "if in the course of events I should become one of thy followers, my name shall be as thou sayest."

In the meantime John had been explaining to his father the cause of his leaving him, how he had been informed by John the Baptist that Jesus was the Messiah spoken of by the Prophets, and that he was destined to become the king and ruler of Judea, if not of the whole world; and that he would make princes of all his followers. He, therefore, sought the first opportunity to join Jesus and become attached to him, for at some future day he should, no doubt, become a person of great power and dignity. James, his brother, would have the same chance of being aggrandized, and his father would be made rich and honored in his old age. This tale John made the old man firmly believe, gaining his consent that he and his brother should follow Jesus in his adventures, and progress to eminence. John then approached Jesus with his father, giving a formal introduction, which took place with a show of reverence on one side, and an easy gracefulness on the other.

"Then thou art the father of my much beloved John?" remarked Jesus inquiringly to old Zebedee, smiling his satisfaction of the interview.

"I am, worthy sir," replied the old man bowing, "and of James, the elder, two of the finest boys that ever called a man father."

"Thou art blessed, Zebedee, in thy children," remarked Jesus; "but art thou willing to part with them that they may follow me?"

"Worthy sir," replied Zebedee in a tremulous voice, "though I love my children dearly, and it will grieve me to part with them, yet having confidence in thee, and for their benefit do I freely commit them to thy charge. But when thou shalt be at the height of thy eminence, which is thy destiny, do not forget the children of old Zebedee. Let them share with thee thy prosperity and exaltation."

"Doubt not, Zebedee," answered Jesus earnestly. "Whatever may be my adventurous career in this world, thy sons shall not be forgotten, but shall receive all the benefit and exaltation that I can confer."

Then Zebedee stooped down low, took up one of the corners of Jesus' coat and kissed it; and as he took leave of Jesus his eyes glistened with joyful emotions.

Simon then brought Jesus a cup of wine, of which the latter partook, and when returning the vessel to the host, he observed:

"I have not acquainted thee, worthy Simon, with the nature of my visit."

"Come this way, sir," said Simon, going under the piazza and pointing to the bench. "We will be seated and confer alone."

They were soon seated, when Jesus proceeded to inform Simon of the nature of his principles and designs: How he wished to improve the mental condition of his fellow men by giving them an insight of their true nature, and of things generally around them, and a right conception of the true God. How he was at war with the impositions of the priesthood and the erroneous notions and prejudices of society. He stated the plans he had adopted to carry out his designs; his desire of having some followers whom he might instruct in his principles and send abroad to spread the good cause. He told of his reception at Nazareth after he had been absent from it for many years; how he had buried his last of kin, and then how he had given his first discourse to his townfolks, and the progress he had made until the Rabbi opposed him. How he had exercised his power over the Rabbi; and finally how the Rabbi exercised his power over him by driving him out of the town, with a narrow escape of his life. "I tell thee Simon," he said in conclusion, "a man is not much of a prophet in his own country."

158

"Exactly so," responded Simon with great animation at the thought suggested. "That is the very answer I give my men when they will not believe my big fish story. But now, good sir, let us go into the house, and I will introduce thee to my women."

"One word more, before we go into thy house," remarked Jesus. "I have made thee acquainted with my designs and wishes; if therefore, thou art willing to join thy fortune with mine, I would advise thee to throw up thy old profession for one more worthy of thee, and more exalting. Instead of being a fisherman, thou shalt be a fisher-of-men."

Simon seemed puzzled for a few moments what answer to make to this proposition by Jesus, but at length he replied:

"Sir, I will take a little while to consider of it, and give thee an answer before thou leavest me."

They then entered the house. In the meantime Judas had been mingling in conversation with the company—first with one and then with another, relating what he had seen or heard of Jesus; praising him for his wisdom, and enlarging and construing things always in his favor. When speaking of the mysterious power he had of curing diseases, he magnified what he had seen and heard into miracles; at the same time hinting that he did not doubt of his being the true Messiah. Then he touched upon points of worldly interest, that all those who followed him would have in prospect. Finally his eulogiums of Jesus and the glowing prospects he pictured in other respects, were greedily devoured and believed by the simple fishermen, so that they were made converts at heart before they were required to be so. But as soon as Simon entered the house in company with Jesus, the company in the yard broke up and dispersed to their several homes. John and James went home with their father, leaving Judas to attend upon Jesus until their return. Judas finding himself alone reclined upon the bench, and a train of thoughts passed through his mind similar to what is here presented:

"Base, low-minded, sordid wretches!" he said to himself, and his upper lip gave a scornful curl. "There is no difference among any of them, except that one is less cunning than another. However learned and noble-minded my new master may be, I see he has very little perception of human nature from external indications, or he would not join himself with such men as these, when the meanest traits of human nature are stamped upon the visages of all of them. Thou art a poor judge of physiognomy, my master, or thou wouldst not have said there was something that pleased thee in the visage of that Simon, on which thou wouldst base thy hopes. I have read his countenance, and pronounce thee in error. I read it thus: There is nothing that he would not be willing to do, with the prospect of sordid gain or aggrandizement. They are all alike; they will follow thee as long as they can see a prospect of serving their grovelling interests, but when that is past, and dangers or difficult-

159

ies encompass thee, they will leave thee to meet thy fate alone. It is a great pity that thy benevolent heart and noble intentions should be sacrificed to such men as these, when I could prevent it, if I dare. But, ah! my own cursed self-interest is in the way. O that I were free! I would do otherwise." Judas heaved a sigh. "No! I must not think of it. I must be as bad as the rest, though their course is of choice while mine is of necessity, therefore there is some excuse for me. Ah! here comes this Simon. I must sound him, and endeavor to bring him to my views, for I shall want more help to carry out the design of my master Saul. I think I shall not have a very difficult task to convert him to be one with me."

Simon, who had re-appeared at the door during the latter part of Judas' reflections, looking around and seeing no one but him, approached the latter and observed:

"As I have done my duties as host to thy master, it will become me to attend to the servant."

"Thou art kind and considerate," replied Judas with a smile.

"I thank thee for the compliment," replied Simon. "Wilt thou take a cup of my wine, sir? It is the best on this side of the mountains."

Judas gave his assent to that agreeable proposal, when Simon went to the black goat skin bottle and found that there was still some wine in it. Bringing it forward he filled two cups, one of which he presented to Judas, and the other he reserved for himself. He then observed:

"Come, let us be social, and without ceremony make each other's acquaintance."

Judas considered this a hint that a little confidential conversation would be agreeable to the host, which was the very thing he desired also, yet he would not show himself too eager for it, in case Simon should suspect any design upon him.

"How dost thou like this wine?" inquired Simon, and then he quickly added: "Thou must excuse my blunt manner of addressing thee, for I know not thy name."

"I think thy wine very agreeable," replied Judas. "As to my name, kind sir, I must tell thee it is not very common in this part of the world, for it is Judas."

"Judas!" echoed Simon. "I have heard that name before, but I know it is not a common one. It sounds well upon the ear, and I am certain it must be respectable."

"I can assure thee that I came of a noble family," replied Judas as he sipped his wine. "There is nothing significant in it of meanness or treachery, any one may know."

"Certainly not," replied Simon. "I should rather think that it signified everything that was great and noble; and if I am not mistaken in thy looks, the name is appropriate to the man that bears it."

Judas stroked his beard and glanced archly at Simon, as he said to himself: "I wonder if he is serious in what he says. If he is, he is a fool, and if not, he is trying to make a fool of me; if he means the latter, I think there are two of us."

"Talking of names," resumed Simon, "didst thou notice what thy master said to me concerning my name?"

"I did not," answered Judas. "What did he say?"

"Why, he said that my name of Simon was not expressive enough of my character," and if I were one of his followers, he would call me Cephas. Now what is there in me resembling a rock? I understand that Cephas means a rock in the Greek or some other language."

"He wished to intimate," replied Judas, "that he saw in thee the qualities of firmness, steadfastness and surety, which are necessary to the support of any great enterprise or virtuous principles."

"Well, perhaps he is right," remarked Simon. "He may see more good in me than I can myself."

"That is generally the case with modest and disinterested men," observed Judas, and his lip curled as he said so; "but a sensible man never should be ashamed to acknowledge any good qualities he is conscious of possessing."

"Thy words have great reason in them, worthy Judas," rejoined Simon, who began to feel and think so favorably of his guest as to venture on confidential ground, "and they remind me of a remark thy master made to me that I cannot understand."

"What was it?" inquired Judas indifferently.

"He was advising me to leave off my profession as fisherman for one more worthy of me, when he said: 'If thou wilt join me, in place of a fisherman I will make thee a fisher-of-men.' Now what he means by that I am not bright enough to understand. Perhaps thou canst explain it to me, worthy Judas."

"Let us take another taste of this wine, mine host," observed Judas, for his design was to render Simon as communicative as possible with the aid of the stimulus. "Perhaps with its aid we shall be better enabled to solve this doubtful part of speech."

"Most willingly, sir," answered Simon, who immediately had resort to the black goat skin bottle and cups, which were filled and soon drank; and then Judas observed:

"That expression of my master's, fisher-of-men, was nothing more than a figure of speech, which, though a bad one as designed to express his meaning, means simply this: A fisherman is one who catches fish, therefore, a fisher-of-men must mean one who catches men, that is to say, in other words, one who by greater cunning and knowledge is enabled to entrap men; to get the advantage of other men; to bring other men under his influence and within his power."

"Well, what does thy master mean that I should do with men, when I get them into my power?" inquired Simon innocently.

"That is the point where my master's figure of speech does not meet his meaning, which made me say it was a bad one," replied Judas. "My master's principles are of an extremely benevolent nature. He wishes to exercise an influence over his fellow men to their benefit; to cure them of their vices and diseases; give them enlightenment, and make them improved, refined and happy mortals. Now such a course is not suggested in the figure of speech he used. The fisherman does not catch fish for the fishes' benefit, but for his own, for when he catches them, he either eats them or sells them to others to be eaten. I think I have explained my master's meaning, also the difference between it and the figure of speech he used. What dost thou think of it?"

"I think," replied Simon, as he gave a comical twist of his mouth, "that the fisher-of-men would not receive much benefit from his toil, if he carried out thy master's principles."

"That is exactly my view of it," remarked Judas, and he gave a short laugh. "Now, worthy Simon, suppose a man carries out my master's figure of speech in all its particulars, how wouldst thou like it?"

"Thou must explain, sir. I am not quite so bright as thou art in this matter," answered Simon.

"Well," resumed Judas, drawing himself closer to Simon, and regarding him with a keen scrutinizing look, "the fisherman catches fish. Why does he do so? Is it not to convert them to his own benefit? Has he the right to do so? Yes; for his superior power gives him the right according to nature. Now, on the other hand, we will say the fisherman catches men, that is, he subdues other men to his power. Why does he do so? Is it not to convert them to his own benefit? Has he a right to do so? Yes, for might makes right, and we know that whatever is said against the theory of it, it has always been so in practice."

"Well! there is something comprehensible in that manner of stating the case," interposed Simon, with a pleasing change of features. "I perceive, worthy Judas, that thou hast been in the big school of the world. Go on, I pray thee."

"Now, sir," resumed Judas, "we will bring this matter home to ourselves and circumstances, and see how it will affect us. Thou wouldst not trouble thyself to catch fish unless thou couldst benefit thyself thereby. Thou wouldst not throw them away or turn them back into the sea."

"By Moses I think not!" exclaimed Simon.

"Neither wouldst thou trouble thyself to subdue men to thy power, unless thou hadst a motive and will in so doing; and when once thou shouldst have them in thy power thou wouldst hold them so for thy especial benefit."

"I certainly would," responded Simon emphatically.

"Well, then, Simon," resumed Judas in a soft persuasive tone of voice, "suppose we were partners in interest, and I should say to thee, "Simon, I have a man in my power whom I wish to hold and guide in a certain manner, until I shall accomplish a certain end. I wish to have thy assistance to that end in view. If thou wilt give it, I will insure thee fifty shekels of gold. What would be thy answer, worthy Simon?"

Simon threw his body back a piece, placed his eyes upon Judas, and regarded him with great intentness for several seconds, as though he would penetrate the innermost man. At length he drew himself forward, and said in a low whispering voice:

"Why, in that case, worthy Judas, if thou wert in earnest, I should say I am thy humble servant."

"I am in earnest," returned Judas, "and the proposals I have just supposed shall be in reality."

"How? In what way?" cried Simon in mingled astonishment and joy.

"Let us pledge ourselves in another cup of wine to be true to each other, then I will explain myself," replied Judas.

Then the two conspirators filled their cups from the black bottle, made many protestations of mutual fidelity, interest and secrecy as they drew closer to each other, conversing in low tones. Judas then stated the relation between him and his two masters (keeping the name of Saul in the background), the designs he wished to accomplish regarding Jesus, the manner by which it was to be achieved, and the different points of interest that might be obtained; so that, at length, Simon was completely prevailed upon to give his assistance to carry out all that Judas suggested. Then a plan of proceedings was adopted, and all other necessary matters discussed, and finally, when they were about to separate with a good understanding of each other, Simon's eyes suddenly brightened as though some lucky thought had just entered his head, and placing his finger to his chin, he cast an arch look upon Judas, and observed:

"My worthy Judas, one more word with thee before we part. An excellent idea just came into my head."

"What is it?" inquired Judas impatiently.

"My wife's mother is generally ailing with one complaint and another," replied Simon. "I will ask thy master to use his power over her. There is no doubt he can ease her complaints; then when he shall have done so, in order to enlarge the report of his powers among the people, I will magnify them into a miracle that he has performed upon the old woman. I will report it all over the neighborhood that Simon's wife's mother lay sick of a fever, and that Jesus laid his hand upon her, when she was instantly cured.'"

"That is a good idea," responded Judas laughing.

VISION TWELFTH

RUINS OF THE HOUSE OF THE VIRGIN AT EPHESUS

On the south-western verge of the plain of Genesareth, there was once a spot admired for its beauty, and noted in history as a much cherished scene in the career of Jesus. The western background was formed of a square-shaped hill with two tops, rising not more than a hundred feet above the plain, the crest of which was covered with trees of various kinds: the cyprus, cedar, pine, mulberry and oak predominating. On the western side it gradually sloped down to the narrow but fertile plain, except at one particular spot where the base of the mount terminated suddenly by a small ridge of rock, presenting a perpendicular and even front of about ten feet above the plain. Around the base of the mount and along the plain at this spot, there were but few trees, but here and there a copse of shrubs or a ridge of thorny pear. The ground was mostly open and covered with luxuriant grass.

The view extending eastward, took in a portion of the lake and a part of the north-eastern mountains—the intervening plain and the mountains surrounding the spot, filled up the scene.

Some days had passed since Judas and Simon had become friends on a basis of mutual interests and secret understanding, in which they had industriously persevered in spreading all around the neighboring villages wonderful reports concerning the man Jesus. They appointed a day when all the people who chose might assemble at the particular spot as above described, where the great and wonderful man, Jesus, would address them, and afterwards use his mysterious power for the benefit of the sick in the curing of diseases. In the meantime, Jesus passed his hours at the house of Simon, or among the family of Zebedee.

On the day appointed a great multitude assembled in the forenoon on the verge of the plain and along the base of the mountain with two tops, roundabout the spot of the rocky ridge that intervened between the mount and the plain. They were of all classes and characters, the greater portion being poor working people who had come from the various villages of the neighborhood; but there were others of higher standing and condition who were attracted to the scene by report of the great man having come from towns and cities on the other side of the mountains; and some travellers even from the Holy City itself, among them some spies from the Sanhedrim and the Government.

The scene was a lively and interesting one, all the people being attired in their best and gayest clothing and ornaments. The long flowing coats, robes and mantles of gay colors, their ornamented girdles and fanciful tires or head dresses of the men, who seldom wore any covering upon their heads except on occasions like the present, and the long white veils and long ear rings of the females, with their jewelled arms and bright colored dresses, presented a scene of interest and gaiety not often presented in that part of the world. Nearly every one carried a small panier in which were provisions of bread, fruit and fish, ready prepared for consumption, while many men—the more humble in attire, supposed to be servants—carried goat skin bottles containing water, and some of wine, which they thought requisite for the occasion. Some of them formed themselves into small parties seated around a tree; some were in indiscriminate groups, and others standing, walking or reclining upon the grass here and there alone; but all were in close proximity to the platform-rock at the base of the mount, from which it was understood Jesus would address them.

The people, generally, seemed to be engaged in discussing the merits of the coming great man—some, in a quiet whispering conversation, while others, seeming to be excited, gave vent to louder expressions.

"I tell thee what," said an old man, one of a small group that he was addressing with evident zeal, judging from his tone and manner, "this Jesus must be something more than a mortal man. No man that I ever saw could do what he has done."

165

"But he denies being anything more than a man," remarked another person. "Did he not address the people as brethren at Nazareth, and made no pretensions to be otherwise?"

"That matters nothing," replied the first speaker. "Some men are not as great as they think themselves to be, while other men are greater than they think themselves to be. This Jesus is known to do wonderful things. It is known that while he was a youth at Nazareth under the name of Jose, that he cured many complaints among his neighbors by simply touching them. Besides, did not Simon's wife's mother lay sick of a fever a few days ago, and did he not cure her instantly? Did he not cure one of our neighbors of a stiff neck by simply rubbing it? And he has done many other wonderful things that I know of. What did he do to the Rabbi at Nazareth? Did he not cast a spell over him and make him declare sentiments he before opposed? When the Rabbi came to himself he said he had no power of resistance, and knew not what he had said or done. He declared when he was under that spell that Jesus was not the son of Joseph and Mary, but that he was the Son of God."

"That last idea was declared by Jesus himself," remarked the second speaker; "but that is to be taken in a certain sense, for he said we are all children of God, if we live in a state of purity and seek after righteousness."

"Did not John the Baptist say," resumed the first speaker, "that this Jesus was the Son of God, and the true Messiah that the prophets spoke of? Did he not say that when he baptized him he heard the voice of God in thunder, saying, 'This is my Son,' and saw his spirit descend upon his head?"

"Well, it is generally known that John the Baptist is a crazy man," returned the second speaker, "and therefore no credit ought to be given to his testimony."

"If John the Baptist is crazy," said the first speaker, "then I am crazy too, for I believe it."

The first speaker then left the group, seeming to be much excited.

A sudden commotion was now seen among the people. All those that were reclining upon the ground suddenly sprang to their feet when their attention was drawn to the slope of the mountain before them. They then saw a body of men descend from a copse above, and when they came to the verge of the declivity they took up a position on the ledge of rock close to the edge, so that they were in view of the people beneath and around them. As soon as they took up their position, there was a loud shout of acclamation by the people and much commotion for a little while, but it gradually subsided as Jesus, standing alone in front of them, waved to and fro a branch of cedar, which intimated that quietness and order were required; then the multitude soon became as still as death.

Jesus appeared in his usual long blue garment open at the top, exposing to view the beautiful curves of his neck, throat and shoulders. His head being bare, displayed his glossy dark hair as it played around his neck and shoulders. He stood erect, with an air of the noble dignity of true manhood; his broad, high, spotless forehead, which seemed so expressive of majesty and wisdom, crowned his dark, fascinating eyes, which beamed with serene love and satisfaction with all around him. On his right side stood Judas, with due deference and humility expressed on his countenance, and John his personal attendant holding his tire and mantle, with James his brother by his side. On his left was Simon who had now assumed the name of Cephas, or Peter, as he was afterwards called, having doffed his fisherman's garb, and dressed himself in a long gray coat with red girdle, since he had undertaken his new occupation of fisher-of-men. He cast his eyes over the multitude with an air of import- ance, congratulating himself on the good opportunity he should have of trying his new vocation, and speculating upon the profits he should make thereby. Beside him stood Philip, a new follower to the new vocation, who was equally disinterested in following Jesus, though not initiated into the secrets of Judas. In the rear stood old Nathaniel with his bell- shaped head, who held converse with old Zebedee with his hoary locks. On either side of Jesus stood two new followers, who, by means of staves, supported a rude canopy of cloth over his head to ward off the sun's oppressive rays.

When quietness was perfectly established, Jesus commenced to ad- dress the people in a mild and melodious voice. His enunciation was slow and distinct at first, but as he progressed with his subject, he became more animated and rapid, more impressive, more eloquent and fascin- ating, so that people seemed to lose all consciousness of their identity and their locality so absorbed were they with the interest of the theme.

"My Friends and Brethren," he said, "it seems, from the best knowl- edge we can acquire concerning the phenomena of nature that the whole universe is subject to change. That, though the principles by which God rules the universe seem to be the same, yet there is nothing that is not undergoing a change. With the social relations of man it is more particularly so. It seems that though the fundamental principles upon which man is constructed remain the same, yet as an individual or in society as a nation, he is ever undergoing a change, making progress towards a better state, or retrograding to a worse. It seems that God having made man with certain senses, faculties and propensities neces- sary for his wants in life, and given him a principle of intelligence, has left him to work out by his experience all that wisdom and power which his wants and pleasures may require or demand. Yes, my brethren, the intelligence and power of man comes through the experience of the past. That experience may be of a happy nature, or it may be sad. In general, it is a sad and painful one he goes through before he becomes impressed with intelligence to benefit him in the future.

"How has it been with our people as a nation? We have gone through a long historical series of sad experiences, from the dawn of our history to the present day. Great have been our afflictions, great our sufferings, and great our shame and misery, which continue along the roll of time without the prospect of an end. What have we gained from all this sad experience as a nation? Nothing but woe and discord as yet. Shall we always remain in this sad state as a nation? Shall we always remain ignorant of the cause of our weakness and misery? No, my friends, there are some persons prompted by the love of their fellow men, who have had boldness enough to look down the long vista of our historical career, who have been enabled to discover, and have been courageous enough to declare, that all our social compacts have been founded on error, ignorance, superstition and tyranny, instead of wise principles and good social laws, which our sad history ought to have taught us. Yes, my brethren, we have gone astray from the principles implanted in us by the God of Nature, and believed the false fabrications of a vile priesthood, who have flattered our vanities by telling us we were the chosen people of their God Jehovah, while they fastened the fetters of mental slavery the firmer upon us. Under such great errors and impositions we have been ruled through all our historical career by despotic priests and tyrannical kings, amidst anarchy, confusion, bloody wars, rapine and general destruction, in which our strength has been weakened, our substance wasted, our tribes lost, and we have been kept in continual ignorance of our natures, and now become vassals to a foreign power. 0, my brethren, had it not been for the machinations of a vile priesthood, we might long ago have learned something of what we are and the phenomena of the universe by which we are surrounded. We should have found out that we all are the children of the great God of nature, and not the chosen people of a fictitious God as represented by them. We should have learned that the true God placed us here on an equality of power and means, to bring our various faculties into exercise, to gain intelligence, improve and excel, so that as we advance from age to age, we should ultimately arrive at a state of excellence far superior to what we are now. Let us pass no more time in vain regrets, for if the past ages have been passed in folly and misery, there is yet hope for a different state of things. Let us shake off the scales from our eyes and look around us, for now the dawn of a new era is about to commence. The day star of hope announces the coming of a new day, which shall disperse all the darkness of the past, and shall reveal to us the various obstacles over which we have hitherto stumbled. It shall show us the little bright house upon the hill, and the path that leads thitherward.

"Now, my brethren, let me impress you with a few observations pertaining to you individually. The true God who made us has endowed

168

every man and woman with a divine principle, independent of the common understanding. This principle is the source of all life, of consciousness and feeling. God has given it to us to cultivate and improve, that it may be productive of blessings in this life, and assure to us a more blessed one hereafter. If you take a seed and plant it in the ground, and cultivate it with tender care it will rise up and grow to a goodly tree, bearing rich fruit and giving you a comfortable shade. So it is with this divine principle which God has given you. If you cultivate it carefully it will expand and grow, bearing rich fruit all your lives, and overshadowing you with a celestial home after you have passed the confines of mortal death. But, my friends, whoever is neglectful of cultivating this principle that is within him, but forgetteth that he has it, or is in ignorance of its existence, passing through a life of vice and wickedness, it will not grow up for him a goodly tree, giving him fruit or shade in a celestial home. My brethren, in order that you may know how to cultivate this divine principle, I will give you some rules or precepts concerning the most prominent and primitive duties of your social position, in the performance of which this divine principle is more or less dependent for its welfare:—

"Firstly, I will speak relative to our duties to our persons. Secondly, of duties to our families. Thirdly, of love and harmony among our relations or kin. Fourthly, of duties to our neighbors. Fifthly, of obedience to our government, if just. Sixthly, of duties to the world at large, making all men brethren. Seventhly, of our duties to ourselves. Eighthly, of duties to our enemies. Ninthly, of obligation to conform to the principles of nature. Tenthly, of our acknowledgment of the Heavenly Father.

"In accordance with the first duty, you must remember under all circumstances, that your bodies are not yourselves. The divine spirit which God has given you to cultivate is the man, and not the body. The body is but the vehicle in which you live, and have connection with the external world. It is the house as it were, in which you live during your residence on the earth. Therefore you must pay such respect to it only as something of less consequence than your inward selves, yet you must perform all the necessary duties to it that its nature shall demand to make it a comfortable and desirable location during the time your spirit shall need it while on earth. You must preserve it from all the inclemencies and ravages of the elements. You must keep it from all impurities without and within—being careful to perform all its private offices in due time and season. You must give it plenty of pure air, and pure water to quench the thirst of the blood, and perform all necessary ablutions. All necessary food must be supplied to it in due time and proper portion, giving sufficient to satisfy hunger and no more, choosing the most simple and wholesome,—remembering that you eat to live, and not live to eat; for if you eat and drink more than its nature demands, you will engender bad habits, which will engender disease and misery. If your bodies should be ailing through accident or otherwise, resort to pure water and fasting, and avoid taking all poisons under the name of medicaments; and thus by conforming to all other rules of prudence, your bodies will recover their usual health and vigor. Regular exercise is also necessary to insure tone, soundness and strength, the development of all its parts and functions until it shall arrive at maturity.

"One thing more I will observe on this head. When the impulses of certain passions are developed within you, study how to administer to their necessary wants, without accelerating or retarding them in the due course of their nature; but let all your proceedings therein be of a secret and chaste nature. By so doing, the body will become a fit habitation on earth for the pure spirit to dwell in.

"Secondly, are the duties incumbent upon us in relation to our families. The most sacred obligation of a man on earth is the relation between himself and family. God has considered it so necessary to the preservation and perpetuation of the species, that he has impressed this obligation upon every kind of animal on the earth. With all other animals it is instinct, but with man it is not only instinct, but a sacred moral obligation also; and whoever proves recreant to this sacred duty, is far inferior to any of the brute creation. It is God's desire that man and woman shall enter upon conjugal love to procreate their kind, for he is desirous that the divine principle in man shall improve from age to age, until it shall arrive at its destined end of perfection. Thus it is that he has implanted in man and woman those divine instincts and moral obligations to induce them to take care of their offspring, and he rewards them in part for their toils by giving them ineffable pleasure in performing their tasks. What man is there who has a spark of true manhood within him, who will not shield with his body and defend with his arm the wife of his bosom, who is the partner of his love, and the child, which is the fruit of this love? There is not one worthy of the name of man who will not. He will toil by night and day also to procure for them all the necessaries of food, raiment and shelter. He will even go so far as to deprive himself of what is necessary for himself rather than see them suffer. He will run hither and thither to serve them in time of sickness, smooth their pillows for their aching heads, and speak soft soothing words into their ears; and do all other things, though ever so humiliating, for their welfare. Such a man is worthy of a loving wife and good children. Such a man feels his spirit chastened, ennobled and exalted in thus performing his duties; at the same time he qualifies himself for an inheritance hereafter, where all the objects of his earthly love will again surround him in the heavenly world. My friends, be you then loving, kind and self-sacrificing one to another in your families, for such will meet the approbation of your heavenly Father.

"Thirdly, - There are duties and obligations that are due to other persons in our family relations, which call into play the noble feelings and sentiments, all of which improve and refine our natures. To your parent's you ought to be obedient if you are under the years of manhood, and deferential and respectful even after you are your own masters; taking care of them in their old age and soothing them under all the vexations of life, and leading them with as much gentleness as possible as they go down to the grave. And then there are, perhaps brothers and sisters who require your tender solicitude, love and assistance; to them you ought to administer all the tender and useful offices that are in your power, being kind and affectionate, slow and mild of reproof, and acting with them in all things for the family's welfare. Many of you may have a little sister or brother whose parents have gone down to the grave. To whom should they look to supply the place of their parents but their elder brother. It is your duty to fulfill that office; therefore watch them, love them, and attend them with the care and affection of which you are capable. And when your younger brother shall need counsel or assistance, give it to him freely, with all thy experience, wisdom and disinterested affection; for he that does not treat his brother in this wise, is not worthy of the name and respect of a brother. To all your other kin, be you gentle, amiable and respectful; by so doing, you will establish harmony in your family, and gain the respect of good men.

"Fourthly, - My friends, are your duties to yourselves, which will embrace several points. The duties to your bodies I have already spoken on; the next is your duty to your understanding or mind, which is one of the most important dependent upon your care. It will become you to gain an intelligence of all things pertaining to your intended calling and circumstances in life that you may prove capable of undertaking all necessary matters of common occupations, acquainting yourselves with some of the beauties of nature's phenomena. By thus acting you will enlarge your minds, gain your own self-esteem and the admiration of all good and wise men. Your next care will be to guard your reputation from the foul stings of slanderers and all evil workers who shall endeavor to injure your just fame. If your honor, honesty and manhood are abused, call forth the slanderer and argue the case before your neighbors, and if he be proved a liar and evil worker, take all just means to punish him; for the slanderer ought not to go unpunished; make him an example for others to dread. Your next duties to yourselves will be to care after your worldly interests, for, though it is not good for a man to be greedy after wealth, yet it is necessary for every one to seek after the honest means of support. Secure to yourselves some honest occupation as a means of gaining your daily dependence for bread, then pursue it with perseverance and be prudent in your expenditures, that your out-goings be not greater than your in-comings; and if possible, save a little against times of sickness or accidental misfortune. Thus you will render yourselves independent of others, and avoid many evils that others encounter. A sensible and generous man may thus act without becoming a miser, an usurer, or a greedy-hearted man of riches.

"Fifthly, - Are our duties to our neighbors. All men as neighbors ought to be treated on social grounds with perfect equality of rights. Whatever we expect they shall concede to us, we ought to be ready to concede to them; for, as in the social compact, there is a mutual interest to support, so ought all our bearings and treatment to each other be mutual. Mutual rights, mutual respect, mutual affability and politeness, when perfectly understood and conformed to, will form a harmonious society. But there are instances that occur among neighbors, which come not under the mutual transfer of obligations, but which appeal to our sympathy, our sense of justice and charitable feelings. Such, for instance, if our neighbor be sick or poor, and needs assistance, he may have no right to demand a share of our wealth; yet it is our moral duty to sympathize with him, and relieve him to the best of our abilities. If he meet with an unforeseen accident, such as his house being burnt, he cannot by force or right compel us to restore him another house; but it will be well for our names and add greatly to our characters of benevolence, if we endeavor to restore his loss. There are many other ways by which a man can do good to his neighbors, and the best criterion by which he should judge how to do so, is to take the Golden Rule, "Do unto others as you would they should do unto you."

"Sixthly, - Our duties to our government, they are conditional, and very simple in their nature. If the government be a just one, founded on rational and just principles of mutual protection of the people, their rights, privileges, lives and property, and in which the people have a voice in the selection of their rulers, then it becomes our imperative duty to implicitly obey all its laws, and respect its rulers; and should an enemy invade the country, then it will be the duty of every man when called upon to go forth to repel the foe; but on the other hand, should the government be one of tyranny, and the laws and rulers be oppressive and unjust, no man is morally bound to obey the one or the other; but he may do so to save himself. If he betray such a government he is no traitor; or if he fight against it he is no enemy to his country, but a patriot who wishes to abolish a bad government with the view and hopes of establishing a just one in its stead.

"Seventhly, - Are our duties to mankind at large. All nations of people are the children of our heavenly Father, wherever found or under what circumstances. Though there is some difference in their natures and appearances, no doubt, God created them with the same motives as he did us. They are born upon the same earth; the same sun shines upon them by day, and the same moon by night; therefore they have an equal light to live and enjoy this life that we have. Like us they are susceptible of pain and pleasure; like us they have the same motives and interests in life; and though their colors are different, and their habits, customs, language and ideas also, yet they are our brethren; they are entitled to the same sympathies, the same love and assistance we have one for the other. Therefore let there be no party or local distinction in our love for a class or nation of men, here or there. Let there be no local hatreds, prejudices or antipathies. Make an allowance for the difference of customs, habits and prejudices; and keep this ever memorable maxim in your minds, that the whole world is your country, and all mankind your brethren.

"Eighthly, - Our duties to our enemies are but few, yet we have some to perform even to them. When a difference or dispute shall arise among nations our first duty is to keep cool, to prevent our nature from being aroused to a state of anger or irritability; for if we allow anger to overcome us it will prevent our seeing the difference in a just light. Our next duty will be to invite our enemies to an argument on the points of dispute, and then with prudence, circumspection and just principles, investigate the matter. If we find our party to be wrong, then concede so much in their favor; and if we find that they (the enemies) are in the wrong, we will draw a line, and say, 'Thus far will we go and no farther; we will not war with you, but we will stand to our point. If you attack us, we will resist and defend ourselves, and the blood of the battle will be upon your heads.' If war becomes inevitable then we can fight with a good heart in a good cause. If we conquer we ought not to demand anything more than the fulfillment of the principles for which we contended before the battle. When treaties are made between us, we ought to adhere to them with inviolable truth and justice; our enemies will then learn to respect us on all future occasions.

"Ninthly, - Are our obligations to conform to our passionate natures. My brethren, many have told you to suppress or extinguish certain passions or principles within your nature. My doctrine is, that you do nothing of the kind, for God never made man with any passions or principles useless or destructive to him. Every passion, principle, or function has its specific duty to perform, all tending to the preservation and happiness of the individual; but it requires the exercise of prudence and patience to regulate them, that they shall not injure ourselves, or be detrimental to others. Therefore, my friends, neither accelerate nor suppress any of your natural passions or emotions; your nature knows how and when to display them, and when to arrest them. When a man is excited with pleasing emotions or ludicrous ideas, he laughs; then let him laugh, it will do him good; for if you endeavor to suppress his laughter he will laugh the more, or it will kill him. When a man is hurt in body or mind he may shed tears; then let him weep for his tears will ease his pain, or if he is excited to tears of sympathy at the distress of another, let them not be suppressed, for they will move him to good offices of charity and benevolence towards the distressed one. A tear of sympathy outshines the brightest of diamonds; its sparkling lustre will penetrate through space, extending to the realms of heaven where God will see it and feel pleased with the donor. If your brother or neighbor offend you and you become excited to anger, give vent to your anger; but first turn aside and take two stones, then beat one upon the other until your anger be subdued. It will be better for you to beat the stones to powder, than to smite your brother upon the cheek; but you must not suppress your anger, for it will generate hatred and the desire for revenge. If the development of your nature is such that the conjugal passion is dominant, then with prudence and circumspection seek for yourselves partners in your love, and give vent in a chaste and proper manner to your natural desires; but seek not to suppress them by celibacy, for it is an error entailing a thousand horrors. In all respects, my friends, suppress not your natural passions or emotions, but so endeavor to regulate them that they shall not produce to you or others any evil results.

"Tenthly, and last. - Is our acknowledgment and love for our heavenly Father. When we investigate our own mortal bodies, we cannot help seeing how beautiful and wonderful they are made, and we cannot help inferring the wisdom and power of the maker. We know, therefore, that there is a supreme wise power in the universe above all other things; and when we understand that this body of ours is only the representative of the spirit within, how much more beautiful and wisely constructed must that spirit be. We, therefore, infer that this great Power has some great design in bringing us into existence, and though we know not what that design is precisely, yet we have reason to believe that it is a good one. We, therefore, hail this great Power as our heavenly Father —the true God of the Universe. The wisdom and magnificence of his works as displayed all around us, we cannot help admiring; and as we are enabled to perceive they all tend to something good, we have reason to believe that he is a God of Love. It, therefore, becomes our duty as rational beings when in contemplation or speaking of that God, that all our aspirations of sentiment and feelings shall be of a pure devoted love."

Jesus paused for a few moments, and then concluded his address with the following remarks:

"Our ancestor, Moses, presented to his brethren a Decalogue or ten commandments, which he told them he had received from the God Jehovah at Mount Sinai for the government of the people. He was the first to break those commandments, for he dashed them to the ground, and slew three thousand of the people before he had made them acquainted with the nature of them. I also present you with a Decalogue, not coming from Moses or the God Jehovah; but mine is founded upon the principles of truth and wisdom, in conformity with the principles of nature. You will compare them, and decide for yourselves which is the best and most capable of adding to man's happiness."

Jesus, having concluded his address, stood aside, when Peter, whose former name was Simon, the fisher-of-men, advanced in front of the people and announced in a loud voice: "As the address of Jesus has been terminated, the people can refresh themselves for an hour, after which, if there are any sick among them, if they will come forward, Jesus will exert himself to relieve them by the laying on of his hands."

This announcement was hailed with a great shout of joy by the people. Then a general commotion ensued; some running hither and thither to the woods and copses, but the greater part seated themselves upon the ground where they were, and immediately unpacked their small paniers of provisions for a repast.

At length about an hour had passed in recruiting their outward man; the paniers and skin-bottles were emptied, and the fragments strewed around; every one was filled, for those who brought nothing received from those who had more than enough.

The time was agreeably passed by the multitude in eating, drinking and discoursing upon the recent address. In the meantime Jesus and his followers partook of refreshments in a retired spot upon the slope of the mount.

At length it was announced that the sick persons were to be brought forward to the base of the rock; then there was a general commotion, a rushing and crowding towards the place mentioned, and for some time a good deal of confusion, but in the course of time all was reduced to order. An open space was maintained by the people around the base of the rock, into which several sick persons were admitted and placed in a row, while, the multitude stood around on the plain and on the slope above, awaiting with the most intense curiosity the forthcoming proceedings.

There were about twenty sick persons in the allotted space when Jesus entered it followed by Peter, Andrew, John and James, and with a serene, benevolent expression of countenance he stood before the applicants for his mysterious favors. He beckoned for one to approach, who did so, when he inquired of him the nature of his complaint. It was a severe headache, without intermission. Then Jesus placed his hands upon the crown of his head and gently moved them down the sides of his face, shoulders, body and legs; this he repeated three times, when the man with a sudden exclamation of joy declared the pain was gone. He went away rejoicing. Another person was cured instantaneously of a severe toothache by similar means; he went away expressing his gratitude and joy. Some patients were afflicted with rheumatic affections, part of whom were instantly cured and others relieved. Some had running sores on their legs or back of their necks, with whom Jesus took a longer time in the process than with the preceding; at length he discharged them with the injunction to bathe seven times in the lake, when they would be cured. They departed in great confidence. The remaining cases were disposed of in a similar manner; some being instantly cured, some relieved, and others were to have the process repeated before a cure could be effected.

At length Judas made his appearance, thrusting his way through the crowd of people into the open space, followed by a most miserable and unfortunate looking man, or it seemed more like some monstrous quadruped than a man, yet it was in verity one of the latter; he was walking on his hands and feet with the aid of two blocks of wood in the former, with his head near to the ground and his back bent in form of an arch; his clothes were in tatters and his head covered with rags; his countenance dark, disfigured and distressing to behold, with a short ragged beard. As he approached Jesus crawling along with his arms and blocks of wood, as substitutes for legs, tears gushed from his eyes, and he cried: "0, Master! for the love of God, do something for me, for I believe thou canst."

Jesus was startled at the sight of this miserable creature, and he looked up to Judas inquiringly.

"Master," said Judas, quite seriously, "this poor creature has come a great distance to see thee, to obtain the benefit of thy powers. His friends have brought him hither in all hope."

"But, Judas," replied Jesus in a tone of expostulation, seeming to be somewhat distressed as he spoke, "I am afraid that my power will not extend so far as to enable me to relieve this poor man."

"Master, thou knowest not the extent of thy power, neither do I," replied Judas persuasively, "yet it may be greater than we think. Let us hope in this case that God will extend his power to thee for the benefit of this poor man. Try, dear Master."

"Well, Judas, as thou sayest, I can but try," responded Jesus.

He then approached the deformed creature, placed his hands upon the back of his neck and along the spine to the pelvic region, where he let them rest a few moments; this he repeated three times, when Judas gave the deformed a wink, who immediately stood erect, and with a sudden spring bounded several feet into the air; then descending he repeated the same several times, shouting aloud with joy. After leaping up and down, slapping his hands and performing many comical actions demonstrative of his astonishment and excited feelings, the cured cripple threw himself at the feet of Jesus and kissed them. The multitude were thrown into the most astounding astonishment. Jesus and his followers were also greatly surprised at the miraculous cure; but the former attributing the miracle to the interposition of his heavenly father, took no merit to himself. He then placed his hand upon the man's head, blessed him, and told him to depart to his friends, rejoicing that God should have been so good to him. The man rose to his feet and re-commenced his joyous frantic actions, giving no one an opportunity to question him, as many of his supposed friends wished to do.

At length, Judas taking him by the arm, led him forth through the crowd, and with hasty steps they made their way to a body of woods at some distance from the multitude, where there was a horse tethered. Then, perceiving that no one was near, they both burst into a loud laugh which continued for some minutes before either could speak.

O, Cosbi! Cosbi!" exclaimed Judas as soon as he could compose himself: "Thou hast nearly killed me. Had the farce been carried out five minutes longer I should have died with suppressed laughter." Then Judas burst into another fit of laughing.

"Oh! God of Moses!" exclaimed Cosbi, with great efforts to restrain his cachinnatory excitement. "What fun! Now the simple multitude will have enough to excite them for a month, and call into play their faculties of wonder."

"Thou hast performed thy part well, Cosbi," said Judas; "but thou must now hasten away and get rid of this disguise, and then follow me in my track, for I shall have more use for thee."

The two conspirators then took leave of each other; Cosbi mounting his horse, rode off, when Judas returned to Jesus and his followers. The multitude was dispersed and went to their homes, wondering upon all they had seen.

VISION THIRTEENTH

Saul was in his chamber, that one as before described. All around was dark and gloomy without; but within several lamps burning perfumed oil gave cheerfulness to his abode by the bright light and pleasant odor emitted. He held in his hand a small scroll which seemed to be a letter that he had just been reading, and was then reflecting upon its contents as he paced to and fro. The general expression of his countenance was one of pleasure. Bright flashes of thought suddenly illumined his eyes, and various movements of his lips indicated the thoughts and emotions as they passed through him.

"He is a bright and ingenious knave, that Judas," he said to himself, and then a cold smile curled his lips. "He has been more successful than I anticipated, and writes of his future prospects in a glowing strain. Bright Judas! cunning Judas! thou deservest thy promised boon; but it will not do to reward thee until thy work is done, and then—ah! no one knows what will be thy reward, or mine either, for the result of this conspiracy or treachery we are enacting cannot be foreseen. Where are my thoughts wandering to? Such must not be. I must have no touches of remorse or stings of conscience before my work is accomplished. As I have started the puppet into action I must concentrate all my energies of mind, blunt all my finer feelings, and arouse all my ingenuity and skill to make every one of my tools perform the parts assigned them, or perchance some momentary weakness may foil the whole design and ruin me irretrievably."

Saul paused for a moment, then striking himself upon his breast, he added: "Courage, Saul, courage! Persevere, and thy ends shall be attained. The day shall come when thou shalt see the hoary heads of this distracted country bend low before thee, and posterity will see millions, now unborn, bend in reverence at the sound of thy name."

Saul then went to his recess from which he took a silver tankard containing wine and a goblet, which he placed upon a small stand; then filling the cup with the beverage he was about placing it to his lips when he heard a knock at his chamber door. Starting at the unexpected summons, he replaced the cup as he exclaimed "Ah! who can it be at this unusual hour? I must see." He then opened the door cautiously, when Judas made his appearance.

"Welcome, Judas," said Saul, as he immediately shut the door and fastened it; "my skillful and trusty agent. No man's visage do I prefer to

178

the sight of thine."

"I really do begin to think there is something comely in my countenance, since the young and handsome Saul takes a pleasure in beholding it," responded Judas ironically, and then he gave a short sarcastic laugh.

"Well, Judas," said Saul gaily, "thou art in time to join me in my last cup of wine, before I retire to rest. Come, take this, and I will get another for myself."

Saul went to the recess and got another cup, when returning, he filled it and added: "Come, drink, and relate thy adventures."

Judas drank his wine with a seeming critical taste, for having taken the cup from his lips he reflected for a moment, then replacing it to his lips, he drained the last drop, and remarked:

"This wine is good, but not of so fine a flavor as that made down by the Lake of Genesareth."

"Never mind the wine," responded Saul impatiently, "tell me of thy adventures in that part of the world."

"0, worthy Saul," replied Judas, "there have been glorious doings in that neighborhood, thanks to thy advising and my performing. There is a complete revolution among the Genesarians; things that were, are now almost upside down. Old Moses and the Holy Priesthood are below the usual price; fishing for fish among the fishermen is voted vulgar, for they have started a new vocation which is called fishing-for-men. The advent of the Messiah, performing miracles, cures, and casting out devils, with the wonderful doctrines of Jesus, form the subject of talk through all that district. The fishermen have thrown down their nets, the publicans have forsaken their inns, and the laborers their fields and vineyards; for they are running hither and thither almost distracted, collecting in multitudes wherever the great man, Jesus, will hold forth, and then spreading all over the country, relating the wonderful things they have heard and seen, and every time they are related they become more and more miraculous."

"Come let us be seated," said Saul as he motioned Judas to the couch, "then thou mayest give me a more particular and connected account of what has been done."

They became seated, Saul having placed the wine on the stand before them so that they could help themselves at pleasure, when Judas having taken another draught began as follows:

"Before I started on the expedition of adventures with my new master, as I must call him," said Judas, as he cast a keen glance at Saul, "I made acquaintance with a young man of a lively, versatile nature, whose morals are not anywise objectionable to our views, and who possessed certain talents which I thought would be of great assistance in accomplishing what I have undertaken. I engaged him to follow me in our travels, but to keep at such a distance from me that our connection should not be suspected. He gladly accepted my offer, when we all started at the time set. We traveled four days on foot, with as much haste as was convenient, through Judea and Galilee, without allowing ourselves or our business to be known. At length we arrived at the village of Nazareth, which is the native place of Jesus, but who had been absent from it about ten years."

Judas then proceeded to relate all that took place at Nazareth, but as these matters are related elsewhere, it is not necessary to recapitulate. However, let it be known that when he spoke of the address of Jesus to the Nazarenes, he gave a very favorable view of it. After stating how they left Nazareth, he went on to say:

"From Nazareth we went on to Bethsaida, where we received a more favorable reception, and where we organized our future proceedings. From the narrow escape Jesus had made from losing his life, he saw it would be necessary to have a body of followers to act as an escort of protection to him, with which I agreed. We then proceeded to avail ourselves of such as could be obtained, whoever they might be, and in this little fishing place we obtained several. I will therefore acquaint thee with the adherents who formed the strength of our party. First, there is young John of Galilee, who received intimation of Jesus from John the Baptist. Thinking that he could make it to his advantage to serve Jesus, he ran away from his father and joined the former in his retreat near Jericho. Then there is John's brother, James; we picked him up at Nazareth, where he had come to seek after his brother John by his father's orders. These young men, with old Zebedee, their father, are very ignorant and silly, far below the common understanding: yet they are grossly selfish, for they will believe any foolish tale told them wherein there is a prospect held out of becoming great worldly men. I accordingly told them that Jesus would certainly become the King of Judea, if not of the whole world, for he was the true Messiah promised; and I held out to them that they should become princes and governors of provinces, and that their father should be made rich. They all believed what I told them, so that they became followers. Young John knows how to read and write, but his brother does not, which makes him think that he is somewhat the superior of his brother. He may be right in that respect, but it has led him into a most egregious error, for he entertains the idea that he has a poetic and a prophetic faculty within him, which he endeavors to cultivate by scrawling the most absurd, silly and monstrous trash that any infatuated fool ever committed to parchment. The next is Simon, whom Jesus calls Peter. This man is a merry, good-hearted fellow in a general way, possessing more intelligence than the rest of the fishermen. He is generous in a certain way, and would not stoop to do a mean, petty thing; however, I found out that his principles would not prevent him from doing anything on a large scale for the sake of gain and power. I found, also, that I could not cajole him like I had the others, so I declared to him in true colors our designs and prospects with regard to Jesus. He understood me and consented to be one of us provided his expenses were paid while traveling; and after Jesus should have made many adherents among the people, and be put aside, that he (Peter) should be assigned the head of a portion of his followers. I told him his interest should be attended to in that respect. He then became one of us."

"Judas," exclaimed Saul with evident uneasiness expressed in his countenance and voice, "How didst thou know that such were my designs in this business? I never told thee such."

"I know it, most worthy Saul," replied Judas as he glanced archly at his employer. "Thou hast told me thy designs in part, the rest I read in thee."

"Proceed, Judas," said Saul indifferently, "I know thou hast a keen perception."

"Then the next," resumed Judas, "is that ignorant, awkward, selfish brute, Andrew, brother to Peter. The latter assured me that he would secure the co-operation of his brother by certain inducements he would hold out to him. He accordingly did so, and Andrew became one of the company, but he was not let into an understanding of the true state of things between me and his brother Peter. There were two more miserable, ignorant, sordid creatures that we induced to join us, with very small offers of gain. They were so poor and so humble in their expectations that for the value of a dead dog's skin they were willing to believe anything, say anything, and do anything mean. One was named Nathaniel, and the other Philip. With this respectable and worthy escort we thought we would proceed to business. Accordingly we—that is, I and Peter—sent them all around the neighborhood for many miles to gather the people, telling them to say that Jesus would address them and heal the sick. At the time appointed a multitude of people of about a thousand had assembled at the foot of the Square Hill with the two tops back of the plain of Genesareth, where Jesus gave another address touching upon the barbarous history of our forefathers, and concluded by giving them some excellent rules of life. After the address the people partook of refreshments they had brought with them; then Jesus proceeded to exert his mysterious power of healing the sick. Some he cured instantly, some he relieved, and some remained doubtful; but the last act was one that established his fame in spite of himself, as a worker of great miracles. I brought before Jesus the young man I spoke to thee about, Cosbi by name, who performed the part of a poor deformed man, bent almost double and walking on all fours like a beast. Jesus was doubtful whether he could do anything for him, but I persuaded him to try. He accordingly did so, when Cosbi sprang into the air performing all kinds

181

of mad evolutions expressive of his joy. The people were struck with astonishment, and no longer doubted that Jesus was the true Messiah. They dispersed, wondering and spreading far and wide what they had seen and heard of Jesus; but I and Peter, after leaving that spot, made great additions to his fame. We then crossed the mountains and passed over into Galilee, passing through many towns and villages where Jesus gave addresses and performed some cures, and as we went along I enlarged upon his wonderful powers of healing. I told them how the deaf, dumb, blind, lame and deformed were cured, making tales to suit all occasions, our followers repeating and adding thereto wherever we went. Peter undertook to relate how the multitude was fed at the expense of Jesus and his followers. He said, at first, that there were a thousand people and five hundred loaves with two hundred fishes for supply. Then the next place where he related it he said there were three thousand people, one hundred loaves and fifty fishes. And at the next village he came to he said there were five thousand people, ten loaves and five small fishes, and all were fed. Then at another place he stated that there were six thousand people, five loaves and two fishes. I now thought Peter had made the tale of feeding the people quite marvellous enough, so I said to him, "Peter, the next time thou relatest that tale, it will be well not to reduce the number of loaves and fishes, for the people will begin to suspect that thou art telling them one of thy big fish stories, and thou knowest they will not believe thee in that thing." "Well, Judas," replied Peter with a wink and a short laugh, "I think thou art right in that respect, but still I must do all I can to make my master's works as famous as possible; however, I will not reduce the number of loaves and fishes the next time I tell it, but I will try what can be done to make it appear still more wonderful." So the next time Peter related the tale of the multitude being fed, he said there were six thousand people, five loaves and two small fishes; and when they had all eaten enough, there were twelve baskets full left.

"I must tell thee one more miraculous adventure which took place without design or anticipation of the result at least. We had left Galilee and returned to the other side of the mountains by Genesareth Lake. One day we concluded to make an excursion to a village on the opposite shore by the name of Gadara, which was built in a cleft of the mountains, the people of that part being Gentiles who eat swine flesh. They were basely ignorant, believing that when a man went crazy or mad, a demon had entered him; they therefore turned him out of society to wander and die where he could. It now occurred to me to avail myself of Cosbi to further advance our cause. So I contrived that he should be upon the spot to personate a madman when we should make our appearance on the road to the village. All things being arranged we crossed the lake and began ascending the mountain towards the village; and as we advanced up the steep road we saw some of the villagers who had come out to meet us, for they had heard of our coming; we had got about half-way when we met them. At this part of the road on one side of us there were many caves in the side of the mountain which were used as tombs; and on the other side of us there was a descent to a hollow of a few feet deep where a herd of swine were feeding upon the scanty herbage found there. Now, just as we met the people and began to pass the usual greetings, a monster looking man came out of one of the tombs or caves and rushed among the people causing them to flee with terror. He stood before us in his tattered garments; his face disfigured with hideous patches of dirt and paint; his hair tangled and matted, and his legs and arms bare. He held a large club which he brandished before him in a menacing manner. He pointed at Jesus, making many grimaces, and lolled out his tongue, and at length said in a blustering voice: "Get thee gone; I know thee—I will kill thee—get thee gone, thou Jesus of Nazareth. Thou art sent of God to drive me out, but I will not go." Jesus looked upon him with an expression of great commiseration, and a slight tremor seemed to come over him as he did so. "Master," I observed, as I caught the eye of Jesus, "is there no possibility of this man's reason being restored?" Jesus responded that he thought there was none. I then urged him to try his power, as he was enabled to do good things when he did not expect them. I instanced the case of the deformed he had cured. He consented at length to try if anything could be done. He caught the madman's eye, and stretched forth his hands as he uttered the words, "Peace be to thee." The madman, who was still making violent gesticulations and grimaces, at length fell upon his knees, seeming to be overcome by some invisible power, and then closing his eyes he remained for some time quite peaceable. Jesus then drew near him, and for some minutes waved his hands over and around him. Then the madman opened his eyes, looking around him with seeming strangeness; at length jumping up, he said in a mild and reasonable manner: "I feel better; my mind has come to me again, and thou art my benefactor." Then he humbly bowed before Jesus and burst into tears. "Arise, my poor man, and depart, rejoicing that God has restored thee to thy right mind," said Jesus encouragingly. The villagers by this time had descended the road again, and many of them had drawn near, as they no longer feared the madman, but were struck with awe and reverence for Jesus by the power he had seemingly displayed. The restored madman rose to his feet, when having made an obeisance to the people he began to caper and jump with joy, and as he neared the edge of the road he slipped and fell over into the hollow among the herd of swine. The swine receiving so sudden and unexpected a visitor with such a frightful mien and disordered dress, became seized with astonishment and fright; they accordingly scampered away as fast as they could. A great many jumped over the cliffs and were killed, while others found their way to the base of the mountains, rushing onward until they came to the lake, when many of them plunged in and were drowned. All was confusion among the villagers. Some ran after their swine, but in vain. The madman was not to be found; he had hid himself in the ravine, and at night Cosbi—for it was he—managed to return to me in safety. We went forward to the village, but the people had become afraid of us, so they desired us to depart from their neighborhood. We did so. A few days afterwards the fame of Jesus was spread around the country—how he had made a wonderful cure of a man possessed of a demon, which had entered the swine after being driven out of the man. Many alterations and exaggerations were added to this at different times, by different persons relating it, but it was firmly believed by all who knew no better."

"It was an interesting adventure, and will answer well for our end in view," observed Saul.

"After the adventure at Gadara," resumed Judas, "we returned to Bethsaida and stayed at Peter's house. Afterwards we sojourned at Capernaum some days, where nothing of importance occurred, except that we took two more followers. One of them was named Matthew, who possessed the rare talent of knowing how to read and write; a most conceited fellow; always with book and reeds in hand taking notes; a great babbler of absurd stories and monstrous fictions. He not having anything better to do, agreed to accompany us and be the writer of our party. I do not doubt if he should be alive when Jesus is dead, that he will make out a most astonishing and wonderful history of him. The other adherent we took into our company was one Thomas, a disagreeable atheist who believes in nothing that does not contribute to his own selfish and vicious principles, yet he will profess to believe anything, if he is paid for it in money or wine.

"As the feast of the passover was soon to commence, Jesus with his honorable and talented company of followers—not forgetting to include my own honorable self—concluded to start for Jerusalem. We passed along by the lake of Genesareth and down the river Jordan, and then came in by the road to Jericho. So here we are, ready for new adventures. But there is one thing more that I must acquaint thee with, worthy Saul. On my return to this city I came across a man who told me that John the Baptist is in prison—sent there by Herod Antipas, Tetrarch of Galilee. John had given offence by using his tongue too freely concerning Herod's family affairs. This man informed me also that John is coming to his right reason; that he begins to perceive that he has acted the fool in considering and treating Jesus as the Messiah. He wishes to see Jesus once more, for he says if Jesus is the true Messiah he can deliver him from prison, and if he cannot do that he (John) will be convinced that

Jesus is not what he thought him to be. Now, Saul, thou mayest perceive if this John gets out of prison and tells the people he has been mistaken about Jesus, he will undo, in part, our good work."

"In that case," responded Saul, "it will not do to let him come out of his prison. I will think what is to be done in the matter. My dear Judas, I have to express my approbation of thy proceedings. I wish thee to continue in the same course until I give thee further orders. Tomorrow I shall have an interview with the High Priest, perhaps after that I shall have further orders for thee. Now let us take a parting cup of wine and terminate our conference till tomorrow."

Then Saul and his agent acted accordingly.

VISION FOURTEENTH

JESUS ADDRESSING THE PEOPLE

The noon day sun is reflected from the white marble structure of the Holy Temple, dedicated to the great Jehovah, which is said to be, literally, "The House of the Lord." From a distant view, it seems to be a mountain of snow, so exquisite is the whiteness of the polished rock, but on a nearer view the spectator can scarcely support the brightness of its splendor on account of the dazzling light reflected from the silver and golden plates with which it is adorned. The roofs and other parts are of cedar wood, beautifully engraved, and the gates are of great magnitude,

186

richly wrought, and ornamented with gold and silver. In the eastern front of this temple is a lofty door-way, rising over a hundred feet in height, the sides and posts of which are covered with plates of gold, ornamented with figures in relief. This doorway leads into the chamber or sanctum of the Holy of Holies, where is placed the Ark, guarded by two golden cherubims. Around the four sides of the Temple is a tessellated paved court, surrounded by a portico with lofty pillars of white marble,— which is named the Court of the Priests, in which is placed the altar. The latter is a massive structure over a hundred feet long and the same in height, covered with plates of gold. In this court also is the great brazen basin, supported on the backs of oxen, which is large enough when full of water for a ship to sail in. This court opens into another exteriorly which is separated by a wall a few feet high, paved in the same manner as the other, and surrounded on its four sides with taller pillars than the preceding one, which is named the Court of the People, none but Jews being admitted therein. Nine gates give exit to another court exteriorly, the eastern and centre one being of surpassing magnificence, which is called the Beautiful Gate. This gate is ninety feet in height by seventy in width, the door being of massive Corinthian brass, covered on both sides with golden plates, sometimes plain, sometimes fretted work, or raised figures in low and high relief; on either side of the doorway is a tower, seventy-three feet high, adorned with columns twenty feet in circumference. Altogether, this handsome porch surpasses anything of the kind of the works of man.

Then by a descent of seventeen steps these gates give exit to another court, and the last exteriorly, called the Gentiles Court, which is paved the same as the others. On the exterior edge of this court there is a descent of a few steps, which is bounded by another line of cloisters around the four sides—the southern side having four rows of columns with fluted shafts and ornamented leaves; this part of the cloister is called Solomon's Porch. On the exterior of this a wide colonade passes around the four sides consisting of chambers with columns forty-seven feet high, and at each corner towers with turrets and pinnacles, to gaze down which would make the head dizzy, from the extreme height. This colonade extends to the margin of the wall on the east, which descends down to the bottom of the valley of Jehosaphat, a distance of seven hundred and thirty feet, formed of massive blocks of rock as large as ordinary houses.

Such was the stupendous structure of the Temple from an external view, being from the bottom of the valley to the top-most pinnacle a height of nine hundred feet, seeming to be one massive mountain sculptured into a fantastic form.

In this stupendous structure, which took many ages in construction, all the wisdom, all the wealth, and nearly all the energies of the Jewish people were expended. And what were the powers by which it was achieved? An ignorant people; a vile priesthood; a gloomy superstition, and a line of tyrannical kings. Such is the Temple of the Great Jehovah, who says, "He dwelleth not in temples built with hands."

The Holy City was crowded to repletion with people from all parts of Judea and from many foreign countries, independent of its ordinary number of inhabitants, for the great feast of the Passover was about to be celebrated with all the pomp and gorgeous ceremony, reverence, superstition and folly that was ever expended upon the occasion. All the streets were crowded with multitudes of people, making it difficult to pass to and fro. All the vacant lots and suburbs were filled with lightly constructed booths for the accommodation of the country people who were formed into companies of tens or upwards, designing to feast together on the paschal lamb. Every public inn was filled with strangers; every dwelling house was filled with visitors from distant parts, who sojourned with their friends on the occasion. The porches of the colonades; the porticoes, and the two outer courts, were filled with people moving to and fro; some in groups discoursing of the news from distant parts; others were dealing, trading and speculating on matters of worldly interests, as great numbers of stalls and shops were allowed for business people of every sort.

The pavements of the two courts were nearly covered with devotees, kneeling or prostrate, with their faces turned towards the temple, spreading broad their phylacteries, performing their ceremonial evolutions, and repeating their usual prayers for the occasion, having performed which, and left the spot, others would fill up the place and go through the same.

The Court of the Priests, which surrounds the Temple, presented a strange assemblage of living beings and incongruous religious ceremonies in performance in and around the "House of God."

Close to and around the Temple were great numbers of the tribe of Levi, in flowing robes and gorgeous tires, acting as musicians and singers. The first, with long brass trumpets, stringed instruments and horns, flutes, cymbals and drums, made the courts resound with terrific inharmonious sounds; then another party chanted psalms of debasing humility, gross adulation and praise, fit only for the ears of an absolute king.

On the southern verge of the court was the vast structure called the altar of burnt sacrifice, from the top of which an inclined plane descended at each end, and at a small distance from either end were numerous cattle pens, filled with lambs and sheep, which mingle their noise with the terrific blasts of the trumpets and the chanting of the priests—altogether forming a horrid din. Then a great number of uncouth looking beings with bare heads, arms and legs, forming a part of the holy priesthood, smeared and bespotted with blood, seize the poor beasts, slaughter them, divest them of their skins, and carry them to the top of the altar where there is a large fire burning, and there roast them.

On the top of the altar were several men in scanty garb, reeking with perspiration, the fumes of wine and other bad odors, resembling demons more than holy men, with long metal instruments poking the fire and turning the carcasses until they should be religiously done. Then vast clouds of greasy smoke, mingled with incense, arose above the altar, curling and ascending up to the skies to regale the nostrils of the great Jewish God, Jehovah. Great numbers of men carried wood to the top of the altar, and then descended on the other side with the burnt offerings, which were distributed among the various owners after abstracting the Lord's share, which was about one-third of the best parts.

Thus the noise of hundreds of noisy instruments, the voices of singers, chanters, and bleating of sheep and lambs, the crackling of burning wood, the hissing, sputtering, phizzing of roast flesh altogether made a mingled din agreeable to the God of the Jews, highly expressive of Jewish piety and religious adoration. But now a sudden blast of trumpets is heard. What is it? It announces that the High Priest is about to visit the Holy Temple. The holy cortege proceeds from the palace of the Sanhedrim, at the south-east corner of the Court of Israel, from which a numerous train is slowly wending its way. Foremost is a detachment of guards headed by some officials, who prepared the way through the dense crowd for the advance of the Holy Priesthood. Then comes the body of the Chief Priests of the tribe of Levi, headed by the Nasi, or president of the Sanhedrim, who are dressed in blue vestments and white ephods, with broad girdles round their waists of many colors, and white linen tires around their heads. Their long flowing beards and grave deportment bespoke them to be what they were not—most holy men.

Next in the train is the great High Priest, who treads the ground with a grave dignity. His vestment is white, reaching to his feet and fringed all around, from which are suspended golden bells, alternating with figures of pomegranates. His girdle is formed of five cinctures embroidered in flowers of gold; over all an ephod of blue of corresponding materials, fastened by two clasps below the throat, resembling two shields of gold, in which were set two precious stones bearing the names of those from whom the tribes descended. His head was covered with a mitre of fine linen wreathed in blue, in the front of which was a plate of gold whereon were embossed the sacred letters, which say "Holy to the Lord." Then followed the Chief Scribes headed by the Abbithdin or vice president of the Sanhedrim, who were dressed in long black vestments with blue girdles and plain white linen tires in form of cones. These were followed by another detachment of guards who brought up in the rear.

As the cortege passed through the courts the people either prostrated themselves or bowed down till their fingers touched the ground. All noise and commotion ceased for a time, but as it approached the temple the very turrets were shook to their foundation by the terrific blasts given from the trumpets, which was followed by singing and chanting, accompanied with milder instruments. At length the High Priest stood before the doorway of the Holy Temple, when the vocal and instrumental music ceased; then all present, excepting the former, fell prostrate upon the ground. Then the High Priest placing his hands upon his breast passed in at the doorway and entered the vestibule alone. Raising the sacred veil he passed into the Sanctuary. Looking at the twelve barley loaves which awaited the Lord, ready to be eaten, and glancing indifferently at the golden lamps which were continually burning, he passed into the chamber called the "Holy of Holies." In this holy precinct there was nothing except the holy ark; not even daylight was permitted to enter, for the great Jehovah was supposed to be favorable to darkness. The High Priest being under the necessity of staying in this dark chamber for some time in order that the people might believe that he was having a communication with the Lord Jehovah, felt inclined to rest himself; but as there was no furniture in the room excepting the holy ark, he coolly sat down upon it between the two cherubims, and having heaved a sigh he said to himself: "0 Israel! Israel! what a despicable humbug is thy religion!" When the High Priest thought that his stay in the holy chamber was sufficiently long, he rose from the ark and with solemn steps retraced his way to the front of the temple, where as soon as he made his appearance he was greeted with a simultaneous burst of music from the musicians and singers, then the cortege being formed he returned to the palace of the Sanhedrim as he had come.

It was now about the first hour past the noon of day. Great crowds of people, both Jews and Gentiles, had collected in the south side cloister of the Gentile Court, called Solomon's Porch—that magnificent production of art! There were four rows of marble pillars eighteen feet in circumference, with fluted columns and ornamented capitals—the two centre rows supporting a groined roof one hundred feet high, and the two external rows forming aisles fifty feet high. This part of the temple was frequented principally by people of business, and as a locality where friends from different parts of the world could meet each other and discourse upon worldly affairs; and at various times lecturers on various subjects would gather crowds to whom they could hold forth. Around the bases of the columns there were many stalls where small articles of every kind could be purchased, and some money changers were allowed to accommodate the people by taking a percentage out of every piece of money they exchanged.

In the central part of this porch there was a great crowd of the people collected who seemed to be much excited, making exclamations of wonderment and curiosity as they pointed to a handsome man standing on a platform in the midst of them. "It is he," said one. "Yes, it is the miracle worker," said another. "The enemy of the Priesthood and the reformer of the Temple," said another. "The preacher of strange doctrines," said another. "He is going to speak!" said another, and then a great many voices cried out "silence!"

Jesus was elevated about three feet above the crowd, with his followers around him. His head was bared, his beautiful countenance being exposed in full view of the people, and as his serene intelligent eyes glanced around upon them, they could not help feeling an admiration and prepossession in his favor. As soon as he found the people attentive he gently raised his eyes for a few moments as though invoking the aid of the Deity, and then he proceeded to address them in a voice distinct, low and impressive.

"Friends, Countrymen and Brethren: I am sensible the address I am about to deliver to you is one of great hazard and difficulty, for there are two opposing powers of great magnitude which I shall have to contend with. But, my friends, as I am impelled by my love towards you as a brother, by my duty to you as a citizen, and by the great obligation I am under to the true God of Nature to do all the good I can in this world— by all these obligations, I say, I am willing to risk my own worldly interest and safety in order to declare my mind to you. One of the opposing powers that I shall have to contend with will be the authorities of certain institutions which I shall be under the necessity to expose and attack; the other opposing power will be in yourselves. I do not mean, my friends, that you will oppose me from any ill will or intention that you have at present, but it will be of this nature: As I proceed in my exposition of matters my views will clash with some of your old established notions which you have been taught to consider good, or not to think about at all. For what has this vast multitude of people assembled in this city and temple today? To celebrate the feast of the Passover, you will say. What is the Passover? The exodus of our ancestors from slavery in the land of Egypt, under the guidance of Moses. So it is said, the Lord set apart this day to be celebrated every year with thanksgiving and joyousness. Now, my brethren, you believe all this to be true, and that the Lord is entitled to your thanks and lasting gratitude for the favor shown to our ancestors, and this institution of the Passover is the manner by which you wish to express your feelings to the Lord. Gratitude and thanks are divine traits in human nature, therefore it is good in you to be grateful to the Lord for any favor shown to our people. It is good of you to be thankful to a man if he do you a favor. It is good even to be thankful to a dog if it has done you a service, but, my friends, notwithstanding all this we ought to inquire whether the claims of our gratitude are well founded, and by investigation be certain that we are not deluded into a false belief. You have been taught to believe that all these statements concerning God, Moses and our ancestors are true; you have not been allowed to doubt them, or if you have doubted them, you have not been allowed to express them. Therefore these established notions you have are your prejudices; and if I, in the course of my discourse, shall endeavor to show you that these statements are not true, but false, your prejudices will take offence, and you from mistaken motives will be apt to oppose me though I am endeavoring to do you good by giving you enlightenment upon the matter. My dear brethren, let me advise you to lay your prejudices aside; give to me your minds as though you were little children, and follow me in a course of investigation of this matter; then I doubt not in a little time and with a little natural reasoning you will be enabled to acquire so great an amount of truth that you will view it in quite another light.

"In the first place, my friends, we must have some fixed ideas of this God Jehovah of whom Moses speaks, and then we will take that as a criterion to judge all other matters by. What is this God represented to be in his principal attributes? What do you wish him to be? I think he is generally represented to be all-powerful, all-wise, ever-present, and all-benevolent. If this character of your God will suit you, it will also suit me to argue from. I wish you, my brethren, to follow me in my investigations with your minds free from prejudice, and guided by simple natural reason, and you will then perceive that there is no truth in this history of the exodus of our ancestors from Egypt—I mean in the manner they left, or that the God Jehovah is not what he is represented to be.

"In the first place we understand our ancestors were in slavery in Egypt, and that the Lord Jehovah was desirous that they should be liberated, but Pharaoh, it is said, would not let them go. Well, if the God of Moses were a wise God he could have suggested means how to liberate them, and if he were powerful he could have put his means into execution without entering into any contest with Pharaoh. Here, then, we may perceive that the story is not true, or that the God of Moses is not what he is represented to be. In another place the Lord tells Moses to demand of Pharaoh to let the Children go. Moses does as he is bid, but Pharaoh will not consent for a good reason. The Lord hardens his heart, which will not allow him to yield. Here, then, we may perceive that the statement is not a fact, or the Lord is inconsistent and cruel. The Lord is then represented to enter into a long contest with Pharaoh to make him give up the children; at the same time he hardens his heart and will not let him do so. The Lord brings plagues and diseases upon the Egyptians and their cattle, punishing the people as well as Pharaoh for not doing what he will not allow them to do. Here we have a tale of the greatest inconsistency and absurdity that ever was related; either the tale is one of the grossest, lying, absurd productions, or the Lord Jehovah is an absurd, cruel, imbecile monstrosity. After some silly contests between the Lord and Pharaoh's conjurers and the Lord killing the first-born of the Egyptians, the Children of Israel force their way out and cross the Red Sea through a valley made by the waters. Now if the Lord could do such wonderful things as this, what is the reason he could not have taken the children out without killing the first-born? Why did he not kill Pharaoh instead? That would have settled the matter at once. And what occasion had he to take them through the Red Sea, when he could have taken them into the desert by going a little further to the north? The fact is that is the way they must have gone into the desert. Thus seeing the statement of the exodus to be a great tissue of lies up to this point, there can be no more reliance on any other part of it. You may then perceive, my friends, that the history of the exodus is not a reliable fact on which the feast of the Passover is founded, and the God Jehovah, if he had anything to do with that affair, is not worthy of our thanks, our gratitude or our notice. I come to this inference concerning this God's actions before the exodus, and I can come to the same after the exodus. He is represented to have been inconsistent, cruel and unjust to the Egyptians, and he is equally so to the Children of Israel after the exodus, as well as to all other nations that they had to do with. Did he not say, according to history, that he had made choice of the Israelites as a favored people? That he would give them a home, a land flowing with milk and honey? Did he not say that they should become as numerous as the sands on the sea shore, and become a great and powerful people? How have his words been verified? In not one instance have these words been true, but quite the reverse. Instead of getting a home flowing with milk and honey, when they left Egypt they wandered in the deserts forty years, until all the people that had left Egypt in manhood were cut off by slaughter, famine, thirst, plagues, scorpions, diseases and exhaustion, —even Moses, his favorite, died before they got land to settle upon. And how did they get land at last? By their own individual barbarous strength; by robbery, bloodshed, treachery and the most ferocious cruelty in war. The Canaanites, with all their ferocious warfare and the aid of the Lord Jehovah, were never completely subdued after many ages of bloody contest. Sometimes they exterminated the people in some parts, while in other parts they failed altogether, and were made slaves. When they could not make any further conquests of their enemies, they turned their arms against one another, and a succession of bloody civil wars continued for many ages. At length they became a prey to every surrounding nation, becoming vassals or slaves to one or the other for the remaining period of their history. One monarch came down upon them and took away ten of their tribes into perpetual slavery, so that now instead of twelve tribes we are but two. And what are the people now? Are we not vassals to the Romans? All these things that I have stated are facts.

193

What then has become of the great promises of your God Jehovah when he said that he would make our people a mighty nation? Is it fulfilled? No, my brethren, it is not, but quite the reverse; we are a miserable, weak and ignorant people, who never had a country to call our own. We never were a mighty, a just or an organized people, for we have always been living in bloody strife, either against the rights of others or against ourselves. What, then, are the inferences from all these facts that I have stated? First, the statements of our history concerning the exodus are not true, and the statements concerning the God Jehovah cannot be true. Secondly, that the existence of such a God as Jehovah is described, is not true, but is nothing more than the fanciful and lying spirit of him who wrote the account of the exodus; therefore the institution of the Passover feast is not founded on true history, and is not entitled to our gratitude and observance. How then, my brethren, shall we account for all these absurd lies and fables? It is very simple, if you will open your understandings and be governed by their dictates like true men. It is highly probable that our ancestors were once slaves to the Egyptians, when, in course of time becoming numerous, they, under the guidance of Moses, managed to revolt and leave their masters. Moses then took them into the desert, and established by the strength of his mind and power of the sword, new institutions and laws to govern them. To him is due the credit of releasing our people from bodily slavery, and to him is due the ignominy of reducing his brethren to a mental slavery under the guidance of a vile system of Priesthood, which has been continued from his days to the present. To the priestly historians must we attribute all those lying tales; to the priesthood must we attribute the established belief of a lying, inconsistent, cruel and revengeful God under the name of Jehovah; to this vile priesthood must we attribute the establishment of this irrational and disgusting ceremony of the Passover feast which today is celebrated. 0, my friends, if you wish to believe in a wise and powerful God, and wish to obtain his favor, why do you make a monster of him by making these disgusting offerings of this day? Do you think that a good and wise God can be pleased with the greasy smoke that ascends from yonder altar this day, or the smell and taste of roast flesh of several hundred thousand slaughtered animals? Is your God nothing more than a monstrous gluttonous animal, that he shall devour the parts allotted to him from the dead carcasses, with the blood, the wine and the oil that are set apart for him? The true God of the Universe, does he stand in need of such as this from us poor mortals? He, who is all good-ness, would he desire or accept it from the needy mortals of earth? No, my brethren, such a thing cannot be possible. You are mistaken in what is the true God who presides over you all; you have been worshiping the figment of your imaginations, which has been established in your minds by erring and wicked men; you have been through the whole course of your history the mental slaves of a wicked priesthood, whose perversity it is my will and ambition to expose. This institution of the Passover I pronounce absurd, and an abomination to the land. This stupendous structure of the temple has been founded upon the ignorance and super-stition of the people; the whole is a gross imposition. The Lord God does not reside in that chamber called the Holy of Holies; the High Priest does not communicate with him there, for the whole affair is an imposition. That great altar is more pleasing to swine and dogs than to the Lord. The roast meats are not sacrifices to God, but the perequisites of glutt-onous priests, who daily gorge upon the fat of the land which the needy people ought to have. And this handsome porch where I now lift up my voice, instead of being a place devoted to disseminate learning to the people, has become a den fit only for thieves and money gamblers."

The address of Jesus was discontinued as a great shouting arose among the people, and great confusion ensued. Some cried aloud, "The profanations of the temple! The traders! The money changers! Down with the money changers!" Then the crowd swayed to and fro and broke into several parts. A young man was seen disguised with a patch on his eye and a hump on his back, who nevertheless could be distinguished as Cosbi, who, having a large club in his hand, was stimulating and exhort-ing several ill-looking men to follow him. "Come, my men," he said, "let us clear the temple of these profaners, these traders and money chang-ers." Then he rushed forth with many ruffians after him, when, coming to one of the money stalls, they upset the tables, beat the changers so that they fled; then there was a scramble for the money, which was soon gathered up. This example stimulated others to follow the same course, so in the course of a short time all the stalls of the traders and changers were upset and robbed, and a great many of the owners beaten.

The mass of the people seeing the illegal proceedings withdrew them-selves as quickly as possible from the scene of confusion, in fear they should be criminated with the offenders; among them Jesus and his followers silently betook themselves away, and quietly passed out of the city. The same scene of confusion and robbery passed all around the portico of the court of the Gentiles until the alarm being spread through the city the Roman guards were sent to quell the disturbance and arrest the offenders. Then Cosbi seeing the guards approaching dropped the patch from his eye, pulled down the hump from under his vestment and made his escape without being suspected of being the originator of the disturbance. He was acting under the authority and at the suggestion of Judas.

195

VISION FIFTEENTH

The scene presented to the mental eye was a lofty chamber in the palace of the Sanhedrim, gorgeously decorated with hangings of purple and scarlet colors, embroidered with gold and silver. Two rows of pillars with fluted shafts ran lengthways, with ornamented capitals supporting a ceiling curiously groined and painted. On one side were window-casements opening into the Court of Israel, and on the other side, looking over the eastern part of the Holy City. On another side was a folding door opening into a suit of private apartments, and on a fourth side was the door of public entrance from the external parts of the palace. At different parts of the walls were pedestals supporting branched candlesticks or lamps of solid gold, and between them were elevated seats covered with the most costly cloths of purple and gold. The floor was covered with a thick matting, over which was spread a cloth of various colors worked in gold and silver. Such was the audience chamber of Caiaphas, the High Priest.

Caiaphas was in this chamber alone, pacing to and fro with a slow noiseless step, his head slightly bending forward in apparent deep reflection; and from the emotional working of his hard features his thoughts seemed to be none of the most pleasant. The numerous lamps emitted a brilliant light, for it was evening—about the fourth hour of the day following that on which he as High Priest made the ceremonial visit to the Holy of Holies. His dress was more humble than that of the day before, his head being circled with a simple tire of white linen, and a vestment of white reaching to his feet, with a plain girdle of blue around his loins. He was a tall spare man, with harsh angular features more expressive of worldly interests than holiness and serenity. There was no sign of ambitious aspirations in his eyes, but rather of satiety and disgust with worldly greatness; for as his thoughts passed through his mind, they would arouse many a scornful curl of the lip and irritable glance of the eye.

As thus he paced the gorgeous chamber a train of thoughts passed through his mind of the following nature:—

"This, then, is the acme of human greatness," he said musingly, "among the people of Israel at least! 0 foolish and accursed ambition! Foolish and infatuated man that I have been thus to sacrifice my peace and quietness, principles, virtue and wealth for this bauble of a priestly mitre! Had I foreseen how little enjoyment and how little true honor is to be gained in this exalted station, I would have eagerly seized the most humble lot in preference, and felt myself fortunate and happy in the choice. Had I known how galling would have been my loss of self respect, and the disgust I feel in being compelled to act the hypocrite, I would rather have been a dog than be sensible to such mortification. The time was once, no doubt, when this high office was worth the struggle for its possession; there was much self-exaltation to be felt in filling it. Then there was some gratulatory pride to be experienced as a High Priest looking down from his lofty station upon the mass of credulous, ignorant people, for he knew that they elected him from their sense of his superiority to themselves. But now the case is different; the people, though credulous as ever, have not the power to elect the priest of their choice. The all-grasping Roman Eagle has taken it to itself to do so, and thus the people are discontented, having no longer the love and reverence for the office. The office has lost its prestige, for the world begins to view it in its true light, as the means established by the cunning and ambitious to sway the rude and ignorant mass, while the intelligent begin to scorn and despise it. 0 horrible! When I reflect that I am daily obliged to be the chief actor of the grossest of mummeries, in support of the vilest system of superstition that ever cursed the society of man, without the respect of the people, or my own self-approbation to compensate me for the sacrifice of my feelings. 0 cursed ambition that— "

The soliloquy of Caiaphas was suddenly arrested as his eye encountered one of the priestly order, who stood a few feet within the door of public entrance, awaiting with respectful demeanor the recognition of his presence before he advanced further; but as soon as he caught the glance of the High Priest, he bent himself in obeisance.

"Approach, reverend Gamaliel," said Caiaphas, as he instantly assumed an air and attitude of solemn dignity.

The man thus addressed was a little above the common stature, with meagre aspect, bronzed complexion, long gray hair, full white beard, and hazel eyes, denoting a man of thought. Upon his high, broad forehead was placed a tall, conical black tire or cap, more for distinction than comfort. He was habited in a long black vestment fringed around the bottom, and a girdle around his loins, of various colors.

At the bidding of his superior he approached within a few feet of him, repeating the obeisance, but not so low as before; then placing his hands upon his breast, with his eyes cast down he awaited to be addressed before he stated his business. This man was Rabban Gamaliel, who was Nasi or President of the Sanhedrim, the High Priestly Court of Israel.

"What news, Gamaliel, from the Sanhedrim?" inquired Caiaphas. "To judge from the sad expression of thy countenance, it bodes no good."

"Most Reverend Superior," replied Gamaliel seriously, "there are others at Jerusalem who wear a sad countenance besides myself. The whole city is in confusion and terror, waging a war of conflicting opinions con-

197

cerning the doings and doctrines of this great Innovator they call Jesus. The greater part as yet are disbelievers in his words and acts, and are enraged against him; but there is no knowing how long they may remain so, for he is making proselytes by his teaching, and gaining many adherents. The same confusion has seized the Sanhedrim. The greater part are aroused to anger and hostility, while a part seem to be stricken with terror, for they timidly hold back their counsels, and refuse to proceed to extreme measures. Some went so far as to say that this innovator is possibly what he is represented to be, the Messiah as promised."

"What! are there such fools in the Sanhedrim?" exclaimed Caiaphas with a start and a curl of his lip. I should have thought that their learning and experience were such as to enable them to estimate the outpourings of Prophets according to their intrinsic worth."

"May it please your Mighty Reverence to consider," replied Gamaliel, "that there are members of the Sanhedrim who do not presume to be equal in wisdom and knowledge with your sacred self; they, therefore, are more liable to view things, in some respects, like the common people. Now this timid party in the Sanhedrim seem to think that there is some truth in the doctrines of this Innovator, and that his works of healing the sick are undeniable facts. Such opinions as these become schisms and heresies in our counsels, for whatever may be the private opinions of any of our members, it becomes all of us, who wish to support our Holy Order and all its institutions, to say and do that only which shall conform to the old established routine of things."

"I believe thou art correct, Gamaliel," returned Caiaphas, feigning an acknowledgment of error. "Pardon my momentary forgetfulness of our most sacred dignity. Pray go on, what decision did the Sanhedrim come to?"

"Most Reverend Sire," answered Gamaliel, "the greater part of the members in their anger would have this Jesus arrested and brought before them on a charge of blasphemy, but I thought it better to arrest their proceedings until I should know your most sacred opinion."

Caiaphas crossed his sacred arms upon his breast, and with every appearance of profound reflection remained silent for some minutes, while Gamaliel, with his eyes turned to the ground, remained in respectful silence. At length, the former, in a voice expressive of doubt and uneasiness, remarked:

"Gamaliel, this is a perplexing business. I know not what to say. What wouldst thou advise?"

"Reverend Sire," answered Gamaliel, "these are troublous times. It therefore behooves us not to be hasty in our proceedings, so that a rash act shall not accelerate that which we wish to arrest, yet the state of things is such that something must be done to stop the progress of this innovator. By his address to the people in Solomon's Porch yesterday,

the low thievish part of the populace availed themselves of an opportunity and excuse to commit acts of rapine and plunder, which they
masked under the pretence of ridding the temple of its profanation. This
class of people, combined with the sincere admirers of his doctrines and
works, make already a formidable force in the city; and according to
accounts I have heard that his influence extends over one-third of Judea
and Galilee. As his influence extends, that of our Order will decrease and
become at length prostrate."

"Well, what wouldst thou suggest as a remedy?" inquired Caiaphas,
eagerly.

"Most Reverend Sire," responded Gamaliel, "before I suggest anything
I wish to introduce to your sacred presence a man who is well acquainted with this Jesus, knowing the general tenor of his doctrines, his power,
his designs and influence in the country. This man is one who has some
interest in the support of our Order and the suppression of the influence
of this Jesus. He therefore wishes to have an interview with your Reverence, to make certain statements and propositions. If it will meet the
approbation of your Reverence I will introduce him, for he is in the
palace awaiting your pleasure."

"Dost thou know this man? Canst thou trust him?" inquired Caiaphas.

"I have known him, your Reverence," returned Gamaliel, "from the
time that he was a little boy, for he was a pupil of mine and an apt
scholar. He is of respectable parentage of the tribe of Benjamin; his
name is Saul, from Tarsus in Cilicia. He is learned and astute with many
agreeable manners; with all he is ambitious, which, when turned to the
cause of our Order, will add to its acceptability."

"Let him be introduced immediately," said Caiaphas hurriedly. "Such a
man as thou describest is needed to prop up our failing greatness."

Gamaliel immediately left the chamber, leaving the High Priest to his
reflections; but he soon returned followed by Saul who advanced within
a few feet of the latter, and made a most profound obeisance. He was
dressed as a citizen, in rich garments, but plain. His head tire was of blue
and white linen in form of a wreath, and his vestment of purple cloth
reaching below the middle of his leg; his underdress of pink silk reaching
below the knees; his legs bare, over which were laced his sandals, and
around his loins a girdle of blue, red and white.

Caiaphas eyed him for a few moments with a piercing glance, the
result of which was he seemed pleased with his appearance; then, in a
complacent tone of voice, he observed:

"It has pleased thy friend and former tutor, our reverend brother
Gamaliel, to make report of thee, which in all things considered give thee
credit as one worthy to be admitted to our presence; I therefore make
thee welcome."

"Most reverend and exalted Sire," said Saul, again bowing obsequiously, "your most gracious condescension in thus admitting me your most humble servant to your most sacred presence, shall be ever gratefully impressed upon my mind and heart."

Caiaphas gave Saul another penetrating glance, as he said to himself: "This man is not an ordinary tool that any one can use. He has features expressive of great energy and firmness; an eye of great intelligence and astuteness; his lips seem capable of pouring forth the most flattering and seductive words; with a bold, lofty forehead, denoting lofty aspirations and desire of command; altogether he seems to be one more fitting to be a king or a High Priest than I am." Then turning his attention to Saul, he observed:

"Our reverend brother has informed us that thou art acquainted with the man called Jesus; that thou couldst reveal many things concerning him, which we may deem worthy of consideration; if so, let us know what they are."

"I could say many things concerning this Jesus," replied Saul with great modulation of tone, "but much may possibly be offensive to your Holy Order. I therefore crave your indulgence and consideration in whatever I may say of an offensive nature, and believe that I, as the humble narrator, am in no wise connected with the enemies of your Holy Order."

"I beg thee, sir, to speak with all due candor and freedom, making no reserve," returned the High Priest.

"I take this as a further proof of your condescension," returned Saul. "I shall therefore proceed to relate what I know of this Jesus, that I consider ought to come before your order.

"In the first place this Jesus possesses great beauty of person, which commands the admiration and prepossession of all who set eyes upon him; then he has a rich musical voice which he modulates with such skill that his words seem to personate all the characters of the subject of his discourse. His learning seems to be unlimited, whatever may be the subject brought before his notice; and no one, as yet, has been capable of coping with him in argument; yet there are some things in which he is defective, and on such points he may be led into error. In his nature he is mild, meek and humble in all things pertaining to himself; full of sympathy, of a loving and unbounded benevolence to all men, excepting those he deems the oppressors of the people. In his dealings and decisions he is scrupulous, exact, impartial and strictly just. He is learned in all the theology of the Jewish institutions and the Holy Order of the Priesthood; and where he sees error, imposition, oppression and injustice, he is indefatigable and bold in denouncing these errors, and speaking the truth to the people."

"God of our Fathers," exclaimed Caiaphas in astonishment, "Is this the man against whom thou wouldst conspire? I never knew a man of so perfect a character as thou hast given this one."

200

"Most Reverend Sire," responded Saul, as he erected himself with an air of assurance, "I came not here to speak otherwise of this man than to represent his true character, and in so doing I think your Holy Order will have greater cause to dread him than if I were to vilify him."

"By the Holy of Holies," exclaimed Caiaphas, as he lifted up his eye-lids and stared upon Saul with still greater astonishment for a few seconds. At length a new light seemed to break upon his mind; the marked expression of his countenance subsided to a softer tone, and he added: "Well, I believe thou art right; thou hast so singular a mode of treating an enemy that I was taken by surprise; but I think I see the point at which thou art aiming thy shaft. What thinkest thou, reverend brother?" he added, addressing Gamaliel. "Didst thou mark the words of thy pupil? He says this man Jesus is learned in all the theology of our institutions and Order of Priesthood, and whenever he sees error, imposition or injustice, he is indefatigable in denouncing these errors and telling the truth to the people. What thinkest thou of that?"

"I think, most Reverend Sire," replied Gamaliel with bitterness of expression, "that this Jesus is a dangerous man to our Holy Order, and that we ought to proceed against him, if for no other cause, even to smiting him to death."

Caiaphas was rather shocked at the vindictive denunciation of Gamaliel against Jesus, for he slightly trembled and remained silent for a time, but at length he observed to Saul:

"There are great reports of wonderful cures of diseases that this Jesus has performed. What knowest thou on that head, worthy Saul?"

"This much, Reverend Sire," replied Saul. "These reports are true in part and false in part. It is true that he possesses a power to cure in certain diseases, and to a certain extent over some others, when upon others he cannot make any favorable impressions. What this power is I know not, nor can any other man account for it that I have heard, and I do not believe that even Jesus himself can. But he considers it to be natural, for he says that other men have possessed it before him, and will after him; he, therefore, does not make any pretensions to a super-natural power as the people believe him to possess. Such instances have been known in other parts of the world, therefore we may know that it can be nothing more than a natural power, though we know not what it is. The cures that he has effected, the people have exaggerated by converting them into great miracles; and when they take into account the hints and assertions of that crazy John the Baptist, they firmly believe that this Jesus must be the Messiah of whom the Prophets have spoken. However, it is quite certain that this belief is fast spreading among the people, and if Jesus should give countenance to it, it will spread with still greater rapidity; for he is a man quite capable of gaining their love and confidence, and as it spreads all his doctrines will accompany it; then

201

there will be a rapid revolution in the minds of men. Old institutions will be undermined, giving way rapidly to the great change of the public mind; then, most Reverend Sire, your Holy Order will fall with a crash like all the rest of mundane things."

Caiaphas could not help being struck with the true picture of things that Saul drew, which formed the subject of their discourse. He perceived that Saul was a man well acquainted with all the mysteries of Jewish Theocracy, and all the secret designs, interests, delusions and mummeries of the priesthood; and knowing this, he felt a shame that all the secrets of one in his position should be open to the penetrating eye of such a man. He felt humiliated as he stood in his presence, and almost dreaded the next time he should look upon his countenance to catch a glance from his eye or a curl from his lip expressive of scorn and contempt. He saw clearly that Saul was a man of great mind and ambitious of power, who had some secret design in thus coming forward to aid him in the cause of the priesthood; but judging his designs to be of no greater extent than to obtain some office, he thought there would be no occasion to fear or mistrust him by holding back any secrets or desires. He therefore determined to consult with him in all confidence and accept his friendship and assistance, for he had great reliance in his superior wisdom. Having made these reflections he remarked to Saul in a more familiar and affable tone than before:

"My worthy friend Saul, it would be folly in me if I did not acknowledge the truth and wisdom of thy remarks. Thou seemest to understand the true position of our Holy Order, and the dangers that menace it from the changes now undergoing in the social mind, and thou hast clearly intimated the ominous state of the future. The character of the great Innovator who is the cause of all this dreaded change, thou hast ably described; and now there is still another thing thou must do to fill up the measure of thy services."

"There are no services, though ever so great, that I could not venture upon to serve one of your most exalted station and reverence; you have only to name them," responded Saul with another most obsequious obeisance.

"We would that thou shouldst suggest the means," resumed Caiaphas, "by which this Jesus can be arrested in his progress without danger to our Order, and yet be so effective that we shall not fear him hereafter. Give us thy counsel on this point, and should we approve and avail ourselves of it, we will leave it to thee to intimate in what manner we can testify our acknowledgement of thy services."

"Believe me, most Reverend Sire," responded Saul, "this man must be proceeded against in a cautious and strategic manner. The ordinary proceedings of the Sanhedrim would endanger your own safety and not effect the desired end in view. It is to prevent this, which is one reason that I come forward to offer my humble advice and services, as I am devoted to the interest and continued support of your Holy Order. That which is done to arrest the progress of this man I wish to see done well. If you arrest him and charge him before the tribunal of the Sanhedrim, you may condemn him and cast him into prison, but you will not achieve the end you desire by so doing; you will exasperate his adherents who will effect his liberation by some means. The community will be thrown into great commotion, and our Roman masters in order to quell it may probably strike a blow at your authority; the mass of the people may probably sanction it, and then when your power is once prostrated you will find it difficult to recover. The cause of Jesus will then become more popular, and his adherents will be ten times more numerous. There are no means to prevent the propagation of his doctrines and his influence over the people except by removing him entirely from the scene of his actions. How is that to be done unless by death? But this penalty the Sanhedrim has not the power to inflict, it has passed from their hands to our Roman masters, and they will not spill the citizen's blood when they do not consider it necessary to retain their power. What way, then, ought you to proceed in order to effect your object in view? Simply this: Let this Jesus go on his own way for a time without receiving any notice or molestation from the Sanhedrim; give some one man authority who is competent to watch over him; let there be spies around him to record all his actions and words; let there be men always ready to do the will of this chief officer who has charge of him, and then it will be an easy matter so to entangle and enmesh him that he will commit some offence against our Roman Rule; or others can be made to do so in his name. Men can be easily procured in this Holy City to bear testimony that they saw Jesus do so and so, or, to say such and such. When this critical time shall arrive then the Sanhedrim may proceed against him; then with the charges against him of a political nature he can be handed over to the Roman Governor, so that between the two tribunals and other influences brought to bear upon him he may be made way with."

Saul paused. Caiaphas could not but admire the strong reasoning of Saul and the deep planned strategy he proposed; yet at the same time in his heart he condemned its wickedness, and for some time he struggled with himself before he could decide to avail himself of the suggestions. But he saw it would be vain for him to struggle against his difficulties, and he at length fell under the spell of Saul's superior mental power. Then turning to Saul, with some trepidation in his manner he observed:

"Thy suggestions, Saul, have the wisdom of a god, and the machinations of a—" he was going to say devil, but checking himself, he said "bold man who is devoted to the welfare of our Order. But who is to accomplish and execute this deep laid scheme? Canst thou suggest that, also?"

"I am the man," replied Saul, as he erected his figure and looked upon Caiaphas with unflinching boldness. "Let that office be mine, and I will engage that in a reasonable time all these measures shall be accomplished. This work I have set my mind upon, and if you promise that the Sanhedrim shall not interfere until I will it, the thing shall be done. Two things I shall require of you to my aid: first, your sanction to do so, and secondly, the use of your signet ring until the matter be accomplished. Now say the word, most Reverend Sire—shall the work be done?"

Both Caiaphas and Gamaliel were struck with astonishment at the boldness, callousness of heart, and seeming pleasure with which Saul offered to execute a plot of deep treachery and wickedness against a man he had portrayed in such glowing colors. They knew not what to think of it. Caiaphas beckoned to Gamaliel to step aside, when they walked to the farther end of the chamber and conversed in whispers.

"What thinkest thou of thy friend in this affair," said Caiaphas to Gamaliel, "is he not a bold and desperate man?"

"He is," answered Gamaliel. "That he is so, is good for our cause."

"What can be his enmity against this Jesus?" inquired Caiaphas.

"I am not aware that he has any enmity against him," responded Gamaliel. "Saul does not act from the impulses of common men; it is more probable that he admires the man against whom he is about to act."

"That is strange," said Caiaphas musingly, and then after a slight pause, he added: "However, dost thou think he can be trusted in this affair, and with my ring?"

"He is all prudence," replied Gamaliel, "and will not endanger us, I am sure; and as to your signet, I will answer that he shall use it only in our cause, and return it in safety."

"It is well. I give my consent," said Caiaphas. Then the two priests returned to Saul.

"We give our consent to this enterprise, depending upon thy prudence in all matters as concern us," said Caiaphas to Saul. Then pulling the signet ring from his finger and presenting it to Saul, he added: "And I loan thee this signet upon one condition, which is, that thou dost not use it for any other purpose than that concerning which we have an understanding, and when this business is over, it must be returned."

"Reverend Sir," responded Saul as he received the ring, "all your requests and wishes shall be complied with."

Saul having made his obeisance of departure, left the presence of his most Sacred Reverence, the High Priest of the Holy Temple of Jehovah, in company of Gamaliel, with whom he conversed for awhile and then returned to his home. Thus terminated the interview between the arch conspirators, and the settlement of the great conspiracy against the best man that ever breathed.

When Saul returned to the public inn where he dwelt, on entering his chamber he found Judas awaiting him. He related to the latter his interview with the High Priest, or as much of it as he thought proper for Judas to know. They then sat down, took wine, and conversed upon the future proceedings of their nefarious plot against Jesus, with as much coolness and earnestness as though they were master architects discussing the plan of an edifice. Saul then determined to write a letter in the name of Caiaphas, to Herod Antipas, Tetrarch of Galilee, who reigned as king in that part of the country, advising him, as John the Baptist was in his power, to make way with him. He told Herod that John was a troublesome fellow and a slanderer; that John had slandered Herod all over the country, and was an enemy to the Holy Priesthood; he, therefore, desired that John should trouble neither of them any more. Saul then gave the letter to Judas, telling him to find a trusty messenger and have it sent as soon as he could. Judas received it, promising to comply with his orders, for he was going to start in that direction with Jesus in a day or two, and he would be enabled to convey it to Herod without an express messenger. Having concluded their business, they separated.

VISION SIXTEENTH

COSBI, WHO FIGURED IN THE SO-CALLED MIRACLES

At the south-western extremity of the Holy City, not far from the cattle market, there was a large spring of medicinal water, much celebrated throughout Judea for its power of curing diseases. Whether these cures were produced from any sanitary qualities of the water, or whether through the means of excited minds in the afflicted, it is certain there were many cures produced, so that the spring was visited daily by the afflicted coming from all parts of Judea and more distant parts.

The spring was walled around in form of a parallelogram, partially covered with an arch, and open on one side, where a flight of stone steps descended to the water. On either side were large magnificent porches where the afflicted assembled and awaited their opportunity of bathing. At a certain time of the day the water gurgled into the pool faster than at other times, so that it was believed an angel stirred the water; then it was the most propitious time for bathing. When near the time of movement the afflicted would be waiting in great anxiety for the sign, and as soon as it was given, all who could run, walk or crawl, would immediately rush down the steps and plunge in; many times there were severe accidents, and even deaths, as the consequence of the simultaneous rush; but poor cripples who could neither run nor walk, were dependent upon their friends to be carried there. After bathing some would consider themselves immediately cured; others would feel relieved, and the greater part, though feeling no benefit, would depart buoyed up with hopes.

It was on a Sabbath, in the early part of the day when a great crowd of afflicted persons were assembled within and without the porches waiting for the movement of the waters. Many of them were paralytics; some had extensive sores in various parts; some, diseases of the skin; some, internal complaints; and many had complaints unknown, all of whom whiled the time away with comparative patience and good humor in relating the histories of their diseases, and the wonderful cures effected at the Pool of Bethesda.

While things were in this state, Jesus, followed by Judas, John, Peter and some others, made his appearance among the afflicted people. Judas and Peter had persuaded their master to make this visit to dispense his power of healing among the afflicted, as they thought it would be a good opportunity to extend his fame by a scheme they had planned, which they wished to put into operation.

It was soon spread from mouth to ear that there was a great man present, who could cure diseases. A crowd soon began to collect around Jesus, who called upon him imploringly in the name of the Great Jehovah and Father Abraham, that he would do something for them to relieve their sufferings. Then Jesus took a stand on an elevated spot, intimating that he would address the people; and Matthew pulled out his note book, his reed and ink horn, which he carried in his girdle to be ready to take notes of anything remarkable that might occur, which he probably could convert into a wonderful tale. Then, Jesus casting a glance of commiseration upon the miserable creatures around him, in a mild and sympathizing tone of voice, thus addressed them:

"My poor afflicted brethren: It grieves me to the heart to see you thus before me. My eyes are wet with tears of sympathy when I behold your sufferings; what then must be your feelings who have to suffer? O that it was in my power to give you instant relief! O that it were possible for me to relieve all mankind! I would immediately sweep all maladies from the face of the earth. But it is not, my brethren. I am a poor mortal like yourselves, with limited powers; yet, what little it has pleased God to give me, I am willing to exert in your favor. But first let me say a few words to you, which, perhaps, may do you some good. What are the causes of your sufferings, do you suppose, my brethren? Is it that you have sinned, or your fathers, or fathers' fathers before you? Does God afflict you because your forefathers have sinned? Moses states in the Decalogue that such is the will and decree of the Lord, and you may think it hard and unjust that it is so. So it would be, my brethren, if the Lord ever made such a decree; but such is not the fact. Let me exculpate him from the charge. God is not guilty of such injustice and cruelty,

207

for he is a God of love and mercy, striving to make all things good. How, then, came these evils with which you are afflicted? It is thus, my friends: When the great God of Nature put all matter into motion by mingling with it his divine essence, he strove to do the best that could be done with the vast material mass by the power of his love and wisdom, and as the various phenomena came forth, they were endowed with fixed and perpetual laws. As long as those laws are unbroken everything goes on well; when they are broken by any means they go on badly, and the result is ruin and destruction. Every phenomenon that continues from age to age in conformity with established principles becomes better instead of worse; and everything that departs from its original principles as it continues from one age to another, becomes worse instead of better, until it runs out and is lost. God never condescends to alter his fixed principles in any of his works. Now, my friends, let me inform you that man is one of those phenomena which are worked out by God's eternal principles. If a man passes through life in accordance with those established principles he does well, and as posterity advances he improves; but if he departs from those principles he deteriorates, he becomes diseased, deformed and useless, and will in time run out and be lost. This is the cause, my friends, of your diseases and deformities in most cases. Either you or your fathers have departed from the established principles of your natures, and brought upon you your miseries as the inevitable results. You call them afflictions and attribute them to God as the author, but it is not so; he is not so cruel and merciless as to afflict poor mortals who have erred through ignorance; he would rather mitigate their miseries if he could without altering his eternal principles of creation. As a proof of this he has endowed some men with powers which can mitigate the sufferings of others and ameliorate their conditions. I am one of those powers which God has suffered to exist to mitigate the sufferings of my fellow men. Man is composed of body and spirit; the body may be unsound but the spirit may be sound, and these sufferings of the body may open your eyes to the preservation of the spirit before it is too late to save it. Then thank God you are not altogether impure and hopeless, for as the body may be past recovery, the spirit may not be so. The body will die and be lost in the elements, but the spirit, if pure, will live and enter into another world of enjoyment. Then, my brethren, gain wisdom from your past sufferings; turn your attention to the cultivation and improvement of the spirit, for that will profit you most. Nevertheless, if there be any hopes, it will be well to attend to the body also; therefore what little power I have I will devote to your benefit."

Jesus having made an end to his address, commanded his followers to so arrange the afflicted people that they might receive the benefit of his touch. The followers proceeded to do as they were bid by placing them in a row at a short distance from each other, when they formed a line of about fifty feet in extent. Then Jesus passed along the line, and to every person he ministered certain motions of his hands, aided with the power of his eyes. With some he stayed a few moments, and with others a longer time, touching them on various parts of their persons, while to others he gave a simple wave of the hand. As soon as he had terminated these proceedings he stood before them and observed:

"My friends, with the blessing of God, and a struggle within yourselves to prove worthy of his blessings, you may become cured. Now, as soon as the waters of the pool are moved, go and bathe seven times a day; and when you do so, pour water upon your heads, calling upon my name."

Jesus, in giving this last order, was not vain or foolish enough to think that his name would be more efficacious in producing a cure than any other man's name, but he did so to make a decided impression upon their minds; for he knew that if their minds could be aroused and concentrated to a firm belief in that effect, the chance of cure would be more possible and probable. He knew also that some of the cures would depend upon the impression he made upon their minds solely, and thus it was he told them to use his name. To give them time for their minds to act favorably, he told them to go through the operations seven times over.

The signal was now given that the waters of the pool were moving, and immediately the afflicted made a rush to the place as fast as their powers of locomotion would allow them. Some ran, some walked, some tottered, some crawled, and some actually leaped and soon got to the steps leading down to the pool, which they descended somehow, and immediately plunged into the waters.

Jesus was now about to retire from the pool when his attention was arrested by some one calling upon his name in piteous strains: "O Jesus, Jesus, thou man of God, have pity on me!" Then Judas and Peter went to the porches from whence the voice came, to discover who it was that called, and in a few moments they returned, helping along a miserably deformed and diseased creature, and brought him before Jesus. He seemed to be a man advanced in years, with a blotched and disfigured face. He supported his body by resting on two short crutches, his knees being on the ground, and his legs which were apparently lifeless, he dragged after him. His head was covered with a dirty linen, from beneath which spread around long gray locks of hair. His eyebrows were enormously large, of a grayish white, and his face was nearly covered with a mass of gray beard, moustache and whiskers. On one side of his neck there was a large swelling, which caused his head to hang on the other side. His dress consisted of a combination of rags of various sizes, shapes and colors; so that altogether he presented a revolting spectacle of misery and misfortune.

As soon as Jesus caught sight of him, he was shocked, and instinctively placed his hand upon his heart to quiet the painful emotions aroused within him.

"Jesus, thou man of God, have pity upon me, and do something to relieve me," piteously cried the poor man, as soon as Peter and Judas placed him before their master.

"I doubt that any power of mine can do thee any good, my poor man," answered Jesus with sympathy and regret. "Thou must look to God above for help."

"I know thou canst help me, kind master, for my dreams have told me so," returned the deformed man pertinaciously.

"Master," observed Judas, "this poor man has long been praying and wishing for thee; he believes strongly that thou canst help him, and will not be satisfied unless thou wilt touch him."

"Well, be it as thou wilt," said Jesus, addressing the poor man. "If thy strong faith and my good will and power will cure thee, be thou cured."

Then Jesus quietly laid his hand upon the head of the poor man, who immediately uttered an ejaculation of mingled joy and surprise, and exclaimed:

"0! forever blessed be thy name, kind master! I feel better already, and if thy servants will carry me to the pool, I doubt not that I shall recover.

Then Jesus gave orders to Judas and Peter to carry the man to the pool, and then he turned from the place and bent his steps towards the temple, followed by John, James and the others.

As Judas and Peter were carrying the deformed to the pool, the former whispered in the ear of the latter:

"Cosbi, thou art an excellent mimic, and thy disguises are perfect, thy father would not have known thee."

"What father does know his son?" said Cosbi laughing, for he was the deformed.

"This will be a miraculous cure when finished," observed Peter dryly. "When I shall tell it to my old acquaintances, they will think that I have improved on the big fish story."

"Well, Cosbi," resumed Judas, "when we throw thee into the pool thou must finish thy cure, and not forget to let the folks know that it was Jesus who wrought this miraculous effect upon thee."

"I think we had better get Matthew to draw up an account of it," observed Peter; "he is a great hand at the marvelous style; then we can recite it to the people."

"0 leave it to me," said Cosbi. "When you throw me into the pool I will give a good account of it. 0! what fun I shall have among the cripples!" Then Cosbi laughed.

210

Then the whole party descended the steps to the pool, when Judas and Peter threw Cosbi into the water among the others; he immediately commenced splashing, floundering, jumping, shouting and clapping his hands, declaring that he was perfectly cured, and that the man of God, Jesus, had done it.

VISION SEVENTEENTH

The Beautiful Gate is the largest and handsomest of nine which gives entrance to the Court of Israel from the Gentiles' Court. It stands fronting the east with a colonnade and range of chambers on either side, the ground being seventeen feet above the other court, and the pillars being forty-seven feet high with the entablature making sixty. This gate is of surpassing magnificence, and is about ninety feet in height and seventy in width; the door being of massive Corinthian brass, covered on both sides with gold plates, as also the joints and lintels, with plain or fretted figures in low or high relief. On either side of the doorway is a tower seventy-three feet high, adorned with columns twenty feet in circumference. All the exquisite art and ingenuity of the Jewish people seem to have been expended on this particular gate, for it was the most gorgeous of all the other parts of the temple. No one but an Israelite was allowed to enter it to the court beyond, for all other nations and creeds were excluded to the court below. When one of the true faith, as he considered himself, passed through the Gentiles' Court and entered at this Beautiful Gate, a glow of pride and vanity ran through him to think that he was one of the privileged; he thought he must be superior to those he had passed in his way; he, therefore, could not help giving support and praise to institutions which had given birth to such vanity and error.

It was about the second hour when Jesus and some of his followers were walking in the Gentiles' Court in front of the Beautiful Gate. Since the remarkable cure that had taken place at the Pool of Bethesda in the morning, his fame had considerably extended, so that whersoever he was seen, some one knew him who would impart this information to others, and crowds of people would gather roundabout him. On the present occasion there were many people gathered in small groups up and down before the gate. They all stared at him as he passed. Some cried aloud that "he was the man of God." Others, that "he was the Messiah," while others approached him humbly asking for his blessing; and others made so bold as to stoop and kiss the selvage of his garment. At length a group of men approached him, and prostrating themselves before him in the most humble manner, when one of them, who acted as speaker for the rest, said:

"Master, we have heard that thou art a good and wise man, that thou art blessed of God, holding a power from him to cure many complaints of the unhappy and afflicted people. We beg of thee to help us, for we are sorely plagued with divers complaints; impart to us, we beg of thee, the virtue of thy mysterious power, by placing thy hand upon us and healing our diseases."

"Is it in me, or in God, thou trustest?" inquired Jesus, who was much pleased with the honest and sensible speaking of the man. "I am nothing more than a poor mortal like thyself, for I cannot lift my finger through any independent will of my own."

"Master," replied the man, "I know that all things come of God, and that we are all dependent on him; yet there are some of his children who have received a greater portion of his grace and power than others."

"Thou hast spoken wisely," remarked Jesus, who could not help being struck with the ideas of the man, being so much more rational than the superstitious notions of the people generally. "It is as thou sayest; and whatever advantage I have over thee through God's favor, I will share with thee and thy companions to your benefit. Arise, then, good people."

Then Jesus placed his hands upon the heads of all of them, at the same time giving them his blessing. Then they departed rejoicing and invoking blessings in return.

Then a tall man approached Jesus, who was dressed in a long black vestment fringed around the bottom, and a girdle of the same around his loins, with a plain linen tire around his head, having a high conical black centre piece, from beneath which his coarse black hair hung down straight, just reaching the nape of his neck, and cropped all around with great precision. His visage was long and meagre, of a dirty olive complexion; his beard black, long, combed out straight and cut even at the ends. The corners of his mouth were drawn down most lugubriously, and his hazel eyes emitted an expression of great gloominess. As this man approached Jesus his steps were staid and solemn; when suddenly arresting them, he confronted him with a look of severity and disapprobation, and said in a harsh tone of voice:

"Knowest thou, man of confusion, that this day is the Sabbath, and that thou art breaking the laws in performing thy acts of jugglery and pretended cures?"

Jesus, when he saw this man confront him, felt instinctively that an enemy was in his presence, and before any dialogue had commenced, he erected his noble person with an air of defiance. The thousand graces of love and amiability that generally played around his mouth, forsook him for a time; they became compressed, and his nostrils dilated and expanded with the current of life rapidly passing through them. But when the man addressed him in the language as above stated, his eyes, which generally expressed loving and amiable emotions, for the moment forsook their wonted offices and now beamed with a powerful fire of high indignation, expressing the dignity of his manhood to be insulted and aroused for defence or war.

213

"Man of folly and conceit," replied Jesus in an emphatic manner, "who art thou thus to question me? Thinkest thou that I am a pagan that I know not when is the Sabbath? I, who when a child, could repeat the laws of Moses, thinkest thou that I know not the law?"

"Then if thou knowest these things, why dost thou break the law?" further inquired the man in black. "Is it not commanded to keep the Sabbath holy?"

"Did Moses or the God that spoke through Moses, give permission that unholy acts may be done on any other day of the week?" inquired Jesus.

"No," replied his opponent.

"Then," resumed Jesus, "if all our acts are required to be holy, where is the difference, whether we do them on a Sabbath or any other day?"

The opponent could not find an answer to this question, so he contented himself by frowning and allowing Jesus to resume. He was one of the dominant religious sects of that day, called the Pharisees, who made great pretensions to extreme piety and righteousness, but practiced only hypocrisy and selfishness.

"What are holy acts," resumed Jesus, "but such as will please God and benefit man. Then let my acts be examined by this test; they will speak for themselves. If they are evil they cannot be holy; therefore they ought not to be done on any day; and if they be good, they are holy, therefore it is no sin to do them on the Sabbath. If thou wert sick and I cure thee, would it be good or bad for thee?"

"In that case, it would be good," replied the Pharisee.

"Well, then," resumed Jesus, "what else have I done for others but cure their infirmities and enlighten their understandings, that they may live a healthy life. Thus to act is to conform to what is holy, whether it be done on a Sabbath or on any other day; therefore I break not the law of Moses."

"But the law requires that thou shalt do all thy work on the six days in the week, and rest on the Sabbath," remarked the Pharisee.

"My labor," replied Jesus, "is to do good. I hold it as the greatest principle upon which all true religion ought to be founded, to do good without ceasing, without distinction of time or seasons as long as we have the power to do so; and I will defy the whole body of the Priesthood to find a law of Moses to oppose it. Which wouldst thou rather do, save thy ox from falling into the pit on the Sabbath, or leave it to the next day when thy efforts would avail thee nothing to save it?"

"In that case," replied the Pharisee, "I think I should prefer saving the ox on the Sabbath; but thou must recollect that this restriction of labor has reference to regular daily labor."

"The law of the Sabbath is good in that respect," replied Jesus. "The intent of the law was for the benefit of the poor laboring class, as a time of rest from labor, recruiting their powers, and a time for recreation. But how is it construed by the Priesthood? They say the Sabbath is the Lord's day; on it thou shalt do no manner of work, excepting to wait on the Priesthood, to prepare their food, their clothing, their houses, or anything else they may require. The law says, also, that the ox, the ass, or the servant shall not labor on that day; yet the priests ride their horses, asses and mules on that day whither they choose. This law of the Sabbath, though good in the intent, is like all the others, construed by the priesthood to their advantage only."

"But," remarked the Pharisee, "the Sabbath is a day which is to be kept holy in commemoration of the Lord's works, for he made the world and all that is in it, and rested on the seventh day, which he commanded to be kept holy."

"The cause assigned in the Decalogue for the observance of the Sabbath, is but an absurd fiction," replied Jesus; "so egregiously absurd is it that no man can give it credence, unless he put aside common sense, general experience and all learning. I will put a very simple case to thee to prove my assertion. Suppose a man shall work for thee daily for forty days, and at the end of that time he has done so much work—we will say he has ploughed forty rods of land. What wouldst thou say, if that man told thee he had done, at a former time, ten thousand times more work than that in six days?"

"I should think, in that case," replied the Pharisee, "that he was either a liar or a crazy man."

"Thou wouldst have reason," returned Jesus. "Now let us apply this to the law of the Sabbath. According to Moses' account when he was in the mountain of Sinai he was absent forty days and nights, while the Lord was making the two tablets containing the ten commandments. When Moses descended he read them to the people, and one of them says that the Lord made heaven and earth in six days." Now, if it took the Lord, with the aid of Moses, forty days to make two tablets of inscription, how can we believe the assertion that the Lord made heaven and earth in six days? There is no rationality in believing it, it is so absurd and ridiculous. We must, therefore, infer that the cause assigned for the establishment of the law of the Sabbath is nothing more than an absurd fiction invented by Moses. If we examine the features of this fiction, we shall find that we are at variance with all the experiences and knowledge we are enabled to deduce from the phenomena of nature, for they amount to positive impossibilities. In the first place, it states 'the Lord created the heavens and the earth and all that in them is.' Now, the word create means to bring into existence. The world and all the other bodies in the heavens are vast masses of matter, which to create is an impossibility, even to God himself, for something cannot be brought out of nothing. An atom of matter cannot be made, neither can it be destroyed. There has always been as much matter as there is now, and there will be the same amount to all eternity. Matter is always undergoing a change of form; but it never was created and never will be destroyed; there the statement is false and silly. There is another point we must notice. It is said that 'the Lord having finished his work on the sixth day, rested on the seventh.' This statement is disproved by the fiction itself in more instances than one, but I will view it in another light, to show its absurdity and impossibility. If we inquire into the nature of God, we are enabled to know this much at least: That he is an eternal active principle, a vital essence or subtle material power of intelligence and action; without an imaginary beginning, but now in action, never ceasing, and will never end. Then to suppose that he after a certain amount of labor became tired and needed rest, is to suppose that his nature is analogous to our own mortal state, which becomes fatigued and exhausted, needing recuperation. This will be to compare God to a poor laborer who sweats and toils, struggling, straining and panting at his work until he becomes exhausted, and then lies down to rest. How inconsistent, how absurd, how silly this conception would be of a God, a child would be enabled to see! This fiction, therefore, needs no further refutation."

"How, then, thinkest thou the Sabbath ought to be observed?" inquired the Pharisee.

"It was designed by Moses as a day of rest from labor," answered Jesus. "Thus far it is good. The working people require one day of rest from labor in the week; but there are other wants the mass of the people require, which they ought to seek on that day. They require intelligence, therefore a part of the day ought to be set apart to the improving and refining their minds. They need recreations or amusements also to buoy up their spirits to cheerfulness, and fortify themselves against the disappointments and hardships of life. Yes, the remainder of that day ought to be devoted to rational and innocent amusements of dancing, singing, Innocent games, exhibitions, walks, races, feats of power and emulation, gathering of kin and social assemblages of all virtuous kinds; and many other ways by which gloom, discontent, sorrow and apathy can be dispersed, the heart made cheerful and all rendered happy. Such is the manner the Sabbath ought to be observed, and such the people will enjoy when their rulers become wise.

The Pharisee having no further objections to urge, Jesus ended his discourse about the Sabbath. The former took his leave with a little more civility than when he commenced the acquaintance of the latter, feeling that his previous notions were somewhat shaken. He thought that Jesus was not altogether an ignorant pagan, and by the time he reached home, he felt that he was a wiser man.

Jesus then left the Court of the Gentiles and the temple, when, having given Judas certain orders concerning his followers, he, in company with John, passed over the Mount of Olives to Bethany, where, in the hospitable home of Lazarus, he passed several days reposing himself after his exertions. Sweetly glided his hours in this retreat surrounded by domestic comforts; his stern, arduous duties being exchanged for humble domestic enjoyments, which were rendered tenfold sweeter by the innocent enlivening discourse of his chaste and beloved Mary.

Here he received a message from John the Baptist, who stated that he was in prison at Sychar, by the authority of Herod Antipas. John told him also that if he were the true Messiah to come and release him, and if he were not, to send word that he (John) should be no longer under delusion and false hopes. Then Jesus held a council with Judas, Peter, and John of Galilee, when it was decided to depart forthwith for Sychar in Galilee.

VISION EIGHTEENTH

The slanting rays of an evening sun gilded the temple roof, which stood on the top of Gerizim, where prayers, incense and sacrifices were daily put up, with other priestly performances, striving to rival the "Temple of the Lord" at Jerusalem.

On the eastern side, stretching north and south, lay the narrow valley of Shechem. On the north-eastern side, at the termination of its lowest slope, stood the walled city of Sychar, which formed part of the dominions of Herod Antipas, Tetrarch of Galilee. Between this small city and the termination of the valley of Shechem, near to the base of the mountain, there was a well which was walled around with stone about two feet from the ground. Of so ancient a date was this well that it was attributed to the times of their ancestor Jacob by the people of Samaria.

The sun was fast disappearing behind the mountains indicating that the day was near to a close. Shepherds and shepherdesses were returning with their flocks of sheep from the mountains to their enclosures around the town, and a sombre haze was spreading over the eastern sky when four travelers arrived at the well, seeming to be wearied with their day's travel. They sat upon the edge of the well conversing for a time, waiting in hope some one would come to draw water, that they might have an opportunity of drinking; but their patience becoming exhausted, three of the four departed for the city with the intention of procuring meat and drink, the other preferring to await their return.

The party of three had not long left their companion at the well when a female of middle age, with a water vessel on her bead, left the city and bent her steps to that spot. She was of dark olive complexion, dark sparkling eyes, and long, jetty black hair tied behind in form of a club, which was adorned with trinkets and braids; her features were agreeable, her form symmetrical, and her vesture gay and graceful.

With a light, bounding step she approached the well; but as soon as she saw a stranger sitting there, she gave a start that caused her to place her hand to the vessel to keep it from falling. Her start was not one of fear or timidity, but rather of surprise and admiration on beholding so handsome a person so unexpectedly before her. Having deposited her vessel upon the ground she gave a slight modest inclination of recognition, and then proceeded to draw her water. The stranger removed from his position, courteously offering the woman his assistance, but she intimated she would rather do it herself. Having filled her vessel she was about replacing it upon her head when the stranger, who was no other than Jesus, addressed her in a mild, sweet and persuasive voice:

"Good woman, wilt thou give me to drink?"

The woman retreated a step with some degree of confusion and distress, looking upon him with an expression as though she would willingly comply but dare not; and after a moment's hesitation she replied:

"How is this, sir? Thou art a stranger to me, yet from thy appearance I take thee to be a Jew. If I am right thou knowest it is forbidden by the Samaritans to eat or drink in company of Jews."

"Thou art right, woman," replied Jesus mildly, "as far as the customs of thy people restrict and command thee; but hast thou not understanding enough to perceive that such customs are wicked prejudices, unjust and inhuman? Wouldst thou treat all persons so who should ask of thee to drink? Wouldst thou refuse thy brother a drink if he should ask thee?"

The woman seemed much troubled at what Jesus had said to her; then stepping aside from her vessel, she pointed to it and said:

"In the name of our father Jacob, take the vessel, sir, and drink—for thou knowest I dare not give it to thee."

Then Jesus took the vessel and drank enough to quench his thirst, and as he was replacing it, she added:

"But tell me sir, what meanest thou by saying, wouldst thou refuse thy brother a drink if he should ask thee?"

"I mean," replied Jesus, who reseated himself upon the well, "that we are all children of the same God, therefore I am thy brother. The God that formed this beautiful world, the sun, the moon and the stars, is the same power that brought us into being as men and women; therefore we are all the offspring of his parental care. Thus we ought to treat each other with as much love and kindness as though we were brothers and sisters of the same earthly parents. If, then, we are brothers and sisters of the same heavenly father, how will it sound in his ears when I shall say in my prayers, that thou, my sister, would not give me to drink when I asked thee?"

"Thy views seem to have reason in them," replied the woman as her timidity and prejudice seemed to soften, "and thy words sound pleasantly upon my ears, suggesting to me thoughts and feelings which I have often experienced in my dreams of happiness, but never realized."

"Ah!" exclaimed Jesus, his eyes beaming with pleasure, "what thou hast just said confirms me of the truth."

"What truth?" inquired the woman somewhat surprised.

"The truth is," returned Jesus, "thou concealest a prisoner within thee."

"A prisoner in me," cried the woman in greater amazement.

"Yes, a prisoner, whose existence thou hast concealed from thy-self," answered Jesus; "one whom thou hast neglected and treated with cruel-

219

ty and injustice, keeping it shut out from the light of God's world to pine and suffer in the dungeon and darkness of thy ignorance. I mean, woman, thy soul—that divine spark of life which the Lord gave to thee to improve and cultivate, but which thou hast deprived of its rightful authority and thrust into oblivion, placing around it the guards of evil customs and prejudices to prevent its asserting its true nature. But when I was speaking to thee of our heavenly father—of our being his children, and our duty to each other as brothers and sisters, then that prisoner within thee heard my voice. Judging that some friend was near, it called aloud to be liberated. Then thou saidst my words suggested to thee thoughts and feelings which thou hadst often felt in thy dreams of happiness. O, woman! woman! let that ill-treated prisoner, thy soul, come forth to see the light. Turn away the guards and break the shackles of customs and prejudices, and let it come forth to the light of day in its native innocence even though it be as a little child. Let me direct it in the way that leads to the true God."

"Who art thou?" inquired the woman, who seemed to be undergoing great emotions of mingled awe and reverence for the person before her. "Art thou a Rabbi or a prophet, for no man has spoken to me like thou hast done."

"I am one who aspires to be a man in his true dignity, having a consciousness that he possesses a portion of the God-head within him," replied Jesus in an impressive manner.

"I know thou must be somebody of greater mind than I have seen in Samaria," remarked the woman with seeming reverence. "Our Rabbi tells us we must worship God upon Mount Gerizim, bring our offerings, perform our ceremonies, pay our tithes, respect our people and hate the Jews. Such are the duties we are told to perform; but no one except thou has told me that 'the God of all nature is the God of all men, that we are all his children, and that we should love one another.' Then that imprisoned soul of mine which thou hast brought to my notice, filled me with wonder and unspeakable delight! Kind and learned sir, wilt thou come and tarry with us in our town? My husband, who is the custodian of the prison, will be delighted to see thee, and make thee welcome."

Jesus saw that the woman was regarding him with a pleasing and respectful expression of countenance, and a degree of uneasy expectancy as to his reply. With these favorable indications and the kind tones in which she addressed him, he thought she would be willing to render him any kind service he should ask of her. Having reflected for a few moments, he at length replied:

"Thou sayest thou hast a husband, and that he is custodian of the prison. Canst thou tell me what prisoners he has under his charge?"

"There are but few," replied the woman, surprised at the question; "for our Lord, the Tetrarch, is very severe, whoever disobeys his commands is soon disposed of by death or otherwise. There are two robbers and two of his servants now in prison. There is an old looking man besides who was lately brought from the fortress of Mareschaeus, whose name is John the Baptist, he having offended our Lord in some way not known to me."

"Wouldst thou do me a service if I ask it of thee?" demanded Jesus.

"All that is in my power to do, I will do to serve so good a man as thou," answered the woman earnestly.

"Well, then," said Jesus, "go to thy husband and prevail upon him to give me an interview with this John the Baptist in his cell."

"It is strictly forbidden," answered the woman, "that any one shall be admitted to see this prisoner, John; but sometimes things are done contrary to the commands of our Lord, and I think it possibly can be again. I know that my husband loves me, and at times my word with him is as powerful as the command of Herod Antipas. I will now return to him, and if possible the thing shall be done. Be thou at this well about the fifth hour of night; at that time all will be still and quiet in the town, then I will send a messenger to thee, who will inform thee if I succeed to thy desire."

The woman then making an inclination of respect took up her water vessel which she placed upon her head, and with hasty steps departed for her home in Sychar.

In a few minutes after the departure of the Samaritan woman the followers of Jesus returned bringing with them some provisions, including a bottle of wine holding about three gallons. Jesus then gave orders that they should seek out a favorable spot in the woods, as near as possible to the well of Jacob, where they would take their supper and pass the night, for by this time it was dark. They then retired to a copse not many yards distant where they spread their mantles and every man made himself as comfortable as he could, and then proceeded to attack the good things they had bought at Sychar. Their appetites were good, and though it was dark, practice and instinct combined showed them the way the food ought to go. The goat skin bottle was repeatedly in request; Peter especially showing a great affection for it. He embraced it with as much true love as though it were a living pet, or child of his own. He took it in his arms and pressed it fervently to his breast; placing his lips to the orifice, with long repeated embraces, he expressed the ardor of his love and devotion; and when at length he tore himself away, tears of sympathy or vinous excitement burst from his eyes.

Having satisfied their hunger and thirst they passed some time discoursing on their adventures and future intended journey. Peter enlivening the talk every now and then with some facetious narrative, and once that night he related his big fish story with an improvement.

The time passed on until it was far into the night. John had fallen asleep, when Jesus arose, then telling Judas and Peter to remain where they were until he should return; or should anything prevent his returning that night they must seek him in the morning at Sychar. He then left them, and bent his way towards the well.

As soon as Jesus had left his followers, Peter whispered to Judas so that John should not hear a word that was said:

"Has our master any idea of the intended fate of poor John the Baptist?"

"No," replied Judas in a similar manner, "he knows nothing of the plot that has been devised for his old companion. It will grieve him sorely when he finds it out, for he loves his old friend, although he knows him to be a crazy zealot."

"When did Cosbi arrive with the letter that Saul wrote in the name of the High Priest?" demanded Peter.

"He arrived four days ago," answered Judas. "He gained admittance to Herod's presence, and delivered it into his hands. The Tetrarch was much surprised at its contents, but said it should be attended to, and that he must wait to carry back an answer. Since then, John has been transferred from the fortress of Mareschaeus to the prison at Sychar, where he arrived yesterday, and Cosbi has received intimation that he must prepare to depart tomorrow; so it is very likely that poor John will be executed in the morning."

"Ah!" exclaimed Peter, "then Jesus has arrived just in time to take a last farewell of his old companion, if he can get to see him."

"John the Baptist will be the first man that Saul will make away with to accomplish his ends," observed Judas with a shudder.

They then said no more, but resigned themselves to sleep.

Jesus had been sitting on the edge of Jacob's well for several minutes, reflecting upon past scenes and times concerning his and John the Baptist's career when they were fellow students and companions; he traced John's history from his most early days, and continued it up to that time when he was languishing in prison, and he could not help giving vent to a deep sigh when he thought of the probable future termination of his career. While he was in this thoughtful mood, a tall figure enveloped in a mantle softly approached him, and said in a low voice:

"Art thou the man who wishes to see John the prisoner?"

Jesus started, but readily conceiving the business of the visitor, made answer:

"I am."

"Then follow me," was the reply.

And the person without giving other explanation or showing his countenance, turned in the direction of Sychar, pursuing the path with a quiet, stealthy step, and Jesus following in a similar manner. The night was dark with the exception of the light emitted by the stars. Mount Gerizim gloomed in the south-west, and the town of Sychar could not be distinguished before them except by the twinkle of a light here and there.

After a few minutes walking they arrived before a large wooden gate which was closed; but on one side of it there was a narrow opening before which stood a sentinel leaning upon a spear, who immediately upon their approach demanded the password. The guide then advanced and whispered something, when the sentinel stood aside, allowing them to pass. With the same noiseless steps they passed along the main thoroughfare for some hundred feet without meeting anybody, then they turned into a more narrow one, and in a short time came to a large stone edifice, in front of which were pillars of great magnificence. Passing along this they came to an inclosure, when the guide opening a small door entered a garden, and having traversed some of the walks they came to the rear of the building, which was the palace of Herod, in the lower part of which the prison for particular offenders was situated. Entering a small door they came to a passage which led them to another door, which, on being opened, they entered a chamber where Jesus saw the Samaritan woman with whom he had discoursed at the well.

The guide then threw off his mantle in which he was enveloped, and presented the appearance of a man of middle age, with an agreeable countenance.

"Husband, this is the good man I have been speaking to thee about," said the woman, with great pleasure lightening up her countenance.

"I know not who thou art," said the custodian addressing Jesus, "or what is thy object in wishing to see the prisoner John, unless it be the promptings of humanity and friendship, which I admire in those who seek an interest in the unfortunate. But my wife having spoken in great favor of thee as a good man, I have consented to comply with thy wishes, and run the risk of the consequences. Thou wilt therefore be prudent and not put me in danger."

Jesus commended the custodian for his kind feelings, thanked him for his good opinion, and spoke in great praise of his wife, acknowledging her services. Then the custodian taking a lamp bid Jesus follow him. They left the room by another door that opened into a corridor, along which they passed for some distance until they came to a wide flight of steps, down which they descended to another corridor, on either side of which was a range of cells with massive wooden doors fastened with bars of iron crossing them. Having come to a particular door the custodian removed the bars, opened it and entered the cell followed by Jesus.

For the first few moments nothing was visible in the gloomy chamber; but gradually the outlines of things began to impress the sight. It was a small rectangular chamber, as though cut out of solid rock, so close and firm were the blocks of stone cemented together. There was a bed of straw in one corner and a vessel containing water, which were all the conveniences of the unhappy inmate. There was a hole in the upper part of the wall to admit air, but no means of obtaining light. In the centre of the floor seated on a block of wood, was an object bearing the human form, to which the custodian pointed as he observed: "Behold thy friend." Then he placed the lamp upon the floor and left the cell.

The light of the lamp was too powerful for the eyes of the prisoner at first, for he shaded them with his hands and admitted it gradually; then turning his sight towards the visitor he endeavored to ascertain who it was. The long dark hair and beard of the prisoner was tangled and matted, scattering around in the greatest disorder; his eyes were sunken in their sockets, and nearly lustreless; his cheeks were hollow; his whole form wasted, and his garments dirty and tattered. Altogether he was a miserable object of tyrannical oppression.

Jesus regarded the unfortunate man for the first few moments in silence, for he was so overcome with painful emotions that he could not speak; but at length recovering his powers he exclaimed in a tone of the deepest anguish:

"0 John! John! is it thus I see thee?"

John the Baptist sprang to his feet uttering a shout of joy; then raising and clasping his hands above him, he ejaculated:

"My God, I thank thee! I said he would come. I knew I was not deceived!"

Then Jesus rushed forward and fell upon John's neck, but spoke not.

"Shed not tears for me, my lord and master," said John in a tremulous voice, as he endeavored to disengage himself from the embrace of Jesus. "It is not for thou to expend the essence of thy virtue upon a poor sinner such as I am. Thy presence is glory enough for me. Let thy tears be reserved for others more worthy. Yet, master, glad am I that thou art come, for this imprisonment bears sorely upon me. I fain would be released from this dungeon to go upon the world once more; not that I love the world, but I love to do my duty to thee, and fulfill the words of the prophets, by proclaiming thy name and office to the lost people of Israel."

"John! John!" exclaimed Jesus, as he retreated a few steps from the prisoner, "let me hear no more of this strain of talking. I should have thought that thy misfortunes would have banished thy former delusions of mind. 0 John, how have I reasoned with thee, entreated thee, and even begged of thee to banish these foolish ideas! How, by my arguments, by showing thee my deficiencies and lack of all necessary powers, have I endeavored to convince thee of thy error, in conceiving me to be what I am not. But all my endeavors to bring thee to right reason

224

have proven in vain, for thy mind is still under the same delusion."

"Is it possible," exclaimed John, as he started back a pace with the greatest alarm expressed upon his haggard countenance, "that I have been under a delusion? Art thou really not the Messiah come to release me from his prison?"

"Have I not always denied being such, and thou wouldst not believe me?" answered Jesus. "How, then, can I convince thee? Thou knowest that I have always loved thee, and would do anything that I could for thy benefit. If it were in my power, would I not release from prison the man I love?"

John seemed to be struck with a new idea, for the glance of his eye became expressive of more rational and serious thought. He remained silent for a few moments, but at length said impressively:

"Then thou canst not release me from this prison?"

"No, John," replied Jesus sorrowfully, who perceived that he began to make an impression of the truth upon the weak mind of the unfortunate man, "it is impossible; if I could, I would. Ought that not to convince thee that I am not what thou hast thought me to be for so many years?"

"Great God! have pity on me, for I am a miserable man," exclaimed John in a tone expressive of utter despair and a conviction of his true standing. "I now perceive that my life has been one of complete delusion."

Then the miserable man threw himself upon the block of wood, covering his face with his hands, a picture of hopeless despair.

"John," said Jesus in a tremulous tone, "sorry am I that this perception of thy error has come so late. Thou canst not blame me for thy delusion, although I have been the innocent cause. From the very first hour when that mysterious power was discovered in me, upon which thou didst conceive thy delusive idea, did I not deny and oppose all thy erroneous suggestions? Was it not the means of discontinuing our youthful friendly intercourse, because thou wouldst not be convinced of my reasons and denial, but still adhered to thy errors? It is true that I could not account for the power I found in me; yet I had sufficient knowledge to be convinced that it could not be as thou didst endeavor to persuade me. Since we were youthful companions, I have been enabled to learn something concerning it, enough to know that it is a natural power, and not superhuman, as thou didst think it to be. Like all other natural principles it is beyond our search to ascertain its true nature; though we cannot account for it, it is nevertheless natural. The great cause of this delusion of thine has been in the nature of thy studies. The dark, gloomy train of superstition which the priesthood prescribed for thee, had the power to weaken thy reasoning faculty, and prevent thee from acquiring just and wholesome ideas of things; therefore when thou didst see this extraordinary power of mine, thy superstition availed itself of the opportunity to confirm and exemplify its doctrines."

"Say no more, my dear Jose," said John the Baptist, as he withdrew his hands from his face and looked up to Jesus with a sorrowful mien. "I must call thee by that name, now my delusion is past. That name brings to my mind the fond reminiscences of our youthful friendship, and the many pleasing incidents of our happy young days. That name is suggestive of all that is innocent and blissful in my youthful career, while the name of Jesus that I gave thee at thy baptism, suggests only my folly and madness. Say no more, Jose, to justify thyself being free of blame in this matter—I know thou art blameless. Thou didst all thou couldst to arrest and exterminate my outrageous folly; but, as thou sayest, my mind must have been weakened before the time of thy mysterious power became manifest, or I could not have been so egregiously deluded by my own erroneous notions. It matters not now, however, there will soon be an end to my regret and sorrow, for I have a presentiment that I shall not be many hours among the living. I have lived a life of self-delusion; it will, therefore, be better that I go down to the grave without sorrow, regret, or notice of the world."

Any further discourse between the two friends was prevented by the custodian rushing into the cell with alarm depicted on his countenance, who said hurriedly:

"My friends, you must part instantly. 0, John the Baptist, pardon me for making the announcement, for I must do my official duty. There is an order received that John the Baptist be executed at the hour of six."

"Executed!" exclaimed Jesus in terror, as he staggered to the wall and leaned against it for support.

John raised his eyes and clasped his hands, and then ejaculated in a tone of great solemnity:

"Then indeed is the delusion of this world over, and the reality of the next begins."

"Come sir," said the custodian to Jesus, taking him by the arm, "not another minute must thou tarry; we must away from the city before the guard comes around."

Urged by the custodian, Jesus left the wall and instantly threw himself upon the neck of John; their embraces were in sorrow and tears—a farewell was faintly expressed, and Jesus tore himself away.

In a few minutes the custodian had conducted Jesus without the walls of Sychar, when the latter made his way to his followers whom he found asleep. Jesus then sat up the remainder of the night lamenting and weeping over the fate of his old friend and youthful companion, John the Baptist. When morning broke, he awoke his followers and related to them the adventures of the night, all of whom gave evidence of great sorrow, especially Peter, who was obliged to resort to the goat skin bottle to supply his waste of tears. However, they prepared to depart on their route through Galilee; and as they were passing by Sychar, they learned that John the Baptist was executed in the middle of the night.

VISION NINETEENTH

"Friend Alexander, from the nature of the intelligence which now I wish to impart to you, the numerous and disconnected parts contained therein, I find it surpasses my ingenuity and skill to convey it to you in the form of a vision; therefore I shall be constrained to use the mode of simple address or relation. I shall so endeavor to impress your mind that you may re-commit it to paper from your memory. To relate all the travels and adventures of Jesus and his followers in detail would be very difficult, even if it were possible to gather all the accounts from the spirits who were concerned therein when mortals on the earth; but as Judas has informed me there was a great sameness or similarity in them, I shall not impose so heavy a task upon you, even if I were able to do so. I shall, therefore, speak of them as a whole—with the exception of the scenes and events, with which I have already impressed you—during his several tours through Judea and Galilee; and I shall then recommence my mode of impressing you by visions with regard to the remainder of his career, where he returns to the vicinity of Jerusalem for the last time.

"Throughout the numerous towns, villages and country places where Jesus passed, he made a great impression upon the people, for he was generally well received by them. Even in places where his fame had not reached, his noble, manly appearance and amiable manners made an agreeable impression, before he broached any of his doctrines. However suspicious they were at first, or whatever antipathies they took to his followers, they had no doubt of his being an intelligent and good man. His most numerous admirers and adherents were among the poor, for he spoke to them in gentle and affable terms. He sympathized with them in their afflictions and calamities. He pointed out in a mild manner the irrationality and injurious consequences of vice. He cured some of their diseases, and he relieved others. He taught them how to live a virtuous life, and with the greatest of patience and in the simplest manner did he endeavor to enlighten them upon their own nature, the existence of their souls, and the existence of a true God.

"With the wealthy he was not so successful; he did not pamper their vanities; he did not flatter them, or bow obsequiously to them; he did not approve of their ambitious schemes or pride of rank, but he made war upon all those things on which they chose to exalt themselves. Although he did not make many converts among them, yet they treated him with general respect.

"The Roman officers treated him with marked respect, for they saw that he was a superior man to the generality of the Judean people. They compared his ideas with those of the Roman and Grecian philosophers, and found that in his, there was a great similarity with their best philosophy. The only enemies he encountered during his travels were the priesthood, and others under their influence. We will not include in this notice his great enemy, who was myself, with Judas my confederate; for the heinous nature of our deeds are partly known to you, and the remainder will be given elsewhere. But the priesthood saw that if the doctrines and influence of Jesus extended over the country the temple, the altar, and even the mitre of the High Priest were all doomed to destruction, consequently, they were his declared enemies. The priesthood would have doomed him to destruction long before they did, had not I thought it necessary to achieve my ends, to allow Jesus to run a longer career. As it was, the priesthood gave Jesus all the annoyance, insult, and petty injuries they could.

"The conduct and doctrines of Jesus were incapable of making enemies, from their incapacity of doing evil. His demeanor was so amiable and just that neither friends nor foes could feel injured by it, and his doctrines were productive of nothing but good results to all those who adhered to them. How, then, came he to have enemies? His enemies were only those whose ambitions and interests were sustained by the follies and corruptions of society. None others were his enemies, and none others sought to do him an evil. Strange as it may seem it is no less the truth, his greatest enemies were his two greatest admirers, Saul and Judas. I, Saul, considered Jesus as the model of a noble man, but my heart being callous and my mind remorseless, I chose to sacrifice him to my insane ambition. But Judas not only admired him as the most amiable and virtuous of men, but he had a feeling of pity when he reflected how Jesus was surrounded and enmeshed by a set of sordid, ambitious wretches; and he wept tears of agony when he reflected upon his own conduct towards him, even previous to his final act of treachery.

"The physical or scientific knowledge of Jesus was very limited, yet he knew as much as any who made pretensions to learning, and more than the generality of men. There was very little scientific investigation in his days. Whatever little was known of the phenomena of nature was acquired through common experience, and that little was kept a secret from the people instead of being used to their enlightenment. The secrets of nature were taught in the colleges of the Egyptians, and some others under the awful name of magic, as something emanating from supernal sources. Now, as Jesus travelled abroad in his youth to acquire knowledge, it is reasonable to suppose that he acquired a portion, at least, of what the colleges taught. It is evident that he had learned some true ideas of the solar system. He knew that the stars and planets were worlds similar to the earth, and that these bodies with the sun did not revolve around the earth; but the ignorance and prejudice of the people were so great he dared not declare it to be so. So it was with many other subjects of which he had a true knowledge. He did not declare them to the people for if he had done so he would have appeared in their eyes as a magician instead of a moral teacher. It was in the moral sentiment that the strength, the beauty and wisdom of his knowledge existed. In this respect he was pre-eminent; in this he was powerful; in this he exemplified all the beauty, greatness and virtue of his short career. His experience and studies gave him a knowledge of the conditions of the people and the state of their minds. His intuitive ideas gave him the power to reform those conditions, and suggest others for the benefit of mankind at large, which if conformed to, would have produced a state of happiness on earth, and a prospect of future bliss. What is there more beautiful, more just, more rational, more in accordance with nature, and more beneficial to mankind than the ten classes of duties he gave to the people in his address at the foot of the mountain at Genesareth? There is nothing that can be produced in the form of a code of morals, so comprehensive and yet so compact. There is nothing to be dispensed with, and nothing lacking. Every form of duty which is capable and necessary to render a people happy is embraced in it; and everything superfluous, austere, cynical, or in anywise opposed to the development of our true natures, is excluded from it; therefore it may be said that his moral obligations are the best ever devised by man.

"Jesus not only gave to the people the most complete code of morals, but he gave them the most sublime and exalted ideas of man's inward self. He gave glimpses of the nature of the soul and of the great God of the universe, not such as is taught in the Jewish theogony under the name of Jehovah. He taught that the soul of man is a refined material element, an ever active essence of immortal existence, and that it originally was an emanation from the great God or active principle of life; that in its original nature it is pure, and by its alliance with grosser matter in the form of organized beings, it is capable of continuing pure, and becoming improved if we live in conformity with the principles of nature. That a man living a strictly good moral life his spirit or soul will continue to expand and improve during his life; at the termination of which it will be enabled to shake off this material body, and continue its existence in another state more suitable to its nature, where it will continue to enjoy unspeakable bliss in pursuing its onward progress. But should a man live a demoralized, wicked life, then his soul becomes impure by the predominating influence of grosser matter; then its original nature dies out, and he sinks down to a level, or below the inferior animals. Then at the termination of the man's earthly existence his soul is too dense and grossly material to be enabled to ascend to that refined state of future existence where the virtuous and intelligent are alone allowed to go.

"This doctrine of Jesus, though not exactly true as regards the spiritual world, was calculated to lead men in the right direction to obtain that desired future existence, and to make them eminently happy while on earth. That he was a true believer in the doctrines he taught, there is no reason to doubt, for all his conduct through life confirms his sincerity. He looked not to anything upon earth to reward him for his toils and sacrifices, in the endeavor to improve his fellow men. Nothing beyond the gratification of his own conscience did he desire to repay him for the loss of time, the expenditure of his small fortune, the anxiety, care and study he made for man's welfare. He coveted not gold, silver, lands, rents or titles, for he saw nothing in this world worthy of acceptance. His eyes were cast on the future state where he anticipated a home and a condition suitable to his refined and exalted nature.

"By these doctrines Jesus did immense benefit for man during his time, in awakening them to a knowledge of their low condition; and had it not been for his enemies in cutting short his career, mankind would have greatly improved from that date; but by the unaccountable changes in the destiny of man, evil predominated over good in his case. Soon after his death his sublime doctrines were either lost or perverted, and others, silly and vicious, substituted in their place. His healing powers and achievements were converted into absurd, lying accounts under the name of miracles, and his history into a compilation of fables. Instead of being represented what he really was, as a handsome, generous, amiable, intelligent man, he has been converted into a myth of an unnatural and impossible origin, of doubtful existence and nature, with such a termination to his career that it casts a diabolical and blasphemous slur upon the God of our existence.

"But what were his followers? If we can view Jesus in the light of one who was the model of true and noble manhood, when we contemplate the traits of character of his followers called his 'apostles,' we may reverse the picture, and then we shall view them as a set of the most contemptible, ignorant, sordid knaves and traitors that ever lived to hatch knavery and treason on the earth. With the exception of Judas, every one of them had the most sordid motive of interest in attaching himself to Jesus. Judas was a traitor, it is true, yet he was a man of noble sentiment and fine feeling in comparison to the rest. Though he was under the necessity of performing the part he did by the manner in which I, Saul, coerced him, yet he was a great admirer of Jesus as a teacher and a man. Could Judas have been a free man in action there is reason to believe that he would have been the only sincere admirer and friend among the followers of Jesus. What were the motives of the two sons of Zebedee, John and James? They thought that Jesus was going to obtain

231

great temporal power—to become a king, and they felt a sneaking inclination to become princes; so they attached themselves to him, hoping that they should realize their wishes when their master should arrive at his temporal eminence. Peter's motives were of the same nature, and he lived to realize them in part. His object was to become a great man somehow, as Judas persuaded him he could be if he followed his directions. His object was to become the governor of a province, if possible, and if not, to wait for the death of Jesus when he was to become one of the heads of the new sect that was founded after Jesus' death; this he lived to see accomplished. Andrew was under the guidance of his brother Peter, for the latter made it appear to his interest to follow Jesus. His mind being of a very low cast, he was obliged to act a subordinate part to his brother. All the rest were only followers in name, for they seldom accompanied him on any of his travels, nor did they take any part in the direction of affairs. Whenever Jesus visited a place where they were, they came to him, and in his absence undertook to repeat some of his sayings, which they soon converted into absurdities and nonsense. Some of those followers went so far as to pretend to cure diseases by their touch, and got whatever fees they could from the silly believers; besides, they were continually begging all they could get from all persons on whom the presence and doctrines of Jesus had made any impression. Thus these low sordid minded creatures, calling themselves the followers of Jesus, cared nothing about him more than to make him the means of gratifying their selfish interest. But the time at length arrived when these disinterested followers began to be tired of following their master, and of their pretended affection for him. Jesus having travelled over the greater part of Judea, Galilee and the countries east of the mountains, his followers perceived that there were no greater prospects of his being made king than in the commencement, and that they were no further advanced than they were at first. They then began to perceive that there was delusion somewhere, but they could not charge it upon Jesus, for he had never held out any prospects of the kind to them; they therefore became dispirited and discontented, and much grumbling and mutual accusation took place among them. At length Judas received orders from me, Saul, that he should persuade Jesus to return to Jerusalem as soon as possible, for it was decided among the conspirators that they would bring their conspiracy to a close. Jesus at length gave orders to return to the city, when the followers determined to assemble all their members at some place before they entered Jerusalem, to consult and have an understanding what were to be their future prospects. They accordingly agreed upon Bethphage as the most convenient spot.

"It was now about two and a half years since Jesus first started on his tour of teaching the people, in which his fame as a wise man and healer of the sick had extended over all Judea and Galilee, besides into

232

the borders of the neighboring countries. The multitude in general considered his cures as so many miracles, as Judas and Peter had taken pains to represent them; but the more thinking part of the community did not give credence to all they heard, but at the same time were convinced that he did great good. It would be impossible to estimate the number of his disciples, or those who admired and determined to adhere to his doctrines. There was scarcely a town or village where there were none, and in some places the greater part of the people were with him. The disciples of every town, village or country hamlet assembled to communicate and discuss with each other what they had heard and seen concerning the great man; and in some places his doctrines or parts of them were committed to writing, and some who could read were appointed to read them every time they met. Thus by this time the seeds were sown which promised a great gain for the future revolution in the minds of men. I, Saul, was aware of all this, so I determined to be the first to gather in the harvest. But I saw before I could make sure of this rich gathering that the man who sowed the seed must be removed so that he could not interfere and, defeat my designs. I then determined to proceed to action; to destroy Jesus was my next intention, and how far I accomplished my design the sequel of events as I am about to relate will make known.

"Jesus and his followers at length arrived at Bethphage, a small town a few miles from Jerusalem. The party put up at the public inn, but there was a room provided elsewhere where the followers determined to hold a council in secret. Early on the next day, before Jesus had risen, the party met in council. There were present Judas, Peter, John, James and Andrew, besides others who were only nominal followers, among whom were old Nathaniel and Thomas. At first there was a conversation in a low tone of voice, which grew louder and louder as it lengthened; the workings of their harsh, repulsive features, the motions of their beards, and their violent gestures betokened that there was much anger and contention among them. Some outburst of laughter, accompanied with comical and sarcastic leers at each other, indicated that jeers and jokes were passing at the expense of each other's mortification. Most of the attacks seemed to be made upon Judas, who instead of making any angry return rebutted them with some observation or stroke of wit that produced a general laughter. After a while there was a little order restored, when Judas proceeded to address them:

" 'Come, my fellow laborers and disinterested followers of our master,' said Judas ironically, 'let me hear what are your complaints, and according to the soreness of them and their long standing, I will judge and treat them according to the best of my skill and the help of the money bag. Come, Peter, be thou the first to speak. Let me hear what are thy complaints.'

" 'Master Judas,' said Peter in a half grumbling tone of voice, 'I have always considered thee next to our master, my superior, and I must say thou hast been kind to me in words, and very liberal in promises as to what shall be done for me; but thou knowest, worthy Judas, promises will not catch fish nor fill the goat skin bottle with wine, and as yet I find they have proved of no more benefit to me. Here I am with no more money in my girdle than when I left Bethsaida. Ever since I left off being fisherman and turned to be a fisher-of-men, I find after all my toils that I am not so well off. It is true we catch plenty of men in our new calling, but our master profits nothing by such a mode of fishing; he lets them all go again, without making anything of them. He gains no money, no houses, lands or titles, and I see no prospects of his becoming king. What chance is there, then, for me in becoming the governor of a pro-vince? I want to know that.'

" 'My dear Peter,' replied Judas in a conciliatory tone of voice, and with a mischievous twinkle of his eye, 'thy complaint is just and reason-able; our master shall be duly informed of it, and no doubt, as soon as he arrives at his Kingly inheritance one of the first acts he will do will be to issue an edict appointing thee a governor of a goodly Province.'

"There was a general laugh at Judas' response, when Peter sat down muttering that he had enough of promises.

" 'Come, blue-eyed John,' said Judas, addressing the son of Zebedee, 'what complaint hast thou to make of me or thy worthy master? Is it that we cannot appreciate thy poetical genius?'

" 'No, Judas, nothing of the sort,' responded John in a shrill, childlike voice; 'I have no complaint to make, but I wish for an understanding. John the Baptist told me that our master was the Messiah, and that he would certainly reign over all Judea. He then persuaded me to join Jesus. I did so, thinking that as I was the first to join him, I should be the first in his favor when he should become King. Now I really believe that John the Baptist has deceived me, or was mistaken.'

" 'Very likely,' remarked Judas, as he regarded John with a comical leer. 'John the Baptist's brains were rather out of order, so Herod Antipas cut his head off to cure him; since then he has not made any mistakes of that sort. So thou must forgive him.'

" 'But mark me, Judas,' resumed John, 'thou didst seem to persuade me that all that John the Baptist said was right, and thou didst intimate that when Jesus should become King, I should become a Prince of the first condition, and that my brother James should be the General of the armies. Now I wish to know if this is to be, for I am getting tired of waiting.'

" 'It is very possible, my dear John,' replied Judas, with mock seriousness, 'that our master may not be King of Judea, but he will be Emperor of the whole eastern world. This will take place as soon as he can make it convenient; he will then be enabled to make thee not only a Prince, but a King, my dear John.'

"There was another general laugh by the company, when John sat down rather puzzled to know in what light to view the answer of Judas.

"Many others made complaint that they had been deceived in their expectations when they joined Jesus, stating that they followed him so long and had rendered him such and such services, and nothing had they obtained excepting what they begged or got as fees of introduction. They ended by saying they must have wages, and that Judas must intimate the same to their master. Judas endeavored to pacify them, but he failed to do so. They became more angry, raising their voices, making threats and taunts until there became a general confusion and din. At this critical state of affairs Jesus made his appearance at the doorway, and looked around the company with seeming astonishment. All the grumblers immediately slank into their seats in the greatest of dismay, and all became in a few moments quite still.

"Jesus, regarding Judas with an inquiring look mingled with a degree of wonder, at length said:

" 'Judas, what means this scene of tumult and discord that I have just witnessed?'

"Judas and the rest were taken by surprise at the unexpected appearance of Jesus; he consequently was much ashamed and confused that the latter should have been witness to so disgraceful a scene, he therefore remained silent for a little while, reflecting upon what answer he should give to his master's question. He saw clearly that it would not do to break up the company of followers at that particular time, as their services could not be dispensed with in accomplishing the designs of Saul and his own interests. He knew also if he were to represent their gross selfishness in its true light Jesus would be apt to dispense with their attendance. He, therefore, thought it best to palliate their conduct and make it appear as little disgusting and offensive as possible, so as not to irritate Jesus against them, and at the same time he thought something must be done to satisfy them for the present. All these ideas passed through his mind in a very short time, when he resolved what answer to give.

" 'Worthy master,' replied Judas, in a lively voice and with a smiling countenance, 'thou hast taken us by surprise in a small matter of private contention, yet it is not of so much consequence as thou mayest imagine. It is simply this: Our worthy brethren in the good cause have been thoughtlessly neglected by me in not considering their necessary domestic wants, and they having met in council, came to the resolve to bring the matter before me, knowing that I command the money bag. They say their garments are become tattered and poor and some of their families are in need of necessaries. As they came upon me all at once, it caused a little contention and display of warmth of temper, which could have been avoided if I had had time to examine them. I therefore propose, worthy master, with thy permission, that our brethren's wants be supplied from the bag.'

"This mitigated representation of the tumultuous scene gave more satisfaction to Jesus than he expected. He thought it right and reasonable that his followers should expect their necessary wants to be supplied; therefore, if there was blame to be attached to any one, it ought to be to Judas, for neglecting their wants, so Jesus was glad the matter was no worse.

"The brethren were very much pleased with the manner Judas had brought the matter to the notice of their master, taking all the blame to himself and saving an exposure of their selfishness. It also gave them a prospect of sharing the contents of the money bag.

" 'How much money is there in the bag, Judas?' inquired Jesus.

" 'There is about one hundred and fifty shekels of silver, my master,' replied Judas.

" 'Indeed:' exclaimed Jesus, who had no idea there was so much money in the whole company. 'Then let every man have ten shekels, but before thou doest it, I will speak to the brethren.'

"This decision of Jesus filled the hearts of his loving followers with delight, more so than if he had given them a thousand lectures on the value of time and the philosophy of their enriching themselves by curtailing their wants. Their eyes glistened with pleasure and their fingers were quite restless, feeling an instinctive desire to clutch the money, but they managed to put a sober restraint upon themselves while their master was addressing them. Then everything being satisfactorily settled and order restored, Jesus spoke as follows:

" 'My brethren, in my former discourses, I have apprised you that it is a duty we owe to ourselves to seek after our daily necessities; at present I iterate the same injunction. But when we do so, my brethren, we ought to be careful that we border our desires by our necessities, and take heed that we do not become covetous after this world's wealth, for it is one of the greatest evils we shall encounter to the progression of our spiritual welfare if we allow our hearts and souls to be devoted to mammon. I do not say this as a matter of moral opinion built upon a slight foundation, but I speak of it as a great fact founded upon the experience of the world. A man whose heart and soul is devoted to the acquisition of worldly wealth, cannot progress in the scale of spiritual refinement and exaltation. He has no time or opportunities to think of the nature of his soul; he has no sympathies or pleasure in the measures required to its development, for he sees not the beauties and advantages attendant thereon. As the mind continually contemplates the objects of wealth the soul gradually sympathizes with them, and they become gradually incorporated with it. The soul, then, instead of becoming more refined and pure, partakes of the grosser material things, and finally becomes tied down by them to this earth so that it is rendered incapable of aspiring to a more exalted state and is forever allied to the gross attractions of earth. It then becomes impossible for it buoyantly to rise up to the spheres of refinement and everlasting bliss, which is allotted to all those who live a life of purity and wisdom. Thus, I may say it is more easy for a ship's cable to go through the eye of a needle than for a man whose soul is devoted to mammon to be able to pass from this earth and enter the regions of the blessed. Let this saying be impressed upon your minds, my brethren, and henceforth profit in spiritual wisdom from my present discourse.'

"When Jesus had ended his short address a messenger from Bethany delivered a message to him and then retired. Then Jesus announced to his brethren that his friend Lazarus was sick, and his family requested the immediate attendance of Jesus; all who chose to follow him to Bethany might do so. Then Judas and the brethren hastily divided the contents of the money bag, and having made all other necessary preparations they took their departure with Jesus for Bethany."

237

VISION TWENTIETH

The sun was descending behind Mount Olivet when Jesus and his followers, or part of them, were travelling on the ridge path and approaching the village of Bethany. As they were entering the skirt of the village a female covered with a veil ran towards them—Martha, the elder daughter of Lazarus. With tears streaming from her eyes and her countenance expressive of sorrow, she stopped before Jesus, and for a few moments remained silent, for her grief prevented her giving utterance to speech. Jesus approached her and kissing her upon the forehead, said:

"Why this sorrow, dear sister?"

Martha at length, in a voice of distress, managed to answer:

"0, brother, dearest brother, our father, Lazarus, is dead!"

"Dead!" exclaimed Jesus in astonishment, and then he clasped his hands and uplifted his eyes as though uttering a secret prayer. The remembrance of his friendship, and all the fond relations connected with his kind old friend, rushed upon his mind and a tear of affectionate regret trickled down his cheek; and many were the painful emotions he felt at his loss.

Motioning to Martha and his followers to precede him, he waited behind a few moments to compose himself, and then he followed them. On entering the chamber of mourning, Jesus saw that there were many of the neighbors and several strangers from the Holy City, among the latter were two Rabbis, who had come to administer consolation to the orphan daughters. The visitors were seated around the chamber on cushions, and the lifeless Lazarus was outstretched on a bier in the centre. The corpse was enveloped in white linen, with a band passing around his under jaw and over his head, and a large purple cloth thrown over him.

As soon as Jesus entered the room there was great commotion among the mourners, but all persons kept their seats excepting Mary, who rose and approached the former. Throwing herself upon his neck she burst into tears, and soon as her sobs would allow her she said:

"0, my beloved, hadst thou been here my father would not have died!"

Jesus, gently pressing the fond maiden to his breast in whispering words of sweet condolence endeavored to console her, and after a few minutes delayed in the expression of his sympathy, he led her to her seat. Then Jesus advanced to the bier, and removing the cloth from the features of the corpse, he regarded it with great earnestness for some minutes.

The settled features of the deceased seemed to have an expression of great ease and resignation. The flesh seemed to be without that clammy moisture peculiar to the dead, nor was there any unpleasant odor arising from it; there was no appearance of exhaustion, and a degree of freshness seemed to pervade it, as though it were a person in a tranquil sleep.

Jesus placed himself at the foot of the bier, then clasping his hands and uplifting his eyes, he exclaimed in a plaintive tone with most thrilling pathos:

"0, Lazarus! Lazarus! My much beloved friend, hast thou departed from us and become released from thy mortal tenement of clay? Dost thou hover in the spirit form on the verge of this terrestrial sphere, looking upon us with glances of love and sympathy? Mutual love was the tie by which thou wert united to us in heart when on earth, and still that love exists, though thy presence has departed from us, and when the time shall come for us to leave this mortal state it shall again unite us. 0, Lazarus, thou wert a kind father, a good neighbor and sincere friend. Thy domestic virtues made all around thee happy. Thy just appreciation and dispensation of virtue, justice, and truth, render thee worthy of being exalted in the realm of spirits. Accept, then, our tears as pledges of our love, rather than of regret at thy departure to a better home."

Having thus apostrophized the departed Lazarus, Jesus turned his regards to the assembled persons, and observed:

"My friends, Lazarus, though dead in the body yet lives in the spirit. It is a dark, cheerless, and more than brutish idea, to think that man ceases to live at death. To entertain this idea will be to rob man of all his noble aspirations in this life, and make his end one of misery and regret. For why should man aspire to be good and noble, if there be no other life after we have passed through the scenes of strife in this world? Where shall he realize all his refined conceptions of beauty, grandeur, magnificence, fadeless love and friendship, eternal truth and justice, if he shall have no other world than this to develope the refined germs within him? That man ceases at death is a contradiction in itself. For what is the living man but a portion of the divine essence of God? If this be so, how can that portion of the Deity be destroyed? Does not everything in this universe have a befitting place? If so, where is the befitting place for the soul of man? It cannot be in this world, for here man's soul is imprisoned, restricted and thwarted in its aspirations and thirstings after righteousness. Where then, can this soul bask in the sunlight of unrestricted freedom, unthwarted in its virtuous tendencies, if there be no other realms but this to live in? Yes, there is another life after this. The divine soul within us scatters abroad its seeds of love, truth, justice,

239

charity and sympathy in this world, but we find it difficult to cultivate them here and bring them to maturity. How then, do they die? No! They mature in some degree here, but they come to perfection in the next world, and are there harvested.

"Man is the greatest of God's works—not in size or bulk, but in the combination of all the elements of the universe, the wisdom displayed in his construction, the quality of the materials, and the exalted end to which he is destined. All these superior excellencies exist in the soul of man. For what is all this extra labor, time and wisdom expended in the construction of man? It cannot be for this life, for the pure soul is never at home here. It must be, then, for another life to come, that one which begins when the body ceases at death. Then the perfect soul will receive its true inheritance. God will be rejoiced to see his work perfected. Then to say that man ceases at death, will be to rob God of the triumph and glory which belong to him.

"Yes, my friends, though the mortal part of Lazarus be dead, yet his spirit lives. He has passed the shades of death, which is only a transition from this world to another of greater beauty and perfection, where all our pure and noble affections and desires will become realized and perfected. His virtues and noble principles will buoy him up beyond the earth's attraction, so that he will not be held to it longer than he chooses. Blessed be his name, and long may it live in remembrance."

Jesus was then about to throw the pall over the head of the corpse, when he started back in dismay and astonishment. "Father of Heaven!" he exclaimed, and then he looked upon the corpse with an intensity of gaze.

The visitors looked upon each other with astonishment and alarm, not knowing what to think when they heard the exclamation of Jesus. Mary and Martha rushed forward to the bier, looking upon the corpse and then upon Jesus in an agony of suspense. In the meantime, Jesus was still gazing upon the corpse. At length he stretched out his hand and touched it upon the forehead; the flesh rebounded with elasticity when the finger was withdrawn. One of the eyelids quivered, and a slight trembling was perceived at the corners of the mouth. Then Jesus cried aloud:

"Lazarus lives in the body! He is not dead!"

A simultaneous cry of terror and amazement now burst from all present excepting Jesus, who instantly drew away the pall, and then passed his hands over the head, down the breast of the now resuscitating Lazarus. Then he gave certain passes with both hands, and repeated them several times over that body which a few minutes before was considered to be an inanimate corpse, but now proved to be a living person, for life, human life, was made manifest therein.

At first his eyes and lips began to move with a twitching motion; then the mouth opened, and a deep inspiration was inhaled; the chest heaved and in a few moments it sank, and the operation of the lungs was renewed. Then a roseate glow came into his face; his eyes opened and closed again. At length, his fingers indicated that the current of life was restored to the extremities. A slight groan was uttered, and he opened his eyes looked around, and seemed to recognize his situation. All this time Jesus continued the waving motions of his hands, commencing at the head, then passing over various parts of the body, and returning to the head by a circular route to renew the process. All the visitors had gathered around the bier at a small distance from it, looking on with a fixed gaze, motionless, speechless and breathless, seeming to be like so many statues, for they gave less manifestations of life than the reviving Lazarus. But as soon as Jesus perceived that Lazarus had opened his eyes a second time, he discontinued his manipulations, and taking the hand of the now living man, he gently raised him to a sitting posture and said:

"Lazarus, my dear friend."

Then two of the visitors supported him behind, as he seemed very weak, while his two daughters taking each a hand, pressed them to their bosoms.

"Thank God, he lives!" ejaculated Martha.

"Thanks to God and our dear brother, our father lives!" said Mary, and she wept with joy.

Lazarus looked around him with surprise and confusion, not being able to comprehend what the scene meant, and after a few efforts at speaking, he said in a faint voice:

"My dear children, have I been ill or sleeping? I know not what all this means."

"Dear father, thou hast been very ill," said Mary.

"I must have been sleeping, child, for I had a beautiful dream," replied Lazarus, smiling.

Restoratives and kind attention soon enabled Lazarus to converse freely. The evening was passed in joyous congratulations. The visitors gradually left for their homes, while Jesus and his followers stayed there that night. Before the morrow's sun arose, the news was spread all over Jerusalem that Jesus had raised Lazarus from the dead.

Very little was known of the human system in the days of Jesus. Anatomy and physiology were very little known. The arterial, venous and nervous systems were not known at all. Psychology or its connection with mesmeric influences was not known, or even a true idea of its cause suggested. All nervous and psychological affections were supposed to be cases where demons had got possession of the persons thus affected; and when any cures were produced, as by the touch or manipulations of Jesus, the demon was said to be cast out, and the powers by which the affections were cured were not known or suspected. Jesus himself did not know anything of the nature of that power he exercised over the afflicted to their benefit. He knew that it was not a supernatural gift, for he had learned that other men before him had possessed similar. What was the nature of it he knew not. Now, when a person is under that psychological state, when the mind is abstracted from the senses, or when all motor power is suspended in the brain, it is not surprising to those of this age that people in the days of Jesus should think a man thus affected to be dead. There can be no possibility in their ignorant minds of accounting for it in any other way, consequently when another man through his superior power shall bring into action the nervous force of a man thus affected, and restore him to his usual state of life and vigor, that man will be considered to possess a supernatural power sufficiently great to cause the dead to rise. Thus the wonderful affair of Lazarus is accounted for. Lazarus was under a state of asphyxia, or suspension of the motor powers. The superior nervous power of Jesus being present, began to awaken the dormant nerves of the sick man, which by certain indications that Jesus perceived, caused him to suspect that life was not extinct. He then exercised his power over him to the full extent, and the result was that Lazarus was restored to himself and family. This view of the matter was not seen in those days, but it was more consonant with the peoples' mind to believe that Jesus raised Lazarus from the dead.

VISION TWENTY-FIRST

A vast multitude of the Jewish people were in the Court of Israel, and under the porticos. Those in the former were generally going through their religious ceremonies and prayers, and those in the latter were mostly walking to and fro. There were many small groups, and some large collections, who seemed to be much interested in discussing some important matter or news. There was a great sameness in their dress, in form and color; though some wore more costly garments than others, as they were all Jews, descendents of Judah or Benjamin, for no other casts were admitted into this court.

"What thinkest thou of the late report concerning this Jesus, the miracle worker?"

This was said by a tall gaunt man in black vestments, whose staid sanctimonious air denoted him to be one of the Pharisees who was addressing one of two other persons, one of whom was attired in a black vestment, with a richly wreathed tire and embroidered girdle. The other was dressed in white, with a large full tire and a girdle of various colors. The two latter were of the sect called Sadducees, and the last mentioned, a scribe and doctor of law.

"I know not what report thou alludest to, there are so many concerning this man," answered the Sadducee in black, as he gave a contemptuous lift of his head.

"It is reported," said the Pharisee, "that Lazarus, the tanner of Bethany, died yesterday morning, and in the evening Jesus made his appearance at the house, and after having eulogized the deceased, and made some observations on the nature of death, he raised the corpse to life."

"Well, I do not believe a word of it," responded the Sadducee in black.

"Nor do I," chimed in the Doctor of law. "When a man is once dead, there is no bringing him to life."

"But there were many persons present; besides two of our Rabbis were witnesses to it," observed the Pharisee. "And the Rabbis stated that Jesus said the spirit of man did not die at all; that death was only a transition state whereby the spirit of man passes from this life to another and better one."

"That makes the matter worse and more improbable," observed the Doctor. "If the spirit of Lazarus passed from his body to another world, how did Jesus get it back? Did he go there, too, after it? All his ideas about a future state are false; and I think, therefore, this report about

243

raising Lazarus alive, must be a deception in some way. Lazarus could not have been dead."

"The forepart of the report is quite mysterious," rejoined the Pharisee; "but I think his ideas about a future state are quite rational and worthy of praise."

"Thou thinkest so because thou art a believer in it thyself," returned the Sadducee, who perceiving Jesus approaching, added: "Lo! here comes the very man. Let us question him, and allow him to speak for himself. Doctor, wilt thou question him? Thou art more learned than I."

"Yes, I will question him, and soon convince thee that he is but a shallow pretender," answered the Doctor of law.

As they were thus conversing there was a great commotion among the people when it was seen that Jesus was approaching. They then opened a way before him as he passed, giving many demonstrations of respect and reverence. At length he came to the spot where the interlocutors were standing, when the Doctor placing himself directly in front of him, made a salutation of much reverence, and said:

"Worthy master, I wish to exchange a word with thee, if it will meet thy pleasure."

"Speak on, I will hear thee," responded Jesus in a cool, independent and dignified tone and manner.

"I have been conversing with some friends," said the Doctor of law, "and we differ much upon a certain matter. Now I wish to submit the same to thee, to hear thy learned opinion."

"What is it?" inquired Jesus.

"A certain man died leaving his wife a widow," observed the Doctor; "then according to the law of Moses, his next of kin, a brother, married her. Then he died also, when the next brother of age married her, and so on until seven brothers had married her, and all died; then the woman died also. Now as this woman married seven brothers, whose wife will she be in the next world?"

"Dost thou think, man of folly," answered Jesus, with a smile at the conceit of the questioner, "that the laws of Moses govern matters with the spirits of the other world? They acknowledge not the laws of Moses, or any other human law though it be ever so wise, for they are above them all; therefore they do not marry, neither are they given in marriage."

"How, then, are the sexes in common?" inquired the Doctor.

"They are not in common," replied Jesus. "Every spirit has its particular conjugal partner, with whom it is destined to unite to consummate the holy offices of love, and with whom it is enabled to enjoy a bliss to mortals unimaginable. This union is independent of all external law or choice."

"But how can these things be, if they are not given in marriage, and

244

have no choice?" inquired the Doctor.

"I will endeavor to reduce the matter to thy comprehension," replied Jesus complacently, who perceived that the former began to be interested in the subject, and put his questions seriously. "Thou must first understand that every atom in the universe has its counterpart in some other atom. These counterparts are of opposite sex, whose natures assimilate to each other so that when the two unite, they form one perfect whole. All the organized beings upon the earth are formed after this principle. Everything has its counterpart in another sex, and no perfect union can be formed unless the two counterparts are precisely adapted to each other. When this takes place, it is a perfectly conjugal union; then the two become one perfect whole and the union is complete and happy.

"Such unions sometimes take place among men and women upon the earth, but they are rare because there are so many artificial restraints to thwart and obstruct the natural inherent powers of the sexes assimilating and developing their attractions for each other. If we take different kinds of salts and mix them, and then throw them into water, making a solution, the particles of every kind will seek out their proper counterparts of the same kind, with which they will enter into union, forming crystals. By the solution, all obstacles and obstructions are removed, when the particles follow the impulses of their natures in seeking their destined mates and proper conditions. So it is with the spirits of mankind after death. Death is the universal solvent which frees human spirits from their worldly restrictions and opposing influences; then they seek out their befitting counterparts, according to the inherent impulses of their being, which destine them to perfect conjugal unions in the spirit world, that they could not accomplish when on earth. Such is the nature of heavenly marriage."

The Doctor of law could not help admiring the beauty and reasonableness of this doctrine of Jesus; his conceit and pomposity were very much diminished. He had no further questions to ask or objections to make, so he bashfully hung his head, and after making an obeisance, he stepped aside.

The Pharisee being much delighted with the new ideas he had received from Jesus, determined to question him on another important subject. Therefore, modestly inclining himself before him, he said:

"Master, I am convinced that thou art a great man—thou hast spoken truly and beautifully of the spirits of the other world. I wish to know of thee which is the best and most perfect of all the moral laws, by conforming to which a man may live wisely and righteously, and finally obtain an entrance to the realms of bliss hereafter."

"The greatest moral law," replied Jesus, "is dependent upon the first, and the first is the foundation of all moral wisdom."

245

"Then what is the first law?" inquired the Pharisee eagerly.

"The first law is," replied Jesus, with great stress upon his words: "Know thyself;" and the second is, "Treat all men with that justice and humanity with which thou wouldst they should treat thee." On these two obligations hang all the moral wisdom of society. With regard to the first, unless a man knows himself to a certain extent, he is not worthy of the name of man, neither is he fit to live as such. If he has no intelligence pertaining to his own nature he is scarcely elevated a degree above the lower order of brutes. It is a man's consciousness of self which makes a man stand erect, and look around him with an air of manly dignity. Why does man toil for food, raiment and shelter, but that he knows such things are necessary for his existence, and that they must be acquired by such means? Why does he make social compacts—make laws—build up walls around his cities, but that he knows security is necessary to his existence? Why does he believe in a God, but that he knows his person is wonderfully made, and that he did not make himself? Therefore he believes a God to have made him. These are some of the most simple items of self-knowledge; but as man advances in life his knowledge of himself becomes of greater extent, more refined and of greater worth. He is enabled to make additions to his domestic comforts from a knowledge of the peculiarities of his desires. He is enabled to keep himself in health from a knowledge of certain effects produced upon him by certain things. He is enabled to cultivate his mind because he knows that knowledge is power within him. He is desirous of cultivating his soul because he has an intuitive impression that it came from God; and he has a desire to live a life of moral purity because he knows they redound most to his benefit and happiness here and hereafter. Such is a slight view of the moral obligation to know thyself. We will now see how the second is dependent upon it.

"Treat all men with that justice and humanity thou wouldst they should treat thee. When thou wishest to judge thy neighbor, or to know how to treat him, look to thyself for the law. If thou knowest thyself, thy sense of propriety and justice will tell thee how to judge him and act with him. If thou seest thy neighbor in distress, needing help, then ask thyself what thou wouldst have in that condition, and whatever thou wouldst should be done to thee in that condition, go thou and do the same for him as far as in thee lies. If thy neighbor is oppressed by an oppressor, what wouldst thou in that case do for thyself? Thou wouldst wish for help to resist the oppressor; then go and help thy neighbor to free himself. This simple manner of viewing and construing things will answer in all cases pertaining to thy neighbors, though they be ever so complicated. The obligation is founded upon a sense of justice, reason and humanity; therefore, it is the best and greatest of the moral laws."

"Master," responded the Pharisee, in a tone of great respect, "I perceive the beauty, reason, truth and justice of all thou hast said upon this subject, but as the laws of Moses place certain restrictions upon our intercourse with men, it may be difficult to understand who is our true neighbor. How, then, shall we understand who is our neighbor?"

"Who is our neighbor?" exclaimed Jesus in astonishment, "knowest thou not that all mankind are thy brethren in humanity, and all men not dwelling in thine own house, but living in the same country, are thy neighbors? I will tell thee a tale that will help thee to understand me."

Jesus paused for a moment, and then said:

"A certain man was attacked by thieves, when they having robbed and wounded him, left him to die on the road. A certain priest was passing by, and seeing the unfortunate man, he lifted up his eyes to heaven, ejaculated a few words of prayer for his benefit, and then passed on. Then came a wealthy man, a great officer and man of rank, who, pompous and proud, seemed to scorn the ground he walked upon. He, perceiving the wounded man, turned up his nose with disgust, as though the very air around would contaminate him; so he passed on his way also. Then came a travelling trader of Samaria, who was riding on a mule, and as soon as he saw the wounded man he alighted from his beast and approached him; then the Samaritan's heart became moved with sympathy and compassion for the poor, wounded man. He poured cordials into his mouth and oil into his wounds, and tore up his undergarment to bind them; then he placed the helpless man upon his beast and gently led him to the nearest inn where he gave him in charge of the host, and putting some money into his hand, he said: 'Take care of this unfortunate man, tend him well, and whatsoever more thou shalt spend, I will repay thee when I return.' Which of these three men was the true neighbor to that man who was robbed and wounded by the thieves?"

"I should say the Samaritan was the true neighbor," answered the Pharisee.

"I perceive," remarked Jesus, "thou understandest me."

Then Jesus left the temple for that day.

VISION TWENTY-SECOND

Jesus was walking in the portico of the Court of Israel, as on the previous day, followed by some of his disciples and a multitude of people, some of whom being prompted by curiosity to see and hear this famous innovator, while others were impelled to do so by a sincere love of his doctrines and a great admiration of the man. They all desired to hear him give one of his usual discourses. Soon an occasion presented itself, for a venerable man with a grey beard, whose costume denoted him to be a Pharisee, stepped forward and with a respectful obeisance intimated his wish to speak to Jesus. This man's name was Nicodemus. He was one of the most learned of the priesthood, holding high rank among them. Having heard of the great wisdom and wondrous works of Jesus, he thought he would question him and judge for himself, free of prejudice for or against him. After saluting Jesus, he regarded him for a few moments with an eye of great scrutiny, though with a respectful bearing, and then he said, in a serious and candid tone of voice:

"Master, all Judea has heard of thy wisdom and wondrous works. Pardon me if I am presumptuous in asking thee a question. I am not prompted to do so through idle curiosity or malevolence, but from a desire to learn the truth." Nicodemus paused.

"Proceed, my friend and brother," said Jesus, blandly.

"With all my studies and experience in life," resumed Nicodemus, "I am not satisfied, nor have I decided what course is the best to pursue or believe in to insure an immortal life hereafter; therefore, my question is this: 'What ought a man to do to insure eternal life?' "

"He must renew himself; he must be born again," replied Jesus, emphatically.

"Be born again!" repeated Nicodemus, in surprise, "how can that be? Thou dost not mean so literally, for such a thing is impossible."

"The language I use," answered Jesus, "is but a figure of speech, and of course not to be taken in its literal sense, yet it is very expressive of my meaning. The idea I wish to convey is this: A man who wishes to inherit immortal life among the angels after death, must so examine and purge his spiritual part of the vices, errors and sins of this life, that he shall be in soul as pure as the babe just born. That I consider is equal to being born again."

"Thy explanation is quite clear," returned Nicodemus, "but still I do not perceive how the soul of a man can divest itself of the errors, vices

248

and sins that man has acquired during life, so as to be enabled to return to its original purity."

"It is possible, nevertheless," returned Jesus. "Look around thee, Nicodemus, at this magnificent structure, the Temple, the greatest and most beautiful work of art ever produced by man, in which all the wisdom, skill and energy of our people have been combined in its construction. What was the design of this unparalleled structure? Was it not a place destined to worship the Great Jehovah in, in honor, purity and truth? And what is it now? Thou knowest as well as I do that it is full of corruption and error. How came it so? It is in this wise: The people are the soul of the temple. They have been led astray, blinded and kept in ignorance, until they have become vicious and sinful; the proceedings in the temple, then, correspond to their corrupt nature. But is it not possible that the people may become enlightened so as to be enabled to see their errors, vices and sins? I think it possible. Then when they shall have reformed the temple will be purged of its corruptions and restored to its purity of use for which it was designed. Now let us apply this to the individual man:

"A man is composed of body and soul. The body is the magnificent temple in which the soul lives during its sojourn on earth, and in which when in its original purity it lifts up its grateful prayers to the Great Jehovah. The soul in its original pure state has an intuitive knowledge of its own divine principles or nature, but when it comes into the world at the birth of the babe it finds itself in total ignorance of all eternal things. It then begins to gather up impressions of the external world, and those impressions constitute the mind. Now the constitution of the mind may be good or bad in reference to the nature of the soul; if good, the mind, soul and body will unite harmoniously; and if bad, the soul and body will become corrupted; then the mind and body will enter into an alliance and mutual dependence, regardless of the rights and welfare of the soul. The soul at length becomes completely subdued; its voice is smothered, and its presence confined to the deepest recesses of the bodily temple where it carries on the offices of life unknown, unsought and uncared for; while the mind and the body, assuming to be the man, pursues a wild, erroneous, sinful and reckless life, in ignorance of its most important part. But as the man passes on in the course of life, wandering in error, vice and sin, the soul gains a knowledge of external things—it then cries with a louder voice, and exerts all its efforts to arrest the man in his course of destruction. Perhaps some dreadful calamity brought on by his reckless career, has prostrated his body or his mind, reducing him to a state of serious self-inspection; then the soul takes courage, and once more sends forth its voice pointing out some of the errors of his course and the necessity of reform. Should the man arrest his evil course at this point, there will be hope, but should he disregard his inward monitor, he will inevitably go on to his destruction. At this standpoint there will be a great struggle between the spiritual and carnal parts of the man. The mind will be wavering, concluding to throw its influence first on one side and then on the other. The body, by its dilapidated state, announces to the mind that the course they have been pursuing is not the correct one; the mind perceives it, and confirms it by its experience. Then the soul speaks in thrilling strains regarding its original purity, petitioning to be released from the road of error, vice and sin by which it is bound down. The whole man becomes aroused and conscious of his miserable and degenerate state. He sheds tears of agony and remorse, and at length awakens to the necessity of repentance and reform."

"But how can repentance restore his soul to its original purity, when all within him is corrupt?" inquired Nicodemus.

"There never was a human soul so corrupt as to have its original nature entirely extinguished," responded Jesus, as a glow of enthusiasm spread over his handsome features, and his eyes beaming with a holy fervor, giving him the appearance of one inspired by powers more than human. "The soul may be led astray by the errors of the mind; it may be polluted with the excesses of the body; it may be battered and bruised through the calamities of life; it may be contaminated with vice, and it may be entangled and covered with sins of the darkest nature, still there is a speck of that divine essence which is concentrated within itself, safe and impregnable to all evil surroundings. Hast thou ever transplanted a tree, Nicodemus, from an uncongenial soil to one more genial? If so, thou didst lop off all the roots and branches which thou didst consider were not necessary, that they might not impede its future growth. Then thou didst place it in better soil, and tend it carefully. At first, there was very little prospects that it would live, for it seemed sickly; all its former growth of leaves and branches withered and fell off; the sickly bark exfoliated and fell off. Then, in course of time new buds and shoots were seen to put forth; the shoots extend and ramify, putting forth leaves and blossoms, and finally it becomes a large and goodly tree, bearing rich fruit. So it is with the human soul, Nicodemus, in its most unfavorable conditions. Let it be torn up from the uncongenial soil; lop off all its excrescences, as near as possible to the centre, and then plant it in a spot more favorable to its true nature. The divine germ of life will feel an instinctive sympathy with its new position; it will swell and expand, sending down new roots; its impure and imperfect parts of former growth will wither and drop off, leaving it unimpeded in its new development. Then it will put forth new germs and shoots, which will give place to wide-spreading branches, expanding in the broad light of day, and drinking in the pure dews of heaven in the evening. Finally it will become a goodly tree, rising up to heaven and bearing delicious fruit, pleasing to the sight of God. Such is the nature of true repentance of sin, Nicodemus, by which

250

the soul of man is born again to its original purity."

"Master," responded Nicodemus in a grave tone and respectful manner, "thy words are wisdom itself, and thy eloquence surpasses that of all other men I have heard speak. I, Nicodemus, a ruler and teacher of high rank among the people, would be proud to be counted worthy of that new birth, which thy wisdom and eloquence have so beautifully made clear. But, sir, there is another point I should like to hear thee speak upon. Will God receive the repentant soul, which was once polluted with the errors, vices and sins of the world, into his realms of beauty and bliss?"

"Will God receive it?" repeated Jesus in a tone and expression of surprise, as he looked upon Nicodemus with sternness, which soon subsided and changed to one of pity. He then added: "0, Nicodemus! Nicodemus! thou knowest not the God of whom I speak. I speak not of the God Jehovah, who is the prototype of Moses' self; but I speak of the great God of Nature, who is the God of wisdom, love and benevolence. I speak not of the God of Moses, who delights in vengeance and slaughter, punishing his people unto the third and fourth generations for the sins of their fathers. No, Nicodemus; the God I wish to bring to thy mind's eye, will receive the repentant sinner with gladness and parental care, to think that the divine spark of man's being has triumphed over all the obstacles and drawbacks to which mortal beings are liable. The repentant spirit is not judged according to what it was, or its progenitors before it, but according to what it is; and if it be found qualified to enter the blessed realms, the portals of heaven are opened to it, when it is hailed with a joyous welcome. I will relate to thee a short tale of domestic life, which will exhibit to thee the relation between a repentant sinner and our Heavenly Father."

Jesus paused for a few moments, and then spoke as follows:

"There was a man who had two sons, to each of whom he gave a jewel of enormous value, telling them at the same time to guard it well, for if they parted with it, or lost it, they would forfeit his love and esteem. The two sons promised their father they would be mindful of his request. Then they wrapped up the jewels and wore them near their hearts. The younger son was wild and reckless, and sometimes disobedient of his father's commands. One day he became angry because his father chided him for a fault. He then demanded of his father a share of the estate, which his sire gave him. He then started for a distant country where he soon got into bad company, and passed his days in riotous and sinful living. In course of a short time he had spent all that he had brought with him, and found himself in a state of abject poverty and misery. So low had he fallen that he had not wherewith to appease his hunger; so he prowled about the market place, shivering with cold, hunger and disease, and feeding upon any offal and garbage he could find. One day

251

as he crouched down in the market place in great misery, he remembered that he still possessed the jewel his father had given him. He instantly pulled it out from his bosom, thinking to sell it and buy bread; but when he unwrapped it, so beautiful and bright was it that it attracted his attention, and his intended purpose was forgotten for the time. It suggested to his mind the reminiscences of his happy past days when he was under his father's roof; how blessed was his condition compared to his present misery. How kind and loving was his father, and reasonable in his requests! He thought of his father's injunction when he gave him the jewel—'Never to part with it or he would forfeit his esteem.' Then another long train of reflections passed through his mind tracing from stage to stage his course of vices and sins, until a heavy sigh burst from his lips, and he exclaimed: 'No! I will not sell thee, dear jewel, but I will take thee back to my father, confess myself unworthy of his regard and crave his pity.' Then the prodigal son arose, and with slow and feeble steps started for his father's home. He left the scenes of his vicious excesses, gained the high road, and travelled on as well as he was able, depending upon charity for a morsel of food. The first day's journey was short, owing to his great weakness, proceeding from the sinful life he had led; but as he travelled on he got rid of some of his rags, for they dropped off from their rottenness. He slept by the wayside, breathing a purer air than he had been wont to do. On the next day, instead of being fatigued, he found himself stronger than before; so he continued his journey with a hope lighting up his countenance. He soon came to a pool where he bathed and washed himself; then a charitable person seeing his deplorable rags, gave him a wholesome garment; so with a grateful heart he continued his journey with renewed strength and hopes. Thus he continued to travel on for many days, improving in strength from day to day; for being withdrawn from his sinful ways, the food he ate and the fresh air he breathed did him good, making him feel like a new man, and he began to resume his former appearance. At length he perceived his father's mansion; then his heart felt overcome with fear, and his countenance expressed dejection. But assuming what courage he could command, he softly entered the enclosure, and saw his father walking in the garden. Suddenly, with a shout of mingled agony and joy, he sprang forward and prostrated himself before him, and with tears streaming down his cheeks, in a piteous and humble tone, he thus addressed him: 'Father! behold thy unhappy and repentant child! I acknowledge the sinfulness of my ways, and the just retribution of my misery for having been disobedient to thee. Although I know I am unworthy to be thy son, yet I would fain ask thy forgiveness and mercy.'"

"'Hast thou preserved the jewel I gave thee?' said the old man in a stern voice.

"'Yes, father, I have it safe,' replied the son sobbing. 'Under all my

252

temptations, recklessness and sin, I thought of thy love and guarded it well.'

" 'Then come to my arms, thou dear repentant child; thou shalt ever be my son,' replied the father, with tears of joy running down his cheeks. 'Forasmuch as thou didst not, under all the errors of thy ways, disregard thy father's love and obedience in that particular, I will forgive all the past, and again receive thee to my heart.'

"Nicodemus," said Jesus, as soon as he had ended his narrative, "canst thou see the gist of this little tale?"

"Most worthy master," replied Nicodemus reverently, "I perceive its application. Worthy thou art to be a teacher over the people of Israel."

Then the parties dispersed, when Jesus left the temple for that day.

VISION TWENTY-THIRD

On the eastern end of the portico of the Court of Israel, Jesus was elevated on a bench at the foot of one of the pillars, with a crowd of people around him, who were listening to one of his moral discourses. All proceeded in good order for a while, to the great satisfaction of the audience, whose attention was absorbed in the interest of the subject. The people gave evidence of some commotion. The crowd was broken into, producing great confusion, when several voices cried aloud, "Make way!" Then the people were scattered, and a body of men with a woman in their midst, thrust themselves forward and approached Jesus. They seemed to be persons of authority, for they forced the people to stand off some distance from the pillar, leaving a large open space, which they enclosed with their own persons. The woman was made to stand alone within a few feet of Jesus, when one of the officials advanced, and thus addressed him—

"Reverend master, this woman has broken the laws of Moses. She has committed adultery, and been caught in the act. Now, Moses says, that any woman found thus guilty, shall be stoned to death. We wish to know, reverend sir, what is thy opinion."

The object of this accusation stood in their midst with her head slightly drooping, indicative of shame, as she was sobbing and crying in great distress. She was tall and symmetrical in form; youthful, but of mature development; a fine rounded arm and well developed bust. Her dark hair hanging loosely around her neck and shoulders, with a white veil attached in front, which obscured the beauty of her countenance; yet from certain glimpses taken, were seen features of great regularity and expressions denoting great ardor of the passions. She was dressed in a loose robe of black, which fell in graceful folds to the ground, over which was a vestment of light blue, terminating a little below the waist, held close to her person by a narrow girdle of red silk, and her ears, arms and fingers were adorned with jewels.

Jesus regarded the accuser with a penetrating glance, when he saw evidences that the former was a stern, hard hearted man, so that the woman could not expect any mercy from him. He also saw that when he had made an end of his accusation, he cast a furtive glance at his associates as a smile of cunning played around his mouth. This Jesus construed as having some reference to himself, and he reasonably supposed that it was a plot devised by the priesthood to entrap him into some indiscreet expression of sentiment, that they might have authority to bring him before the Sanhedrim under accusation. He, therefore, thought it prudent to be careful as to what he should do or say in this matter. Then, turning towards the woman, he regarded her fine person and unfeigned distress with emotions of commiseration. He resolved to investigate her case, and if she proved to be one worthy of mercy, to save her, if possible, from the dreadful penalty attached to her crime. Then, catching the glance of the woman, he exchanged with her one of pure sympathy, when he addressed her in a voice of mildness:

"Woman," he said, "is this accusation against thee just or unjust?"

The woman, as soon as she caught the glance of Jesus, instinctively perceived that the heart of the man before her was open to mercy, and that his mind was governed by just principles. A flash of hope immediately passed through her mind, and a thrill of courage gave her heart a new impulse. Then, immediately stooping at his feet, she took up the hem of his garment and kissed it, and said in an imploring tone of voice:

"0, most worthy and reverend sir! deign to listen to my tale, and then thou shalt be my judge, and whatever doom shall be pronounced from thy lips, I will receive it with resignation."

"My ears are open to the self-justification of the unfortunate, and my heart can sympathize with the oppressed," replied Jesus. "Woman, relate thy tale."

Then the accused, erecting herself from her humiliating position, remained silent for a few moments, in which she regained her composure; then confronting Jesus with a countenance void of timidity or shame, but of a firm reliance of the justice of her plea and good feelings of her judge, in a voice clear and firm, mingled with a degree of pathos, she proceeded to give a sketch of her history relating to the subject of her accusation:

"It is not often, reverend sir," she said, "that a woman under the base accusation such as mine, has the good fortune to meet with a judge whose mind is free from common prejudices, and whose heart is moved with the sublime impulses of sympathy for the unfortunate, but such I deem my good fortune under the present disreputable charge, as I stand before thee. How can a woman who is accused, expect mercy or justice, when the minds of her people and judges are made up of unwholesome prejudices, vicious customs and tyrannical laws, which are entirely opposed to her nature? How can she expect justice when the hearts of her judges are callous and unsusceptible to the fine impulses of mercy, because the unfortunate woman is under the ban of the public mind for daring to assume certain rights which she has inherited from her Maker, though not acknowledged by the blind and inefficient laws of man? If she be tried by her judges, she is proven guilty or innocent; if guilty, she is condemned for being what God in his wisdom designed her to be, and

255

not being what her judges in their ignorance and vile prejudices considered she ought to be; and if she be proven innocent, she blasts her own nature by conforming to the vile commerce of man, instead of assuming the divine right and fulfilling the tender offices of love assigned to her nature by God. I will now to my tale:

"I am the only child of parents who have a small estate, to which, at their death, I shall inherit by right. Not far from my parents' mansion, lives a neighbor whose estate joins that of ours, who has an only son, with whom my parents were desirous of uniting me in marriage. Without my consent an arrangement was made that he should be my husband. When the matter was made known to me I refused to agree to their arrangements, for good reasons: I entertained a pure and holy love for another man, whose love for me was equal to mine. The other reason was, I considered the son of our neighbor not worthy of me, for he was ugly, coarse, ignorant and vicious, having habits not congenial to the marriage state. He was a great wine bibber. My parents at first tried persuasion to gain my consent, but without avail; then they commenced a course of restraint and coercion, and when the day appointed for the marriage came, they compelled me, in spite of all my protestations, to go through the ceremony. I was at length forced to become the wife of a man I never had loved and never can love. Three years of a most wretched life I have lived with that man, in which I have experienced all the horrors that a poor mortal can suffer. Every day I had to submit to abuse, taunts, insults the most revolting, and severe beatings, and then at night I was made the mortifying receptacle of his vile lusts. Not long since the man for whom I entertained a pure love, I met by accident, when we renewed the expressions of our holy passion for each other, and under the influence of our ardor we embraced, as nature taught us to unite in the body, to consummate the destined end of our mutual love. The rest is known to thee, reverend sir. Picture, then, to thyself, the wrongs I have sustained and the stigma brought upon me, though no unnatural act of mine has been the cause. If the marriage rites have been broken, it was not by me, for I never married the man. The fault is attributable to my parents, who forced me to do, in spite of my inclinations, what I could not prevent. Judging then, reverend sir, thou to be a man of reason and mercy, I submit my doom to thy decision."

The woman ended her tale, and the breast of Jesus was painfully moved with emotions of profound compassion for the much injured criminal, and the people around who had heard and comprehended her, shed tears of sympathy, while the priestly officers looked at each other with expressions of uneasiness.

Jesus remained silent for a few minutes with his eyes cast to the ground, which he passed in recovering his serenity and collecting his thoughts, while all others around awaited in silent, solemn expectation his decision upon the case. At length, raising his head and turning upon the chief officer a stern and fearless glance, he said in a loud and emphatic voice:

"Thou wouldst have my opinion in this case?"

"If it so please thee, reverend sir," answered the officer.

"Then thou shalt have it," replied Jesus, as he pointed to the woman, and added, "This woman is not guilty of the charge."

"Not guilty!" exclaimed the officer, with astonishment, the same being echoed by all the others. "Not guilty! Why, sir, this woman was caught in the act!"

"It matters not; I say she is not guilty," repeated Jesus, with great assurance, "which I will prove to thee in a minute."

Then Jesus went close to the officer, and placing his foot quickly behind him and giving him a push on the breast at the same time, the man went staggering backward, and after an ineffectual struggle to regain his balance, at length came softly to the ground, much to the astonishment of the priests and the people, who, as soon as they saw there was no harm done, gave a loud shout of laughter. Jesus, however, hastened to help him to rise, when the officer began to give demonstrations of great indignation.

"Peace, man," said Jesus, soothingly. "I mean thee no harm. My act was intended as a simple mode of illustrating this case before us. Didst thou fall of thine own will, or the will and force of another?"

"I certainly fell by thy will and force," answered the man, angrily.

"Such is the case of this poor woman," rejoined Jesus. "She fell not into crime by her own will and power, but through the will and power of others; therefore she cannot be amenable for the results. It would be injustice and cruelty to punish her for the results of other persons' bad conduct. She never married that man called her husband, therefore she could not have broken the marriage rites, or the laws of Moses."

"How, sir! Not marry him?" exclaimed the officer. "Do not her parents and all her neighbors testify that she is his wife?"

"I say she is not his wife," returned Jesus with great emphasis, "neither in the sight of God or man; therefore she has not broken any law of Moses or of God. What do the Levitical laws say regarding marriage? They state what men and women shall not marry. But do they state that a woman shall marry a man against her will and inclinations? They do not, nor any other law of ancient script. By what right, then, do the parents of this woman force her to a marriage union with that man, against her consent and inclinations, for such is the actual case. It is by their own despotic and selfish wills that they have accomplished it—then it is to them, and not to her, the evil results are to be attributed. The Lord is represented to say when instituting the marriage of man and woman, that, 'The man shall cleave unto his wife and they shall become one flesh.' This implies that there is a mutual consent and love existing with both parties previous to their union as husband and wife. For without this there can be no union. But how is it with this wronged woman? Without her consent; without any impulse of love, she has been compelled by brutal force to become the wife of that vile and profligate man called her husband. Therefore this violent course of proceedings has been in violation of all the laws of God, of Moses, and the instincts of humanity. What right, then, has that man to call her wife—to make her life wretched and her body the sink of his lusts? He has no right. And nothing but blind ignorance, sordid interests and tyrannical customs will support him in it. And not being his wife by right she is not under any obligations to conform to any of the marriage rites and duties. Consequently whatever she does of her own free will, she is not amenable to him. She was given to him as wife by despotic force, how then could she have anything to do in the solemn consummation of the marriage rites, when she was a coerced prisoner? A marriage to be just and pure must be consummated by two free consenting parties, who are moved towards each other by the divine impulses of holy love, which is to be the bond of union between them, making them one flesh and one spirit. Was there any holy love between this man and this woman? No, there was none. He was impelled like the wild rampant beast of the forest, with the hot, lustful passion of the brute. No soft, thrilling impulses of love hovered around his heart filling it with tender sympathies and sweet, joyous desires for the other sex. No refined essence traversed the labyrinths of his mind, disseminating the divine intelligence that the holy offices of love in the flesh were the preparatory means, by which God designed to perpetuate the spiritual part of mankind. No; he knew nothing of this pure and holy love.

"How different was the state of this woman previous to the forced marriage with that man! She became acquainted with a man whom she thought capable of making her happy; a love was engendered between them, which was tender, pure and holy. They lived in blissful anticipations that they should become as one flesh and one spirit, their only desire being to live for each other, fulfill their duties on earth, and thus render themselves happy and worthy of their God. But sad has been the lot of this truly loving woman; for her wicked parents, whose mercenary souls aspire to naught but worldly wealth, deprived their daughter of her natural rights, her earthly happiness and prospects of future bliss, by forcing her to this unhappy marriage. Like a dog did they treat her, forcing her from her home, tearing her from the man she loved, and forcing another she loathed to be her master. How did that man treat her? Did he love her? No; but he gratified all his filthy cravings, as a drunkard would with his wine cup, in loathsome excesses and vicious revels. Cruel taunts, jeers, quarrels and beatings filled up her miserable days until years of anguish passed. At length the object of her true love comes across her path; they renew the expressions of their mutual love and the miseries of their wrongs; but their afflictions are forgotten for the moment in the happiness of each other's presence, and the sweet impulses of their holy passion bring them into closer embrace when they forget all worldly prudence, or that there were enemies around them. This woman fell into the embrace of her true lover; by so doing she complied with the laws of her being, and her duties to God, by whose divine impulses she had been swayed. What right has her enemies to accuse her of crime, of adultery? She broke no law of marriage, for she never married. What her enemies call her marriage was a violation of her natural and civil rights, committed by her parents. Let them, then, answer for the results. If there is a crime committed, it is of their doing, and the blame or sin of the matter will be upon their heads. That man can have no claim for outraged rights, for he is not her husband by right, divine or human. The laws of Moses she has not broken for they were not conformed to in the ceremony of the marriage, but the laws of God she alone fulfilled. Therefore, you members of the Sanhedrim, it is my opinion that this woman is not guilty of the crime charged to her. You expounders and defenders of the Mosaical law must understand that there are other laws of greater authority than those established by Moses, which have existed from the commencement of the world. I mean the laws or principles of love, established by God himself, and made inherent in man and woman at the time of their creation. Now, if there be a conflict between these laws, which ought to be suppressed that the other may rule? Shall the law of God he suppressed that the law of Moses shall rule? Or shall the law of Moses give way that the law of God shall predominate? If this case be investigated by wise and impartial men it will be found that no law has been broken by this woman, but that the case will bear this complexion.

"The parents of this woman were moved by worldly considerations to marry their daughter to the man called her husband, by which they proved themselves deficient of parental affection and duty. The daughter refused to comply as she loved another. In this she stood upon her natural rights, in which no law or person whatever has a right to oppose her. Then her parents forced her to comply with their wishes, in violation of all law, human and divine. This tyrannical coercion took from the daughter all responsibility for the results of this wicked marriage; she, therefore, is not guilty of any crime in committing the act with which she is charged; but on the contrary in doing what she has done she has conformed to the principles of her nature in accordance with her natural rights and her duty to her God. If such, or similar to this, be not the opinion of a just and impartial judge, I will consent to cast the first stone at her."

When Jesus had ended his defence of the woman there was a great

259

excitement among the people, who clamored loudly for her release. The priests were much excited also, talking loudly and violently, as though they were of opposite opinions as to what should be done with her. Some were for freeing her on the spot, while others were opposed to it. At length the people became so excited that the priests began to fear for themselves; so they withdrew, leaving the woman in the presence of Jesus and the people. Then Jesus turning his attention to her, observed in a mild, compassionate tone of voice:

"Woman, thy accusers have left thee. Thou hast heard my opinion, now depart in peace, and for the future be more circumspect."

The woman fell at his feet and embraced them.

THE HOLY CRADLE, PRESERVED AT ROME

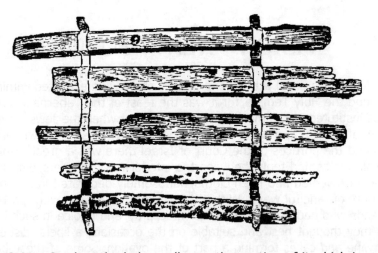

La Sainte Creche—the holy cradle—or the portion of it which is preserved is, in fact, only a part of the grating that was placed across the stable trough in Bethlehem to hold the fodder for the animals that fed there. It became the cradle of the infant Savior when he was laid within the rough trough by his mother, and came in time to be regarded as one of the most sacred things on earth. This broken piece of the grating was taken from Bethlehem at the time of the Mussulman invasion in the year 642, and was carried to Rome, where Pope Theodosius took charge of it as one of the most precious of relics.

Whether or not the grating now shown is the true relic, it is certainly extremely old, says the New York Tribune, and is interesting for that reason and because of associations that have gathered about it since it became one of the mementoes cherished in the imperial city. It is one of the greatest treasures of the ancient Church of Santa Maria Maggiore.

It consists of five worn bars; these are of wood—worm-eaten and gray, and looks as though it might be oak powdered with flour. The bars average about ninety centimeters in length—nearly a yard—and the entire grating is suspended in a crystal case by silver ribbons.

This case is supported on carved gold and silver feet, and its full length is a metre, its height half a metre. It is surmounted by a beautiful enameled statue of the infant Jesus.

During the year this magnificent reliquary is enclosed in a golden case and disposed on one of the altars of the church. At Christmas time it is exposed to view, and the festival of the nativity terminates with an imposing procession in which the relic is carried, the solemn occasion being presided over by a cardinal.

VISION TWENTY-FOURTH

More than usual activity and priestly show were exhibited within and around the Holy Temple, for it was the feast of the Tabernacles, which was instituted in commemoration of the event when the Jews' ancestors had left Egypt, and were living in booths and tents in the wilderness. Around the porticos of the Court of Israel there was a great display of small booths and tents, between the interior rows of pillars, which were made of woolen and linen cloths, handsomely decorated in an endless variety of fanciful ways. Within these slight structures were parties of friends who had assembled to converse, pray, and rejoice in such modes as they thought best and suitable on the occasion—a liberal dispensing of wine and cakes forming a part of the ovation. Some of these booths and tents were of a public nature, where strangers from all parts assembled and paid for their entertainment. The people were in their best attire, and the priests in their most splendid holy-day vestments. Large bands of musicians and singers were stationed at various places, producing a continuous din of inharmonious noises. All faces were gay, and every one at liberty to exercise his wit and humor, provided all were kept within the bounds of good nature, for that day was a day of rejoicing. Jesus, as usual, made his appearance about the middle of the day. He was walking along the southern portico followed by some of his disciples and attendants and a great crowd of admirers and strangers who wished to see and hear something to realize the wonderful reports they had heard concerning him. The faith of the common people in the virtue of Jesus in curing diseases was very great; for a great part considered themselves safe for the present or future if he would touch them, or they could touch him or his garments; yet their respect and reverence prevented them from crowding upon him. However, many as he passed along bent before him, beseeching him to place his hand upon them, while others stealthily seized the corner of his dress which they kissed, or touched with it some particular part of their bodies. He had gratified the wishes of many on that occasion by touching them, and many had gratified themselves by touching him, when at length a man was led before him by two friends, who seemed to be blind, for his eyes were closed. His head was covered with a large roll of linen, coming down low in front near to his eyebrows, and his face nearly covered with a full red beard and whiskers; his dress being of the ordinary kind—a long blue coat and broad girdle.

262

"Master," said the blind man as he crouched down before Jesus in a suppliant posture, "have pity on my misfortunes, and do something to relieve my affliction. I know thou art a good and wise man, possessing a gift from God. I, therefore, beg thee to extend it in mercy to my benefit."

"I am afraid that no one can aid thee save God," responded Jesus with a feeling of distress, for he saw clearly this was a case beyond his power to relieve.

"But, master," resumed the blind man, "I dreamed last night that I met thee in this temple, and that thou didst spit upon thy finger and passed it over my eyes, when I immediately saw. I beg thee to do so; I feel convinced my dream was not of vain import."

Jesus still hesitated to comply with the man's request, when Judas whispered in his ear: "Master, comply with this man's request, and remember the cures at Bethesda Pool and other places. Thou hast greater powers in thee than thy modesty will allow." Jesus then consented to do as the man requested him, when he spat on his finger and observed:

"I will do as thou wishest me, but remember the result is of God and not of me, if any good comes to thee."

Then passing his finger across his eyes, the man immediately sprang to his feet, opened his eyes, and stared around him in astonishment, and at length exclaimed:

"Praise Be to God and Jesus of Nazareth! I see! I see!"

Some minutes were now passed in the joyful demonstrations of the cured blind man and the wondering excitement of the people around him, when at length he returned to Jesus, fell at his feet and expressed his gratitude. Then Judas told his friends that they had better take him home, in case the light should injure his newly restored sight. They accordingly did so; but Judas, before they went, managed to whisper to him a few words, and said:

"Cosbi, meet me tonight at the usual place."

Jesus then resumed his walk, but his progress was soon interrupted by a body of Scribes and Pharisees who approached him, when one of the Superiors thus accosted him:

"We wish to know by what power thou doest these things in the temple, whether it be of God or Beelzebub."

Jesus regarded the questioner for a few moments with mingled surprise and contempt, but at length made answer:

"I will ask thee a question, and according to thy answer I will give thee mine. By what power or authority dost thou move thy finger?"

The Superior Scribe remained silent for some time, for he seemed puzzled with the question; but at length he replied:

"Well, I suppose it must be through the power of God, for the psalmist says, "In thee we move and have our being."

"Thou sayest well," replied Jesus. "Even so is my answer to thy question. All I say and do, is of God—and more especially that which I say and do in the temple."

"But how are we to know that thou speakest the truth?" inquired the Superior. "A man in the Courts of the law cannot bear testimony of himself."

"That is true, as regard the Courts of law," responded Jesus. "But I must remind thee that the things of God are not regulated according to the customs and practice in the Courts of law; one is of God, the other of man. Now I assert that everything that comes of God has a testimony within itself, whence it comes and by what authority it acts." Jesus then pointed to the sun and added: "Seest thou yonder bright luminary which dispenses its light all over the earth? Does not that bright orb testify of itself from whence it came and what is its mission? Is it not from God? Is it of God?"

"Thou art right in that respect," responded the Superior; "but there is a great difference between the sun in the heavens and a man in society."

"Not so much as thou thinkest," rejoined Jesus. "The light of that sun testifies that it is a part of God's works, and that it came from God. Even so the light that shines within me testifies that it came from God, and that my spiritual self is a part of God. Not of me alone, for all men could give the same testimony of themselves, if they would withdraw themselves from the wickedness of the world, and uncover the light which is in them."

"This is really blasphemy!" exclaimed the Superior in great indignation. "This doctrine must have come from the Arch Fiend himself. Thou shalt be denounced before the Sanhedrim, as a reviler of God, in asserting that thou art from and of him."

By this time the other Scribes and Pharisees had approached near to Jesus, forming a semi-circle before him; they stood and listened with surprise and indignation at what they considered his madness and assurance.

Jesus, perceiving that the Superior would not or could not argue with him any further, and feeling his spirit aroused by the observation of the latter, thought that if they would not believe his testimony concerning himself, he would see if they would believe him if he testified against them. Jesus and the Priesthood were naturally enemies to each other, always acting in antagonisms. The latter were reasonably afraid that the former would injure their worldly interests, by enlightening the people upon their true condition. And, Jesus knew that the people could not improve as long as the Priesthood held them in mental slavery. They consequently appeared in his eyes, the Great Evil of Society, which he was determined to attack and destroy with the weapons of reason and truth. He, therefore, thought this a good opportunity to give them a true picture of themselves, and scatter a little knowledge among the people of their priestly rulers.

Having discontinued his discourse with the Superior, he addressed himself to the whole body of the Scribes and Pharisees before him, in language more than usually emphatic, severe, sarcastic and ironical.

"You Scribes and Pharisees," he said, "it seems you will denounce me before the tribunal of the Sanhedrim for testifying to the truth of myself. What will you do if I testify against you?"

He paused for a moment, and then altering his tone of voice to one of irony and sarcasm, he resumed:

"Most Just and Holy Order of men, you sit on the seats of the High Tribunal established by Moses, as the rulers of the people of Israel, dressed in the vestments of your sacred offices, assuming a solemn dignity on the occasion, drawing down the corners of your mouths and wearing that solemn grave expression of countenance denoting wisdom, which is lacking in your minds.

"When walking abroad among the people, your gait is one of solemnity and sedateness, and your garments are precisely cut to the fashion of sanctity. When you sit under the porches of the temple, you spread broad your phylacteries that the people may notice them, and with all the formula of pious mummery, you perform the customary evolutions and prayers, when at the same time neither sanctity nor piety dwell in your hearts. 0! base and ridiculous hypocrites, why do you call upon Father Moses or Father Abraham to testify to the truth of your speech, knowing there is no truth within you, and that you wish to deceive the people? Why is all this masking, this hypocrisy and deceit? Because you wish to blind the people and make fools of them, that you may impose upon them heavy burdens of taxes, of offerings and presents, in order that you may live a life of laziness, and gorge upon the good things of the land, which you rob from the poor and needy. 0! you base hypocrites! unworthy the name of men, for true manhood is not in your natures. How long will you be the pest of the nation? Though great pretenders to humility, you are greedy for the high distinction and reverence of men. You expect the highest seats in the chamber when you go to a feast, and to be treated with all possible marks of reverence by word and action. You are not content to receive the ordinary salutations of men, but when they make their salute they must bend so low that the fringes of their girdles touch the ground. When you are addressed, you are not content to be called by your proper names, but the speaker must say in a most reverend tone of voice, Rabbi, Rabbi, Rabbi. Indeed, in my serious judgment, a mad dog is more worthy to be called Rabbi than such a conceited, puffed-up set of hypocrites as you are. You base set of robbers, what benefit do the people receive at your hands, for the plunder you take from them? You take from them the greater portion of their lands, houses, the finest and fattest of their flocks, their cattle, harvest, wine, oil, gold and silver. What benefit do the people receive for the deprivation of so much of their wealth? You give them in exchange a long sanctimonious prayer, a blessing ejaculated with a pious snuffle; the singing of an old song, and a little discordant music. Such are the benefits your holy order of thieves return to the people for the loss of their substance. By a system of barbarous superstition, a code of cruel laws, and the enforcement of tyrannical customs, you prevent the people from becoming enlightened, and thus you shut out from them a knowledge of the true God, and the true Heaven, keeping them within the same bounds and anticipations that were established by their barbarous ancestors. At the same time you will traverse both sea and land to make one convert to your own evil system, under the pretence of glorifying God.

"O! you blind and infatuated fools! Your minds possess a wonderful contractility and expansibility. They are so contracted that they cannot receive a simple truth that I state; yet their expansibility is so immense that they will take in as true all the absurd and ridiculous statements constituting the system of superstition which this temple embraces. Truly do you realize the old adage that 'You will strain at a gnat and swallow a camel.' Mark me, you men of deception, hypocrisy and perfidy, the time will come when this vast temple with all its corruptions shall tumble to pieces, and the Jewish superstition shall be scattered to all parts of the earth. Then the masks of her priests shall be torn from them, and they will be exposed in all their follies and corruptions. Tremble now in anticipation of the true character with which the world will esteem you. Shrink within yourselves at the loathsome image they will form in their minds, when speaking of the Scribes and Pharisees, for terribly disgusting will it be."

Jesus could not proceed any further in his severe rebuke of the Scribes and Pharisees, for they burst forth in most direful demonstrations of rage. They rent the air with their shouts of execration and anathema. They spat towards Jesus; hissed through their teeth; jumped up and down; tore their beards and rent their garments. They would have sprung upon him and killed him, but were afraid of the people. Then throwing their head tires upon the ground, they ran from the portico towards the palace of the Sanhedrim, uttering the most dreadful denunciations against him. In the meantime the followers and disciples of Jesus had closed around him as a means of protection of his person. The people were much astonished and dismayed, many of them leaving with the priests, and many remaining on the spot.

Jesus perceived that he had irreconcilably offended the whole priesthood; therefore, taking the advice of his friends he concluded to leave the temple and remain in seclusion for some days.

VISION TWENTY-FIFTH

The sun had set, and night's dark curtains were spread over the Holy City; a gloomy mist hung around the stupendous temple when the audience chamber within the palace of Caiaphas was resplendent with artificial light, emitted from numerous golden lamps, which were supported by pedestals around the walls. There were several persons present, nearly all of whom were in the priestly garb, and a few in citizens dress awaiting the presence of the High Priest, Caiaphas. Some walked to and fro in companies of twos and threes, while others stood in small groups, or leaned against the pillars, in conversation. In one of the groups there were about six persons, all dressed in the order of the priesthood, who seemed to be much excited by the subject of their discourse. They were all members of the Sanhedrim Council, deputed by that most sacred body to communicate to the High Priest certain resolves of their pious and charitable determinations.

Since the visit of Saul to Caiaphas, when the former explained his plan of entrapping Jesus, which terminated in an understanding among the conspirators, Caiaphas had placed an injunction upon the proceedings of the Council with regard to all matters relating to Jesus, so that they should not spoil the deeply laid conspiracy against him. At the same time very few knew anything of the secret proceedings that were going on, therefore the members thought it very strange that Jesus should be allowed to insult the Holy Order, and, as they were willing to prove, break the laws of Moses, besides blaspheming against the Most High Jehovah in the course of his preachings to the people. They thought that he ought to have been arrested long ago, and brought before the Council on the charge of blasphemy, if on no other charge. How it was that all propositions of the kind were defeated, they could not tell. But after the severe rebuke they received in the temple by Jesus, their sacred dignity became lowered in the sight of the people, and their mortification so great thereat that they determined to unite all their voices and powers in giving vent to their vengeance upon the offender. They accordingly met in council, discussed the matter in indignant terms, and finally resolved to petition the High Priest to give his consent to the arresting of Jesus and bringing him before the tribunal. They accordingly met in the audience chamber to submit their request to Caiaphas.

"By the God of our Fathers!" exclaimed one of the deputed priests, "I think this conceited pretender has been allowed grace enough. It is high

267

time his blasphemous and insurrectionary doctrines should be silenced before the people. If he is allowed to go on much longer, there is not a member of our Holy Order who will be allowed to walk the streets of the city in safety. We must unite our voices and compel his Reverence to consent to our resolutions. Did you notice how the insolent dog told us that we drew down the corners of our mouths, and assumed an expression of wisdom on our faces because we had none in our heads? He must have alluded to thee, brother Jacob, because the corners of thy mouth hang down very much."

"I do not know that he alluded to me in particular," responded Rabbi Jacob, rather testily—he having a very large mouth with the corners drawn down—"any more than to thee, when he said we assumed wisdom in our faces because we had none in our brains."

"He said our sanctity and piety were in the cut and fashion of our garments, instead of being in our hearts," observed Rabbi Abraham, with some degree of indignation in his manner. "Now this is a gross personal insult as well as blasphemy against our Order."

"He said worse than that," observed Rabbi Seth, "for he called us vile hypocrites, fools, knaves and thieves. He certainly must be a great calumniator, for I never heard such epithets used among ourselves when in dispute, and I think we ought to know whether they are applicable to us or not."

"Now if we relate this to his Reverence, and he does not give his consent to have him brought before the Council, I shall begin to think there is something very mysterious between his Reverence and this Pretender," observed Rabbi Moses.

By this time the tapestry over the doorway leading into the interior chamber, was moved aside, when the High Priest, Caiaphas, made his appearance, followed by Rabbath Gamaliel, the President of the Sanhedrim. Caiaphas was habited in an unofficial costume, consisting of black vestments and plain white tire. His countenance was sad and careworn; his step grave and solemn as he advanced to the centre of the apartment and received the homage of all present. Having made a courteous acknowledgement of the respect shown to him, he proceeded to confer with several persons around him, seeming to dispatch their business with ease and expertness; and after a while he pointed to the group of deputies from the Sanhedrim, inquiring of Gamaliel their business. Gamaliel made answer, when Caiaphas said: "Let them approach and state their desires." Gamaliel gave the intimation to the deputies when they approached the High Priest, and after making their obeisance, the Abbithdin, or Vice-President, spoke as follows:

"We are commissioned by our Most Holy Council to appear before your Most Sacred Reverence, praying you to review the late restrictions you placed upon their proceedings, to the effect that 'No measures shall be entered upon, or against a certain man named Jesus,' who has become obnoxious to us in many respects, as a blasphemer and transgressor against the rites and holy ordinances of our holy religion and temple, as well as being a professed enemy of our Holy Order. We, having a proof that this Jesus being a transgressor in all these particulars mentioned, desire that your Reverence will remove from us your injunction as mentioned, so that we may arrest this profaner of all that is sacred and holy, and cause him to be brought before our Sacred Council to answer the charges against him. Such is the desire of the Sacred Council, and may the blessings of our fathers, Abraham and Moses, rest upon your head."

The Abbithdin bowed low and stood aside, when Rabbi Jacob advanced and spoke as follows:

"May it please your most exalted Reverence to comply with our petition. The proceedings of this audacious pretender have become most outrageous. This arch blasphemer not only transgresses and bids defiance to our Mosaic laws, profanes the Holy Temple and its sacred rites and ceremonies, but he has entered into an open contest and war with our sacred Order before the people. Yes, even in the Holy Temple did he accuse its sacred servants of the most flagrant crimes. He exhibited us in the most wicked and unjust light, bringing down upon us the contempt and ridicule of the rabble of the city. It is not safe for any of our Order to walk the streets of the city, and unless this bold pretender to virtue be arrested in his progress the whole of our sacred institutions will tumble down."

Caiaphas having heard the address and petition of the deputies, seemed to be much perplexed. He remained silent for some minutes, then motioning Gamaliel to approach, he conversed with him for some time in a low tone. At length turning to the Abbithdin, he replied:

"I am sorry that the Sacred Council cannot abide my pleasure on this matter. But you may inform them from me that measures of a secret nature are in operation to accomplish all they desire, in so complete a manner as to prevent a recurrence of the grievances they complain of. Let them wait patiently a little while longer, when all they have asked will be complied with."

This answer seemed to satisfy the deputies, who making their obeisance, took their departure from his sacred presence.

"Gamaliel," said Caiaphas, as soon as the deputies had departed, "this dark business must be brought to a close. The members of the Council are irritated, and begin to look cool upon me for staying their proceedings. The people are in commotion and much divided upon matters, the greater part being still adherents of our old institutions, but a great portion are followers of this new teacher. Things cannot proceed thus much longer, for there will be an eruption before long which will produce a general consternation. If we are to act in this matter we must do so soon if we wish to preserve the existence of our Order. Didst thou not say thy friend Saul would be here tonight?"

"Yes, your Reverence," replied Gamaliel, "I expect him every instant, as it is about the time he promised to be here. No doubt when he comes he will give your Reverence such information on this matter as will allay all cause of uneasiness.

"I hope he may," replied Caiaphas in a despondent tone, and his countenance was expressive of inward uneasiness. "To tell thee the truth, Gamaliel, I like not this business, and were it not that I am under obligations to support these institutions and all pertaining to them, I would wash my hands from this affair. 0! God of my Fathers! Is it possible that within the precincts of this Holy Temple, treachery and murder should hide their odious hands under the garb of sanctity!"

"Hold!" exclaimed Gamaliel in a tone of authority, as he regarded the High Priest with a look of stern rebuke. "Caiaphas, such words must not be uttered within or without the precincts of the temple, not even by Caiaphas. Remember, we are but men, and not Gods who are perfect. It becomes us then, to act as men in conformity with the views and interests of our associates."

"Pardon me, Gamaliel, for the indiscreet sentiment I uttered," said Caiaphas, who felt himself humbled by the rebuke of his inferior in office, but knowing that which he had inadvertently said would be highly displeasing to the Order of Priesthood, he was afraid to resent the check he had received. He then added: "I will be staunch for the future, and remember that I am the Head of the Holy Order. I will imitate the zeal of those deputies who were here just now. Didst thou notice how eager they were to hunt down that young man, Jesus, like the savage hunters of the wilderness do the wild animal? It seemed to me as though they could lap his blood with as much zest as any blood-hounds could do."

"Your Reverence," replied Gamaliel, "must attribute their zeal in our case to a fervor of sanctity."

"Fervor of sanctity," repeated Caiaphas to himself; "if that be it, I think the Sanhedrim are not lacking of it."

Further converse between Gamaliel and Caiaphas was prevented by the entrance of Saul, who was followed by Judas at a small distance. The former made his approach to the High Priest while the latter kept at a distance. Saul having made a very obsequious salutation then turned to Gamaliel and saluted him also. Then erecting himself, he cast a fearless eye upon Caiaphas and awaited the word of reception.

"Our reverend brother informed us that thou wouldst be here about this hour," observed Caiaphas in a courteous tone of voice. "I am glad to find thee so punctual, worthy Saul. Dost thou bring us any satisfactory information concerning our secret understanding?"

"I am enabled to come before your sacred presence," replied Saul with great sweetness of tone, "to lay before your reverence such an account of our enterprise as I think will meet your satisfaction. That much to be feared, yet magnanimous individual, Jesus, has been allowed to go to as great an extent as prudence will permit. His power extends over the minds of the people in every part of Judea and Galilee, and proselytes to his doctrines are being made every day, so that it may be fairly estimated that he can command fully a third of the population."

"I see not the necessity for this course," observed Caiaphas. "It seems to me that thou hast done the very thing which we wished to prevent in extending his doctrines and influence over the people."

"This course of my polity," replied Saul, no wise disconcerted, "has been an indirect way of accomplishing your wishes in the end. Although I sacrifice your wishes in one respect, yet I gain the end in view. You cannot do as you wish with this man in your Council of the Sanhedrim; it will, therefore, be necessary to bring him within the grasp of our Roman Masters. Thus it is that I have made him a very popular man all over Judea and Galilee. Now for any one to be popular and not be a Roman, is almost equal to the doom of death, for it will take very little to make our Roman Masters believe that he is their enemy."

Caiaphas and Gamaliel exchanged glances with an expression that would say, "Mark well the astuteness of Saul."

"Having accomplished this much," resumed Saul, "I caused my agents to persuade Jesus to return to Jerusalem, as I wished him to make himself popular here so that I could bring the enterprise to a close. They accordingly came, and Jesus has been teaching in the temple for several days, many wonderful cures being reported in his name. But I must inform you that the most miraculous cures he is said to have produced, the credit is due to one of my agents, a very ingenious young man who performs the parts of deaf, dumb, blind and deformed persons to the very nature. Judas, my principal agent, persuades Jesus to try his powers upon the man, whatever may be his pretended affliction. The cure is then very easily effected, when Jesus gets the credit and his popularity extends. There was a mysterious case that took place at Bethany, which has increased his fame more than anything he has ever done before."

"Thou needest not relate the case of Lazarus," remarked Caiaphas, "I have heard it related, and I think I understand its nature."

"Well," resumed Saul, "altogether his fame is very great in the city, and his power over the people is increasing accordingly. It now becomes us to arrest his career, that he shall not get beyond our control."

"In what way dost thou intend to accomplish that end?" inquired Caiaphas.

"Since he gave that severe rebuke to your Sacred Order," replied Saul, "I have caused it to come to his ears that the Sanhedrim are determined to arrest him and charge him with many crimes, if he return to Jerusalem. And I have managed that a council shall be held tomorrow evening by Jesus and his followers to take into consideration what course to pursue. In this council my agent will endeavor to persuade him to retire for a time into privacy, or go to some distant country out of the authority of the Sanhedrim, where he may continue his teachings. While these matters are being discussed tomorrow night I wish your Reverence to send an officer to Bethany with a letter of compromise to Jesus, setting forth if he will forego his teaching and agitation in the city all process of arrest shall be stopped, and that he shall have full liberty to go and come from the city without molestation. This offer on your part my agents shall persuade him to accept. Then comes the grand finale of my scheme, which shall put him into your power and finish my engagement.

"When the terms of compromise are agreed upon according to the tenor of your letter, then my agents shall not cease until they persuade Jesus to make one more visit to the city to take a farewell of his friends. A great supper will be prepared at a certain place where he shall meet and address them for the last time, and as I suspect, will bid them a last farewell. In the meantime great preparations shall be made to give him a reception in the city different from what he will expect or wish. As this is the most important point, all our powers must be brought into use."

"What kind of a reception is it that thou intendest he shall receive?" inquired Caiaphas, wondering.

"We intend to hail him as King of Judea or Israel, the temporal and spiritual king as promised by the prophets. I shall also employ some persons to tempt him to say something disrespectful of the Roman Emperor, or in opposition to his rule over us; if we succeed in this respect it will be well, and if not it will be of no great matter. We shall be enabled to make out a case afterwards, which will arouse the fears and jealousy of our Roman Masters that will induce them to take part with us in disposing of this man."

"Well, what is to be the final result of all this deep laid scheme?" inquired Caiaphas.

"The result must be," answered Saul, "that when at night he is feasting and communing with his friends and followers, and the remainder of the citizens are in their peaceful homes, the Sanhedrim will receive word from my agent, when they must send their officers and arrest this Jesus. He will then be in their power, and a little more ingenuity will put him in the power of the Roman Governor.

Caiaphas glanced inquiringly at Gamaliel and said:

"What thinks Gamaliel of this addition to the scheming of thy friend Saul?"

"I think, your Reverence," replied Gamaliel seriously, "that it is a most consummate plan. It will work effectively, and is worthy of its propounder."

"Worthy Saul," said the High Priest after a few moments' reflection, "we thank thee for thy past services; from them we anticipate great results of deep interest to us. I must also express my admiration of the great skill and forethought thou hast displayed in devising such an ingenious and consummate course of action, so efficient in producing our end in view. As well as a master mind in devising all this, thou must have a master man to act as thy agent in executing perfectly all thou designest. I should like to see this man of thine."

"Your wish can be easily gratified, your Reverence, for the man is here," replied Saul.

Then the latter went to Judas and brought him before the High Priest, when Judas made the fringe of his girdle touch the floor, so respectful and humble was his salutation. Then the glances of Caiaphas and Judas encountered each other. Like two friendly wrestlers they contend for a time, as to which should prove the stronger. At length Judas, in courtesy to the High Dignitary before him, averted his glance to the ground, when Caiaphas observed:

"I perceive, worthy Judas, that thou art not a puling babe, but a man of strong mind, courage and perseverance."

"I thank your Reverence for your compliment," replied Judas with a slight curl of the lip. "Our merits are not altogether our own as we are all depending upon one another for our good qualities, but as to our bad ones, nobody will own them. If I have any good ones the merit is due to my friend Saul, for I have been his pupil for some years."

"It matters not who has been our tutor," rejoined Caiaphas, "we are entitled to the merit of our good actions, and as such I thank and commend thee for the good service thou hast done us. Fail not to make thy demands upon our Treasurer in our name whenever it shall suit thee to do so."

The parties then took leave of each other for the night.

273

VISION TWENTY-SIXTH

Several days had now elapsed since the last visit of Jesus to the Temple, when he so severely rebuked the Scribes and Pharisees. Great had been the excitement through all Jerusalem; great the indignation evinced by all the Priesthood and their adherents, and great were the apprehensions of the friends of Jesus. Though the latter were numerous, they were mostly of the poorer class, and consequently weak in comparison to his enemies; therefore, they were doubtful of being enabled to protect him, should he again visit the city. It was rumored about that the Sanhedrim had given authority to have him arrested as soon as he should make his appearance. His friends, therefore, sent him word of the state of affairs, advising him not to come to the city if he valued his safety. Jesus on receiving this intelligence was much grieved—not in consideration of himself but as to the check the object of his labors would receive at Jerusalem by his absence. But on mature reflection he saw that his cause would receive a greater blow if he allowed his enemies to take advantage of him and put him in duress. He thought it would be prudent not to risk his personal safety, and therefore he resolved to make the house of Lazarus his home until something should be decided on among his followers. There was another consideration which had a slight influence in producing this decision. Great and noble as were his exertions in the good cause he had undertaken, as he had sacrificed nearly every earthly prospect to it, yet there was one earthly hope and prospect he looked to and sighed for. It was the hope of earthly bliss he entertained in the consummation of his love when he should be united to Mary, the daughter of Lazarus. When he was in eager pursuit of his labors the idea did not cross his mind, but now finding himself checked and baffled, "would it not be as wise," he thought, "to resign from my labors at present and settle down in domestic happiness with Mary?"

In the meantime the followers of Jesus had been scattered in all directions, some of them having returned to their homes, and others were at different places in the vicinity of the city. Judas and Peter being the only persons who then attended upon their Master, through them all notices were transmitted and all other regulations carried into effect.

Since the last interview with the High Priest, Saul and Judas had agreed on what further proceedings were necessary to achieve their diabolical designs. Several interviews had passed between them, and Judas had passed frequently to and fro between the city and Bethany, having had many private discourses with Jesus. At length something definite was decided on. Messengers were sent to all the followers and to some private friends to meet at Bethany on a certain night when a supper would be prepared for them, and then they could determine upon their future proceedings. Accordingly the time arrived when the following scene and incidents form the subject of the present vision:

The sun had descended behind Mount Olivet and the shades of evening began to overshadow the humble village of Bethany, which was built in the cleft of the mountain, when an air of great bustle and importance was visible within and without the dwelling of Lazarus. All the followers, and some disciples of Jesus had arrived. Some of them were in conversation with their Master, while others were strolling about the yard or garden, awaiting the time when they were to assemble around the supper table.

Within the centre of the public room was a long table covered with a white cloth with a raised form on either side covered with cushions, having ample space for about twenty persons to sit or recline at their ease. Mary and Martha were there arranging the vessels and provisions as fast as two female servants could bring them in. Plates were arranged along the outer edge of the table at equal distances, and large dishes containing bread, fruit and vegetables along the centre, with smaller vessels intervening containing salt and other condiments, and at one end of the table was a large metal dish which was intended to receive the roast kid which was to be served at the last minute. When all things seemed to have received their appropriate place, Martha gave one more glance along the table to see if there was anything lacking, when she suddenly exclaimed:

"Mary, my dear sister, we have forgotten the flowers! What shall we do?"

"The flowers!" echoed Mary, with a start, "why we must have them. Get the vases ready and I will hasten to the garden and gather some directly. They are the silent offerings of my affection, which I will place before the man I love. I would rather forget anything else than that," added Mary, as she left the room and betook her way to the garden.

Mary having gained the garden with a step as buoyant and nimble as a young gazelle, bounded along the path to the farther end, which was terminated by a thick hedge of prickly pear; then she stooped down to cull the flowers of her choice which were growing in an ornamented parterre which was close to the latter, when she thought she heard the voices of men close by. At first she looked around with innocent surprise, but as the voices continued and she distinguished the name of Jesus, a suspicion and a dread seized upon her mind. She ceased culling the flowers, remaining for a few moments breathless and motionless as a multitude of fearful thoughts passed through her mind. Then suddenly regaining courage she softly crept close to the hedge, which formed an embankment of earth about three feet from the ground, on the summit of which grew a thick planting of prickly pear and other shrubs, closely knitted together with creeping vines. She discovered that there were two persons on the other side seated on the ground, who were conversing in audible tones, though not loud. She listened with an increased keenness of sense, not from an idle and mischievous curiosity, but from a conviction that one more dear to her than herself was in danger, when she heard the following discourse:

"Tell me, Judas," said one of the voices, "what part thou expectest me to perform this night, for the whole affair is so complicated I cannot see clearly through it."

"Peter," the other voice answered, "thou art rather dull of comprehension this evening. I think if thou hadst the goat-skin bottle here it would sharpen thy wit. Now mark well, Peter, what I say. It matters not much what subjects may be discussed tonight, or what resolves may be made, provided one thing be agreed on. If we agree to break up the party and return to our homes, or if we agree to continue the good cause, as it is called, in another country, it will be all the same to us. But there is one thing thou and I, with the aid of others, must persuade him to; that is, whatever course we shall agree upon, we must persuade him to make one more visit to the city, to take leave of his friends and address them for the last time. If it is possible we must make him go tomorrow, for everything is being prepared for his reception, and the banquet to be given at night; then our work will be finished. Now dost thou understand, Peter?"

Mary did not stay to hear any more, for she thought she had heard enough to convince her that there was treachery of some kind intended towards the man she loved—that man for whom she was willing to give up her life if required. With the few flowers she had gathered, and a quick, stealthy step, she left the treacherous spot, when having retreated unobserved about midway in the garden, she ran the remainder and entered the house. What to do she knew not at the time. She was harassed with conflicting thoughts, knowing there would be no opportunity of making a disclosure to Jesus at that particular crisis, for all the company were waiting with keen appetites for the feast. At length she placed the flowers in the two vases, which she placed midway upon the table, it being the spot assigned to the master of the feast. Martha observed that Mary was pale and seemed discouraged. She inquired of her sister what was the matter, but the latter making some excuse, did not choose to divulge what she had heard.

At length the smoking fat roast kid was placed upon the big dish, cut up into pieces; then the signal was given that the feast was ready when Jesus, preceded by old Lazarus carrying a lamp, and followed by Judas and Peter, was escorted to a seat at the table, which happened to be in the middle, between the vases of flowers. John and James his brother took their position on either side of Jesus—the former on the right, and the latter on the left. Judas and Peter sat together on the opposite side of the table, and all the others took up the remaining places at their choice. When all were seated, Jesus took some bread and salt which he held up and solemnly invoked God's blessing upon the repast they were about to partake. Then the process of eating roast kid and other good things commenced.

Jesus ate like a man of prudence and intelligence ought to eat—not with the desire of gratifying his palate or to satisfy any inordinate habit, but just sufficient to satisfy the demands of exhausted nature, and he made choice of the plainest and most simple of the food set before him. During the meal he took a cup of water, and after the meal his custom was to take one cup of wine. Having satisfied the demands of his hunger, he reclined back upon his seat awaiting the termination of the repast of his companions.

All the powers of Judas were concentrated in his brains in thinking how he should work out the designs of his fellow conspirator, Saul, and very little active force was assigned to his stomach; he accordingly made a short and hasty meal. John also made a short and delicate repast, for his mind being occupied of late in the construction of a new poem of a very grave and mystical character, he had very little time and inclination to dwell upon the grosser elements requisite to the stomach, so that he forsook his platter and washed his fingers. But Peter perceiving that three of the company had withdrawn from the table, he felt ashamed that he had been so dilatory in not having half accomplished his repast. He thought, however, he would make the best of the remaining time, so he re-applied himself with renewed vigor. Soon the contents of his platter vanished, when he vociferated to the servants for more kid. Peter's example was followed by the rest of the feasters, every one vying with his neighbor in the rapid motions of his jaws and the celerity with which he caused to disappear the enormous quantities of viands, fruit, bread and vegetables. Kid, kid, kid, resounded from one end of the room to the other, so that the attendants were kept running to and fro between the guests and the big dish, until the kid entirely disappeared.

At length all the company finished their repast and washed their fingers in basins of water which were carried around by the servants, when the latter proceeded to remove the platters, dishes and fragments of the feast; after which they placed a cup opposite to every guest and filled it with wine. It was the custom for every guest to wait till the head person at the feast should take up his cup of wine to taste or drink before any one else should do so. Jesus took up his cup and was about placing it to his lips, when an incident occurred which produced great surprise and some confusion. A female entered the room covered with a long white veil, and having approached Jesus she crouched down before him. All present looked on with much astonishment, not being able to guess what was her intention; but Judas and Peter regarded her with a degree of suspicious uneasiness, and they would much rather she had not come.

"What wouldst thou, fair maiden?" inquired Jesus of the female.

"I wish for thy blessing, and permission to testify my regard for thee," responded Mary in a most suppliant tone of voice, for she it was.

"Thou shalt have both, fair maiden," answered Jesus.

Then he placed his hand upon her head and blessed her. Then Mary, rising, took from her bosom a small ornamented vase containing a precious oil of great fragrance which she began to sprinkle and rub into the hair of Jesus with delicacy of action and manner.

"What means this indelicate intrusion?" demanded Judas in an authoritative and surly tone of voice, addressing himself rather to the whole company than to any person in particular. But Jesus, taking the matter upon himself, made answer:

"Judas," he said in a mild yet serious tone of voice, "there needs no rebuke in this matter. The damsel comes here with an innocent and kind intent, to testify her regard for me and gain my good will. She is the daughter of our host, and as such is privileged above all others."

"I think," returned Judas sulkily, "the damsel had better have saved her money for another purpose, or given it to the poor, than to have bought that costly ointment."

"Cease, I command thee," said Jesus imperatively, as he cast a stern and indignant glance upon Judas. "Thy words are impudent and ill-timed."

Judas replaced himself in his seat somewhat mortified at being thus rebuked in presence of the whole company. There was now a general silence for a few minutes for an unpleasant feeling had been aroused among all present. In the meantime Mary continued to anoint the hair of Jesus, and as she smoothed and rubbed it she brought her mouth close to his ear, when she whispered:

"Beware of traitors in this company. Go not to Jerusalem." Then she made a hasty obeisance and left the room.

Jesus slightly started on hearing the warning voice, but immediately perceiving the impropriety of making it known, he collected all his powers and assumed as placid a countenance as possible, yet he was much troubled. "What can it mean? Whom does she mean?" he said to himself, and then a train of suspicions was passing through his mind, from which he was aroused by the voice of Peter, who said:

"If the master please to recollect we have not tasted wine yet."

"Ah! Peter," answered Jesus, smiling, "I see thou hast a true friendship for the juice of the grape, for thou never forgetest it. I have been forgetful, but I will make amends to thee."

Then taking up his cup of wine he drank a portion, and the example was followed by all present, and the discourse was resumed. Some minutes were passed in general discourse on important subjects, when at length old Nathaniel, with his bell-shaped head, observed that "He had lately seen in the northwest of Galilee some itinerant preachers and doctors, as they professed to be, who presumed to teach the doctrines of Jesus, and undertook to produce certain cures by working through faith. This power they pretended to have derived from Jesus, and every itinerant had a book which, they said, contained his doctrines as delivered from his mouth."

This statement of old Nathaniel greatly surprised the whole company, and some, especially Peter, felt indignant that anybody out of the company should undertake to do what they did, without authority. They began to fear that they should lose their business and influence among the people. But there was another idea this relation suggested which gave them more gratification. They saw that as certain itinerants could go about the country, preaching the doctrines of Jesus, and producing cures, they certainly could do the same; therefore they did not feel so dependent on their master as they did a few minutes before. "Should anything happen to deprive them of Jesus," they thought, "they could easily start on the business by themselves, for they could preach what they had learned from his mouth, and produce cures by touch and through faith." These ideas were not openly expressed, but conveyed from one to the other by whispers and hints, so they were generally understood.

Jesus remarked upon this matter, that "he did not wish to restrict any one in preaching his doctrines or in working cures, if they had the power to do so; for he would be glad if they spread all over the world. But he was afraid that those itinerants would lead the people into many errors, and say many foolish things in his name. He, therefore, desired that the people should discountenance all teachers who could not show authority from him."

Judas having heard this subject discussed to the end, rose and said:

"Will the Master please to inform the brethren what the purport is of our assembling?"

Then Jesus rose from his seat and stood erect, when casting a glance around the company, intimating his intention to address them, he spoke as follows:

"My dear brethren and fellow-associates: I presume you are partially aware of the critical circumstances by which we are surrounded—the difficulties and dangers which menace us in the prosecution of our good cause. To take this into consideration, and decide what shall be our best course for the future, is the object we have to consider at this meeting.

279

After you have discussed this matter, I shall be influenced according to what I perceive to be your inclinations, rather than by any I have of my own; for I shall consider it to be my duty to sacrifice my own inclinations, as I have always done, to your interests and pleasure, provided our good cause is always paramount in your thoughts and designs. Grieved as I am at the thought of the dangers that menace us, yet it is a source of gratification to me in one respect. It is evident our labors have not been in vain. The great body of the priesthood, the Sanhedrim, is at last aroused. That vile body of knaves and impostors are up in arms against us, and why? They perceive that a light has been shed over all Judea and Galilee by which the people have been enabled to see the gross ignorance and mental slavery to which they have been bound by their priestly rulers. Thousands, tens and hundreds of thousands of the people have already shook off the trammels of priestly superstition. Thousands of new-born aspirants to truth hail the prospect of a general emancipation from the mental slavery imposed upon them by their barbarous ancestors. The minds of the people have been aroused; their united voices begin to murmur like the low rumble of the distant thunder, which announces that a storm is nigh. The pinnacles of the mighty temple begin to totter, and the holy priesthood to tremble; the latter are afraid the former will fall with a mighty crash, and bury them in its ruins. This, then, is the cause why our enemies are up and opposed to us, endeavoring to thwart our proceedings. They think to destroy our good cause and work by aiming their shafts of enmity at me, aiming at my destruction; and should they achieve that point they will extend their persecutions to all of you. I shall not quail at any dangers that menace me. From the commencement of my labors I resolved to devote all my energies, time and worldly goods to the cause I uphold, and now, I am willing to sacrifice my life if it be necessary. No, my brethren, if I have a fear, it is for you and the good cause of our labors. Should our enemies prevail over me they will assuredly extend the same persecution to you, and perhaps to the many thousands who have shaken off their priestly yokes. These probable results are to be considered, and our future proceedings made with prudence and caution. If I go up to Jerusalem, my enemies are ready to lay hold of me, throw me into prison, and perhaps aim at my life. Therefore it behooves me, on whom the prosperity and safety of our cause depends, not to risk this venture of my personal safety. What, then, shall we decide upon doing? That is the subject of our consideration. I can see but two courses to choose from; for neither of which will I express any preference, that you may unbiasly select that one which you think most acceptable to you. The first is: We may depart for a distant country where we may labor in our cause free from the molestations of our present enemies. The other is: We may abandon our labors in the good cause, and separate for the present, every one to his home or to some place of retirement, until the times and circumstances shall be more favorable to our endeavors. One of these two courses we must adopt. I shall, therefore, leave it to your free choice as to which it shall be, and whichever you may decide upon, you may expect to receive my assent."

Jesus having ended his address, reseated himself, then placing his hand over his eyes he waited in a reflective mood for some one to respond to his words. The greater part of the company commenced a low, muttering conversation, while Judas and Peter conversed in low words and significant glances. But before any general understanding took place, John rose from his seat, when it was immediately suspected that he was going to make a speech. John cast his glance around the company, then uplifting his eyes with a solemn expression of countenance, he seemed as though he were under some supernal influence.

"John seems to be in one of his poetical rhapsodies," observed Judas to Peter, in a whisper. "Open thy ears, Peter, thou wilt hear something sublime, no doubt."

"My dear brethren," said John, in a shrill voice, "last night I had a dream. If it were not a dream, it was a vision, and if it were not a vision, I know not what it was."

"Perhaps he took a cup of wine too much," observed Judas to Peter, with a sneer.

"Yes, it must have been a vision," resumed John, "for I heard a voice behind me, as though coming through a brass trumpet, which said: "I, am the First and the Last, the two ends, and the middle of all things. I was before there was anything in existence. I am all in all of the Present, and shall be when there will be nothing. Now John, what thou seest and hearest, write in a book, that all mankind may read and understand." And behold! I looked up, when I saw a beacon on a hill burning brightly in the surrounding darkness, and there were several men who furnished fresh fuel for the flames, working merrily and zealously. Then there was a great convulsion in the heavens, with thunder and lightning; then a troop of demons came out of the darkness and approached the front of the hill with the intent of extinguishing the beacon; they shouted and shrieked, endeavoring to frighten the tenders away, but they could not, for more fuel was added and brighter grew the flames. Then the demons cast water upon it without avail, for the flames grew higher and brighter, spreading all over the heavens and dispelling the darkness. Then the demons became discomforted, for they could not abide the light, and they all ran away howling."

"Now, brethren," resumed John, after relating his vision, "what does this vision portend? The beacon is our good Master, Jesus, spreading his pure light amidst the surrounding darkness of the people; we are the tenders, who by our labors are enabled to spread that light and increase

281

its greatness, and the demons are our enemies, who will finally be over-thrown and dispersed by that light. Therefore, it is my opinion, brethren, that we keep united and continue this good work, even if we have to journey into a far country."

John sat down, when casting his regards around he encountered a look from Jesus, which seemed to express an approval.

Some few minutes were passed in exchange of whispers and looks between Judas and Peter, when at length the latter rose to address the company.

"Brethren and fellow-workers," said Peter in an easy off-handed man-ner, for be it remembered he had much improved in understanding and speech since he used to relate his big fish story at Bethsaida, "it is natural enough for our brother John to be influenced by dreams and visions through the supernatural for understanding of a matter when he cannot find it in his own mind. It seems natural to me when I have no money in my girdle to cast an eye upon the girdles of others. So it is similar with brother John. When he finds he has not an idea in his head by day to answer a question, he resorts to the wild phantasies of a night dream to make good his deficiencies. But here is a matter concerning our present and future safety, which must not be decided by dreams and visions, but by sober present thought and cool judgment. The question is, shall we continue our accustomed course of labors in some other country, or shall we break up and retire? I feel no hesitation in saying that we ought to do the latter. We have been following our beloved master near upon three years, and what have we accomplished to our benefit? I doubt not that every one of you, like myself, have been dis-appointed in your expectations. It is true the people have received much benefit, and in course of time the world at large may be much bettered; but I think it not natural or just that the laborers who undergo all the toil to do all the good, should not have a remuneration for their services. Now what have we received for our toils and sweats but insults and deprivations?, and we are now in danger of losing our liberties and our lives. I do not speak in this manner with the intent of attaching any blame to our beloved master, for if there be any to blame it must be our-selves in entertaining expectations that cannot be realized in conformity with our master's principles. No; our master is everything he professes to be, and no words that I could utter would speak his full merit."

Jesus, who had been attentively listening to Peter's speech, was much astonished at his open avowal, that he and some of the others had been disappointed in their expectations in following him. He now began to perceive that the souls and hearts of his followers were not in the good cause, but that they hankered after worldly gains and distinctions. This sudden understanding of things filled him with sadness and alarm. He now thought of the warning voice of Mary. That there were some traitors in the company he felt almost convinced, which made him cast an eye of distrust on all around him; and when Peter referred to him in laudatory terms, he loathed the very sound as well as the signification of the words. Suddenly extending his hand towards Peter, he observed in a deprecatory tone of voice:

"Peter, if thou lovest me, thou wilt not speak of me in that strain."

Peter looked up to Jesus with seeming unfeigned astonishment before he replied. He thought by the manner in which his master addressed him, Jesus had no longer any confidence in him; he, therefore, became alarmed. At length, assuming his usually simple and candid expression of countenance, he replied:

"Didst thou doubt, O my master, the love of honest Peter?"

Jesus made no answer, but covered his eyes with his hands, seeming to be undergoing distressing emotions.

"God of my Fathers!" exclaimed Peter in a loud voice, as he seized his beard with both hands, which he gave a tremendous pull, tearing out some of the hairs and then scattering them upon the ground. "Have I lived to this day, to have my love and loyalty doubted by the very man I love the most? O, my beloved master, thou knowest I love thee! If thou canst not believe the words of honest Peter, look to his acts. See what I have sacrificed to follow thee. Was I not a wealthy fisherman by the beautiful waters of Genesareth, and the principal man in the whole village of Bethsaida, until thou madest me a fisher-of-men? Have I not forsaken that beautiful lake, that neat little village, my three boats, my nets and fishing hooks? Have I not forsaken all to follow thee? and yet thou doubtest whether I love thee."

How long Peter would have continued in this strain is not known, had not Jesus desired him to be at peace, for he was satisfied as regards his loyalty and love. He then put the question to his followers, whether they would follow him into a distant country to prosecute the good cause. All were opposed to it, with the exception of John. Then he put the question, should they break up, and every one retire to his home or elsewhere? This was answered in the affirmative, with the same exception. Then John left his seat and threw himself upon the neck of Jesus, when they both shed tears of sympathy and regret.

There was a pause and silence for a few minutes, for the affecting scene between John and Jesus had impressed the whole company with sad feelings. At length this unpleasant scene was terminated by the entrance of old Lazarus, who, with some degree of alarm depicted on his countenance, announced that there was a messenger from the palace of Caiaphas, who desired to be admitted to present a letter to Jesus. This announcement filled every one with surprise and unpleasant feelings; none more so than Judas and Peter, who by their sundry exclamations expressed their wonder as to what it could mean. After a short consultation Jesus gave orders for the messenger to be admitted, when Lazarus left the room. In a few moments the latter returned, followed by an elderly man who was dressed in the priestly garb, with certain insignia denoting that he was an officer of the palace. As soon as he entered he made a respectful obeisance, and then said in a firm and distinct tone of voice:

"I am commissioned by his most high Reverence, Caiaphas, the High Priest of the Holy Temple, to place a letter into the hands of the man called Jesus, and when its contents are read, I am desired to receive what answer he may deem proper to send."

The officer then presented the letter to Jesus, which was a small scroll tied around with a silken string, and a large seal of wax suspended to it. Jesus received the letter, and told the officer to retire until he should be recalled to receive his answer. The latter retired accordingly. Jesus then broke the string of the scroll, unrolled it and read it to himself, and then reflected for a few moments, while all the company seemed excited to the highest pitch of curiosity to know its contents. At length, handing the letter to Peter, he said:

"Peter read that letter to the company, that we may form some opinion of its contents, and be enabled to send an answer."

"My dear master," replied Peter, "I never read or wrote a letter in my life. I have always been too busy to learn. I have always been employed in catching fish or catching men, that I have had no time to catch the meaning of these hieroglyphics. There is brother Matthew, he is a great scholar, for he always has his ink horn and reed in his girdle. He can read the letter, no doubt."

The letter was then handed to Matthew, who rising from his seat, made sundry formal preparations, and gave several significant leers and hems to draw the attention of the company to the important task entrusted to him to execute. At length he read it in a loud, distinct and important tone of voice:

"Palace of the Sanhedrim.

"Caiaphas to the man called Jesus. This comes greeting.

Brother in the flesh, peace be unto thee and to all under thy command, in the name of the Lord Jehovah.

"Certain rumors have come to my ears that thou, from misconception or from some other cause unknown to me, hast been preaching certain doctrines in the precincts of our Holy Temple, which transgress the Mosaical law, and hold up to ridicule and contempt the sacred rites and ceremonies of our sacred institutions. And furthermore, that thou hast inveighed against and scandalized our Sacred Order of Priesthood. These direful transgressions have been borne with for a long time by the Sacred Council of the Sanhedrim, without proceeding against thee in any manner, thinking that with time, thou wouldst be enabled to see the error of thy ways. But now the Council are much exasperated against thee, and determined to arrest thy course by punishing thee according to the powers they possess. Therefore, as I wish to be lenient to thee, and enable thee to avoid the penalty of thy conduct, I send thee this letter, proposing to shield thee from all harm if thou wilt pledge thy word of truth that thou wilt cease thy teachings in the temple, and withdraw from the neighborhood of the city. Send me thy word of truth to this effect, then thou and thy followers shall be free of any arrest within or without the city for the time of ten days, which will be allowed thee and thy followers, if thou and they should wish to pass to and fro on matters of business, or to take a farewell of thy friends. Let this be a compact between us, and may God speed thee in all just ways.

"CAIAPHAS."

This letter seemed to have made a favorable impression on all of the company with the exception of Jesus, for he began to be mistrustful of all around him, and of all that transpired. The warning voice of Mary still rang in his ears, but as he had promised to conform to their wishes and inclinations, he could not oppose them in this single matter without showing some reasonable cause; he was, therefore, compelled to be guided by their opinions.

"What is thy opinion of this letter and our action thereon?" he inquired of Judas as he knew the latter to have a keener wit and clearer perception than the rest of his followers; he, therefore, placed more confidence in his opinion.

"As my master honors me by asking me the first for an opinion, I will give it with all sincerity," replied Judas, with great deference of manner. "It is this. I think all of us ought to accept the favorable terms his Reverence has thought proper to offer us."

The opinion of Peter and all the rest were to the same end, so that Jesus had no alternative but to coincide with the others. He then ordered the officer to be sent for to receive his answer, and when he made his appearance Jesus spoke to him as follows:

"Tell Caiaphas, the High Priest, that I, Jesus, having taken counsel with my followers, have agreed to accept of the proposals contained in the letter, and that we give our solemn word of truth to conform thereto, according to the requests made therein."

This answer being considered all that was required, the officer made his obeisance and departed.

As soon as the officer was gone, Judas rose from his seat to address Jesus and the company. He seemed considerably excited, for in the importance of the measures he was about to propose he was naturally anxious and worried so that his usually cool and steady demeanor was not at his command. However, with a great effort he prevented his master from detecting his wicked intentions. At length with a slight

285

hesitancy and tremulous voice, he said:

"If my worthy master please, and the brethren generally, I wish to make some suggestions. It has been decided in this assembly tonight, that the union of our brethren and their obligations as followers of our worthy master, shall be dissolved for the present; that every member shall be at liberty to return to his home or go wheresoever he please. It behooves us, therefore, to consider in what manner and when we shall sunder our ties of brotherhood as a body, for some manner of regular proceeding is necessary in order to give satisfaction to our brethren present, and to do what is right and seemly in the eyes of our numerous disciples and adherents who reside at Jerusalem, and those as well spread throughout the country. It will not be commendable or convenient to dissolve this union now, and at this place; such a proceeding will be productive of many inconveniences. Besides it will give cause to our enemies to spread many disreputable reports injurious to our characters and detrimental to our cause. No! such proceedings would not be to our interests or honor, but would detract very much from our glory. We must have a little more time to make all necessary arrangements—to call our friends and adherents together that we may give them a just understanding of the true nature of the causes and reasons for which we have resolved upon this measure. But how, when, and where is this to be done? They are the next points of our consideration. I must acknowledge that not more than an hour ago I could not conceive how these points were to be achieved. I knew the proper place ought to be the city. 'But how,' I said to myself, 'can we accomplish this when we are surrounded by dangers, and the very life of our master menaced by our enemies?' These questions were answered quite satisfactorily when the officer who has just departed, brought the letter from the High Priest, making the liberal proposals as are therein stated. We now have no occasion to fear for our safety, neither for our master or ourselves. Upon the pledged word of the High Priest we may go to Jerusalem without molestation—call around us all our disciples and friends, explain to them the nature of our circumstances, settle our affairs, and make any other arrangements we choose; and after exhorting them to remain true to the good cause, take an affectionate farewell of them. I will now propose, if it will meet the approbation of our master and my brethren, that in three days from the present our brethren here present shall assemble at this house to escort our master to the city, where his friends and disciples will be ready to receive him, and testify their admiration and gratitude for his inestimable services. Our ovation shall then terminate at night by a feast, to which none but the most prominent friends shall be admitted. After that I shall proceed to render an account of my stewardship, and divide the remainder of our joint stock of money among the brethren. I am happy to inform my brethren that not long since I received a donation of a hundred shekels of silver; thus the amount to be distributed is greater than would be generally supposed."

As Judas progressed in his speech, the brethren were somewhat divided in their opinion about the proposed final meeting at Jerusalem. Some were doubtful of their safety in spite of the letter from the High Priest to the contrary. But when they heard Judas speak of the distribution of the common funds and the donation he had received, all their minds were made up in a second. Judas knew the nature of their sordid souls; he had only to shake his money bag at them and promise them the contents when he could carry any point he wished with them.

Jesus was quite indifferent to all that was said and decided on, after he knew the bent of their inclinations. He listened to the speech of Judas, but made no objections; neither did he exhibit any pleasure at what was proposed. He seemed to have fallen into a state of apathy, or rather of disgust for all around him, and anxiously wished for the termination of the meeting.

Then Peter addressed the brethren in a few words expressing his approbation of the measures proposed by Judas, and asked them to testify their refusal or approbation of them; which they accordingly did by unanimously voting an approval of them. Then Peter desired Jesus to express his approval or rejection of the proposals. Jesus rose, and with his eyes gently closed, in a mild tone of voice, he said:

"My dear brethren, I have before expressed to you this evening that all measures discussed and adopted by you at this meeting, I shall assent and conform to. I repent the same concerning the measures proposed by Judas. If they meet your views and wishes I am willing to assent to them and comply with your requests; I, therefore, have nothing more to say upon the subject. How these measures are to be accomplished I must refer you to Judas, for he will know best how to achieve what he has proposed."

Judas was therefore appointed to make all needful arrangements, and thus terminated the meeting. The assembly broke up, and the brethren departed their several ways.

VISION TWENTY-SEVENTH

Three days had elapsed since the events transpired as represented in the last vision. The sun had risen high in the heavens, denoting that it was about noon. The day was bright, clear and fragrant with sweet odors, and the foliage of the mountain scenery was beautiful to the sight. The palm tree was in its full bloom.

This was the day appointed by Judas for Jesus to make his last visit to Jerusalem under the false representation to receive the addresses and condolence of his disciples and friends—the expression of their grateful and loving hearts, and to sympathize with each other in the fears and hopes pertaining to their good cause.

Judas, under the direction of Saul, made great preparations for this day, as they intended to play their most important part, to entrap their virtuous and unconscious victim into the meshes of their iniquitous designs. A great deal of money had been expended in bribing certain persons to perform acts deemed necessary to their scheme of treachery; also for the sumptuous provision of an evening banquet, so that no labor or expense had been spared to render sure their contemplated plot.

There was a great number of people assembled in the village of Bethany, all attired in their best and cleanest clothing. The greater part were thronging around the residence of Lazarus, most of whom carried in their hands branches of the palm tree. All of the followers of Jesus were there dressed in white vestments, with girdles and mantles of various colors, and their heads were enveloped in handsome tires form- ed of blue and white linens, wreathed around a blue centre covering. Judas and Peter were busy in superintending the arrangements. In front of the yard gate there was a handsome grey mule, the body of which was covered with a scarlet cloth, and its head decorated with slips of the palm tree. Upon this beast it was intended that Jesus should make his entry into the city, that he might not be thronged or pressed by the people, and everybody should be enabled to see him.

All were ready and anxious for the departure, excepting Mary and Jesus, who were in the garden conversing. He, upon this occasion, had changed his ordinary dress for one of white, with a blue girdle; his head being covered with a superb tire of blue and white linen. His mien was pensively grave, as with tender expressions he endeavored to give assur- ance and consolation to the distressed Mary, who was leaning upon his arm, as she looked up to him with tears in her eyes and an expression of sorrow in her countenance.

"My dearest Jose," she said, sobbingly, "I have never opposed or contravened thy wishes before, for I always deferred to thy superior wisdom; but in this case I feel strong in my convictions that if thou goest to the city this day, thou wilt meet with treachery and destruction. Was not the traitorous conversation I heard enough? Why, then, wilt thou voluntarily throw thyself into the arms of thy enemies?"

"If it were possible, dear Mary," replied Jesus, much affected, "I would comply with thy wishes. No earthly influence could be greater with me than thy sweet endearing voice. But, Mary, if I fail to perform my duty and promises this day, I shall sacrifice all the good reputation I have gained among my people, and I shall fail giving support to that cause for which I have labored."

"What matters all this in comparison to the sacrifice thou wilt make, if thou becomest the prey of thy enemies?" asked Mary. "Thou mayest intend to do one thing, but thy enemies will work it that thou shalt do another. What dependence hast thou to do anything of thine own wish, when thou art surrounded by wicked men who will make thee do another? What confidence or trust is there to be placed in traitors?"

"It is possible, Mary," answered Jesus, "that thy construction of those men's words may be a wrong one, and if we knew all they might admit of another meaning. It seems my followers are discontented, and afraid to continue their labors with me, and that they wish for a dissolution of the brotherhood. This I have consented to, and when we assemble this evening at the banquet, it will be for the last time, for then I shall resign all claim to their services. It is possible, Mary, that when thou didst hear Judas and Peter say that "If they could persuade me to consent to this measure, that their task would be finished," they had reference to the dissolution of our brotherhood; but as thou didst not hear all that was said, It seemed a traitorous design to thee."

"I know not what they had reference to, dear Jose," replied Mary, as again the tears coursed down her beautiful cheeks; "but I feel convinced from that and other instances, that they are conspirators and traitors to thee. If they have not already betrayed thee to thy enemies, some unaccountable presentiment tells me they will do it. Therefore, my beloved Jose, if thou valuest the love of thy Mary, that love which was engendered in my heart from the days of my early childhood, and which has been cherished and expanded to an intensely holy passion for thee—0! by this holy tie which unites our hearts in tender sympathies, I beseech thee to comply with my request, and forbear this intended visit to the city today."

"0, Mary! Mary!" exclaimed Jesus with great emotions of distress. "Dear maiden of my earthly affections, spare me from complying with thy request. Thou knowest that of all things on earth whereon a man could look for happiness, all my hopes, dependence and love are centred in thee. My love for thee is without measure, making me subservient to thy will in nearly all respects; yet there is a love and duty which I must acknowledge is of more paramount importance than the earthly love which unites us in heart. I mean my duty to God and my fellow men. These, Mary, take the precedence. Ask me not to neglect them through any worldly fears or considerations. Mary, I must be firm and true to the last, in performing the last act and fulfilling the last promise that is expected of me. I must go to Jerusalem. Then let me banish all fears of danger, and hope that all things will terminate well. Let us comfort ourselves with the pleasing anticipation that when this last duty shall be performed we shall be enabled to become to each other what we both have so long ardently desired."

"Then be it so," replied Mary, with comparative composure, "since it is thy wish and thou sayest, thy duty, I will not tempt thee any longer to disregard them. But mark me, Jose, these eyes of mine will know no sleep until I know the termination of thy day's adventure. When the shades of evening come upon us I will repair to the Garden of Gethsemane, and in the northern bower I will pass the evening in prayer for thy safety. Between the hours of five and six, if all go well with thee, send a message to me at that place, and if any danger menace thee, I conjure thee to flee and come thyself to that spot, there thou wilt find one heart at least to shield thee. Promise me this much, and I will endeavor to keep from despair."

"Mary, I promise thee," replied Jesus. Then the loving pair took a tender and affectionate embrace, when Jesus took himself away and returned to his company, who were anxiously awaiting him.

He entered the house where he took a friendly leave of his host, Lazarus, and his daughter Martha. He was then escorted by his followers to the spot where the mule was tethered, and with the assistance of Judas and Peter he was soon mounted upon the animal.

As soon as he was thus elevated to the view of the people, he was greeted with a loud shout of joy—many exclamatory laudations and blessings invoked upon his future career. Jesus acknowledged the greetings of the multitude with a graceful inclination of his person, and supported with calm dignity the unusual position in which he was placed. The order of procession was now formed and the word given to advance. Judas was on one side of him and John on the other close to him; then Peter and Andrew and two others of his followers were in front, and another four behind, all of whom carried in their hands branches of the palm tree. Several aged men who were representatives and heads of various small societies of his disciples, walked two by two in front, and an indiscriminate crowd followed in the rear. Thus they left the village taking the south-western road, which descended to the Kidron and thence leading on by a bridge to Jerusalem. The road was narrow and rugged, with a steep descent as it curved round the shoulder of the mountain of Olivet, with the luxuriant forest foliage above it on one side, and beneath it on the other. Having descended this road about half way, and turned the shoulder of the mountain without any important incident, they came in view of the Kidron, and then the stupendous structure of the Temple burst upon their view.

Though Jesus had passed this spot hundreds of times before without receiving any extraordinary impressions therefrom, yet at this particular time some unaccountable power within him caused him to halt and contemplate with a serious gaze the interesting scene before him. His comprehensive eye seemed to measure the stupendous wall from the depth of the valley to the high colonnades of pure white marble; thence over the tesselated pavements, ascending by flights of steps still higher up the mountain; then, another range of marble porticos with their high, white pillars, spreading at equal distances around; then, another pavement with a flight of steps, ascending higher and higher, and then, to crown the whole, the view takes in the magnificent Temple itself, with its tall pinnacles piercing the clouds and its golden roof dazzling in the rays of the sun. Vast! stupendous structure! nine hundred feet from the valley base to the topmost pinnacle! Almost too vast for a mortal eye to embrace. Yet it was the work of man.

Then Jesus cast his eye around the city noting the many magnificent palaces of fanciful forms, with their gilded roofs and gorgeous decorations; the numerous white marble towers of great strength and magnitude, and no less great in their symmetry of structure and general beauty, especially those built by the great Herod. The towers of Hippicus, Phasaleus and Mariamne were there, towering high towards heaven, mementoes of the strong will and tyrannical power of that great bad man. And then the eye of Jesus glided rapidly around the scenery exterior to the walled city, taking within its scope many pretty villages embossed with gardens and deep verdure, and the graceful slopes of Mount Olivet with their rich verdure, its cottages and villas half exposed and half hid by beautiful groves. What a beautiful and magnificent scene was here for the contemplation of this great good man. Having terminated the tour of his inspection, he heaved a deep sigh and exclaimed:

"0 Jerusalem! Jerusalem! thou art sublime even in thy madness and folly! Magnificent and stupendous thou art beyond all other mortal achievements! Yet great as thou art the day will come when all thy mighty structures will be toppled to the ground. Hadst thou been founded in wisdom and benevolence for the true benefit of man, thou couldst have bid defiance to the destroyer for many ages of the future. But, 0 Jerusalem! thou wert conceived in the days of barbarous ignorance; thy parents were superstition and tyranny, therefore thy days of duration are drawing nigh. As the human mind becomes disenthralled from its barbarous impediments of superstition, so will thy gilded roofs and pinnacles topple down and mingle with the dust."

The cortege resumed its progress down the steep uneven road amidst the acclamations of the people who had come from the various villages and towns to greet the friend and instructor of mankind. At length the base of the mountain was reached. They were then in the valley of the Kidron, or Jehoshaphat, as named by some, and then they crossed the magnificent arched bridge which extended across the stream to the other side. At this spot another demonstration in honor of Jesus was given. A body of young men dressed in white vestments lined each side of the bridge, standing in even rows waving to and fro branches of the palm tree. The center of the bridge was strewn with palm branches, and along the sides the young men had strewn their mantles of various gay colors. As the cortege passed along the young men burst forth with united harmonious voices, singing a song of praise and honor to the great good man, as the deliverer of the people from mental slavery, the benefactor of the poor, and the exalted of the Lord.

This point being passed they took their route eastward, between the stupendous wall and the brook of Kidron, the multitude increasing in number at every pace, and the acclamations of joy and praise becoming louder and louder. At length they arrived at the Golden Gate, on each side of which was a tier of magnificent pillars of the most beautiful workmanship, and a colossal gate covered with plates of gold extending from pillar to pillar. Here they came to a halt, for their progress was contested by a band of Roman Guards, which was drawn up in front of the gate. The multitude stood aside while Jesus and his followers stood in front of the guard for a few moments awaiting the challenge of the sentry. An officer at length advanced to Jesus, and said in a tone of authority:

"Who art thou, that comest to this city followed by a multitude. Art thou a friend or foe to its rulers?"

"We come as friends, with peace and good will to all men, having nothing less in our intents than obedience to its rulers," replied Jesus.

"Wilt thou be responsible for the peace and good order of this multitude?" demanded the officer.

"I and my followers will do our best to keep the peace and promote good order," responded Jesus.

"Then thou mayest pass," returned the officer, and orders were instantly given to throw the gate open.

The cortege took up their march, passing through the gate, the people following while the Roman guards brought up in the rear, in case their power and authority should be required to quell any disturbance that might possibly arise.

They passed through the main street leading in the direction of the Temple, the multitude becoming greater and greater, and the commotion among them intense. The porches, the windows, and house-tops were thronged with the people, a great many being dressed in white, with palm branches in their hands, distinguished the friends and disciples of Jesus from the old adherents of the Priesthood. The former made the city resound with the shouts of welcome and joy as the cortege passed by; while the latter, though looking on with intense curiosity, held a mysterious silence.

Jesus deported himself with a noble, serene dignity, like a good and wise monarch who feels assured that his throne is in the hearts of his people. Sometimes he acknowledged the demonstrations of the people with a graceful bow or a smile, but said nothing to augment their excitement. At length they arrived at the colonnade of the eastern front of the Temple when Jesus alighted at the steps and ascended to the upper walk where he was received by many worthy disciples and friends.

While introductions and congratulations were passing, the Roman guard pushed through the crowd and formed themselves into a cordon in shape of a half moon, keeping the multitude back from thronging upon Jesus. Thus under the semblance of being of service to him they were ready to check any tumult among the multitude.

Some time had now passed between Jesus and his friends, when the multitude began to be restless; a great many called aloud for an ad-

293

dress, while others whose motives were reckless or hostile, uttered cries and shouts of an impudent and treasonable nature. At one part of the crowd a number of ill-looking men seemed to be more active and vociferous than the rest who seemed to be headed by a young man whose wild and reckless dark eyes denoted him to be Cosbi, of previous notoriety. He seemed to be urging his ruffian companions to some deed of tumult or insurrection; and after some turbulent demonstrations had been given by that party, a banner was unfurled having upon it the Lion of Judea, the old national emblem of Judea. Then the voice of Cosbi was heard above all the rest, urging the crowd to follow him:

"Come on, my braves," he said, in a loud animating voice. "Let us make him King; Jesus shall be King of the Jews."

The attention of Jesus was now drawn to the multitude by this outcry, when seeing the old banner of Judea unfurled he immediately directed the Captain of the Roman guard to seize it and arrest the tumult.

The officer perceiving that Jesus did not encourage this act of folly and insurrection, immediately ordered his soldiers to seize the banner and the man that bore it. The order was executed immediately as regards the banner, but the bearer made his escape among the crowd.

Jesus then stood upon the uppermost step of the colonnade, when stretching forth his hand he commanded silence and order, and after a little while when all excitement had subsided he thus addressed them:

"Friends and Brethren, it pains me to think that some of you present have mistaken the motives with which I make this visit to the city. Some of you have mistaken the nature of the doctrines I teach and the good cause I advocate, thinking that they bear reference to our political state and rulers; and some of you have mistaken my character in supposing that I would sanction the tumultuous and imprudent conduct which has just transpired. I feel it necessary to say a few words upon these points. In the first place, let me state I come not here, as I have been in the habit of doing, to make war upon absurd dogmas and priestly institutions. Nor do I come to meddle with your political state or rulers—to speak disparagingly of the one or the other; but I come with motives of brotherly love and social good feelings, to make known to you that I have resolved to retire from my labors. This is the motive of my coming, and in doing so I wish to explain the cause of my resolution to my friends; to express to them my best wishes; to strengthen them in the hopes of our good cause; to renew to them the assurances of my love, and to bid them that tender farewell as becomes a brother. Such is the motive of my visit. On the second point, I say some of you are mistaken in the nature of my doctrines and the cause I advocate, if you think they sanction turbulent and unlawful proceedings of a political nature. Who has ever heard me, in any of my discourses, deliver aught in favor of discontent, anarchy, insurrection or revolution against our political rulers?

There is not one can charge it upon me. I come not among you to preach confusion or rebellion, but peace and good will to all men, that you may so moderate your conduct as to bear and forbear with one another. I have never spoken of your rulers, or disputed their right to govern you; but I have endeavored to enlighten your minds, and taught you patience to submit to the present state of affairs until your own intelligence would suggest and establish a better. A good government does not consist in being governed according to our wishes, but in its being according to the nature of our wants. If you are weak and cannot govern yourselves, quarrel not with your rulers, because they are stronger than you; a government requires strength, and any government is better than anarchy and confusion. Some of you, I have said, are mistaken in my character in supposing that I would interfere in political strife. Some pretended friends have shouted, "Let us make him King." 0, my friends, how great is the mistake or wicked the intent of those who cry thus! How poor and trifling is the ambition they wish to inspire and enthral me with! How low is their conception of my nature to think that I would be pleased with a golden sceptre and the power to work mischief among my fellow men! No, my friends, my kingdom is not of this world. I aspire to something more exalted. I wish to rule over the minds and hearts of men with the sceptre of reason and the power of love. I wish to free the minds of men from the phantoms, the demons, and all other evil spirits which are engendered by ignorance and superstition; the enemies of men's immortal souls through which they have so long wandered in error and confusion. I wish to eradicate from the hearts of my brethren all the tares and rank weeds of envy, hatred, malice, revenge and sordid interests; to cultivate the heart, and sow therein the seeds of love, truth and justice towards one another. These are my designs, this is my ambition, and the basis of the good cause I advocate. How mistaken, then, are all those who attribute to me an hankering after political strifes or worldly aggrandizements. Be prudent, then, my brethren; let the light of the truths I teach be admitted to your understandings. Live a life of peace, harmony and justice, and attend to the cultivation of that immortal principle within you. Then you will progress in all that is good from day to day and age to age, until you will arrive at that degree of perfection when you will know what is true government, and how to govern yourselves. When that day arrives you will be free men, but if you neglect or despise the truths I have taught you, the little freedom and happiness you now enjoy will become less, and you will finally become extinct as a nation, to wander over all the corners of the earth a poor, despised, degenerate race."

When Jesus had terminated his explanations a man of middle age approached him by way of the colonnade, who by his dress and deportment seemed to be a civil officer. As he made a very obsequious salutation, Jesus observed that the expression of his countenance was of great worldly intelligence and shrewdness, which he endeavored to mask by assuming an air of great simplicity.

He was a native Judean and a Jew, but he was of a certain political party called Herodians—a set of selfish unprincipled men, who were willing to advocate and serve their foreign oppressors for their own individual interest. They accordingly were employed by their Roman masters as spies throughout Jerusalem and Judea, to discover and make report if any of the people were disaffected or plotting against the government. This man had been bribed with the money of Saul, under the management of Judas, to endeavor in the course of conversation with Jesus to get him to say something against the despotic sway of the Romans so that he might be charged therewith and handed over to the mercy of the Roman tribunal. But Jesus immediately perceived of what class he was, therefore he was on his guard not to commit himself.

"Master," said the Herodian, in a courteous manner and with an oily tongue, as soon as he had risen from his profound bow of salutation, "it is well known throughout Judea that thou art a man of wisdom and excellent deeds, whose opinions are founded on truth, virtue and justice. Thy independent spirit gains thee the respect of all men, at the same time thou fearest no man. Will it please thee to answer me a question?"

"Say on," answered Jesus curtly.

"I wish to know," said the Herodian, "which is the best government, this under which we now live, or that under which our fathers lived?"

"That government which is best administered will prove the best," answered Jesus with a triumphant smile curling his lip.

The Herodian not expecting so dubious an answer to his question, was somewhat disconcerted, and forgetting his assumed simplicity, a glance of malignant expression escaped from his eyes. But after a few moments he rallied himself and said with a smiling countenance:

"Truly so, great sir, thy answer is a wise one, but doubtful in its application. I wish to know, by comparison of the two, which is the superior. There are advantages in both, and no doubt defects in both; but be it remembered that under the Judean rule the people paid no tribute. Now, speaking in candor, dost thou think it just to pay tribute to Caesar?"

"Hast thou a coin in thy girdle?" asked Jesus of the Herodian, and perceiving his vile intent by the nature of his question, determined to answer him in a manner that he could not gain his desired point.

"I have," answered the Herodian.

"Then show it to me," responded Jesus.

The Herodian immediately pulled from his girdle a small leathern bag, from which he took a small silver coin called a denarius, which he presented to Jesus, who examined it for a few moments, and then said:

"Whose effigy is this?"

"Caesar's," answered the Herodian.

"Then if it be Caesar's," returned Jesus, "render to Caesar that which is Caesar's, and to every man, that which is his."

This answer of Jesus was an equivoque. It was not a direct answer to the Herodian's question. Such an answer would not be tolerated in this age, but at the time of Jesus it was considered a fair mode of getting rid of an unfair question. The Herodian knew as much, and he knew also that his question was not a fair one; he thought best to push the matter no further. He therefore remained silent for a few moments, then he stealthily proceeded to move away as he found that Jesus was aware of all his insidious cunning and designs.

"Stay yet awhile," said Jesus to the Herodian, "I have a question to ask thee which thou art in courtesy bound to answer, as I did thine."

"Say on, master," said the Herodian, as he drew himself up with an assumed courage.

"Tell me why thou art of that class called Herodians," said Jesus; "is it that thou art aware of the superiority of the Roman rule that our people are too weak and degenerate to rule themselves; or is it that thou art too grossly interested to be a patriot?"

This question seemed a difficult one for the Herodian to answer. He thought to himself, "If I tell the truth, and say I serve the Romans from interested motives, he will condemn me for a vile man; and if I say the superiority of the Roman rule, I must acknowledge the degeneracy of our people. I prefer the latter." Then raising his eyes to Jesus, he answered:

"I am a Herodian because I am aware of the superiority of the Roman rule."

"Thou hast answered well," responded Jesus. "Now hear me say a few words in confirmation of thy own statement."

Jesus paused for a minute, and then observed:

"The Roman rule is the best and safest for our people, and why? Because it is the strongest, most permanent, adapted to coerce, and keep in bounds a people who are too ignorant and capricious to govern themselves. The Judean people are not capable at present, and never have been capable of establishing a wise, orderly and powerful government. Their minds are not constituted of the right elements out of which to construct a good government. They never have had a good government, and as long as they are of the same nature, they never will have one of their own. A good government must be founded upon good and just principles. These principles must be established facts derived from a knowledge of man's true nature and the nature of things by which he is surrounded. When the mind of a people consists of principles of this nature, then it is capable of constructing and establishing a good government; but if the mind of a people does not consist of such principles, then the government it establishes will be more or less imperfect. Now, if we examine the mind of the Judean people generally, we shall find that there is not an established principle that has received its origin in an established fact, which is derived from a knowledge of themselves or of anything around them. Of what materials are the ideas which constitute the mind of the Judean people? Are they philosophical facts and conceptions founded upon truths? Not a whit; their ideas consist of nothing but erroneous conceptions, absurd fables, odious lies, grand misconceptions, wicked perversions, base prejudices, and crazy hallucinations. If this be the truth, how is it possible for any just principle to emanate from the people whereby to establish a government that shall be just, strong, benevolent and harmonious.

"What are the leading principles upon which the government of the people of Israel formerly, and the Judean people latterly, have been established? Firstly, the belief of a powerful, inconsistent, vindictive, jealous, cruel and revengeful God, possessing all the traits of human nature, the only exception being to a greater extent, and according to the history given of him, possessing the character of the barbarous people that worshiped him. This God of their making is an impossibility in nature, and awful in its destructive effects on the people. Another principle of their belief is, that this God made the world and all other things in a wonderfully short time, by his bare word, for man's especial benefit. Man was made from the dust, and woman from man's rib. He wished man to improve and be happy, so he made a tree of evil to tempt and ensnare him to do wrong—man and woman both do wrong accordingly; then God curses them and all their posterity for doing what he made them do. Then this God repents having made man, and he concluded to drown mankind, and does so, all but one family; then mankind spread all over the world and became worse than ever. This God concludes that he will select one people from all the rest, make them his chosen people, and show them all kinds of favors above all others. So this God selects a poor ignorant lot of slaves to be his favorites, and calls them the Children of Israel, who were our original ancestors. This people, with the aid of Moses, God releases from the Egyptians, and by way of showing his favors and protection in the commencement, he leads them through and about the wilderness for forty years, slaughtering them by thousands; famishing them with hunger and thirst, and afflicting them with diseases until the whole of those that originally left Egypt are killed off. Then the rising posterity have to fight their way out of the desert and steal another people's land to get them a home. Not one instance here stated is a fact, but in reality nothing more than the most absurd and ridiculous lies, under the pretense of giving an account of their origin and of all other things, yet this forms the basis of the Judean mind.

"It follows, then, as a matter of course, that all their institutions sub-

298

sequently established, should partake more or less of the same barbarous, absurd and false character. If we examine all of the Judean institutions we shall find them to be the same. Their rules are despotic, cruel and unjust; governing in the name of the imaginary demon God they have instituted, instead of a being wise, benevolent and responsible to men. The pillars of their government were made to support their absurd and destructive superstitious system instead of being the supporters of the interests and wants of the state. Their laws are sanguinary, partial and unjust, instead of being such as are needed to promote the general interest and security of the people. Their customs are odiously absurd and vicious, capable only of engendering conceit and error in themselves, and making all their neighbors despise and hate them as a nation. In their infatuated conceit they believe themselves the chosen people of God, and that all the rest of mankind are excluded from his favor. They, therefore, to make themselves a distinct people, cut off a portion of their body as a mark of their exclusive holiness, and as a sacrifice to the honor and glory of their God. All others who do not the same, they consider as outcasts from God, whom they treat with the greatest contempt, cruelty and injustice. Is it surprising, then, that all other nations should mark our people as objects of their wrath? They set apart a portion of their people as a distinct class, as a Holy Order of Priesthood, to live in laziness and fatten upon the labors of the rest of the people. It is from this body of exclusives that all their absurd, cruel and despotic laws and customs emanate in the name of God. It is this body which continues from age to age the same system of mental slavery and darkness, which constitutes the mind of the people. It is this vile body of men who have been the originators and supporters of all the errors and calamities of our people through all times to the present, and will continue to be so until some fortuitous circumstance shall destroy them. They are the makers of that imbecile state of mind of the Jewish people, which renders them incapable of forming a good government among themselves, or of submitting to one when it is made for them. I say our people never had a good government of their own; yet they pretend that all their institutions and laws are derived from their God; that they are, in fact, the chosen people of God. How is it then, when they have the God of heaven and earth on their side, to guide, legislate and fight for them, that they have never been enabled to establish themselves as a secure and happy people? Read their history as given by their own priesthood, and you will find there has always been confusion, anarchy and bloodshed, or external war. Every nation around them has crushed or enslaved them at different times. Where, then, was the power and majesty of their government? Where was the power and majesty of their God, Jehovah, who could not shield and protect his chosen people? All this was wanting. Is not this sufficient proof that all their pretensions were lies, and all their institutions false and vicious? Let us glance down the history of this chosen people of God, and see how their own acknowledged facts will confirm their pretensions. Firstly, they were found as slaves to the Egyptians. Next, they were slaves under the despotic rule of Moses for forty years in the wilderness. Next they were many generations in continual war with the Canaanites, fighting for the possession of other people's lands and goods. Sometimes subdued by the Philistines, the Amalekites and others; then by the Assyrians, the Arabians, the Persians, the Egyptians again, the Chaldeans, who carried off ten of their tribes, which were lost forever; then by the Grecians, and lastly by the Romans, whose vassals we now are. Does not their whole history give the lie to all their pretensions, and prove the falsity of the principles of which the Jewish mind is constituted? Here, then, we have demonstrative proof that our people were never capable of forming a government fit to govern themselves. What, then, is the inference but this? Any government that is strong enough to hold them together with some degree of order, must be better than any one they may institute for themselves. Therefore the Roman rule under which we live must be the best under present circumstances."

After hearing this address, the Herodian and Judas thought it of no use to endeavor to make Jesus commit himself with their Roman Masters, by any trap they could lay for him, so they relinquished their attempts.

Jesus having received information as to the hour the banquet would commence, dismissed his followers, and passed the remainder of the evening walking around the colonnades, conversing with some of his particular friends.

VISION TWENTY-EIGHTH

JESUS

It was about the fourth hour of the evening, when a spacious apartment in the upper part of the house of one Simeon, who was a disciple of Jesus, was opened for the reception of the guests who were to be present at the farewell meeting of their beloved Master.

The scene presented was not one of a very costly nature, for there was nothing luxurious or ostentatious about the apartment. Plain bare walls, huge beams and long boards for the roof, washed all over with white, and an uncovered floor, formed the boundaries of the room. Numerous lamps attached to the walls and some suspended from the roof, gave forth a sufficient light for the large space embraced. On one side of the room the floor was elevated about a foot higher than the rest, where a long table and seats were placed for the principal personages, and on the other three sides were similar, but longer; all of which were covered with plenty of good cheer, of a plain and substantial nature, consisting of roast meats, bread, fruits, vegetables, and vessels containing water. In the centre of the floor was another table, without seats, on which were vessels containing wine and an extra supply of provisions in case they should be required. Every table was provided with a number of male servants who were dressed in yellow vestments, with long knives stuck in their girdles, and napkins in their hands. The meats were cut in small pieces by the servants, to be handed to the guests, who, if they had not knives of their own, made use of their fingers and teeth in all other respects as needed.

The host, a venerable and zealous disciple of Jesus, passed to and fro, giving orders to the servants and inspecting all things that nothing should be lacking, and when the proposed time arrived he gave the announcement to the guests assembled below that all was ready.

Then Jesus, his followers and disciples entered the apartment, in numbers sufficient to fill all the seats, so that there were no guests ill-provided, or lacking of anything essential to their comfort. Jesus took a seat in the middle of that table, on the exterior side, which was elevated above the rest, and his followers were seated around him, with John and James at his sides and Judas and Peter opposite. The other tables were soon filled up by the numerous guests, when the servants went around distributing the various meats and giving such attendance as was required. When all were ready for the feast, Jesus rose from his seat, and with uplifted hands and eyes implored the Almighty Father of Heaven to give them his blessing on this occasion. Then the feast commenced. All solemnity and reserve were banished. Everyone partook of the good things before him, for fingers, teeth and tongues were in rapid motion. Care, trouble and anxiety were for the time forgotten; their hearts began to expand with generous feelings, and their minds to create noble sentiments as their stomachs were filled. As each person satisfied his hunger small parties began to assemble around the room in conversation, and by the time when all had finished it became general.

Then the servants removed the remains of the eatables and supplied to each guest a goblet of wine, and general conversation was continued. Thus some time had elapsed, during which Jesus remained absorbed in thought. John and James seemed very much depressed, and made but few observations to any one. Judas and Peter conversed in whispers or with significant glances, and the rest of the followers seemed uneasy, as though they were apprehensive of some impending evil. At length Jesus rose from his seat, and placing his hands upon his breast and his eyes on vacancy, he remained silent for some time. The general din of conversation almost immediately subsided, and in the course of a few seconds all became still as death.

Then Jesus slightly bowing and glancing around the room, addressed the assembly in a voice of plaintive pathos:

"My beloved friends and brethren, the hour has at length come in which the sorrowful task compels me to address you for the last time and bid you farewell, and then tear myself from you, perhaps forever. O! my friends, let it not be considered affectation in me when I say that of all the trials and labors I have undergone—of all the insults and hardships I have endured since the commencement of my public ministration, this present moment brings to my heart the keenest pain and the greatest sorrow. You who are parents can judge of the pangs of the father when separated from his children. You, therefore, can judge of the agony which at present rends my breast, for I view you all as my children. You have been born to me from the depth of darkness, through the active animating influence of the light which I have in a degree shed upon the world. As the universe was born out of chaos through the active powers and love of God, making all things his offspring, so have I called you forth from the chaos of human thought and made you my offspring. As a father is pleased when he sees the impression of things dawning upon his child's mind, even so have I been pleased when I shed upon you the light of true philosophy, to see it make its way to your understanding, creating a new life within you by which you have been enabled to comprehend your true nature in part; to catch glimpses of the True God in nature around you, and look back with horror to the murky darkness from which you have emerged. 0! my friends, my pleasure did not end here in considering you as my children. As a father in the fullness of his love for his child, with glowing, sanguine hope, anticipates all that is beautiful and good with regard to its future career, so it has been with me when I anticipated your futurity. In the fullness of my love and desire for your benefits I have seen you so exalted in perfection that when compared to your former selves, you seemed as angels of light compared to demons of darkness. Judge, then, of my love as a father towards you. 0! Judge of my anguish in being separated from you! In my early youth I was educated under the same institutions and influences that others are in our country. The same measure of false and vicious notions were meted out to me that others received. I did not cast them away from any preconceived opposing view, but threw them into the sieve of my reason—sifted them thoroughly, and then I perceived that nearly all fell through, and after further casting out all that were imperfect and worthless there was but little worth preserving. I thus became early convinced that the constituents of the human mind of the people, at least by whom I was surrounded, were false, vicious, absurd, indifferent or doubtful. I said nothing, but continued my investigations. At length the time came when I was enabled to travel, and I availed myself of the opportunity. Travel withdraws a man's mind from a great part of the vicious influences of an erroneous education. The mind becomes free and gradually acquires strength from the acquisition of new and strange ideas. He is enabled to view in a cool and unbiased manner those ideas he has already acquired, and consequently is better enabled to see their truths or falsehood. Thus it was with me. My mind became gradually freed from all the erroneous notions which were given me as so many truths by my early instructors, and which were replaced with facts that I gained in the course of my travels. I was at length enabled to take a comprehensive view of the human mind, comparing it as it is in the unthinking mass of mankind, to the unprejudiced lover and investigator of truth, and then I was enabled to draw certain inferences, which are true as regards the mind of man generally. In the course of my travels I have found men with minds similar to my own, but I will not include them in the statement I make.

"I observed that the minds of mankind did not consist of an assem-

303

blage of facts, or a true knowledge of themselves and the external universe, but quite the reverse. Their minds consisted of false impressions, even of physical things generally, as well as everything else. False conceptions of their own nature; false conceptions of external nature; false impressions of the origin and power of nature; untrue history of man and things; a vast amount of wild fancies and imaginations; a vast amount of foolish and vicious prejudices, and a vast amount of desires, which they transformed into beliefs, and considered as so many facts. I perceived that mankind generally were not desirous of investigating their ideas to discover whether they were true or false, but rather received them as they came, and judged of them only by the rule—whether they would suit their interests and habits or not. I observed that when men reasoned, it was not to discover the truth of the thing, but whether it would conform to their preconceived conceptions of that thing, or to their interests. I perceived that man had no general conception of what is good or evil, but every one decided it to be so, whether it suited or not his end in view; and that all the moral qualities varied with men as their situations differed in life; for what was good and virtuous in one man's estimation, was bad or vicious in that of another. I perceived that mankind in the mass had no true conception of the true God of the Universe, though nearly all men believed in Gods. The nature of their God was always according to the conception they had of themselves, with this difference: They gave greater extension of attributes to their Gods.

"Having arrived at these inferences of the human mind through my investigations and experience, I felt a deep sorrow continually oppressing me, in contemplating man's imperfect moral nature. I sometimes thought that man would be a more consistent and happy being if he had less capacity for intelligence; then his ideas would have been bounded by his simple wants and his actions would be more harmonious and virtuous. And sometimes I thought if God had created man with an intuitive knowledge of all that is necessary for him to know in this life, it would have prevented all the destructive conflicts and aversions of which mankind have been guilty, and are prone to. But after further investigation and mature reflection I perceived it to be man's inevitable destiny to gain perfection and intelligence through his worldly experience; not the experience of a lifetime or an age, but in the course of a succession of ages. I saw that the minds of all other animals were stationary, and the mind of man progressive; that man's spirit and mind were coexistent, destined to struggle together through this life until they should exalt themselves above all gross material influences, when they would become capable and worthy of entering upon another and better state in the future. Then I said to myself, "Is it possible that this state of perfect intelligence may be brought about sooner by individual exertion? Is it possible for a man who is endowed with the light of truth to enlighten

304

his fellow men—to banish from their minds their errors and misconceptions of things, replacing them with a knowledge of facts?" This I concluded to be possible. I then determined to devote my time and exertions to accomplish that desired end. Such, my friends, are the ideas which initiated me into the course I have of late pursued. How, then, have I filled the task I imposed upon myself? You have seen some of my labors, but you know not all. I have endeavored to do much for the amelioration of my fellow man's condition, and though I have not accomplished all I designed, yet this present assemblage can testify that my labors are not in vain. When I entered upon my labors, I found two great obstacles to contend with. One was, the almost impenetrable darkness of the people's minds; the other was, the formidable opposition of the priesthood, whose shafts of wit, scorn and hatred I have defied; but at length their vindictive malice and temporal power have endangered and circumscribed me in my proceedings, yet in spite of all, I have sown so many good seeds that the harvest in time will be goodly and bountiful.

"I have endeavored to enlighten my brethren in humanity, as to the nature of the true God, and that the one they worshiped under the name of Jehovah was only the picture of their barbarous ancestors. I have endeavored to convince them that they possess immortal souls, which emanate from God's own divine essence. I have taught them a code of morals which, if complied with, will preserve the purity of their souls, and render them happy on the earth. I have shown them that death is but a transitory state leading to a new and better life for all those that are prepared to follow it. I have endeavored to enlighten them concerning their mortal nature, and I have shed glimpses of that future life, which we all should endeavor to obtain. This, and much more that I need not state, have I done for my fellow men; the great aim of which has been to make them happy while on earth, and to render them capable of greater happiness hereafter.

"I need scarcely tell you that I am desirous of doing more, but, my friends, I am under the necessity of informing you that it can not be. The circumstances by which I am surrounded are such, it is not me alone that danger menaces, but others whom I cherish will be in danger also if I persist in my course. I have aroused the great Order of the Priesthood; they are up in arms against me because they perceive their priestcraft is waning among the people. They give me the option to retire from my labors or incur their dread vengeance. It is not with regard to myself that I dread their power and vengeance. No, my friends, it is for your safety and the cause I advocate that I have reason to fear. Willingly would I sacrifice this life of mine, if it could assure me these dear objects of my desires and ambitions would be saved. But if by further opposition to their wishes I should drive them to hostilities against us, the sacrifice of my life would not appease their vindictive ire. I must, therefore, submit

305

to the proposals they make me; and though the keenest of agony rends my heart, I must resign myself to the sorrowful separation.

"My friends, it is my intention, after I separate from you this night, to retire to domestic privacy where I shall reflect upon my labors and what I would further have done, had I possessed the power and liberty to do so. When the shades of night shall envelop my domestic cot, I shall not forget to petition that God I taught you to adore, to protect my beloved disciples and further their cause. Before I leave you, I wish to make a few prudent remarks, which will be necessary, considering our circumstances. When I retire to privacy I would advise you also to return to your homes. Some time of quiet inaction will be commendable in the present excited state of feelings of our enemies, until some more favorable opportunities shall occur to renew our labors. Though you may be separated by waters and land, you can be united as one body by the doctrines I have taught you, and the love I have aroused in your hearts, one for the other. Wherever you may be, or under whatever circumstances of life, whether happy or painful, let me conjure you to hold on to the principles I have taught you. They will be your guides under all difficulties and doubt, and as you spread them through the land they will prove the salvation and glory of all Israel. Whatever may be your afflictions in life never despair, but be hopeful, courageous and zealous in all you undertake in the good cause. In all other respects where I have not expressed my views, follow my example as far as you think I have acted prudently. Be assured, my friends, that though we have many obstacles to encounter in propagating our principles, and though the prospects at present may be somewhat saddening, yet they are of so true and divine a nature they must eventually triumph over all obstacles. Yes, my friends, I foresee the time—though demons should howl and raise up tempests and earthquakes to oppose it—the seeds I have sown will spring up to be stupendous trees, spreading their branches all over the earth, so that all who will, may be nourished by their fruits and become renewed In their nature. The time will come when the earth will be a comparative paradise of happiness, and man shall become so exalted in his nature that he will be comparatively perfect, and deemed worthy at death to be admitted to the presence of his God."

Jesus having finished his address, sat down, and glancing to the right he saw that John who sat next to him seemed to be undergoing very painful emotions. Thinking that his distress was caused by the thought of their coming separation, he threw his arms around his neck endearingly and drew him close to his breast as he whispered words of comfort in his ear. But John, instead of making answer, burst into tears, sobbing violently. Then some few minutes passed in a low conversation by all present, which was terminated when a venerable looking man with white locks of hair flowing around his neck, and hoary beard, made his person distinguished above the rest by standing up at one of the other tables. All voices were immediately hushed and all eyes cast toward the old man, who it was understood was going to speak.

Stretching forth his trembling arms with a countenance expressive of painful emotions, he thus addressed Jesus, in a loud, piercing voice and tone of lamentation:

"0! my beloved Master, hear the voice of thy loving and humble disciple, on the part of myself and in response of these my brethren. From the depths of our hearts we possess a boundless love for thee. From the depths of our understandings we acknowledge thy great wisdom, and the soul-awakening efficacy of thy divine doctrines. But how shall we express the depths of our sorrow, the anguish of our hearts, and regret of our minds, at the thought of losing thee? We have no words to express our affliction, but if tears can speak, then we will be eloquent. 0! my beloved master, this is a trying moment for us. We, who were once groveling in the darkness of a gross superstition and among the mists of man's common errors, have been brought forth by thee to the light of a new and happy life. Thou hast impressed upon our understandings a knowledge of our true nature. Thou hast revealed to us the divine principles of the true God. Thou hast made known to us that our spiritual selves are allied to God, and that by living a life of purity and righteousness we may return to him. Can we, then, ever fail to appreciate thy worth among us? Shall we ever cease to regret the loss of thy presence? Can we ever cease to love thee, and feel grateful for all thou hast done for us? 0, never! never! Our hearts and our minds shall be forever devoted to thee, whether thou art living on the earth or in the bright realms of bliss on the other side of death. 0! my beloved master, my brethren join me in making a request of thee. We wish thee to suggest some simple mode or manner by which at certain times we may recall to our remembrance thy cherished love and services; for we know that in the course of natural events we cannot have thee always in our presence, but we wish to renew thy image in our hearts and minds."

The old disciple resumed his seat with tears trickling down his cheeks, and in a few moments after Jesus arose. Then, with an expression of softened sadness on his countenance, in a calm and sweetly toned voice, he replied:

"I thank our venerable friend for his feeling address, and I thank all the brethren, in his name, for their expressions of love and sympathy. Their sorrow and regret at our separation are equally felt by me; but we will hope that this sad event will be productive of more brighter days and more important events. With regard to the request of the brethren I will suggest something in compliance therewith, which will be equally pleasing to me. Call the servants to fill your cups once more with wine, and then I will state it."

The servants, according to orders given, immediately filled every man's cup with wine, when Jesus taking up his, resumed:

"In this cup, my friends, I pledge you my sincere and undying love." He then sipped of the wine and resumed: "Now follow my example, and give me your pledge, as I have given you mine; and at every annual recurrence of this night, do this in remembrance of me."

Then the whole assembly, with one exception, raised their cups to their lips, and with an almost simultaneous voice cried aloud:

"Beloved master, we pledge thee our love!" Then they drank their wine.

Jesus glanced his eyes around with an expression of delight at the demonstration of pure love and reverence towards him; but when his regard embraced his followers who were near to him, he saw that Judas was not present. A sudden chill of apprehension or disappointment passed through him, as he observed:

"Where is Judas? I see him not."

"Judas requested me to state the cause of his absence," replied Peter. "He said that some unforeseen business compelled him to leave for a little while. He will soon return."

"He should have spoken to me," returned Jesus coolly. "He is lacking at the most interesting part of our meeting."

Then Jesus cast his eyes upon John, and noticed that he seemed stupefied under some distressing emotion, and that his cup of wine remained untasted.

"How is this, brother John? Thou hast not pledged me in thy wine," remarked Jesus with surprise.

"0! master!" shrieked forth John in a half frantic and doleful manner, "I cannot."

"Cannot! What meanest thou?" returned Jesus in astonishment.

"Master, I am not worthy," John answered hurriedly, as he aroused himself and looked up to his master with a countenance expressive of mingled shame, terror and desperation. "Let me confess before it be too late. There is treachery among us, master. Thou art betrayed! Judas has betrayed thee to the Sanhedrim. He is now gone for the officers and guards to arrest thee. Flee master, while there is yet time!"

At the announcement of this intelligence, Jesus staggered for a moment as though struck by an unseen powerful blow. All bodily and mental functions were paralyzed for a time, his gaze being firmly fixed upon John with an expression of terror. At length he so far recovered his powers as to speak in a low, hoarse voice, in varied tones expressive of horror.

"Judas has betrayed me, sayest thou? and thou knewest this, and didst not reveal it until the remorse of thy conscience compelled thee!"

"Master! dear master!" exclaimed John as repentant tears streamed down his cheeks, "I have not known it long, and then I was constrained to be silent."

"0, John! John!" ejaculated Jesus in tones of agony, "this is a terrible blow to me—not that Judas has betrayed me, but that thou hast participated in his crime. Thou knewest that I loved thee as a father does his child. I would rather that Judas had betrayed me a thousand times than have my faith shaken in thy love. This— "

Before Jesus could finish his last sentence, Simeon, the host, rushed into the room with terror depicted on his countenance, and having with hurried steps approached Jesus, he said in accents of alarm:

"0! master Jesus, flee for thy life this instant! Thou hast been betrayed. Judas comes here with officers of the Sanhedrim and a body of the city guards to arrest thee. A servant of mine has just brought the information. Flee, I beseech thee—there is not a moment to lose."

Then Jesus uplifting his eyes and clasping his hands, exclaimed:

"I perceive that my last hour draws nigh; but yet I have one duty to perform which I must struggle to accomplish." Then turning his regard once more upon John, he observed: "Thou hast shaken my faith in the fidelity of man more than the treachery of a thousand such persons as Judas. God forgive me. My hopes of man's perfectibility begin to fade before my view." Then suddenly springing from his place he waved a farewell to all present and left the room followed by Peter and Andrew.

The assembly now broke up in the greatest confusion, every one departing as quickly and privately as he could to his home or place of sojourn.

A few minutes afterwards, Judas, followed by some officers of the Sanhedrim and a detachment of the Roman guards, entered the room, when he found it deserted.

VISION TWENTY-NINTH

On the north-western slope and at the base of the mountain of Olivet there was once a beautiful spot of ground which was set apart as a place of pleasure resort by the people of that vicinity, and frequently visited by the inhabitants of the Holy City. It was a place where most of the verdant beauties of nature peculiar to that region were concentrated, which, with a little fanciful addition of art, made it a desirable retreat for any one wearied with the monotony of the city, or desirous of passing an hour in solitary reflection amidst sweet odors and green waving foliage.

It was enclosed by a thick hedge of prickly pear, knitted together with creeping vines and supported on the exterior by a low wall of stone, leaving an entrance on the side facing the Kidron, and one on the side by the road leading to Bethany. Within this enclosure were trees of nearly every species that grew in the country around, of fruits and sweet odorous germs, with shrubberies and flowers bordering the walks around the sides. There were natural arbors, shady nooks and cool retreats, and the ground was covered with a soft carpet of grass. On the elevated or northern side there was a promenade, a favorite place of resort with the young people, where the foliage of the trees on each side was so dense that the branches interlaced with each other, forming a beautiful natural arbor, impervious to the sun's rays. At the interior edge of this arbor there was a mountain spring, gushing forth its crystal waters, which were received in a white marble basin below. This pleasant spot was called the Garden of Gethsemane.

It was about midnight, for the moon rode high in the heavens, and its silver sheen gliding between the interstices of the foliage, gave the scene an air of soft melancholy, so congenial to the feelings of doubtful lovers and soothing to the feelings of all oppressed with sorrow. The stars emitted their usual twinkling light, adding their beauty; and the air being redolent with sweet-scented flowers, affected the senses with a pleasing languor. Within this tranquil, enchanting spot not a living thing was to be seen excepting the phosphorescent night fly that flitted to and fro like, as the imagination may picture, some fairy spirits at a revel. Not a sound was to be heard excepting the tree insect with its shrill grating noise pursuing its industrious habits; or the night owl in pursuit of prey, for the Garden of Gethsemane was reposing in its solemn tranquility.

At length the midnight stillness was broken by the sound of footsteps as three men enveloped in their mantles entered the garden by the entrance fronting the Kidron. The foremost of the party was a tall, portly figure who, as soon as he entered, betook himself to a clump of trees, followed by the others; and having gained the more retired spot he tore the mantle from his head, disclosing to view the person of Jesus.

Great was the change of that handsome countenance within the last few minutes. The usual serenity of his dark brown eyes had vanished, giving place to wildness and sorrow, denoting the great anguish of his heart; his lips were compressed, and his cheeks haggard and pale. For some moments he seemed too much overpowered to speak, but at length resuming a slight command over his emotions he addressed the two followers:

"Peter and Andrew," he said, in a mild though sorrowful tone of voice, "you have given your last proof of attachment to me, as much as I could expect or desire under the nature of circumstances. It now becomes your duty to look to yourselves, and hazard not your own danger by mingling with mine. We must part here."

"Master, dear master," replied Peter in a sobbing voice, "is it I who have loved thee ever since we first knew each other? Is it I who has been thy faithful follower through all thy journeyings, difficulties and various adventures, who shall desert thee now in thy present calamity? No, my master, I cannot. Ask of me my life, it shall be freely given; but do not bid me to depart from thee."

"And I, dear master," said Andrew, imitating his brother's tone and manner as well as he could, "cannot think of leaving thee. If Judas has betrayed thee and all the rest have deserted thee, still thou shalt have Peter and Andrew as faithful followers, whithersoever thou goest."

"My friends," responded Jesus, "my labors are at an end for the present. I am no longer capable of continuing my efforts. I never shrank at toil nor danger, neither shall I do so in the future. But this unexpected treachery and ingratitude that I have experienced from those I loved and trusted, have completely unmanned me. I shrink from placing further confidence in man. I am now a proscribed man, who needs some hole or corner to hide himself from his enemies. I therefore need no attendants or followers. So I advise you, my friends, to return to your homes and secure yourselves from the danger my presence may bring upon you, if you should be found in my company."

Peter and Andrew both vowed they would not leave Jesus, renewing their protestations of love and fidelity, when the latter being at length wearied with their importunities, consented that they should abide with him that night. He desired them to secrete themselves among the herbage, and watch if his enemies should approach, to give him warning if they did so, and in the meantime he would leave them for the solitude of the northern arbor, where he would commune with himself and pray. They promised to do as he requested them. Then Jesus left them and

311

made his way to the grove at the northern end of the garden.

Jesus had no sooner disappeared among the foliage of the trees when Peter, looking up to his brother Andrew, with an expression of low cunning and heartless villainy, observed:

"Andrew we have chased our game to a cover. We must take care that we do not let him escape. His last act is performed, except so far as the Sanhedrim shall dispose of him. We must now look to ourselves, seek a new master, or become masters of our own. Since he has not made me a Governor of a Province as I once expected, I will take up his profession and become a master teacher myself. Now Andrew, thou must hasten to the city and look out for Judas, who with the officers and guards, like bloodhounds are scenting around for their victim. Thou must put them upon the right scent, Andrew, by informing Judas that I have him safe at the northern grove in the garden of Gethsemane. Now hasten thee away, but do not return—thou wilt then escape all suspicion of treachery."

Andrew, having received the orders of his brother, immediately left the garden to execute them, and Peter seated himself at the foot of a tree. From the folds of his dress he drew forth a small bottle containing wine, of which he drank with seeming thirst and satisfaction; then reclining himself at his ease, he entered into a retrospective view of his past career, from the time he joined Jesus up to his betrayal. Among his train of thoughts the following were some of the most prominent:

"Peter, thou hast become ambitious and restless. But art thou better placed in the world and more happy, in leaving thy simple and honest business of fisherman to follow a new vocation for which thou wert not fitted? My poor master called me a fisher-of-men, meaning that I should save men from their errors and wickedness, but Judas construed it to mean the deceiving of men so as to profit by them, and I have followed the principles of the latter. What has my experience taught me but this? That it is more easy, profitable and joyous to follow the calling of fisherman than to do what I have done; to lie, scheme and deceive, seeming to be honest at the time, is more difficult than to catch fish. The earnings of the one is by fraud, while the gains of the other is by honest labor; the latter producing the most happiness. Ah! I almost wish I had never quit my business of fisherman."

Peter's thoughts came to a pause for a few moments when under the influence of regret for his past happy occupation. In the meantime he applied himself to his wine bottle to receive consolation under his distressed state of mind, and having given it a most fervent embrace, he resumed his cogitation with a more encouraging prospect.

"Well, there is no use in repining for the past. When I look at it, there is nothing great in being a simple fisherman all one's days. A man to be thought something of must do as other great men do. Besides the

312

people cannot see anything great in virtuous simplicity or honest toil. They must be cheated, deluded and imposed on, by great pretensions and assumptions, and then they think one a great man. Ah! ah! I have done my part for them in that respect. The fisher-of-men has caught many of them in his net, and at last I have caught, or helped others to catch, my kind unsuspecting master. Ah! what would the world say to that if they knew all? He who was so kind to me that I should return it with ingratitude and treachery! He that loved and trusted me that I should conspire against him and hand him over to his bitter enemies. Traitor that I am—I like not that name of traitor! I must endeavor to wash it out of my memory."

Peter then renewed his application to the skin-bottle, from which he took a deep draught, thinking to wash from his memory the name of traitor. He then resumed his reflections and continued them for some time after, but now and then he discovered something which he wished to erase from his memory, so that he resorted frequently to his bottle, until the wine overpowered him, when he fell asleep.

In the meantime Jesus had retired to the grove at the extremity of the garden, when he paced up and down the walk looking around him in the hope of seeing somebody, but finding no one, he leaned against a tree and gave way to his sad thoughts and painful emotions. In a short time a retrospective view of his past career passed through his mind. His hopes, designs, labors, disappointments, and the calamitous termination of all that was dear to him, glided like phantoms before his mental eye: the surprise and indignation of his youthful mind and feelings when he became enlightened upon the perversity and weakness of human society; the philanthropic desires that warmed his breast and his bright anticipations when he devised a plan, as he thought, which would ameliorate the condition of his fellow men; then the zeal and energy with which he labored to execute all he had designed. Thus far his reminiscences gave a momentary soothing to his wounded feelings. But a sudden revulsion took place, straining every nerve and fibre in his being with horror and agony. His disappointment and crushing conviction of the vile, sordid nature of the men he had admitted to be his followers; his abused confidence and love; their worthless professions and their blasting treachery, were present to his mind in all their astounding horrors, so overwhelming and crushing he could scarcely believe it to be real. But when he thought of the tender love he bore John of Galilee, to find him as one of the traitors, this filled up the measure of the bitter draught of affliction he had to drink. He felt that all confidence in man's virtue was irretrievably gone from his heart. Even should he escape the vengeance of the Sanhedrim, all his hope, all his energies and prospects of the future were blasted. He writhed with the intensity of his sufferings; he groaned aloud in his agony, and his forehead became covered

313

with a clammy sweat, that oozed forth from the intensity of his dolor. A coldness gathered around his heart, when his arms fell to his sides in the prostration of all his manly strength. For some minutes he remained in this weak and almost insensible state, when at length he began to revive, then uplifting his eyes and hands, he fervently ejaculated:

"Great God! in thee have I trusted. For thee and my fellow man have I labored, and now my recompense is treachery, ignominy and destruction! If it be possible with thee let this persecution cease. My principles and love are strong in thee, but the flesh is weak."

Having made this short but reverend address to his Father in Heaven, he felt himself somewhat more composed; then leaving the tree he once more paced up and down the walk, looking around him with restless anxiety, as he said to himself:

"Now I am a miserable fugitive indeed—deceived, betrayed and pursued to the death! No one to pity me, but deserted by all who formerly professed their love. Even the maiden of my heart, whose love I prized above all earthly blessings, seems to have deserted me, for she is not here according to her word. What shall I do? Whither shall I flee? I am not coward enough to flee before my pursuers like a hunted beast. I would rather die a sacrifice to their ire. 0, horror! horror! More blessed is the lot of the meanest thing that crawls than mine at present. I am sick of this life and of my fellow-men. I would rather be a jackal, and nightly prowl around the tombs feasting on the dead, than to live on dependent and confiding in man's professions of love, sincerity and gratitude; then I should not have the agony to experience that all are hollow-hearted, sordid-minded creatures."

"There is yet one whose heart is true to thee," said a soft, sweet voice in a saddened tone. Jesus turning suddenly around beheld his beloved Mary. With a sudden spring he clasped her in his arms, and gazed upon her for a few moments with delight; then approaching her pale cheeks with his lips, he imprinted upon them many tender kisses.

"Mary! dearest Mary!" he frantically exclaimed, "thy presence has snatched me from the madness of misanthropy. 0! my heart has been sorely bruised, and my mind driven to madness! But, Mary, hast thou heard anything of what occurred at the banquet?"

"Dear Jose," said Mary in a firm voice, though sad, "I passed the whole evening in this garden awaiting a message from thee, until the midnight star shone above me; but receiving none from thee, I left for home in hopes that all was well with thee. As I entered the village I met one of thy disciples who had just come from the city. He gave me the fearful intelligence of thy betrayal, and the breaking up of the banquet. Then I instantly fled for this place thinking that thou wouldst first come here if thou shouldst escape thy enemies. But now, dear Jose, compose thyself, and we will endeavor to decide what is best to be done."

314

"Mary," said Jesus in a tone of anguish, "all is lost to me. I am now a fugitive surrounded by traitors and false friends, and dare not show my head by day. I now repent because not heeding thy solemn warning and advice, but my sense of duty to my fellow men and the dignity of my own character compelled me to disregard all thy just suspicions. In that I have erred."

"Reproach not thyself, dear Jose," replied Mary in a tone of great tenderness, "there is nothing in thy conduct to merit reproach. Thou hast been mistaken, deceived and unfortunate; but even thy errors, if any there be, only prove the superiority of thy nature over other men. Thou didst judge from the purity and sincerity of thine own heart that all men were, or ought to be like thyself; and when cunning and false-hearted men made pretensions of love and loyalty to thee thou didst believe them, thinking it impossible that they could be otherwise but true, until thy sad experience taught thee the wickedness of man. But come, my beloved; we must not waste time in discoursing more than is necessary; thy safety must be looked to. A swift horse will carry thee out of the reach of thy enemies before the dawn of day, and it shall be my care to provide thee with one; all other considerations must be dispensed with for the present."

"Dearest maiden of my heart!" exclaimed Jesus, as he fondly drew Mary to his breast, "since thy beauteous image again blesses my vision and thy sweet voice again impresses my ears, more than half of my former anguish seems to have been dispelled. This scene which just now seemed so gloomy, now brightens up with a pleasing aspect; and even life I begin to think could be endured if I were placed in some secluded nook near the neighborhood of thy heart. 0! sorry am I that I should have neglected so pure and holy a love as thine so long. Had I devoted more attention to thee, and less to the false hearts around me the present calamity might possibly have been avoided."

"Cease, dear Jose, to regret the past," returned Mary affectionately. "I know thou lovest me; that is sufficient. I have waited in patience many a long day to hear thee say so, and can wait as long again if it be necessary for the happy day when we shall become one in spirit and flesh. But now, let us say no more; let us hasten to find a place of concealment for thee until I can find the means of escape."

"Mary, there is one thing more I must say to thee," said Jesus in a hurried manner, as though he became sensible of the preciousness of time. "It may happen that I cannot escape, but become the victim of my enemies; therefore, at the present time I wish to impart to thee a secret, in case I shall not have another opportunity."

"Proceed then, dear Jose; but be quick," responded Mary.

"I wish to acquaint thee," resumed Jesus, "that thy former neighbors at Nazareth, known to thee as Joseph and Mary, were not my parents."

"Ah! is it possible!" exclaimed Mary. "Who, then were thy parents?"

"That is still a mystery to me," returned Jesus. "It is upon that I wish to speak, and ask of thee a boon. Know, then, that when I returned from my travels and re-visited my native village of Nazareth, I found my foster mother, Mary, in her last hour of life. When I entered her presence she was speechless, but sensible of her situation. She recognized me immediately as I stooped to embrace her. Pointing to a small casket that was in the hands of a Rabbi, who stood at the side of the couch, she uttered a shriek of joy and fell back, when her spirit departed from her body. After the first outpourings of my regret and grief were over at the decease of my kind mother, as I thought her to be, the Rabbi placed the casket in my hands, telling me that he had promised the deceased he would take care of it till I should return to my native village; he thus acquitted himself of his promise. As soon as convenient I opened the casket, within which I found an article of jewelry and a document in writing, beside a quantity of money. The document I immediately read, and to my great astonishment I was informed that the worthy Mary and her husband Joseph were not my parents; but it asserted they knew not who my parents were. It seems, according to the statement, Joseph and Mary were travelling to find a favorable place for a settlement, when one night as they were resting after their day's journey they were accosted by a beautiful woman, who appeared to be of high rank, and who presented me, then an infant in arms, to them, with a large bag of gold, desiring them to take and rear me as one of their own children. The worthy pair, who were in needy circumstances, consented to do so. The unknown female then taking a bracelet from her arm, gave it to them, requesting that they should never part with it excepting to myself when I should be a man grown. She then departed, and nothing more was ever known or seen of her. This secret had always been kept from me by my foster parents.

"I have now revealed the secret, whose son I am not; but whose son I am I know no more than before. Since then I have made search and inquiry to discover my true parents, but so far I have failed. I will now communicate to thee the boon I would ask. It is to take charge of this bracelet which has been transmitted to me from one of my mysterious parents, whoever they may be. It is the greatest prize I retain upon earth, and I know not any one to whom I could entrust it better than to thee."

Jesus then took from under the folds of his dress a golden bracelet of curious workmanship, set with several precious stones, which was attached to his person by a silken cord. Untying the latter, he gave it to Mary, and added:

"Here it is, Mary; take it, wear it, and keep it as long as thou livest, as a memento of my undying love for thee."

Mary took the bracelet and fastened it upon her arm, as she observed:

"Dear Jose, thy request shall be sacredly complied with as long as I live; but I can assure thee that it will not be long, if any fatal chance shall deprive me of thee. Now come, let us leave this spot that we may carry out the measures of safety to thee.

The loving pair then started from the spot where they held their conversation, taking their course along the walk which led to the gate by the Bethany road, when five or six men who were concealed behind some trees, suddenly burst upon them. The first who made his presence known was Judas. Two others were officers of the Sanhedrim, and the rest were Roman guards.

"This is the man," said Judas, as he pointed at Jesus. "Seize him."

Then the officers and guards immediately surrounded Jesus and laid hold of him. The true nature of the case immediately flashed upon the mind of poor Mary, when she uttered one loud piercing shriek and fell senseless into the arms of her lover. The heart of Jesus sank within him as he bent over the beloved insensible form clasped in his arms, presenting a picture of silent grief and mourning, like the weeping willow on the margin of a stream.

The scene was sad and affecting. Even the officers and guards seemed to be moved with deep emotions, for they conversed in whispers and seemed loath to disturb the grief of the betrayed man. Judas was restless, as though smitten with compunction. At length one of the officers tapping Jesus upon the shoulder, said in an authoritative voice, softened with a tone of compassion:

"Come sir, grief is useless now. We arrest thee through the power of the Sanhedrim; thou must go with us."

Jesus raised his head gently and glanced upon all around, even upon Judas; yet there were no signs of irritation, vindictiveness or fear expressed in his countenance, but there was a pensive sadness tempered with a serene resignation. At length he said in a tone of mildness:

"The first thing to consider is how to dispose of this maiden. She is all innocence, purity and noble mindedness. Under the impulse of her pure and ardent love, she sought this interview with my unfortunate self. She is void of all blame, whatever may be charged to me. I wish, therefore, that she may have a trusty escort to her home, which is not far from hence."

"Be not uneasy on that point, sir," said one of the officers, "I will take charge of the maiden and see her safely conducted to her home."

Jesus expressed his thanks, and then resigned his charge to the officer, after imprinting a last kiss upon her brow. The officer and one of the guards carried off the unconscious Mary, Judas leading the way and giving instructions as to the best manner of conveying her home. Then one of the guards blew a horn, calling together some other forces that were in the garden. In the meantime Jesus remained passively in the custody of the other officer and guards.

A few minutes after the horn was blown the tramp of marching men approaching was heard, and in a few seconds a detachment of the Roman guards made their appearance. They had in their custody a man enveloped in a dark mantle, who was ushered forward, when the captain of the guard said to the officer of the Sanhedrim:

"We found this fellow asleep at the lower part of the garden, and thinking him to be one of the companions of the agitator Jesus, we have brought him before thee to dispose of as thou shalt think fitting."

"I will examine him," said the officer.

He then ordered the new prisoner to be brought in front of Jesus, and to uncover his head. This order being executed, revealed to view the countenance of Peter. The latter looked upon Jesus with a firm unconscious gaze as though he knew him not; while Jesus, wishing to save Peter from all danger, did not manifest any recognition.

"Knowest thou that man?" said the officer to Peter.

"No," replied Peter in an emphatic voice, "I know him not."

At the sound of Peter's voice and the consciousness of being denied by him, Jesus felt an inward shock; his feelings were so stung with the base ingratitude and selfishness of the man he could scarcely retain the composure of his countenance; notwithstanding he was determined to save him from all danger if possible; he therefore exerted all his efforts to recover his equanimity. The officer not believing the assertion of Peter, thought he would try him again.

"Art thou sure?" he said. "Look again upon that man, and tell me if thou knowest him."

"I tell thee I know not the man and never saw him before," answered Peter with still greater vehemence.

Then the officer turning to Jesus, inquired, as he pointed to Peter:

"Knowest thou this man, who denies all knowledge of thee?"

"I know something of him now, but I knew him not before," replied Jesus calmly and distinctly.

In this response he spoke the truth, for he always believed Peter to be a sincere admirer and follower of his; but his last act had convinced him that he was a traitor as well as Judas. For all that, he was so tender of heart that he would do nothing to commit his false friend to danger.

By this time Judas re-appeared, when perceiving under what difficulties Peter was placed, he whispered in the ear of the officer that Peter was a friend of their party, and must be dismissed. The officer accordingly released him, pretending to be satisfied of his innocence.

When the officer had discharged Peter the glances of Jesus and Judas met, both regarding each other for some moments with an unquailing eye. The glance of Jesus was strong from the consciousness of innocence and goodness in the man, while that of Judas was more from habit and self-command. At length Jesus observed:

"Judas, after all thou hast done, in proving thyself my worst enemy, I must commend thee in one respect, if the subject will admit of commendation. I must acknowledge thee to be the most persuasive, skillful, ingenious, self-commanding villain that I have ever seen. Throughout the whole time thou hast followed me, thou hast been plotting my destruction whilst I considered thee a true admirer of myself and a trusty follower in all respects."

"Sir, in the last part of thy observation thou art mistaken," replied Judas in an unassuming and candid tone of voice. "I will also commend thee, and point out one defect in thy nature. I must acknowledge thee to be the most learned, most virtuous and benevolent of men, with most amiable qualities; but in one respect thou art lacking as a man fit for society. Thou hast not the power of penetrating the disguises of men by which they hide the sordid sentiments of their minds, and cover over their hollow heartedness. Thou hast been led into danger by thy credulity in believing men to be what they profess to be, instead of reading the true sentiments of their minds, and the desires of their hearts. Thou hast believed that thy followers were devotedly attached to thee, and that their motives were void of all sordid interests, while they in every respect were quite the reverse. And now I acknowledge that I have proven a traitor to thee, and all the time to have been working for thine enemies; yet I must solemnly declare that there is not one man among thy late followers who admired thee for thy virtues, except Judas."

Judas paused for a moment, when placing his hand to his brow, he added in a tremulous tone:

"Master, if thou knewest the cruel fate which has impelled me to action, thou wouldst as much pity me as execrate me."

Jesus regarded the speaker with astonishment, and at length replied:

"Judas, thou art an enigma to me; I cannot unriddle thee."

Then turning to the officers, he observed:

"Officers, do your duty. I am ready."

Jesus was led from the Garden of Gethsemane towards the city, and Judas followed in a disconsolate mood.

VISION THIRTIETH

THE NASI

In the palace of the Sanhedrim, which was situated in the Court of Israel of the Temple, there was a spacious and magnificent chamber called the Chamber of Gezith, or the Council Chamber of the Sanhedrim. It was lofty as well as spacious; the roof being of curious grain work, was supported by two tiers of pillars, with vermicular flutes and capitals representing graceful foliage. Corresponding pedestals were around the four walls, with windows between them at the upper part. Between the pillars and in the center of the chamber was a range of seats covered with cushions in the form of a half moon, elevated about two feet from the floor. These seats were allotted to the seventy members of the Sanhedrim when a great council was held. Opposite to them were two small ones for single persons, at about twenty feet distant, in the centre of the half circle or radiating point. In one of the latter the Nasi or President of the Council was seated; and in the other the High Priest when he attended. The first person seated on the left of the half moon range of seats was called the Abbithdin, or Vice-President, who exercised some peculiar authority over the Council.

It was about the middle of the day following the night on which Jesus was arrested, when a grand council of the priesthood was held. Every member was present in his seat, some reclining with their legs down, some up, and some under them, but all with their faces towards the High Priest and Nasi. On the right of the two latter were certain officers who attended upon their orders, and on the left at some distance was

320

the accused Jesus, with officers around him and guards behind. There were also a great many citizens who filled up the other parts of the chamber. Between the accused and the President were some witnesses in the prosecution against the former. Everything being in formal order the trial of Jesus commenced.

The Nasi or President rose from his seat, when all present became immediately as silent as death; then with grave and solemn attention all eyes were directed towards him. In a clear voice and tone of great solemnity he proceeded to depict the state of the country as regards religious matters. He said that "of late, a vast amount of heresy and blasphemy had spread among God's chosen people; that it had proceeded from the labors and designs of one particular man who acknowledged the name of Jesus of Nazareth, though by some he is called Jesus the Messiah; by others, Jesus the Christ, and lately it could be proven he had assumed the title of King of Israel." He then dwelt for some time on the heinous nature of blasphemy, the wickedness of the blasphemer, and what the Mosaic law said upon that head. He then concluded by stating that the base agitator was at last arrested in his wicked career, and was now here to answer the charges against him, and at liberty to defend himself if he could. The Abbithdin was then called upon to read the charges. The latter then rose from his seat, and having unrolled a document he proceeded to read it in a loud shrill voice, without intonation or pause. After getting through a tiresome preamble, he came to that part where Jesus was charged with being guilty of blasphemy. The various specifications being as follows:

Firstly-In the course of various speeches, sermons and lectures, the man Jesus had been heard to deny the divine authority of Moses and the special acts of the Lord in the deliverance of the people of Israel from the Egyptians.

Secondly-This man Jesus has been heard to assert that the people of Israel were not a chosen people of the Lord, or of any God; but on the contrary they were base ignorant slaves and idolaters, wild, reckless, cruel and savage.

Thirdly-This Jesus has said that Moses was a cunning impostor, and all his pretended revelations and intercourse with a God on Mount Sinai was a gross imposition upon the ignorant minds of the people.

Fourthly-This Jesus asserts that the God Jehovah, as revealed by Moses, bears not the stamp of a divine nature, but is merely a conception of Moses, bearing an analogy to his own stern, cruel, ignorant and fallible nature.

Fifthly-That all the attributes of Jehovah as given to him in the Scriptures are strictly human with a great extension, which may answer well for a tyrannical King, but not for a God.

Sixthly-This Jesus asserts that the accounts as given by Moses of the

321

creation are nothing more than lying fables without a fact or resemblance to truth; and that all else as attributed to the Lord in the Scriptures
are nothing but absurd fictions, fables and lies.

Seventhly-This Jesus asserts that the most sacred Order of Priesthood as established by Moses at the Lord's command was not initiated
by any Lord or God; that this order of men were not wise, just, pious,
learned or charitable, but a gang of cunning knaves, who rob the people
of the fruits of their labor, and keep them in mental darkness by their
vile impositions and despotic rule.

Eighthly-This Jesus boldly asserts that there is no such thing as the
God we style the God Jehovah. That the character, history and attributes
of that God as spoken of in the Scriptures, are nothing but fictions, having no real existence except in the ignorant minds of men.

Ninthly-But this Jesus boldly asserts that there is another and true
God, which God he calls upon the people to worship in spirit and truth.

Tenthly-But the greatest of all his blasphemies is the assertion that
he is a son of this God, and that he has a power derived from him to
minister unto men. Under this claim he pretends to be the true Messiah
or Christ, and moreover to be King of Israel.

The Abbithdin having read these charges against the accused, sat
down when a general murmur spread among the seventy Judges, with
many demonstrations given of indignation and disgust. After a few minutes the Nasi arose, when he commanded the witnesses to stand forth
and give their testimony of the truth of the charges preferred against the
accused. Then several men stepped forward, among whom were Judas
and Cosbi, who testified, one after the other, to the truth of the charges
—some in part, some general; but Judas made a long statement of the
truth of the whole.

During all this process Jesus did not appear to shrink or seem anywise distressed. He listened and looked around him with great firmness
and calmness; but when Judas gave his testimony he manifested a more
lively interest therein, but gave no symptoms of indignation. This part of
the proceedings being gone through, the High Priest turning his attention
to the accused, addressed him in a stern and solemn voice:

"Perverse and wickedly infatuated man, thou hast heard these solemn
and dreadful charges brought against thee for blasphemy against our
most holy institutions. Scandal against our most sacred Order of Priesthood, which is the same as blasphemy—and what is worse, the denial
of our Great God Jehovah, and his providence over his chosen people.
Thou hast heard the witnesses confirm these charges. Now what hast
thou to say in thy defence or in mitigation thereof? Speak, man, thou
hast liberty to defend thyself."

When the High Priest had addressed Jesus, the latter erected himself
to his full height, his eyes flashing vividly, his lips expressive of energy,

and his whole air prevailing with the dignity of noble manhood. Like a noble stag at bay he was conscious of being surrounded by deadly enemies, yet he was determined that he would not succumb until he had made an effort in his self-defence. Extending his arm towards his judges, with an undaunted mien and bold voice, he thus addressed them:

"You men of Judah, who are self-styled the Sacred Order of Priesthood of the Holy Temple, and thou, Caiaphas, who sittest in the highest seat of this despotic and remorseless tribunal, hear my words. Not in defence shall I speak them, for that I know will be useless, but as a justification of those charges on which is founded my offence. I do not flatter myself that anything I can say will enable you to see things differently from that manner in which you are determined to see them. I do not expect that my words will so affect you as to render you just and honest, for that would be a greater miracle than I am capable of performing; nor do I consider that I shall so move your hearts to sympathize with me as to cause you to treat me with benevolence and leniency. No! none of these are my motives for speaking, for I may as well expect to find diamonds in dunghills as to find such philanthropy in your minds and hearts. My motives for making answer to these charges will be to justify myself in the sight of my friends, that they may transmit the same to posterity, when I hope my motives and services to mankind will be better appreciated. To answer these charges in detail and give full explicit explanations of the whole, would require more time and patience than you would wish to expend, and more strength than I could command; I must, therefore, resort to some other mode or means of treating them. If what a man states, can be proven the truth, then that man has not committed a crime in stating it, though the truth he states may be the means of crushing him; for however base all other things may be, truth in itself is all purity. Therefore my object will be to show that the statements I have made, which you bring against me as charges of a guilty nature, are so many truths, through which I have not violated the laws of a true God or the principles of nature. The first eight charges against me which you in your Mosaical wisdom and liberality exhibit as specifications of my blasphemy, are so homogeneous in their nature, of the same fabulous authority from first to last, that to avoid wasting your precious time I will class them together and speak of them as a whole. I will put the matter contained in them in the form of two single questions, and then discuss them. First, are the incidents alluded to in the charges true as related in the Scriptures, and are they of divine origin and authority? Or, secondly, are they false, as I have intimated them to be—the lying inventions of ambitious and cunning men, which constitute the charges against me? The author and founder of all those wonderful things and events as related in the Scriptures, and which I deny, is Moses, who asserts that he acted as agent of a certain God called

323

Jehovah. Now the subject to be considered is this: Is there anything in the character of this God as declared by Moses, that any man of common sense or reason can accept as of a divine nature? Is there anything in the works attributed to him, or of his actions during the history of our people, which a reasonable man can accept as the doings of a Deity? Did anything transpire in our forefather's history which was attributed to a providential interference of a God, that is not more reasonably accounted for by the limited knowledge of man, under the various phases of his turbulent passions? Let these things and events be examined by the light of philosophical reason, then we may discover that Moses with his limited knowledge and unlimited ambition is the author of all these things, even to the existence of the God Jehovah himself. Yes, Moses and his successors are the authors of all these absurdities which are given as of divine authority. Let us look at this Jehovah as he is represented to be by Moses. It is asserted and acknowledged by all that this God is all-powerful, all-wise and all-benevolent. Now let us take these acknowledged attributes of the Great Jehovah as criterions for our judgment, and examine his works, actions and sentiments as they are stated in the Mosaical books, and you may then be enabled to understand some of my doctrines, and perceive that I have not blasphemed against any God—not even against your Jehovah. Let us look at the account of the creation. Did Jehovah in the beginning create the heavens and earth out of nothing? Philosophy tells us that there never was an atom of matter created or destroyed. Did he make day before he made the sun? Did he make the sun to rule the day and the moon to rule the night? These are impossibilities, for the light, day and moonlight are all of the same source, which is the sun. Did the Lord feel tired after working six days so as to require rest on the seventh? This account of the creation could not have come from a wise God, or by his authority, for it shows the greatest perversion of facts. Whence came they, then, but from the ignorant conceptions of man—whoever was the author it matters not.

"We will pass over many of the no less wonderful parts of creation, and come to Adam and Eve in the garden. God saw everything was good around them, so says the Mosaical account; yet he had planted in the garden a tree of evil to tempt them to do what he did not want them to do. The consequence was they did what he tempted them to do, not knowing any better in their innocent and ignorant state. They sinned and displeased God. This is a most absurd and ridiculous statement, totally destructive of the attribute you wish to give to your God. Would a wise and good father put temptation in the way of his innocent children to tempt them to do wrong—to tempt them to do what he did not wish them to do? No good father could be found to do the like. Yet this stupid account of the creation makes a wise and benevolent God do worse than that; for he not only tempts his children to sin, but he curses them for-

324

ever afterwards for falling into the snare he laid for them. Shall we doubt then for a moment that this silly fabulous account is the production of ignorant men, and not from a wise and benevolent Deity? No man of sense and candor can do so. What authority have we that Moses acted by divine authority when he took upon himself to be the Chief of his Brethren in their exodus from Egypt? We have none other than that given by himself as stated in the book of Exodus. Well, was there anything in the acts of Moses that no other man could do, which would compel us to believe that he must have received supernal power to do these things? I think not. Any other cunning impostor can do as much at the present day. We have only Moses' bare word for his first intercourse with God, which any reasonable man may know is only a silly, lying fiction. Moses said he did not see God, but he saw something like a fire in the bush. Perhaps he saw the sun through the bush when it was setting; that is more probable than a fire that would not burn shrubs and reeds. But he heard a voice saying, 'I am that what I am.' Now Moses knew no more than he did before, after the Lord had thus condescended to explain his nature and person. This cognomen of the Lord is thought to be, even at the present day, the most sublime conception of the Deity, when in fact it is nothing but nonsense, for it does not convey an idea. Can it be supposed that if this God Jehovah wished to reveal himself to any mortal he would have given such an indefinite and mystical description of himself as that? This Jehovah is represented to say that 'he is the God of Abraham, Isaac and Jacob.' We have reason to doubt the truth of this assertion. A wise and impartial God never could have said so. If he made man he was the God of all mankind, and his impartiality would not allow him to favor or love one race of people more than another. He would not have exclusively cherished a set of poor ignorant slaves and idolaters in preference to the rest of mankind much their superiors. Upon what authority rests the assertion that the Israelites were the chosen people of the Lord? Nothing else than the impudence of Moses and the vanity of the people. But what sort of a being must we conceive this God to be, if we take as true the picture drawn of him in the Scriptures? It is asserted by all the Priesthood that 'he is all powerful, wise and just.' If we search the Scriptures with reason for our guide, we shall not find what is said of him to confirm this assertion, but quite the reverse. He could not be wise in selecting the Israelites as a chosen people—a nation so ignorant and stiff-necked that he could do nothing with them, according to his own account. Neither could he have been good and just in showing favor to them in preference to the rest of mankind. The fact is there is not such a being in existence as the God Jehovah. It is a figment of the imagination, invented by our ancestors after their own natures—an image of themselves bodily and mentally, and with the same passions; though by some means they have reversed the fact, and said that 'God made man after his own image.' They represent their God with a person exactly like themselves; with eyes, nose, ears, and every other bodily parts, even to the most private, which decency requires to be covered; and if our ancestors had found themselves with tails, they would have given one to their imaginary God. They have given him all human passions, as love, hatred, revenge, vindictiveness, cruelty, hope, fear, hesitation, doubt, sympathy, pain, pleasure, a tyrannical will like their Chiefs, a love of homage, praise, flattery and adulation, like to any poor mortal; a very limited knowledge of things, like themselves, and a great changeableness of mind on all matters. In fact, the only difference between their God and themselves is, they have given to him greater extension of person and power. Who then is there of sound sense and a lover of truth, can see these things and not know that the existence of the God Jehovah is a fiction conceived in the mind of men, and therefore cannot be true. In making these statements, I speak not from any impulses of vindictiveness, nor do I wish to decry anything I know to be good, just or true in the institutions of our ancestors; but in all respects and at all times I feel myself impelled by the love of truth and the love of my fellow men, whom I wish to bring out of their mental darkness. When I disprove the God as instituted by our ancestors I do not wish to assert that there is not a powerful Being of wisdom, love and beneficence existing in the universe. This brings me to the ninth and tenth charges against me, upon which I will make some remarks.

"That there is a great and wise power existing, by which this vast expanse of universe is controlled and maintained in its present state, is as true as the existence of the God of Moses is false, I will maintain at the sacrifice of my life. The existence of this Being is evident to every mortal of healthy, common understanding; but as regards his nature, it is difficult or impossible to acquire a true knowledge thereof; yet there are some men more favored than others, who possess some glimpses of this Universal Power or God. These evidences of Nature's True God were as evident to our ancestors as to men of the present day, but they, in their eager desire to have some comprehensive conceptions of him, through the means of error and imposition, supplied from their imaginations all they lacked in true knowledge; thus it was that Moses instituted their God Jehovah. Although my knowledge of this Great Power of the universe is limited, yet there are some of the principles of his nature which come to my consciousness through an intuitive perception. Though I know but little of what he is, yet I know sufficient to disprove and defend him from the erroneous conceptions of common people, in what he is not; and though the present occasion will not admit of my stating all that I do know, yet the tenth charge against me compels me to bring to your notice some principles pertaining to this Deity, which I deem necessary as an explanation and justification of the assertion I have made, which you deem blasphemous. You charge me in the tenth specification of asserting 'that I am a Son of God,' and that 'I possess a power above other men derived from him.' This you term impious and blasphemous, but I fearlessly reassert the same to be true. Though mankind generally have not arrived at a state of beatitude and perfection, yet there are many who are worthy of, and truly to be considered the children of God. Who are they? They who have been born with pure instincts and refined capacities of understanding. They who have managed to live free from the trammels of vice, error and cupidity, or having been once thus enthralled, have been fortunate enough to renounce them. They who continue to live according to their true principles of nature, guided by the dictates of their reason and the refined conceptions of an exalted mind; judging and valuing all things of this world as naught compared to that which their thoughts, desires and exertions aspire. Such as these are the true children of God, and as one of them I claim to be a son of God in that sense. This I do not assert from the impulse of vanity or idle boasting, but from the consciousness of my just claims and merits. As a proof that I speak the truth, is it not known to you all that I possess a power above what is the common lot of men—a greater development of the spiritual power with which I am endowed by the great God of Nature? This power I have exercised to the benefit of thousands of my fellow men, who can testify to the truth of what I say. This power I know is limited, and I have not presumed to make it appear greater than it is; therefore if the people, not understanding my nature, have thought or represented me to be otherwise than I am, do not charge the blame upon me when they call me the Messiah, the Christ, or the King of Israel. I have given no sanction or encouragement to be thus styled, and I am of opinion that all these false accusations have originated through the workings of my enemies.

"Now, Men of Judah, my accusers and judges, I have made an end of the explanations I thought necessary to justify my pretensions and acts in the eyes of my friends and posterity. In rendering your judgment I ask not your pity or mercy. I know such would be useless, for I know that you thirst for my blood, and therefore I patiently await my doom, and let my blood be upon your heads."

When Jesus had ended his defense a solemn silence reigned throughout the Sanhedrim Council. The heads of the members drooped upon their breasts, and the countenances of many of them gave evidence of great grief and compunction. They were impressed with the truth of all that Jesus had said, yet they viewed him as an enemy to their Order, whom it was necessary to destroy—thus there were contending emotions within the breasts of nearly all of them, between pity and vengeance. At length they were all startled from their silence by a cry uttered by the High Priest, who having risen from his seat, threw his tire

327

upon the ground and seized the hair of his head, which he pulled and tore, while gnashing his teeth and exhibiting several frantic gestures of rage and grief.

"Members of our Sacred Order!" ejaculated Caiaphas with great force, "you have heard the defense of this arch blasphemer. He has denied the existence of our God Jehovah. He has denied the divine authority of Moses and vilified his character. He has aspersed our sacred institutions and maintains the existence of another God. What need have we of further consideration? Is he worthy of death or not?"

Then Caiaphas stripped off his girdle and rent his outer garment from the top to the bottom. Then the Nasi uttered a loud shout of execration and followed the example of Caiaphas in tearing his garment. Then the Abbithdin sprang to his feet and followed the example of his two superiors. Then the seventy members sprang to their feet and vied with each other in tearing their beards, their garments, and jumping, shrieking, and shouting, "Death to the Blasphemer!"

These frantic demonstrations of rage lasted for some minutes, when they rushed toward Jesus and surrounded him. Some struck him upon the cheek; some spat upon him, and others taunted him with being the "Messiah," the "Christ," the "King of Israel," and all heaped the greatest abuse and indignities that their vindictive rage could suggest to a fallen foe. But Jesus bore all with great fortitude and resignation.

At length Caiaphas ordered the guards to remove him, when once more the Council took their seats to consider what was farther to be done. They knew that though they had pronounced death upon their victim, they had not power to inflict it. They therefore resolved to make out a case, that he was a disturber of the peace and an enemy to the Roman rule, aspiring to be King of Judea; then they would bring him before Pontius Pilate, the Governor, and if they succeeded in gaining the consent of the latter, they would execute him.

Then the Council dispersed.

VISION THIRTY-FIRST

Northeast of the Holy Temple and adjacent thereto was a magnificent palace and fortress called Antonia, said to have been built by Herod the Great. It was a quadrilateral structure with a high tower in each angle, and a stupendous porch facing the north; a flight of marble steps ascended to a terrace which was surrounded by a balustrade of small pillars in front of the entrance and marble pillars of great girth and height in form of a semicircle, supported the arching porch that gave entrance to the great Hall of State. Within this semicircular space of the porch, on one side there was an elevated seat or throne, which was ascended by a flight of steps, all of which were cut out of white marble. This throne was called the Gabbatha or seat of judgment where cases were sometimes heard and judgments or decrees given by the Governor of the Province, who at the time referred to was Pontius Pilate, a severe and strict man under the Roman sway, but one who was not altogether insensible to justice and good feelings. Like most men in high office he was swayed by self-interest, which consisted in serving the power that placed him in his high station with great fidelity and zeal. But when any of these interests were not endangered in any of the cases brought before him, he was capable of listening to the pleadings of truth or injured virtue, and his clear mind and better feelings would cause him to render a judgment in accordance.

It was early noon of the day following the trial of Jesus at the Sanhedrim, when Pontius Pilate, Governor of Judea, was seated on the Gabbatha, which was furnished with soft cushions of silk and covered with cloth of purple dye. He was a portly man about the middle age of life, with an air of conscious power and dignity of station; yet at times there would be a softness of expression in his glance and an easy unaffected smile on his lips that indicated his general expression of sternness and harshness to be more assumed than natural. He wore a tunic reaching to his knees, of yellow woollen cloth, over which was a robe of scarlet silk, his legs being covered with buskins ornamented with figures in gold; around his brows was a circle of gold, from beneath which his dark hair flowed in curls around his neck and shoulders.

Such was Pontius Pilate, the fifth governor of Judea, appointed by Tiberias Caesar, Emperor of Rome. On the right side of Pontius sat a man of similar station, though of greater title. He was a tall slim person past the middle age of life, with a haughty and scornful expression of

329

countenance. He wore a purple robe worked in figures of gold, and a golden diadem upon his head, with numerous chains, bracelets and rings of gold adorning his person. This magnate was Herod Antipas, the youngest son of Herod the Great, who was appointed Tetrarch or King of Perea and Galilee at the pleasure and will of the Roman Emperor. Herod Antipas had come to Jerusalem on the occasion of the approaching festival of the passover, where he was accustomed to sojourn some weeks, as he retained a palace there. He formerly had been at enmity with Pontius Pilate, but on the present occasion they had become friendly, so that Pontius invited him to sit in judgment with him, in the case of the accused Jesus.

On the right and left of the Gabbatha were detachments of the Roman guards, and in front were a great number of the members of the Sanhedrim; among whom were Caiaphas, the Nasi and Abbithdin, with several officers, having in custody their victim Jesus. The eyes of the Holy Priesthood seemed at times to glisten with a demoniac pleasure as they regarded the victim in their power; but as Pontius glanced at Jesus with an expression of compassionate interest, the pleasure of their looks changed to one of uneasiness, fearing the Governor could not be prevailed upon to comply with their murderous wishes. At length all the parties being ready for the examination of the accused, Pontius addressed the members of the Sanhedrim in a tone of authority, though respectfully:

"Say, you Reverend Sires and Ministers of Jehovah's Holy Temple, why bring you this man before me as a culprit? What charges of evil doings have you against him?"

"Most gracious Sir and mighty Governor," answered the Nasi, as he advanced a few steps towards the Gabbatha, holding in his hand a small scroll of writing, "this man has been guilty of grossly insulting and blaspheming against our most holy institutions and the God we worship under the name of Jehovah, and for whlch he has been arraigned before our sacred tribunal, tried and condemned; but as we have not the power to inflict the penalty which is assigned to his guilt, according to our sacred laws, as we are restricted therein by our present rulers, we bring him before thee—"

"To do what you dare not do, but wish to have done," interrupted Pontius Pilate, "which means no less than this: You wish me to take this man's life. I feel myself highly flattered in the preference you show me in this pleasant business, and my august master, the Roman Prestige, must be highly honored thereby. But let me inform you, Reverend Sires, that between the compact of the Judean people and their rulers, the latter do not meddle or judge of any matters assigned to the tribunal of the Priesthood. You may accuse a man for transgressing your sacred laws, try him, condemn him, and punish him to a certain extent, but not touch his life, for that is the property of the State. Nor are we authorized to do so in matters pertaining to your religion."

"We wish not, your Highness," replied the Nasi, "for you to judge this man or condemn him according to our sacred laws, but we bring him before you to judge and condemn him on certain offences committed against the State, which in course of our investigations have come to light, wherein he has been guilty of treason against the State, and contempt of our gracious and august master, the Emperor."

"Ah!" exclaimed the Governor with a sudden change of countenance, from one of indifference to one of sternness, "that is a matter that must be looked into. What are the charges against this man of a treasonable nature?"

"Your Highness will please to hear read the charges specified in this document," replied the Nasi, as he unfolded the scroll and proceeded to read as follows:

"1st-This man has been heard to speak disrespectfully and contemptuously of our most illustrious and gracious Emperor Tiberias Caesar, many times in several places.

"2nd-He has denied the justice and lawfulness of paying tribute to Caesar.

"3rd-He has denounced the Emperor as a tyrant and usurper of the rights and power of the Judean people.

"4th-He has endeavored to incite the people to rebellion against their rulers.

"5th-He has caused the standard of Judea to be raised, and the Eagle of the Romans to be treated with indignity.

"6th-He has proclaimed himself to be the rightful King of the Judean people, and by many ways he has endeavored to withdraw the people from their allegiance to their rulers. All these charges we have witnesses to verify."

"Who are the witnesses to confirm these charges?" inquired the Governor, as he cast a suspicious glance over the members of the priesthood, for he was well aware that they were moved by hatred and interest to the prosecution of the accused Jesus. He was doubtful of their veracity, and afraid that their malignity would push them so far as to swear falsely to the charges they had brought against the accused. He felt an interest in their victim, and was in hopes that he should be enabled to free him; but if anything of a treasonable nature was proven against him, he was bound to see all such offenders strictly punished. Accordingly with much regret he ordered the witnesses to be produced.

"We have several witnesses among our own body who can testify to the truth of our charges," returned the Nasi.

"Then let them proceed," said the Governor.

Then various members of the Sanhedrim stood forth, one after the

331

other, and made several statements in seeming confirmation of the charges against Jesus. Having given their testimony, they cast glances of triumph upon their victim as though to assure him his doom was sure. Jesus still retained his cool state of indifference and serene resignation, as though nothing unusual had happened to molest him. But the Governor felt distressed and embarrassed, and with much reluctance proceeded in the case. After a few minutes of reflection he cast his regard upon Jesus, and said:

"Unfortunate man, what hast thou to say in thy defense to the charges these men bring against thee?"

Jesus raised his eyes to the Governor with an expression of awakened interest to the serious crisis, and a slight flush of indignation suffused his cheeks, as he made answer:

"Your Highness may observe that my enemies have taken advantage of me. They knew I would not be prepared to answer certain charges, of which I was ignorant to the present time. All I can do in the present case is to declare my entire innocence of all that my enemies have imputed to me. I solemnly declare the charges against me are false, vindictive and wicked inventions, designed to work my destruction."

"Hast thou no friends who can bear testimony to the truth of that which thou hast affirmed?" inquired the Governor. "Look around thee, for if there be anyone who can speak in thy favor, he shall have a just hearing."

"There are thousands in the city who can bear testimony to the falsity of the accusations brought against me," replied Jesus, "for everybody that knows me and my principles can prove that my doctrines, my examples and actions are the very reverse. But my friends have all deserted me, as they are afraid of persecution from the same men who persecute me."

The Captain of the Roman guards now left his position at the head of his men and advanced in front of the Governor, and having made his obeisance, he remarked:

"If your highness please, I wish to state that there is one present who can testify in favor of the accused."

The priests shrank back in dismay when this announcement was made, and the eyes of Pontius Pilate sparkled with delight as he hurriedly said:

"Sayest thou so? Then let that witness stand forth and speak, whoever he may be."

"It is I who wish to testify," replied the Captain.

"Speak on, man," said the Governor, "and be not afraid to tell all thou knowest, that will bear in favor of the accused."

"I wish simply to state the occurrences that took place on the evening previous to the arrest of the accused," answered the Captain in a fearless and candid manner, "which I think will go far to disprove, or altogether to confute the charges brought against him."

The Captain then stated that on the day Jesus made his entry into Jerusalem, he, with a company of soldiers, was appointed to preserve the peace and watch the actions and manifestations of Jesus. He described the entrance into the city, and the passing through it to the front colonnade of the Temple as very orderly and void of all insurrectionary and treasonable designs on his part. He described how the friends of Jesus received him, and how all was peace and harmony until a crowd of ruffians under the pretense of being his friends, endeavored to raise a tumult; how they uttered various treasonable cries, and how, at length, they raised the standard of Judea. Then he stated how Jesus requested him to arrest the disturbers, pointing out especially the man with the standard. Then he stated how Jesus addressed the people, exhorting them to be peaceful, to avoid all seditious actions and expressions; how some of them had mistaken his character and designs; that he had no ambition for worldly aggrandizement; that he wished only to reign over their hearts and minds. Then he stated how certain men put questions to him endeavoring to make him say something offensive of Caesar or the Roman Rule; how Jesus answered him without committing himself; how one of them put the question, "Whether the Roman Rule was the best government for the people?" And how Jesus spoke at great length explaining the history of the people, proving that they were not capable of governing themselves, and that the Roman government was the strongest and best for them. The Captain then concluded his testimony by saying: "All that I have said, I swear is true, by the Roman standard."

"Then, by the Gods, this man is innocent of the charges!" cried Pontius Pilate with great energy, as he sprang from his seat in the excitement of the moment. "It is not necessary to continue this investigation. This man has done nothing to merit death, and unless some stronger proofs shall be given of his guilt, I shall free him."

Then Caiaphas advanced a step in front of the Governor, when erecting his person with a haughty and imperious air, he remarked:

"I beg your Highness to consider that this man has been charged with treasonable designs and actions against our Imperial Master, Caesar, on the testimony of many reverend personages; yet their testimony you consider invalidated by the counter testimony of one other man. Is this the usual course of Roman jurisprudence? I doubt it much; I therefore, shall object to this decision."

The Governor, who had never been friendly with the High Priest, Caiaphas, was aroused to great indignation when he found his authority and judgment was disputed by him. But knowing that Caiaphas had some favor and influence at Rome, he thought it would not be prudent to show any hostile feelings towards him; he, therefore, endeavored to curb his anger as much as possible in making a reply.

"Most Reverend Minister of Jehovah's Temple," he said, in a slight ironical tone of voice, "what you say touching your Reverend witnesses may be true in ordinary cases. I must acknowledge that the evidence of one counteracting the evidence of many is not in strict conformity with the Roman jurisprudence. But, most exalted Sir, I wish you to understand that in me is the power to accept or reject such testimony as in my judgment seems fitting. Now, according to my experience I find it possible for twenty Reverends to testify to a lie, and that one honest and simple man may speak the truth, though not a Reverend."

"Sir!" exclaimed Caiaphas in a tone and manner greatly excited with furious indignation, "this language is insulting to the dignity of my office and standing. I shall protest against your decision as unjust, and I will bring the case before our Imperial Master Caesar. I doubt not he will decide otherwise."

"Proud and haughty priest" returned the Governor with equal hauteur, "follow the bent of your will and if Caesar shall disapprove or counteract my decision I shall consider that he disapproves of me. I shall now dissolve this tribunal for the present, and in the evening you shall have my final decision."

The tribunal was then dissolved for the time. Pontius, accompanied by Herod Antipas, entered the palace under the excited feelings of suppressed anger and hatred. Jesus was re-conducted to his prison, and the Holy Priesthood left the palace for a time.

About two hours afterwards the persecutors of Jesus began to reassemble in the porch of the palace and in front of the Gabbatha to await the decision of the Governor and the fate of their victim. Like a pack of bloodhounds with anxious and restless eye and keen appetite, they anticipated the delight of feasting on his blood.

In the meantime the Governor and Herod Antipas had taken a repast, when they discussed the subject in private, whether Jesus should be made a sacrifice to appease the vindictive demands of the Priesthood, or whether he should be freed. Pontius Pilate was conscious that Jesus had done nothing to merit so great a punishment. He viewed the latter as an enthusiast in the cause of religion and morals, who had given offense to the priests by his doctrines, but was quite innocent of any evil intentions to the State or its rulers; he therefore would save him if possible from the malignity of his enemies. Herod was also conscious that Jesus had done no evil to the State, and that the charges against him were lying inventions of his enemies; but he was a man so void of sympathy with injured innocence, and had so little regard for justice and truth that he would not hesitate a moment to commit acts of the greatest turpitude, when he thought it would suit himself or any party to which he was joined. He was a professed worshiper in the temple of Jehovah, and supporter of the Priesthood; whether from motives of conscience or self-interest, was best known to himself. He therefore advised Pilate to decide in favor of the latter. It was then determined between them to give Jesus a private examination, before the Governor should give his final decision. Accordingly the guards were summoned to take Jesus to the Hall of Judgment, and to exclude all others excepting the guards.

The Judgment Hall was a chamber of great architectural beauty, consisting of twelve sides, with as many massive pillars supporting a concave dome, through which the light was admitted. On one of the sides the judgment seat was elevated some feet above the floor—the latter being of tessellated marble, which was divided into various compartments by small balustrades; in one of which, near the judgment seat, Jesus was standing, surrounded by the guards. The countenance of the prisoner bore the expression of passive resignation, as though all hopes and desires of earth had left him, and sweet serenity had filled their place.

At length the solemn stillness of the Hall was disturbed from its repose by the echoing footsteps of the Governor and Herod, as they entered and advanced to the elevated seat.

"I think your Highness had better take my advice," said Herod to Pontius Pilate, when he had seated himself by the side of the latter. "This Caiaphas is an astute and resolute man, quite capable of working his ends; his political enemies he generally finds means to clear from his path. Should you offend him by refusing to condemn this Jesus to the doom he and his order wish, he will seek an opportunity to revenge himself on you. He has great influence with the Emperor at Rome, which enabled him to be appointed to the High Priesthood. I therefore advise you to keep friends with him by giving this man into his power.

"I am not a man over-fastidious in what I do, where prudence suggests," answered Pontius; "but here is a case in which, if I comply with the desires of these priests, I shall not only sacrifice an innocent man, but I shall humiliate myself. But let us question this man. Perhaps we may discover something to justify me in deciding against him."

Pilate then ordered Jesus to be brought nearer to him, which being done, he spoke to the latter as follows;

"Unfortunate man, what hast thou done to these thy accusers, who seek with hatred to undo thee?"

"I know that I have greatly offended them," answered Jesus mildly, "but that has been in fulfillment of my office, which is the duty I owe to God and my fellow-man. In performing this duty, I have said and done nothing that is not in conformity with the eternal truth."

"Truth!" exclaimed Pontius in doubt and surprise. "What meanest thou by truth?"

"Truth, as regards these, my accusers!" responded Jesus, with a degree of animation lighting up his countenance. "My accusers, who style themselves the Most Sacred Order of Priesthood, Ministers of the Holy Temple of the Great Jehovah! To speak the truth concerning them, is to strip them of their lofty and imposing titles; to expose the falsity and base impositions of their pretensions; to lay open the wickedness of their hearts; to display the meanness and ignorance, the cunning and sophistry of their minds; the absurdities of their dogmas; the lying assumptions of their history, and the multifarious evils attendant upon their very existence, as blind guides and evil teachers of the people. This is the truth which has offended them, and for which they seek to destroy me.

"By the Gods!" exclaimed Pilate in astonishment, as he lifted up his hands, "if that be the truth, it is no wonder those priests should endeavor to destroy thee. Truth indeed! Why, man, that is the most dangerous thing a man can meddle with; it generally destroys him who uses it. My experience in life tells me that a man cannot prosper in society by speaking the truth. It is a complete bar to the favor of all the magnates on earth. A man may be forgiven for murder or treason, but if he utters the truth of all he knows concerning men, he will not be forgiven, and will draw down upon himself the hatred and hostility of those he has offended. Unfortunate man, thou hast greatly offended thy adversaries, and produced thy own destruction." Then Pilate turning to Herod, remarked: "What should we think and feel, my Lord, if all the truth were spoken concerning you and me?"

"It is horrible to contemplate," answered Herod, as he gave his shoulders a shrug. "This fellow must be a great disturber of society, and a great worker of vexation among his superiors. There is no doubt in my mind that he is guilty of all that is charged to him. I suspect if he were to tell the truth concerning himself we should find that he is ambitious to become a King, and has been endeavoring to arrive at that exalted station by raising the people to insurrection."

"I have before stated," replied Jesus with energy "that I have no desires, hopes or ambition for worldly aggrandizement. My ambition is not founded on the things of this world, but it points to others of a superior nature in a more exalted state; and as far as my influence over my fellow man extends, I wish to guide his mind and heart in that direction."

"Your Highness may do as you please in believing this man's tale," observed Herod to Pilate, as he screwed up his features expressive of contempt. "But the way in which I view the case is this: That this man is a low-born fellow with a little learning and great ambition, who is desirous of raising himself from his low degree to some point of elevation; he is, therefore, a dangerous character, and no doubt is guilty of all that is charged to him. I am told that he is the son of a poor mechanic, Joseph the carpenter. Ah! ah! such presumption in a low-born thing like him

336

aspiring to be a King! He ought to be made an example of, and warning to all others of his low station."

"Herod Antipas," cried Jesus, with a degree of indignation in his tone of voice and expression of countenance, "thou doest me wrong. I am not worldly ambitious, neither am I of lowly birth. Thou art mistaken in considering me the son of a mechanic. I have proofs to show that I am not of low degree, but the offspring of some great personages, though I know not who my parents are. It is possible, if the truth could be known, that the blood which courses through my heart comes from as proud and kingly a sire as thou art."

At the conclusion of Jesus' reply, Herod gave a sudden start of horror, and gazed for some moments upon the countenance of Jesus expressive of alarm. But at length having recovered from his emotion in a degree, he turned to Pilate and said in a low, husky voice:

"By the Eternal God Jehovah, this man must die a felon's death! He has insulted my dignity, and like a serpent suddenly springing up in my path, by some unaccountable means he has caused my blood to chill with horror. Your Highness must consent to his death, for I will join my influence with his adversaries to compass it, and woe be to those who thwart it."

Pilate sprang from his seat to the floor, and with a wild and hurried step walked to the extremity of the Hall where he paced to and fro for some minutes, wringing his hands and beating his breast in the greatest agony of mind and feelings. At length having overcome the ebullition of his emotions he seemed to subside to some point of determination. Then turning to the Captain of the guards, his pallid countenance expressive of great inward strife, he said:

"Bring the prisoner to the porch."

Then Pilate rushed from the Hall to the porch, and hastily mounted the Gabbatha around which the Sacred Priesthood were assembled, awaiting with intense suspense the decision of the Governor. As soon as the guard appeared with Jesus in their midst, Pilate arose, and the eyes of the Priesthood were immediately fixed upon him, glittering like those of serpents' when they are about to spring upon their prey.

"Most holy and merciful Priesthood of the Great Jehovah," said Pilate in a bitter, sarcastical tone of voice, "behold the man for whose blood you thirst. I give him into your hands. Let his doom be as you will, but I declare before the Gods that I give my consent to his death as a sacrifice to the peace of the State rather than to justice. Take him into your power.

A loud shout of joy burst from the throats of the Holy Priests when they discovered that their desired end was obtained. Their gestures exhibited the wildest demonstrations of their hearts' content, and loud acclamations of thanks, praises and eulogies were given to Pilate as the wisest and best of Governors. Some time was passed in confusion, in discussing the mode, time and manner of executing their vengeance upon their victim, which was at length settled by the High Priest, who decided that Jesus should meet his death on the morrow in a formal manner.

The victim still retaining the serenity of his nature, and mild, sweet expression of countenance, was conducted by the guards back to his prison to await the consummation of an ignominious death as the reward for his virtuous and noble aspirations. Pilate retired to his private chamber to brood over the event with feelings of remorse. Herod returned to his own palace in a state of gloomy and unquiet apprehensions, and the Priesthood returned to their quarters elated with their triumph.

VISION THIRTY-SECOND

THE CRUCIFIXION

The following night and morning after the condemnation of Jesus to death with the consent of Pilate, great preparations were made for the execution. As to the mode or manner of executing a criminal, there was none established by law, it being done in various ways, according to the will and pleasure of the authorities. But when great vengeance was sought to be wreaked upon the unfortunate victims, the crucifix was generally resorted to as the most cruel and ignominious of deaths. This mode was selected by the priests for the unfortunate Jesus. If there had been a more cruel and debasing mode known at the time, they would have chosen it; for their hatred, rancor, scorn and desire of vengeance knew no limits. They not only wished to glut their vengeance in inflicting agonies upon their victim, but they wished to set before the eyes of the people an example of their power, which was to impress them with horror, fear and submission to their wills; accordingly they strove to make this execution as terribly impressive as possible.

The usual place of execution that was selected was an elevated piece of ground without the city, called Golgotha, or Place of Skulls, from the quantity of such relics generally found there of criminals who had been previously executed. On the summit of this hilly spot a high and massive beam was erected with a transverse piece fastened near to the top, upon which the hands of the criminal were to be nailed with the arms extended; and on a small ledge below on the main beam his feet were to be fastened in like manner. Thus fastened, the criminal was allowed to linger in agonies until death put a period to his sufferings.

It was about noon on the following day when the procession to the place of execution began to form in front of the palace and fortress of Antonia. Thousands of people were collected to see the tragic sight; some being moved from hatred to the condemned man; some from sympathy and admiration of the man they considered to be a model of human perfection, wishing to see how he, they considered blameless in life, would deport himself in confronting death; and some were moved from an idle curiosity and a love of general excitement, without any great love or hatred for the condemned. Besides, thousands of his disciples were present, who mourned in silence the sad fate of him they loved, yet whose cause they dare not openly espouse.

The Roman guards were numerous, enclosing a space where the procession was forming, and keeping the strictest discipllne to maintain order and prevent a rescue or rising of the people. At length everything being ready the procession began to move along the main thoroughfare or street to the north-eastern gate of the city, to the place of Golgotha.

A small body of the Roman guards were in advance, clearing the route of people and all obstructions. A few paces behind came Pontius Pilate and the High Priest on horseback, the former dressed in his robe of State, and the latter in his sacerdotals, as though going to a high festival of the temple. As these representatives of the two great powers of the State passed by—one being the strong arm of political power, and the other the strong power of superstition, which kept the minds of the people enchained, the multitude became impressed with a fearful and solemn awe. All noises and clamors were suppressed for the time, but they gazed on intently with countenances expressive of great terror.

Then came a body of the Priesthood headed by the Nasi, and judging from their deportment, they wished to make their appearance one of a solemn nature; yet from the sparkling of their eyes and curling of their lips, it seemed a joyous ovation to them. Then came another body of Roman troops, in the midst of whom was the much persecuted Jesus, the man of virtue, intelligence and truth, who had labored for the enlightenment and amelioration of his fellow-men; the man who had sacrificed all his worldly interests of time, wealth, consideration and ease to enable mankind to arrive at superior conditions. The last of his sacrifices was now about to be made. His life was about to be given up to appease his enemies, glut the vengeance of despots, tyrants, superstitious bigots, cold-hearted knaves, and all wicked men of sordid interests, who constitute the class opposed to the advancement of mankind from the errors and vices of old established notions. The virtuous victim was not cast down; he bore himself up with conscious dignity as the lover and dispenser of truth, virtue and justice, indicating that all was peace within. Sometimes a sweet smile would play upon his lips of gratefulness and brotherly love as he noticed the tearful demonstrations of sympathy given by some of the spectators. Slightly bowing his head, he acknowledged the signs of their heartfelt love, and passed on. Then followed another body of the Priesthood, headed by the Abbithdin, of a similar appearance to the former, and the rear was brought up by another division of troops. The multitude then followed indiscriminately. Both sides of the main street were densely thronged with the people. All the porches, windows, avenues and housetops were filled with spectators. Some uttered exclamations of hatred and disapprobation as the Priesthood passed, but no one thus saluted the victim—not even those who were not his admirers. On the contrary, tears poured fast and copious from the majority of the people; deep sighs were heard and distressing wailings as well as lamentable expressions were uttered. There were scarcely any, excepting the priests, who did not lament the fate of so excellent a man.

Thus the tragical procession moved on to the fatal spot where he was to make the last effort of his pledges to the people. At length they arrived at the gate at the boundaries of the city through which they passed, and thence along the country road by several suburban villas and fields of culture, until they came to a gently rising hill, upon the top of which they saw the fatal cross where he was destined to pay the forfeit of his life. At the foot of this hill were assembled a multitude of females—the fair maiden and the sober matron, all of whom seemed to be bowed down with grief. The two daughters of Lazarus were there, having come to take the last sight and wave the last adieu of the only man of the world for whom they cherished a love greater than that of a sister's. Mary was pale, though she seemed composed; some fixed idea or resolution seemed to support her on this trying occasion, but Martha gave vent to tears and great wailings. When the procession arrived at this spot, there was a halt made to make some further arrangements; when Jesus perceiving the women on either side of him, and recognizing the daughters of Lazarus, he desired one of the guards to go to Pilate, requesting the indulgence of a few minutes' stay, and permission to bid adieu to the females. The guard did as he was requested, when Pilate consented, though Caiaphas wished to oppose it. However, the Governor would not be overruled in this respect, so that permission was given, when Jesus, taking a prominent position among them, thus addressed them:

"Weep not, Mothers and Daughters of Jerusalem; weep not for me! rather weep for yourselves, your sons, your husbands, brothers and fathers. For me there is no occasion to weep—all is peace and tranquillity within me, and a serene pleasure pervades me from a consciousness that I have done my duty to you all, to my country at large, and set an example to be followed by other men for the love and benefit of all mankind. No one knows as well as myself how well I have loved you, and no one knows, excepting me, how I have labored, studied, hoped and aspired to do great things to your benefit and make you all happy. It behooves me, then, to speak in these last moments, and I doubt not you will accept my words as the truth. I have long seen the errors, the vices and unhappiness of our people as a nation, and I have been enabled to see the causes thereof. My love for my country as a whole—for your fathers, husbands and brothers in particular, and you as my sisters—have stimulated me to do what I have done. I knew the evils I should have to encounter, the risk I should run, and the probable forfeit I should have to pay of my life in the end; but this did not deter me from the undertaking. No personal sacrifice could deter me from doing what I conceived to be my duty. I ventured upon the task, and I have been prosperous in sowing the seeds of reform. At length the strong arm of political power and superstitious hatred have put a stop to my endeavors to do more. I am doomed to a mortal death, by which my enemies think to put a stop to the object of my labors, and then they think to triumph over me. But how foolish and narrow are their conceptions! They know not the events of the future which will result from their actions as well as mine. Women of Jerusalem, I have not labored in vain. I have done much good to thousands of my fellow countrymen, as they can testify. I have led them out of the darkness of a vile superstition, corrected their errors and vices, and gave them an idea of what is true life; and the seeds of reform that I have sown shall rise up into a bountiful harvest among the seekers of truth. My words and my love to you all shall not die; though I as a mortal man shall be no more, yet the babes that now suckle at your bosoms shall receive the benefit of my labors, my love, and the sacrifice of my life. My enemies think when they have sacrificed

342

my life, that they have destroyed me and my influence. How grossly dark are their conceptions of the nature of man! No, mothers and daughters of Jerusalem, it is not so. They cannot destroy me, but they free me from the toils and vexations of an earthly life, and give me admission into a spiritual one which is full of beauty, interest and happiness. Yes, women of Jerusalem, after I have drank of the bitter cup of death, my spirit goes to another world far superior to this. Where I go my enemies cannot come until thoroughly reformed, now, for their gross natures, their ignorance, vices and wickedness so much outweigh their virtues, that they are allied to the grosser matter of earth. But you, my friends, who have wept for me in pure sympathy, who have forsaken the darkness of Mosaical superstition, and aspire to the true light, by following my doctrines, this world of beauty and bliss shall be open to you. There we will all meet again, and embrace each other in pure friendship and love."

Then Jesus turning his regard to Mary and Martha, gazed upon them for a few moments with great tenderness, regret and love, and at length resumed his discourse:

"Now, my dear sisters, I must bid you adieu. Believe me, that to the last beating of my heart, I shall be sensible of your kindness and tender sympathy with me, which will tend to assuage the bitter moments of a cruel death. Weep not for me, mothers and daughters of Jerusalem, but weep for the city of your birth; for the time will come, and it is not far distant, when the remaining two tribes of Israel will be scattered to the four winds of the earth—their name as a nation will be lost, and they shall become the thing of reproach, scorn and disgust to all the other nations of the earth as a people, so far lost to everything noble, as to destroy the only man who endeavored to save them. Woe, woe to Jerusalem!"

Jesus having ended his address, the procession was ordered to move on. Scarcely had he withdrawn his eyes from taking the last look of the daughters of Lazarus, when a piercing cry was heard, and Mary was seen to fall insensible to the ground. A young man, who was at no great distance, rushed to her assistance, and taking her by the hand, he saw something which caused him to start with astonishment, and for a few moments checked his benevolent intentions. However, he soon recovered his presence of mind; for, by gently placing his arm around the maiden, he raised her from the ground, and while her sister Martha and the rest of the females were engaged in looking on the procession and the last looks of Jesus, he slipped out of the crowd unperceived, carrying the maiden with him.

In the meantime the procession continued its course up the hill, and at length arrived at the foot of the cross.

VISION THIRTY-THIRD

The young man that had taken the insensible Mary in his arms, hurried from the tragic scene as quickly as possible; and as the people of that vicinity were nearly all present at the place of execution, there was nobody to obstruct him in his progress, or be witness to the cause of his flight. As the maiden he carried was of light and delicate frame, he was not incommoded with her weight; therefore he was soon enabled to pass from the view of the multitude, and out of the reach of any of her friends who might be in search of her.

On he went with unflagging energy. Leaving the main road he turned into a path which he pursued for some distance; then making several other turnings he came to another road, and soon arrived at a small house which seemed to be known to him. He gave a signal by making a peculiar noise, when immediately a rough-looking man made his appearance. A few words were rapidly exchanged, when the latter disappeared behind the house, and the former rested himself with the maiden in his arms. After a few minutes had elapsed, the man of the house reappeared, leading a dark brown horse of great beauty and vigor. Then in course of a little time the young man with the assistance of his companion, was mounted upon the animal, with the maiden enwrapped in a mantle. Giving a signal of adieu to his companion, he started at full speed along the road to the eastward. In the course of a few minutes, he came to the branch of the Kidron, opposite to the northeastern slope of Mount Olivet. Along this he continued for a few minutes, when he plunged through it to the other side; thence taking a road among the hills called the Scopus, he soon arrived at the solitary dwelling of Hester the Sibyl.

The young man rode into the yard and forward to the porch of the house; he then called aloud for assistance, and two male servants made their appearance, who enabled him to alight with his burden. Leaving his beast in charge of the domestics, he rushed into the house and entered the private apartment of the Sibyl—the latter being present with two of her handmaidens.

The mistress and her companions were greatly alarmed at the appearance of the young man, who without ceremony or remark went to a couch and relieved himself of his fair and insensible burden.

"Cosbi!" exclaimed the Sibyl in great alarm, "what means this? What maiden is this thus insensible?"

"Dear mistress," said Cosbi—for he it was—as soon as he could recover his power of speech, for he panted for breath after his great exertion, "give orders that thy handmaidens do their best to restore the maiden to consciousness and health, and then I will explain all this seeming mystery to thee."

Cosbi then threw himself upon a seat to recover his exhaustion, while the Sibyl and her attendants proceeded to administer to the insensible Mary. After some minutes' exertion and application of restoratives, the insensible Mary began to give some signs of returning sense. She sighed deeply, then uttered a faint moan and turned her head from side to side.

"She is recovering," said the Sibyl to Cosbi; "but it will require some time yet before she returns to consciousness. She must have received a terrible shock. Now, Cosbi, inform me who this maiden is, and explain the nature of her swoon."

"I will certainly do so, dear mistress," replied Cosbi in an undertone, "but thou must first bid thy handmaids to retire, for what I have to say is of secret importance."

The Sibyl then told her attendants to retire, but to remain within call, as she would do herself what was further necessary for the recovery of the invalid. Then the attendants, after making their obeisance, left the chamber, when Cosbi immediately sprang to his feet and advanced towards his mistress, his eyes sparkling with joy. Then taking her hand, he pressed it fervently to his lips and observed:

"Kind and beloved mistress, Cosbi's heart now beats with great joy. During the whole of our acquaintance I have been anxious to do something by which I could testify to thee my gratitude and love for the kindness and fostering care that thou hast ever shown to me. The time has now arrived. I can now administer a soothing balm to the sorrow which has so long pressed upon thy heart."

"What mystical language is this, Cosbi?" cried the Sibyl with impatience and vexation depicted upon her countenance. "Be more explicit, I pray thee. My heart is ready to snap asunder with suspense."

"Be patient a little while, dear mistress," returned Cosbi, "and interrupt not the course of my narrative. Thou must also be guarded not to interrupt the recovery of that afflicted maiden, who has been stricken insensible by the shock of unmitigated woe; for her history is connected with the tale I have to unfold."

"That maiden's history connected with mine! Who can she be?" cried the Sibyl in astonishment, as she rushed to the couch and gazed upon the prostrate Mary in a state of suspense and wild conjecture. Then returning to Cosbi, she added, "I know her not. 0! Cosbi, if thou hast love and gratitude for me, do not keep me in suspense any longer. Hasten with thy narration."

"I will do so," returned Cosbi coolly. "Thou must remember the last night I was in thy presence, previous to my leaving thee to serve my new

345

master. 0! cursed be that day when I engaged to render him service, for I now know the fatal results of it."

"Yes, Cosbi, I remember the night to which thou alludest. What of it?" answered the Sibyl eagerly.

"Dost thou remember telling me," resumed Cosbi, "that if in the course of my travels, I should see a certain bracelet like the one thou didst show me, I should endeavor to trace up the history of its owner?"

Yes, yes; I did tell thee so," shrieked out the Sibyl, as she rushed towards Cosbi, placed her hands upon his shoulders, and gazed upon him with an intensity of gaze, as though she would penetrate the depths of his soul. "Hast thou seen it?—knowest thou anything of it? Tell me quick."

"I have," answered Cosbi.

"0 where is it? Tell me immediately, or I shall die."

Then Cosbi taking the Sibyl by the hand, led her to the couch of the prostrate Mary, and taking up one of the hands of the latter, observed:

"Here is the bracelet, if I mistake not. It now remains for thee to solve the mystery how this maiden came by it. I am afraid that though its absence has been the means of inflicting upon thee thy past sorrow, its recovery will be the means of still greater."

While Cosbi was making these remarks the Sibyl was intently gazing upon the bracelet which was around the wrist of Mary, as she held her hand. At length raising her eyes and uttering a pious ejaculation, she exclaimed:

"It is the same! What mysterious circumstances have brought it into the possession of this maiden, and now so unaccountably brought to my view? Who is this maiden, Cosbi?"

But before Cosbi could reply to the question the eyes of Mary opened, and she looked around her with surprise and timidity. Becoming conscious that she was amidst strangers in a strange place, she faintly inquired:

"Where am I? What has passed?"

"Make thyself easy, fair maiden," said Cosbi in a soothing tone of voice; "thou art among strangers, but friends. I am acquainted in part with the unhappy state of things which have thus sorely impressed thee with a poignant sorrow. We sympathize with thee in thy sore affliction, and will tender thee all the consolation that kind friends can impart."

"Ah! now I remember what has happened!" cried Mary, as she started from her recumbent position and looked around her with an expression of the wildest horror. Then wringing her hands in agony, she exclaimed: "0 God! why hast thou been so cruel as to suffer the wicked to prevail over the righteous? Yes, he is gone; by this time, his handsome person is become a mangled corpse, exposed to the gaze of a cruel world and the scoff of his enemies." Then uttering another lamentable wail, a gush of

346

tears came to her relief.

"Of whom does she speak?" inquired the Sibyl of Cosbi, as she drew him aside and spoke in a low tone of voice. Some new apprehension of evil seemed suddenly to cross her mind as she put the question, for her cheeks became pale and her lips quivered with intense painful emotions.

"She speaks of the man who has gained her heart's purest affection," answered Cosbi in a solemn tone, and with a distressed expression of countenance. "The renowned Jesus, who pays the forfeit of his life today, for being a better and wiser man than his enemies, was the tender lover and affianced husband of this afflicted maiden. May the Gods forgive me for what I have done! I, too, have been among his persecutors, though ignorant of their designs, and the results of the evil I did him.

Jesus the affianced husband of this maiden, sayest thou?" inquired the Sibyl, as she trembled violently.

"It is even so," responded Cosbi. "She is the daughter of Lazarus, of Bethany, who formerly resided at Nazareth in Galilee, whose family Jesus has been intimate with from his childhood."

"And what connection is there between this man Jesus and the bracelet this maiden wears?" inquired the Sibyl as she gasped for breath.

"I know not," answered Cosbi. "But I perceive, dear mistress, this subject deeply affects thee. As soon as we can question the maiden, we shall know all."

"My suspense will not allow me to wait longer," said the Sibyl.

She then turned to the couch of Mary, addressed to her some words of consolation, and advised repose to recover her agitated feelings. Crossing the apartment she went to a recess, from which she took a small vessel containing a soothing cordial, a portion of which she prevailed upon the distressed Mary to take; then smoothing the couch and adjusting some pillows she recommended her to take sleep. Then taking her hand on which was the bracelet, she observed:

"Would it not be better to take off this bracelet? Its weight and pressure may mar thy slumbers."

Mary started and drew her hand quickly away as she replied:

"No; I cannot part with it. I dare not part with it an instant, unless I find some one who has a greater claim to it than I have. Till then, I must retain it and press it close to my heart. Yes; I must keep it to the day of my death, but by the sad turn of events, I feel that will not be long."

"Dear maiden," said the Sibyl soothingly and affectionately, "thou hast aroused within me a great interest concerning this bracelet. If thou wouldst not consider it imposing upon thy delicacy, or too much intruding on secret matters, I would wish thee to tell me from whom thou didst obtain it."

"Thy request shall be granted," replied Mary. Then she rose from her recumbent position, looked steadfastly at the bracelet for a few mo-

347

ments, kissed it and observed to herself: "It is well perhaps as it is. I have waited long and patiently in this life, in hopes that my wishes would be fulfilled, and met with nothing but disappointment. My last hope now is to be united to him in that beautiful world in which he taught me to believe. My time will not be long before I go; I must, therefore, endeavor to find a friend to take charge of this sacred relic. To whom can I better entrust it than to this kind woman? I will tell her the whole truth." Then Mary, looking up to the Sibyl, resumed her reply:

"I received this bracelet not long since, from one of the greatest, wisest and best of men, the only man that has gained my soul's affection. His love was pure and ardent for me, as mine is for him. Our beings were united by one sympathy, love, hope and desire. His many virtues raised up enemies against him, who conspired against him and finally worked his destruction. In the last interview I had with him, he confided to me a secret concerning his supposed parentage, to this effect: The persons we both had been taught to consider his parents, were not such. He said he had lately discovered it, and that he still remained ignorant who his parents were. He said that he had received from his foster mother a bracelet, which had been left with him when an infant, and was supposed to belong to his true mother, whoever she is."

"Who, then, is this man of whom thou speakest? Speak quickly, I pray thee," cried the half frantic Sibyl.

"He is the unfortunate man called Jesus, who is now undergoing an ignominious death at Golgotha," answered Mary, sobbingly.

The Sibyl clasped her forehead, as she uttered a dreadful moan. In this position she remained some moments, her bosom heaving with violent emotions. Then suddenly starting and apparently shaking off her intense grief, with an air of desperate resolution she seized the hand of Mary, as she observed:

"Dear maiden, I must have this bracelet. If this unfortunate man is not deprived of life, or should there be any delay, it is possible that I may save him."

Mary yielded the bracelet to the Sibyl, when the latter turning to Cosbi, observed:

"Cosbi, see that my servants prepare me a horse immediately."

Cosbi left the apartment to execute the order of the Sibyl, when the latter bending down to Mary, spoke a few words in a low tone, concluding by telling her to "hope for the best. She must instantly depart for the city, and in the meantime, she would leave her in charge of Cosbi and the female attendants."

The Sibyl then rushed from the apartment.

VISION THIRTY-FOURTH

On a commanding site of the northwestern part of Jerusalem stood the palace of Herod Antipas, which he occupied on his casual visits to the city. It was a small but superb edifice, designed by Greek architects, and built principally by the most skillful workmen from Greece. A small retinue of officers, menials and guards were maintained, sufficient to support and display his kingly rank as Tetrarch of Galilee, Perea and Iturea, but nothing demonstrative of political power.

The day had nearly closed, for the sun was sinking in the western horizon, when Herod was seated or reclining upon a couch in one of his magnificent chambers, which was decorated with all the gorgeous display that inordinate wealth could produce in those days, to please and pamper the meretricious taste of a despotic ruler of the people. There was an air of disquietude and disgust upon his countenance, as though naught but disagreeable and painful thoughts were passing, or had pass-ed through his mind. There seemed to be a surging up of reminiscences before his mental eye, of past follies, vices, crimes and acts of ambition, which did not repay him with the felicity he had anticipated, causing him to feel a disgust and loathing for the very objects he had acquired at the sacrifice of virtue, truth and justice. He had seized, with a tyrant's grasp, all the pleasures of life, without heeding the rights or just claims of others, and devoured them with an inordinate appetite, leaving himself in his latter days but the dregs of his unhallowed feastings. Now he regarded all things with apathy, or a painful remembrance of some evil deed of which he had been guilty in their procurement. From time to time he sipped from a goblet of precious wine, but his libations did not chase from his mind his disagreeable thoughts, for as the exhilarant produced its effects, they rose up before his conscious eye in more vivid colors and with more ghastly horrors. At length he tried to shut out the pictures of the external world and the images of thought in sleep. He closed his eyes and in a few minutes he seemed lost in oblivion. But even this relief was denied him, for one of his household officers entered the chamber in haste, and said hurriedly, as he approached him:

"Gracious Lord, pardon the intrusion, but I thought it proper to make the announcement."

"What is it, fellow, that thou disturbest me?" demanded Herod in an angry mood, as he started from his recumbent position.

"My Lord," answered the officer, who trembled before Herod's angry glance, "there is a woman who desires an audience. She says her business is of the greatest importance; that it is a case of life and death, and does not admit of a moment's delay. Shall I admit her to your lordly presence?"

"A woman! A case of life or death!" repeated Herod in surprise, his angry mood giving place to an aroused curiosity. "Knowest thou who she is?"

"She is called Hester, the Sibyl of Scopus," answered the officer.

"I have heard of that woman, but know her not," said Herod, whose curiosity began to be vividly excited. He found anything that would arouse his interest for a few minutes would be a relief to the dull monotony of the hours he passed so wearily; he therefore determined to see the woman, and gave the officer permission to admit her. The latter left the apartment, and in a short time returned followed by the person known as the Sibyl; then the officer, by a signal from Herod, retired from his presence to an inner chamber.

With a hasty step the Sibyl hurried across the chamber, with a wildness in her eyes and a firmness expressed on her compressed lips, as she stood before the Tetrarch and slightly inclined her person, as she observed:

"Herod Antipas, the nature of the interview I seek of thee forbids all ceremony and punctilious marks of respect."

"Thy unceremonious and abrupt appearance before me lacks much of the dignity due my rank," replied Herod, with some degree of surprise and hauteur, "but go on, woman; state thy business—I will hear thee."

"The virtue of my cause will excuse my rudeness," returned the Sibyl, "when thou shalt understand that thy word can save the life of an innocent and virtuous man."

"My word save a man's life!" exclaimed Herod, with a scoffing laugh. "It has generally been the reverse.

"That is too true, I fear," replied the woman, "but now is the time to do an act of mercy and justice which will atone for some acts of less virtue. Herod Antipas, there is a man of virtue and wisdom, whose life is now at stake, if he has not already lost it, when a word from thee could save it, if it pleased thee to do so."

"Who is this man for whom thou pleadest my interference?" demanded Herod.

"He is the renowned Jesus, a man of inestimable virtues and great wisdom," replied the Sibyl, in a hurried and distressed tone of voice. "He is about being made a sacrifice to the hatred of his enemies. I beg thee to intercede with Pontius Pilate to save him from the horrid fate they design him."

"The renowned Jesus!" exclaimed Herod, with a laugh. "What right have I to save the life of a common malefactor—a public agitator and blasphemer of the Holy Temple?"

"0, King! have mercy upon this man and save him. He is not what he is represented to be by his enemies. His life is not the only one dependent upon thy word of intercession, for mine is enwrapped in his," said the Sibyl in a beseeching tone of voice. Then she fell down before him in an humble, crouching position, and added:

"King Herod, save this man's life, I beseech thee; thou knowest not what joy it will bring to thine own breast in after times."

"It is useless, woman, to plead for this man's life. I will not intercede for him, for I like him not," answered Herod angrily.

"If he was thine own son, wouldst thou not endeavor to save him?" inquired the Sibyl, as she intently fixed her gaze upon him.

"That would probably alter the case," replied Herod, laughing. "However, as that is not the case I must tell thee, woman, I like not the man. A word of mine might have saved him yesterday, but he, low born fellow that he is, had the presumption to tell me, that the blood which coursed through his heart probably came from as kingly a Sire as I am. For this audacity in placing himself on an equality with me I gave my word for his condemnation, when I might have saved him.

A groan of anguish burst from the Sibyl, who after a few moments, rose from her humiliating position and stood erect; when casting a look of the most intense severity and awe-inspiring solemnity upon him, the haughty monarch seemed to quail with an indefinable dread.

"Herod Antipas," the Sibyl said at length, in a low tone of voice and emphatic manner, with her hand raised and finger pointing upward, "I now perceive that this unfortunate man's fate is not to be classed with the ordinary results of human action. The Gods have interfered in this, and in their wisdom, preordained it to be so; not with the view of inflicting misery upon him, but to punish and eternally condemn his unnatural parents. Herod, that unfortunate man, when he told thee that the blood which flowed through his heart came probably from as kingly a source as thine, told the truth."

"Woman! what meanest thou by this insolence?" cried Herod in terror and rage.

"I mean to inform thee," replied the Sibyl, with particular distinctness and emphasis of enunciation, "that man Jesus whom thou wouldst not save from an ignominious death, but gave thy word and influence to destroy, that unfortunate man is thy son!"

Herod sprang from his couch and rushed towards the woman with the greatest of astonishment and terror depicted upon his countenance. After gazing upon her intently for a few moments, he at length said in a voice husky and harsh:

"Woman! who art thou that comest here with this damning tale? What meanest thou by saying this Jesus is my son?"

"I mean," returned the Sibyl, "that thou art his father, and I, unnatural wretch that I was, am his mother. Herod, look upon this care-worn and sorrow stricken face of mine, and see if thou canst discover any relics of the beauty that once fascinated thy lascivious nature, under the form of the beautiful and innocent Glaphira, the princess of Iturea. Herod, behold in me the victim of thy lust, the unhappy mother of that Jesus, who is the offspring of our sinful connection. Yes, Herod Antipas, as true as I am Glaphira, who once loved thee and confided in thy honor and pro-fesssions, thou gavest life to that man whom now thou hast helped to destroy."

As the Sibyl made this astounding declaration to the ears of Herod, he seemed to be struck dumb and motionless for a time with aston-ishment and horror. His eyes were firmly fixed upon hers with an ex-pression of maniacy. With his lips distended, all the functions of his nature seemed to have ceased, and like a statue he stood motionless, the representative of terror. At length a revulsion took place; a deep sigh found escape from his breast; his lips trembled, as he falteringly replied:

"Glaphira! is it really thou? I think I can recognize some remains of thy former self. Yes, it must be Glaphira. Ah! it now seems to me that I have wronged thee. But what is this thou tellest me, that I have a son by thee—that this man Jesus whom I have persecuted is my son? By the God of Israel, Glaphira, this is horrid. Ah! it cannot be true; I cannot believe it! Say it is not true, Glaphira."

"Doubt it not, Herod," returned the Sibyl in a softened tone of voice, as she perceived that he was affected with a degree of contrition for the past, when he had recognized her. "Shouldst thou require a proof that he is thy son, I have it here to give thee."

The Sibyl then produced a pair of bracelets from her dress, which she held before him, as she resumed:

"Dost thou remember these bracelets?"

Herod seized the bracelets and regarded them intently, and the Sibyl continued:

"When I was young and beautiful, the innocent and respected daugh-ter of a princely house among the noble families of Iturea, thou wert fascinated with my person and didst woo me, and didst prevail over my innocent heart to love thee. I was of simple mind, for I confided in all thy protestations of love. One day thou gavest me these bracelets, and didst observe at the time, "receive these bracelets, Glaphira, as a testimony of my undying love for thee. Should I ever prove unfaithful or cruel to thee, may the Gods cause them to be the proof of my faithlessness, and bring punishment upon me in my latter days." Dost thou recognize them now?"

"I recognize the ill-fated baubles," answered Herod in a surly tone of voice, "but what proof are they that Jesus is my son?" * * * * * * * * *

To make the parentage of Jesus clear the history of the bracelets must be related. Iturea was one of the countries assigned to the despotic sway of Herod the Great, which was governed by a Noble or Prince in his name. Glaphira was the daughter of this noble, who at the time referred to was a maiden of great beauty and virtue. Herod Antipas, the youngest of Herod's sons, having occasion to visit her father's court on matters of court business for his father, saw this young maiden princess, and soon became enamored of her beauty; but not having any honorable intentions of marriage, he sought to gain possession of her person only to gratify his lascivious passions. He loved her not; yet he made great pretensions that he did, and soon gained the pure affections of the maiden. On one of his visits he made her a present of a pair of golden bracelets of beautiful workmanship, and made the memorable remark, "that if ever he should prove faithless or cruel to her, may the Gods cause them to bear witness of his wickedness, and bring punishment to him in his latter days." He finally prevailed over her chastity, and having gained the object of his desires, he did not renew his visits but entirely deserted her. Glaphira, in the course of time, finding that she was about to become a mother, and afraid of the disgrace she should bring upon her family and friends, left her father's house clandestinely, and sought out her faithless lover in Judea. She found him, but instead of being received with love and tenderness, he treated her with scorn and contumely, and discarded her from his presence. She then fled into a distant country, living in secret till she gave birth to a son. Her bosom was now filled with rage, which prompted her to seek vengeance upon her cruel lover, so that she had no place in her heart for the affections and duties of a mother. She found that her infant would be a hindrance and disgrace to her wherever she went, and a clog to whatever she wished to do. She therefore determined to get rid of it. One evening she left her place of concealment with her child, and travelled some distance with it, when she found two travellers, a man and his wife, resting on the roadside. She prevailed upon them to take the child and rear it as one of their own; to make no inquiries concerning its parents, and with the child she gave a large sum of money in gold. Besides, she gave one of the golden bracelets that Herod had presented to her, requesting the travellers that they should keep it for the child, and give it to him when he became of man's age, with the information that he was not their son. This agreement being made with the travellers, she gave her child a last embrace, and then resigned it to their keeping, and departed. She was never more seen or heard of by them. These travellers made their way to a village in Galilee by the name of Nazareth, where under the name of Joseph the Carpenter and Mary his wife they were considered to be the parents of the child.

The child grew in health, strength and wisdom, under the name of

Jose, believing that the good woman, Mary, was his mother, and the simple, honest old man, Joseph, to be his father. Thus he continued until old Joseph died, when receiving some money he left for foreign parts to finish his education. Mary, his foster mother, from some cause unknown, had not revealed to him that she was not his mother. Jose was absent many years, when returning to the village of Nazareth he found his supposed mother in the arms of death. She however recognized him, and her last action was to point to a casket in which was the revelation in writing that she was not his mother, and how he came into her possession. In the casket also was the golden bracelet given to Mary by Glaphira, as a clue for him to discover his parentage. This was the first intimation that Jesus had of the truth of his parentage. He kept the matter a secret to himself, and during the three years he was travelling and preaching reform, he endeavored to discover his parents, but all in vain. At last on the night that Judas betrayed him, he revealed his history as far as he knew it to Mary, the daughter of Lazarus, in the garden of Gethsemane, and confided to her the bracelet to keep as a memento of his love. Mary wore it from that moment with the intent never to part with it unless the parents of Jesus should discover and claim it.

In the meantime, Glaphira, the princess of Iturea, gradually lost her desire of vengeance against her faithless lover, and the yearnings of a mother began to spring up in her bosom. She regretted that she had parted with her child, and would willingly have regained it, but she could not find any clue to the people to whom she had given it. She travelled for many years in many directions to find it, but without success. At last she determined to adopt a new course, solely with the view of recovering her child if possible, for that was the paramount object of her existence. She took up her residence in the vicinity of Jerusalem, and assumed the character of a Sibyl, thinking thereby she should be enabled to acquire the principal secrets of persons of high station, and thus find a clue to her long lost child, for the idea never entered her head that her offspring could be found among the lowly.

When her confidential servant, Cosbi, was about leaving her to enter the service of Judas, she revealed in part to him the nature of her sorrow. She showed him a bracelet, and desired him to make inquiries and search after its counterpart, and of the person in whose possession it should be found. Cosbi promised to do so, but during all his travels with Judas and Jesus, he met with no success. At last when Jesus was being led to execution, Mary, the affianced of the victim of treachery, becoming insensible, Cosbi discovered the bracelet upon her wrist. He instantly conveyed her to the house of Glaphira, and thus the latter became re-possessed of the bracelet, and learned that Jesus was her son. The rest is known.

When Glaphira told Herod that Jesus was his son, and showed him the bracelets as proof, bad a man as he always had been, he felt an instinctive horror at the possibility of its being true. He therefore said to her:

"I recognize the ill-fated baubles, but what proof are they that this Jesus is my son?"

"The proof is certain, Herod Antipas," replied the Sibyl; "but there is not time to explain the particulars now. Let it suffice to say the bracelet has been returned to me in a providential manner, and I have discovered that this Jesus is the offspring of our united folly and sin."

"Then the Gods have cursed me!" exclaimed Herod as he struck himself upon the breast in the excitement of his terror and anguish. "In conformity with the invocation I made to them when I gave thee these bracelets the Gods are about punishing me for my wickedness. O! Wretched, impious man that I am! That impious invocation is about being fulfilled. My wickedness is made manifest by these bracelets, and my punishment begins now that I have arrived at the gray haired age."

"There is now no time for self-accusation, Herod," said Glaphira mildly, "consider the object of my visit. I wish, if it be possible, that thou shouldst save our son from this ignominious death. Hasten, I beseech thee, to the Governor, and if there be time, prevent this execution."

"Yes! yes!—I will! I will!" exclaimed Herod, arousing himself suddenly, as though he had just awakened from a dreadful dream. Then he called aloud for his attendants. Soon an officer appeared, and Herod gave orders to prepare a horse, as he wished to ride forth. At that instant, Pontius Pilate made his appearance. Herod then rushed towards him, and said in a hurried and fearful tone of voice, his countenance being of a ghastly pallor:

"What has been done with the man Jesus?"

"He is crucified," answered Pilate, as he looked upon Herod and the Sibyl with surprise, not being able to comprehend the scene before him.

"Crucified!" echoed Herod with a sudden start of horror, his eyes gleaming with wildness, and his countenance expressive of the greatest distress. "Then God's curse and vengeance are upon me for the iniquities of my life, which commenced in faithlessness and cruelty to this woman, and now culminates in my being a participator in the murder of my son."

Then Herod struck his forehead and staggered across the chamber, where he stood for some moments, swaying to and fro like a reed bending before the wind, and at length he fell prostrate and insensible upon the floor.

Glaphira, whose feelings had been aroused to the highest pitch of mortal agony by the announcement of Pilate, uttered one loud, piercing shriek, rushed from the chamber, and left the palace. In a few minutes she was mounted upon her prancing steed which had brought her from her home, when, giving direction and impulse to the mettlesome crea-

355

ture, she darted like a meteor through the city in the direction of the place of execution. On, on she sped, but heeded not what she saw; for palaces, towers and the people glided before her vision like the wild and fanciful images of the mind in a feverish dream. At length she passed the bounds of the city, and quickly sped along the country road to the base of the rising ground called Golgotha. Springing from her steed, she rushed up to the fatal spot and stood transfixed with reawakened horror at the dreadful sight that burst upon her vision.

The sun of day had set, but still a twilight remaining enabled her to distinguish all things around and within the fatal spot. All spectators of the dread tragedy had long since departed; a single sentinel, who paced to and fro at a short distance, was left to guard the bloody cross. With suspended breath and eyes motionless, Glaphira gazed upon the dread object before her. Her maternal eyes, which once looked down with a mother's fondness upon her innocent offspring, now beheld the hand-some form of manhood naked, lacerated, bleeding and outstretched upon the felon's cross. His handsome head, whereon sat the majesty of wisdom, was now encircled by a wreath of thorns, as a scoff and mockery by his cruel persecutors. His beautiful lustrous eyes, which were so expressive of pure and holy emotions, were now lustreless and gently closed by their lifeless lids. His clear transparent skinned cheeks, that used to mantle with the glow of health and the blush indicating the pure susceptibilities of his soul, were now blanched with the pallor of death. And his symmetrical lips, from between which were wont to flow words of eloquence, wisdom, truth and justice, were now closed in death, but still expressive of his mild, sweet nature, even in the last bitter pang. His manly, symmetrical limbs were relaxed and powerless. The Divine and Great Spirit of Jesus had departed, and all that was left of that amiable, wise and benevolent man was an inanimate corpse.

The scene at length became dark and solemn. No one was there to bear witness to the soul-crushing agony of the afflicted mother, except the sentinel who was pacing to and fro. Glaphira's horror stricken form began to relax, as the consciousness of her misery gleamed upon her mind. A deep sigh and a moan escaped from her; then her lips moved as she half audibly uttered:

"Yes, he is my son. The same outline of features as when I saw him a babe. What cruel God or Gods have thus controlled his fate? Why should the innocent and just in this life suffer for the iniquities of the wicked? Why should an innocent child suffer for the iniquities of his parents? Why should truth, honor, virtue and beneficence be sacrificed, and all the base and guilty passions of man be allowed to triumph? Either the Gods are unjust, or we poor mortals know not how to judge of destiny. 0! my heart grows cold! I have now naught else to live for. Now let the gloomy wings of death overshadow me at the feet of my ill fated son."

Then Glaphira crouched down at the foot of the cross, and before the sands of another hour had run, the stars gleamed over the lifeless bodies of an ill-fated mother and her murdered son.

VISION THIRTY-FIFTH

SCENE WHERE SAUL AND JUDAS FOUGHT

The shades of night hung over Jerusalem—a murky mist, more than usual, seemed to enshroud it; scarcely a twinkling star could be discerned to mark the boundaries between the earth and the heavens, so intensely gloomy was the scene around.

The spirits of the inhabitants corresponded with the scene, for a profound sadness pressed heavily upon the hearts of all those who were awake, as they with tears and sighs were filling the air with their wailings. Troublous dreams haunted those who had fallen into slumbers; some produced through fear of persecution, and others from the stings of guilty consciences. The cruel deed of murder just perpetrated at the place of sculls, was the subject of thought by the murdered man's friends and foes. His manly person extended naked, bleeding and maimed upon the cross, presented itself with great terror to the minds of the guilty, and the inward whisperings of self accusing consciences began to agonize the souls of his murderers. Every howl or whistle of the wind as it echoed through their habitations seemed to bring to their ears the cries of murder and vengeance from the murdered man on the cross.

358

Among his friends the hours were passed in tears, prayers and wailings. Thus some hours had passed toward the middle of the night, when the moon, broad and deeply red, like a ball of fire, was seen to struggle up through the murky atmosphere over the western hills. Brighter and smaller it became as it ascended into the heavens, and the mist was gradually dispersed; then the stars with their twinkling light began to deck and enliven the scene. The stupendous walls, the palaces, towers and temple of the Holy City began to assume existence and form. Mount Olivet, with her rich foliage, stood out in relief at her side, and down the deep valley of the Kidron the running stream vibrated incessantly with the moon's reflected light. Just above the stream, at the base of Olivet, the square marble monument of Absalom could be plainly discerned, and not far from thence, a few feet in the rear, with the facade cut out of the solid marble rock, with a tier of pillars, was the excavation in the mountain, called the Tombs of Jehoshaphat; and before these solitary tombs, a man closely enwrapped in a mantle was pacing to and fro.

That lonely man was Judas, the traitor. His steps were stealthy as those of a robber proceeding to a deed of crime, and as he paced, his head was bowed down, as he revolved many disquiet and apprehensive thoughts. Every now and then he would start and listen, as though he heard something to arouse his suspicions or confirm his fears, and then resume his restless motions.

Judas, as soon as he had betrayed his confiding master, found that he had aroused a great part of the people against him, and that it was no longer safe for him to remain in the city. He was afraid to venture abroad by day from his place of concealment; but as soon as the tragedy of the crucifix was over, he sent to Saul, desiring him to come to him without the city at the Tombs of Jehoshaphat, and be prepared to fulfill his promises with him; then he would leave for a distant country. Saul promised to meet him and comply with all his requests. Thus it was that Judas was at that particular spot.

Previous to the last treacherous act of Judas, he was bold, persevering and cool in contemplation and preparation of his crowning act of villainy; but now the deed was done all his fortitude and callousness had forsaken him. He shrank aghast at the consciousness of his guilt, and though he previously thought himself a victim of necessity, in being obliged to do what his conscience would not approve, now he considered there was no circumstance that could justify treachery and murder. When he first joined his betrayed master, he had no true or sublime ideas of a God, or of a future state; for the rude, barbarous notions taught him of the Mosaical Jehovah did not fill him with reverence, or influence his moral conduct for the better. But since then he had learned many sublime principles, and formed many noble conceptions of a true God and future state from Jesus, which frequently presented themselves

359

to his mind and sank into his soul. Now that he found himself a traitor and murderer of one of the kindest and best of men that he had ever seen, his inexcusable wickedness and ingratitude glared upon his conscience; so that he trembled with inward agony and awful apprehensions of a future fate, which before had never given him any uneasiness. He found that he had something to dread more than the loss of his mortal life. This new view of his wicked acts filled him with regret, remorse and anguish, and an indefinable terror shook him to the soul, subjecting his former boldness to a state of cowardice before his own self-inspection. Again he started and listened, for he thought he heard somebody cry: Traitor! Murderer! Then he trembled violently, and a cold sweat oozed from his forehead.

"Wretch that I am," he said to himself, "would that I had never been born, or that I had remained an abject bondman, subject to all the ills of servitude, than to have been tempted by that demon, Saul, to do deeds of the blackest dye for the sake of wealth and freedom. 0, Saul! Saul! thou hast made me a demon like thyself, and if there be a God who shall hereafter judge of man according to his deeds in this world, how great will be the transgressions thou must answer. Thou hast not only thine own iniquities to answer, but mine also; for through thee have I acted throughout this deep scheme of treachery, injustice and cruelty. Would that I had the power of recalling my acts, not all thy wealth, the gift of my freedom, or thy sophistry could force me to repeat them."

Judas gave another start, for a new suspicion suddenly crossed his mind, which he seemed to contemplate for a few moments with a fearful interest. At length he continued his walk, and the train of his thoughts went on:

"And after all that I have done for him, it is possible that he will fail me in all his promises. Can he be so desperately vile as to rob me of all those benefits for which I have served him so faithfully at the sacrifice of all virtuous principles? 0, no, he cannot be so perverse. He cannot be like a diseased dog, willing to bite one of his own species. But let me not be too confiding or sanguine in my expectations of this man. Shrewd as I am and learned in all his secret ways, I may yet be mistaken with regard to his ultimate designs concerning me. Villains, with all their guarded shrewdness, are but the dupes of each other; for as soon as their banded interests are severed, they seek each other's destruction. What reasons have I to depend upon Saul for a grateful recompense of my services? Do I not know that the great principle of his morality is, to use and sacrifice all things to the accomplishment of the object he has in view, and the securing of his personal safety? Now that my services are ended according to our understanding, he may consider it convenient to prove false to me, or consider me a man too many upon the earth. Ah! Something like an instinctive presentiment tells me that he will seek to rid me of my life! What if I forestall him by taking his? This is a convenient place for a deed of blood and I have a trusty weapon with me. It shall be so; for it is too evident we two cannot walk within the same sphere."

Judas then placed his hand within the bosom of his dress, from which he drew a long dagger or two edged knife, which he clutched with a tenacious grasp, while his eyes emitted a fearful excitement. He then continued to pace to and fro for a few moments longer, when he stopped to listen, as he thought he heard footsteps. This time he was not mistaken; footsteps were audible and distinct, seeming to be approaching him. He immediately concealed his dagger, and endeavored to assume his usual composure. In a few moments the expected person made his appearance, when Saul, enveloped in a dark mantle, stood before him.

"My dear Judas," said Saul in a pleasant tone of voice, as he threw off his mantle from his head, "I am here at thy request. What wouldst thou with me?"

"The nature of my business with thee, Saul, is not so difficult to imagine, I should think," replied Judas tartly, as he cast a furtive glance at the former. "I wish for an acknowledgement of my services and the fulfillment of thy promises, according to the compact we made in the ravine by the Lake Asphaltis. Thou knowest, from the nature and results of the dark service I have rendered thee, that the greater part of the people of the city are much excited against me, so much so that I dare not go in public. I must, therefore, retire into some distant country. Thus it is I call on thee for the fulfillment of my rights, according to thy word."

"I acknowledge the justice of thy claims, dear Judas," replied Saul in a tone of kindness and apparent sincerity, "and the prudence of thy determination in leaving this country, though I shall deeply lament thy loss and companionship, as well as thy great services. As thou hast been true to me, it behooves me to be the same to thee. I have accordingly prepared myself to fulfill thy expectations."

The moon by this time had risen high in the heavens, no cloud impeding its silver rays, so that the scene around was lit up with a soft tranquil light, rendering the actions and features of the two men clearly distinguishable. Judas regarded Saul, as the latter spoke, with a serious searching glance, and Saul maintained one of a pleasing and frank nature, though at times a momentary restlessness was perceptible.

"Hast thou brought me money?" demanded Judas.

"Yes, my friend, I have brought thee two hundred shekels; it is all I have at command at present," replied Saul, as he drew from under his mantle a bag containing money. "I will provide thee with more hereafter, wherever thou goest."

Judas received the bag from Saul, and for a few moments he lifted it up and down, endeavoring to ascertain its contents by its seeming weight, and then observed:

"Hast thou the bond of my servitude? which is of more consequence to me than this bag of money."

"I have it," replied Saul, as he pulled from his girdle a small scroll of parchment, which he unrolled and presented to Judas. "Freely and with pleasure do I restore to thee all claims I have to thee as bondman. Here it is; take it and examine it by the light of the moon, to satisfy thyself that all is correct."

Judas took the document and proceeded to examine it, but at the same time he kept Saul in view, as though he was suspicious of his motions and designs. Saul, thinking that Judas' attention was wholly absorbed in the perusal of the document, turned suddenly aside and drew from under his dress a dagger, with which he sprang upon the latter, aiming a deadly thrust. But the vigilant eye of Judas was too quick for his movements, for quickly throwing up the arm and hand that held the document, he warded off the assassin's blow, and quickly dropping the bag of money which he held in the other hand, he struck his assailant a powerful blow in the breast that sent him staggering backward some distance; then quickly seizing his dagger from his girdle, he stood in a defiant position before his enemy, who a moment before was his professed friend and admirer.

Saul finding himself repulsed in his attempt at murder, was at first disappointed and thrown into confusion; but he soon recovered himself and made further preparation for renewing the attack by rolling his mantle around his left arm, with the intent of parrying the passes of his antagonist, and then he looked upon his enemy with an expression of smiling hauteur rather than of an excited hatred.

"Saul!" said Judas, as his eyes flashed with intense indignation, "this last act of thine convinces me that thy heart is blacker with sin than my long experience of thy villainies had enabled me to suppose."

"My dear Judas," responded Saul in his usual tone of voice, expressive of kindness and consideration for his opponent, though a malignant smile curled his lips, "I must confess that there is seeming reason in thy charge, yet it is not thus I would speak of thee. I would rather compliment thee, dear Judas, for thy shrewdness, for I did not think thou couldst have suspected my intentions, and thus have prepared thyself to thwart me in my attempt."

"Monster! Demon that thou art!" exclaimed Judas in desperation, "couldst thou not allow me to depart in peace and safety after all the services I have rendered thee in the accomplishment of thy iniquitous designs? After having made me sacrifice every noble principle, all sense of noble manhood and humanity, all ties of virtue, religion and morality —making me a base instrument to execute thy black crimes. Now thou wouldst recompense me by taking my life like any common assassin.

"Judas," replied Saul in a cool, emphatic manner, "thou knowest that I am a man resolute and unscrupulous in all things that endanger me in the achievement of my designs. In thus wishing to effect thy death I am not different from my former self. I hate thee not, Judas, but admire thee as a brave and serviceable man; yet in the nature of things it is fitting that I should seek thy life."

"Monster, what have I done that thou shouldst seek my life?" demanded Judas. "Have I betrayed thy secrets? Have I exposed thy hypocrisy, thy villainies, thy unbounded and unscrupulous ambition?"

"No, Judas, thou hast not as yet," returned Saul smiling; "but as thou art possessed of my secrets, and as there are no further interests to bind thee to me, thou possibly may be induced to make known to the world what I am. Thou mayest possibly betray me as thou hast thy late master, Jesus. Under such apprehensions and dread, I could not pursue my course with equanimity, for I view thee as being in my way; therefore, Judas, thou or I must die this night. Thou wishest to leave here for a distant country. Let it be so; but it must be for the dark shores of death and eternal oblivion, where thy tongue will be forever at rest, and Saul will not have occasion to fear thee. Come then, Judas, let us decide this contest with our weapons, for we are equally armed, and we understand each other."

Saul then renewed his attack upon Judas, and the latter fought with equal vigor in his self defense. The glances of their eyes emitted a terrifying fury, and their sinews strained as they dealt the murderous blows and thrusts for the first few minutes, without material advantage on either side. Saul had parried and received the blows and thrusts of Judas with his mantle on his left arm, and Judas had thus far received no wounds. But at length Saul pierced him in the shoulder, which caused Judas to retreat a pace; in doing so, he happened to stumble against the bag of money that had been thrown down just before, which caused him to stagger. Saul perceiving this, instantly rushed upon him before he could recover his balance, and with a powerful thrust he plunged his weapon into the breast of his adversary. Judas instantly fell to the ground uttering a groan and dropping his dagger. Saul was about to repeat the blow, when Judas cried out appealingly:

"Saul, stay thy arm—there is no need of further strife; thou hast given me my death wound. I fain would say a few words to thee, while I have strength to do so."

"Say on, brave Judas. Thy shrewd suggestions were always welcome to me, and will be no less so now, I doubt not," replied Saul, as he threw down his weapon, crossed his arms upon his breast, and waited the further remarks of the dying man.

Judas pressed one hand upon his breast, from which the blood was running fast, and managed to support himself with the other as he sat recumbent upon the ground, and at length he observed, in a faint voice:

"Saul, the shades of death will soon draw over my eyes, therefore consider my last words as given in sincerity and truth. I do not regret my fate; considering what evil I have done, I deserve no better; but I did not think I should die by the hand of Saul whom I have served so faithfully. Let me tell thee, that dark conspiracy we planned and executed against that good man, Jesus, never met with my sincere approbation. It was thy coercive measures that forced me to do what I have done against him. I acted in conformity with thy wishes, under the promise of being a freeman. Now behold the reward thou givest me! Saul, thou hast been terribly cruel and unjust to me, and possibly the time will come when there will be a retribution. When I served that good man, Jesus, I listened to his doctrines, and in spite of my will they sank deeply within me. He frequently spoke of the true God and of a future state, with great wisdom and eloquence. I now believe that all his ideas were founded on truth and reason. Should the doctrines of this Jesus be true, as I firmly believe they are, there is some possibility, Saul, that we shall meet again. Should it prove so, Saul,—then— "

On uttering the last word, the eyes of Judas closed, and he fell back a corpse.

"Poor Judas!" ejaculated Saul as he looked down upon the corpse. "Thou hast gone from this envious and treacherous world to the deep shades of death. Of all men of my acquaintance thou hast proved worthy of my high estimation. Thy qualities were worthy of great standing, and a better fate than thou hast had. The loss of no one do I regret more than thee, though I have been thy murderer! * * * * * * * * *

"How mysterious is my destiny, or the controlling power of my career in life! How antagonistic are my actions with my desires in some respects, for the very man I admire most I seem destined to destroy. Two men have fallen through me—the wise and virtuous Jesus, and my faithful servitor, Judas. Did their deaths proceed from any evil in me towards them? No; I admired them both, and could not feel evil towards them. Whence, then, comes this anomalous state of things that I should destroy those I admire the most? Whence this universal strife and disposition to destroy our fellows? Is it an acquired disposition of man, subject to moral control, or does it proceed from inevitable necessity inherent in the mysterious powers of nature, which men call Gods, and their wills as Fate? Ah! according to my worldly experience, I find that man's moral freedom is but a fiction! He knows not what is good or evil, neither can he refrain from doing what he does. As his existence is without his choice or control, so are his actions. He knows not the powers that control him, or what is his ultimate destiny. Like everything else around him he is a being of inevitable necessity. The man of today is but a link between the past and the future, in which position he is compelled to perform a part in the great chain of existence, which is destined to some great ultimate by the mysterious powers that control us. He lives and plays his part of today according to the influences produced by those who preceded him, and those who surround him; then he passes from existence, and posterity assumes the results of his career, modifying and continuing the same from year to year, until the grand design of human destiny shall be achieved. How, then, can my actions be evil? Am I not like all other mortals, a creature of inevitable necessity, dependent upon my predecessors or those around me for my impulses to action, which are without my control? I do but enact a part in the great chain of existence, which are under the guiding influences of the Powers of Nature or the Gods. Jesus and Judas were the necessary preliminary actors to the great and noble end assigned to me to accomplish. Their careers of life furnish the materials and foundation, upon which the more important one of mine is to be established; it then becomes necessary that they should give place to me. After their toils and labors I have removed them to the peaceful retreat of the grave in order that I may enter upon my glorious career without obstruction. Saul! Saul! the glorious field of thy ambition is now open before thee; the path is now free from obstruction. All circumstances, time and prospects are favorable. The minds of men are prepared to receive thy bold and daring influences to control them to thy will. Rush forth, then, and embrace the opportunity to achieve thy long cherished design. It must be so. I was not born to pass this life like other men amidst puling affections and trifling actions; for I see within me the impress of grand and stupendous works pertaining to the social state of man, which give me impulse to action. Yes; I must and will achieve the glorious objects, which the desires and impulses of my nature command me to do. If the results shall prove good, then all mankind will receive the benefit, and I shall be honored and praised through all posterity. And if my deeds prove an evil, then the responsibility will rest with the Gods, who create, control and dispose of the destiny of mortals."

Saul having ended his soliloquy, he looked down upon the lifeless body of Judas, and after contemplating it for a while, he gathered it up and carried it into the Tombs of Jehoshaphat, where he secreted it. After some time he returned to the spot, when he re-possessed himself of the bag of money that he had given Judas, and then quietly left the scene of the murder and his impious resolve.

FINAL COMMUNICATION

The spirits having ended their communications through the media of visions, Saul once more addresses me through my inward perceptive power of clairaudience:

"Friend Alexander, I congratulate you on the progress you have made towards the accomplishment of the task we have required of you. So far you have achieved a great and important work for the benefit of your fellow-man, of which posterity will be enabled to see the value, should the present age not appreciate it and do you justice.

"From the facts we have furnished you, you have produced a comprehensive history of that heinous tragedy, wherein I was the principal wicked actor. You have delineated things in a simple, natural, pleasing and truthful manner, suitable to the comprehension of the mass of mankind, and of that exciting nature as to command the perusal of it. It is a sad thing for me to reflect on, that mankind have been for so many ages wandering in error and delusion concerning the character, history and doctrines of Jesus of Nazareth; all of which must be attributed to my wicked ambition as the original cause. But now, as I am enabled to make an atonement to mankind for my past wickedness, I am in hopes that the evils of the past will be remedied in the present age by giving to mankind an explanation of all their delusions, which they will be enabled to obtain when they peruse your book. When they do so, they will immediately perceive its truth, reason, consistency and conformity with the principles of nature. He that shall peruse and appreciate its truths, will give a test of his intellectual progress worthy of the age he lives in.

"Friend Alexander, I have now informed you of all that is necessary to render clear the True History of Jesus of Nazareth, which I hope through your exertions, will not fail in accomplishing the designs I have in view. You will now issue your book to the world, calling upon the heads of the various Christian sects to read it and preach the same to the people, that they may emancipate themselves from the mental slavery and darkness under which they have existed for so many centuries past.

"All that I have imparted to you has been concerning man's mundane affairs and mortal nature. I would like to inform you concerning our supernal world—our natures as spirits, and the happy conditions of those who are exalted in mind and virtue; but the reason why I do not, is that I cannot. The nature of spirits and their surroundings are quite different to what they are with mortal man. Man's ideas are limited to his earthly life, therefore it is impossible for a man to receive impressions of things and a state of existence, which cannot be conceived by his earthly ideas. We spirits have the power of impressing man's mind as far as his ideas can comprehend us, but we have not the power of creating ideas in him; therefore, you may perceive that it is impossible for the spirits to communicate plainly the facts of anything concerning their natures or the supernal world.

"I must now conclude my address by informing you, that Judas joins me in expressing our thanks and gratitude for your services. We have it not in our power to reward you further than by the promise, that when we shall meet in the spirit-world, we will prove to you what we express. We now withdraw from you our guardian influence, hoping that you will pass the remainder of your days in harmony and peace, until death shall bring a change, when you will enter the spirit-world and obtain the reward of your labors. We now leave you, Farewell."

THE END.